White County Tennessee

INVENTORIES AND OLD WILLS

1831–1840

WPA RECORDS

Heritage Books
2024

HERITAGE BOOKS

AN IMPRINT OF HERITAGE BOOKS, INC.

Books, CDs, and more—Worldwide

For our listing of thousands of titles see our website
at
www.HeritageBooks.com

A Facsimile Reprint
Published 2024 by
HERITAGE BOOKS, INC.
Publishing Division
5810 Ruatan Street
Berwyn Heights, MD 20740

Originally published
December 1, 1936

— Publisher's Notice —

In reprints such as this, it is often not possible to remove blemishes from the original. We feel the contents of this book warrant its reissue despite these blemishes and hope you will agree and read it with pleasure.

International Standard Book Number
Paperbound: 978-0-7884-7775-1

W.P.A. RECORDS

The WPA Records are, for the most part, carbon copies of the original that was typed on onion skin paper during the Depression. Since these records were typed on poor machines by people who did not type in some cases and at the same time, they were read by persons not always sure of the older handwritten materials, the results are often less than perfect.

We have made every attempt to make as clear a copy as can be made from these older papers. Sometimes there are water stains and burned edges around the paper. This is the results of a fire at the home of one of the workers, Mrs. Penelope Allen, who was over most of the project. Sometimes, the index will be misleading in that they index by the middle name when a list of names are given in one family, i.e. "... the children of John Smith are, John, Jr., Mary Warren, and Oscar Sims. The indexer would list a Warren and a Sims in the index, when they should be Smith. Mountain Press has acquired a rather large number of finished and un-finished manuscripts. Many of these latter manuscripts are being typed and index now.

The WPA Records are now very scattered between the Tennessee State Library, various Public and Private Libraries and other collections. Some day, there is a hope that all of these can be collected and stored in one place. In spite of their many mistakes and problems, these are still the most complete collection of Tennessee records found anywhere.

TENNESSEE

RECORDS OF WHITE COUNTY

INVENTORIES & OLD WILLS

1831-1840

COPYING HISTORICAL RECORDS PROJECT

Official Project No. 165-44-6999 (1968)

WORKS PROGRESS ADMINISTRATION

MRS. JOHN TROTWOOD MOORE

STATE LIBRARIAN & ARCHIVIST, SPONSOR

MRS. ELIZABETH D. COPPEDGE

DIRECTOR OF WOMEN'S & PROFESSIONAL PROJECTS

MRS. PENELOPE JOHNSON ALLEN

STATE SUPERVISOR

MRS. RHEA E. GARRETT

SUPERVISOR SECOND DISTRICT

Copyists

Mrs. Arrie England
Mrs. Helen Howell
Mrs. Elma Lee Hickerson
Miss Laura Taylor

Typist

Miss Hattie Ferrell Winfree

December 1, 1936.

WHITE COUNTY
INVENTORIES & OLD WILLS 1831-1840
INDEX

(NOTE: Page numbers in this index refer to those of the original book which this copy was made from. These numbers are carried in the left hand margin of the copy.)

WHITE COUNTY
INVENTORIES & OLD WILLS 1831-1840

P 1 Inventory of the estate of John H. Pistle Decd. returned upon the oath of Enoch Murphee Adm. made before the Justice of the Peace, at April session A. D. 1831.

3 horses 7 head of cattle 6 head of sheep 18 head of hogs, 1 axe, 1 plow, swingletree clevis and trace 1 cutting machine 1 clock 2 beds and furniture 2 tables 1 chest 6 chairs 1 spinning wheel 1 Reel 1 Loom 3 bedsteads, 2 ovens 1 skillet 2 pots. 1 sifter 1 pail 2 piggins 1 churn 1 coffee pot, 1 set cups and saucers Dosen plated. 1 set Knives and forks, 1 crock 1 jar Lard 1 pot fork Flesh fork and shovel 1 pot rack 1 side saddle 1 bride 1 blanket, 3 pieces upper leather. 1 candle stick 2 Bottles 1 strainer some corn & Bacon 2 Sleighs 1 pair harness half dosen spoons 1 set warping spools 1 sad iron 1 pair shears 1 pan 1 pair cards 1 salt cellar and pepper box 1 bee stand 1 half bushel measure 1 washing tub 1 Basket one promissory note on John B. McCormick for $5 - 1 Ditton on Jonathan F. Farrington for $6. one negro a female named Lucinda about six year of age. 2 cow hides 1 small chest meal tub and bread tray.

Enoch Murphree Admr.

Recorded 2nd May 1831.
Test Jacob A. Lane clerk.

Amot returned an oath at April Sessions A. D. 1831 by Robart Cook Guardian to the heirs of Elijah Sawyer Decd. Towit:

Return of the exution of the estate of Elijah Sayer Decd. for the year 1830 from January Court till April Court 1831 — Robart Cook bought for the ares of Tobias Bartlett and Peggy Sawyer Legatees

Septr. 20 To 1 Slate and 4 pencils	$ .50
" " " 2 quirs of paper	.62½
Oct 30, To fee paid clerk for County Seal to power of Attorney to C. Sims	.75
June 29 To Paid John W. Gough for Schooling Tobias Bartlett	3.50
1831 Jany 7, To Paying Jesse H. Vermillion for teaching Bartlett Tobeas and Peggy Sayer in the year 1830	4.00
Jany 19, To Paying Sally Sayor part of her legacy left her by the death of her father Elijah Sayor Deceased	10.00
The above Settled and paid upon as Guardian to said children.	
	$19.37½

Robart Cook

Recorded 3rd May 1831
Test Jacob A. Lane clerk.

Partition & Division of the Slaves belonging to the estate of John Pistole Decd. made at January session A. D. 1830.

State of Tennessee }
White County } Persuant to an order of White County court made at October session 1829. We the undersigned met at the late residence of John Pistole Decd. and preceeded to make partition and division of the Slaves of the estate of said John Pistole Decd. amongt the
P 2 heirs of the said Pistole in the following manner Towit: A boy Charles and a woman Anica was alotted to Stephen Pistole at $425. Sinnon a man and Chaney a girl was alotted for Benjamin Wilbute at $425. Jeffry a man and binda a girl at $450. was alotted for John H. Pistole. Jenny and her child

Phillips $20.43 Jonathan C. Davis $2.25 Ann Jones $3.92¾ Benjm Williams $1.25 Lewis Phillips $6.04½ Robt. Johnston $6.50 Wm Glenn $14.00 Jememiah W. Beshears - 50 cents Bad Thomas Williams doubtful $1.12½ John Pistole $1.50. George Long $1.00 Russell Gest- $1.00 John Paine $9.25 Franky Thomas Bad $2.87½ Vinct (?) Henry $3.60- Charles S. Golden 3.93 A. B. Lane $5.00 Jesse Lincoln 37½ cents Jno. W. Goff 86½ cents Wm Brown Senr 62½ cents John Stome 62½ cents Wm Crownover 41½ cents. Wm C. Brittain $1.00 Jermiah Webb $3.25 - Wm J. Bennett 50 cents Horbart Long 50 cents. - amonts belonging to the estate of M. Anderson Dest. created since his death.

On Wm Anderson $1.71- Wm Terry $15.90½ cents Anthony Dibrell $1.62½ Joseph Nwell $4.09½ salt works $37.60½ Jabor G. Mitchell 25 cents Noah Phillips $3.00 Nenjamin Gapaway $12.62½ R. Johnston $10.50 Nathan Austin 25 cents Russell Gist $4.75. John Paine $7.79¾ Alexnd. Lowrey Senr. Thurs. $2.88 - Nancy Collins $3.62½ John W. Ruthedge $7.08½ Wm J. Bennett $14.18½ which included $4.62½ in first Inventory. -- N. B. Briggs 18¾ cents Glenn & Usury $6.19½ John Chuchimm $2.37½ - - Jesse Lincoln $17.26½ Berry Hamlett $1.00 James Dillon 37½ cents John Jett $1.69 Wm Brown snr. 96½ cents Christopher Hoffman 25 cents - Nicholas Cook $15.75 Wm Roberts 75 cents Washington Duncan 62½ cents N. Haggard 75 cents - C Horbert $1.75 David L. Mitchell $2.75 Duncan Wade $3.62½ Wm Dun 33 cents James H. Jenkins $1.65 John Brown 25 cents Peter Howard $9.87½ John Vincent $3.25 Andrew Gamble 75 cents Wm Simpson 75 cents John Haley Saner $1.00 Simon Histt $1.37½ James Kitchener $2.33 1/3 George W. Isham 93½ cents John H. Anderson $10.15

Of Partnership amunts owing ferm of Anderson & Hill paid to Admr. vis.

On Thomas Green $4.56¼ James Young $3.00 Wm Merry - 98 cents John White Junr. 75 cents Elisha Swift 62½ cents Spencer Mitchell $5.25 Ralph Matthew $6.87½ Henry Williames $1.51 Stewart Warrener 62½ cents John Chisum $8.06¼ Elijah Ward $3.56¼ Joseph Henry $4.82½. Some of the foregoing amounts created before and since the death of M. Anderson were recorded to what they appear in the foregoing tists by receipts of Bark & Hider which was sold to Jesse Lincoln as before shown amounts on the book which had been paid with Bark & Hider an not noticed here. The foregoing Inventory was made out under the directions of John H. Anderson and so far as it goes is according to my belief founded upon his opinion correct.

P 4

Anthony Dibrell

Recorded 15th June 1831
Test Jacob A. Lane clerk
White County Court.

Report of Settlement with Anthony Dibrell, May Anderson & John W. Roberts Admrs. of the Matthias Anderson Decd. commissioners on oath of October Session A. D. 1830.

State of Tennessee]
White County]

We the assigned commissioners appointed by the County Court of White County at the Term A. D. 1830 have proceeded to make a settlement with Anthony Dibrell May Anderson and John N. Roberts administrators of Matthias Anderson who acts for said admrs. find that the following errors have been recorrected by said adm. from the following persons debtors to said estate viz:

1826	July	15	Rcd. of Wm McKey for horse sold before death	$55.00
"	"	18	Rcd. of Henry Williams the amount of his amot.	1.51
"	"	29	Rcd. Thomas Roberts the amount of his amot.	.50
"	"	30	Rcd. of George Long the amount of his amount.	1.00

				Amount
1826	Augt	1	Rcd. of Nathl Austin the amount of his amount	.25
"	"	5	" " Wm C. Madkiff amount of his amount	.36½
"	Sept	9	" " Jacob Stepes the amount of his note	.56¼
"	"	"	" " Benjamin Weaner the amount of his note	1.91
"	"	"	" " Joseph Newell the amount of his amount	1.22½
"	"	"	" " Stwart Warren the amount of his account	.62½
"	"	"	" " John Marlow the amount of his note	8.00
"	"	"	" " Jonathan C. Davis the amount of his amount	2.25
"	"	"	" " Wm Taylor the Amot. of his note	2.00
"	"	"	" " John C. White the amount of his note	2.37½
"	"	"8	" " Wm Massey the amount of his amount	.98
			Amot forwarded.	78.55¼
			P 5 Amount brought forward from Page 4	78.55¼
1826	Sept		Rcd. amount of Elisha Swift. the ballacne of his amount	.62½
"	"	"	Spence Mitchell Jur. bal of his amount	.75
"	"	"	Wm Austin balance of his amount	.25
"	"	"	Jeremah Webb the amount of his amot.	3.25
"	"	"	John Slaan the balance of his amount	1.37½
"	"	"	James H. Pass the amount of his amount	2.18¾
"	"	"	Joseph Kerr the amot. of his amot.	2.79
"	"	"	William Simpson the amot. of his amot.	.75
"	"	"	Simon Hiett the amot. of his amot.	1.37½
"	"	"	N. B. Brigs the amot. of his amot.	.18¾
"	"	"	James H. Jenkins on his amot.	1.65
"	"	"	John Brown on D.O	.25
"	"	"	for Leather sold since the death of M. Anderson from Sundre Persons	53.25
"	"	"	of Genye Dawson half a partianship Note	1.75
1826	Sept	Rcd	amot. of John Williams on a Note	1.00
"	"	"	Robert Kimbill amot of Do	1.25
"	"	"	of James Hudson Amot of Do	2.75
"	"	"	Wm Yarbro Amot. of Do	5.25
"	"	"	Ralph Matthaws on his amot	6.87½
"	"	"	On certifiacte and care of Dubany vis Jett	4.00
"	"	"	$2.25 of Which int. $4. were applied G. L. Cookes Note	
"	"	"	Bibbs due Anderson & Hill	28.22¾
1827	June	14 Rcd.	John Jett on his amot.	1.69
"	"	"	Harp Arnold on his net the amot. of Thos Williams Note.	6.68
"				
"	July	4	Rcd of James Irwin on his note	5.93¾
"	"	"	" " Saml. V. Carrick on Parteanship amot.	.55
"	"	"	" " Tho's Roberts on his note	3.00
"	"	"	" " Josiah Burgess on his note	.62½
"8	"	"	" " John Bell on his note	.25
"	"	"	" " Geo hesson on Sane	1.18¾
"	"	"	" " John Brown amot. of his note	3.30
"	"	"	" " Charles Lowry the amot. of Do	4.61
"	"	"	" " William Hunter on Do	2.00
1827	Aug	11	Rc. of Amount John Thomas Amot of note	4.06¼
"	"	13	" " " Elisha Webb amot Do	1.62½
"	"	21	" " " Wm Iwin Amot. of Do	1.50
"	"	"	" " " " James Young amot	3.00

Year	Month	Day			Account	Amount
"	"	"	" "	"	George (negro) for his hire	10.00
"	Sept	1	Rc	of Amount	Jas Henry on his note	3.43¾
"	"	"	" "	"	William Lyda the amot of his note	3.81¼
"	"	"	" "	"	Thomas Greene on partianship amot.	4.56¼
"	"	"	" "	"	W. P. Duncan on his amot	.50
					Amot forwarded	$260.67½

P 6 Amot brought from Page 5 — $260.67½

Year	Month	Day			Account	Amount
1827	Sept	1	Rcd.	of	William Usrey on Partianship Note	16.25
"	"	"	"	"	Wanett Henry on Note	1.37½
"	"	"	"	"	John Serryfield amot. of his note	5.12½
"	"	"	"	"	Joseph Jones amot. of his note	4.06¼
"	"	"	"	"	James Frisby D.d	4.06¼
"	"	"	"	"	John Walker Amot. of his note	10.00
"	"	"	"	"	John White on amot.	.75
"	"	"	"	"	George McGhee on Note	1.00
1827	Sept	17	"	"	Benjamin Hunter Do.	2.00
"	"	20	"	"	John White Ser. amot. of note	67.75
"	"	22	"	"	Jess Stewart amot. of his note	.25
"	"	"	"	"	John Chisum bal amot	8.04½
"	"	"	"	"	Saml V. Carrick the amot of his note	14.00
"	"	"	"	"	Asa Certain on his note	3.93¾
"	"	"	"	"	Briggs & Yarbrough on their note	1.75
"	"	"	"	"	Hugh Gracy amot. of his note	15.00
"	"	"	"	"	Jo. W. Glenn amo. of Do.	4.18¾
"	"	"	"	"	Jas. Newell on amot	1.59
"	"	"	"	"	Matthew England ba. on note	.37½
"	Dec	13	"	"	Jas Kerr Amot of his note	6.37½
"	"	"	"	"	James H. Jenkins on his note	20.38½
"	"	"	"	"	Ben Hunter on Do	3.75
"	"	8 "	"	"	Noah Phillips on Do	93.50
"	"	"	"	"	Miller & Judson	12.75
"	"	"	"	"	Jas. Wm Duncan	4.25
"	"	"	"	"	Eli Sims Tucker amot. on claim	6.50
1828	Mar	15	"	"	H. Burton on Judgement vs John Barr	23.50
"	"	"	"	"	N. Olaham for leather sold	34.50
"	"	"	"	"	Wm Gist on his note	3.87½
1828	Mar	15	Rc	of	Barnett & England Do	6.50
"	"	"	"	"	John Duncan on note	21.00
"	"	"	"	"	Stephen Wallis on Do	41.03
"	July	15	"	"	Eli Sims Trustee on July claim	2.00
"	"	21	"	"	Wm Brown on note	2.81¼
"	"	"	"	"	Wm & James Irvin on note	11.37½
"	"	"	"	"	George (negro) for hire in the year 1828	20.00
1829	Feby	1	"	"	Samuel V. Carrick for hire of bed in 1828	65.00
"	"	"	"	"	Geo W. Isham amot. of his note	1.03½
"	Apl	19	"	"	James Anderson Sr. on his note	2.31¼
"	"	"	"	"	Elijah Isham Snr. on Do	1.75
"	"	"	"	"	Robert Montgomery amot. Do	5.68¾
					Herbert Long for books bot at sale	20.12½
						$833.21¼

P 7

Amot brought from Page 6 — $833.21¼

1829 Apl 19 Rc. of John Evans amot of note — 11.00

"	"	"	"	"	Wm Rodgers amo. bot by hire at Sale	.59
"	"	"	"	"	Nachl Evan bot by hire at sale	.50
"	"	"	"	"	Jonathan Clumy amot. of note	4.12½
"	"	"	"	"	Leach & Lacy on a note	10.00
"	"	"	"	"	Lewis Phillips part of his amot	5.25
"	"	"	"	"	Elijah Ward amot of his amot	3.56¼
"	"	"	"	"	Chas. S. Golden Do	3.93
1829	Apl	19	ro.	of	James Dillon on amot.	.37½
"	"	"	"	"	Jas. Harley ser. Do	1.00
"	"	"	"	"	N. B. Briggs Same	.18¾
"	"	"	"	"	Jas. Catchend amot of amot	2.33
"	"	"7	"	"	Peter Howard on Do	9.87½
"	"	"	"	"	Duncan Wade amot	3.62½
"	"	"	"	"	Wm Glnn amot of amot	14.00
"	"	"	"	"	Glenn & Ussury Do	6.19½
"	"	"	"	"	Jas Kerr on Do	5.28
1830	Jan	16	"	"	Scott Harry part of his note	8.97½
"	"	"	"	"	Jho N. Alstoah on amot	9.46¼
"	Feby	13	"	"	John Paine on Do.	17.02½
"	March	3	"	"	Wm Ussury partianship note	15.00
"	"	13	"	"	Noah Phillips on his note	38.15
"	June	16	"	"	Balance of Briggs & Yarbrough's note	1.56¼
"	"	"	"	"	Pleasant C. Farley on note	.37½
"	"	"	"	"	Resa James on partinaship note	2.65
"	"	"	"	"	Wm C. Bruttom on anto.	.39
"	"	"	"	"	Rubin Robinson on note	18.75
"	"	"	"	"	Ben McClan	1.25
"	"	"	"	"	Spence Mitchell partianship	4.50
"	"	"	"	"	Jess Lincoln for rent of Ten yard	36.43¾
"	"	"	"	"	Same for him of Glenn in the year 182	30.00
1830	June	16			Same the amot. of his amot	17.64
"	"	"			Alexd Winfree constable on his rect. ($15.75) of which $2.75 was in a hide & sold to Jess Lincoln	13.00
"	"	"			John Anderson amot. of his amot	10.15
"	"	"			Wm Crowder amot. Do	4¼
"	"	"			Russell Gist amot of amot (in part)	.25
"	"	"			Wm J. Bennett amot Do	14.18½
"	"	"			Alexd Lowrey sr. on partianship amot	5.00
"	"	"			James T. Holman Amot of amot	17.00
"	"	"			Dr. Bobt Johnson on Do	10.50
"	"	"			Wm Anderson amot. of amot	1.80
						1189.02½

P 8		amot brought from page 7				1189.02½
1830	June	16	ro.	of	Joseph Nwell on amot.	3.39½
"	"	"	"	"	George (negro) for his hire 1828	6.04
"	"	"	"	"	Jno. N. Alstadh on amot.	17.53
"	"	"	"	"	Samuel Driskell amot. of his amot.	17.93¾
"	"	"	"	"	George (negro) for his hire in 1828	20.41¼
"	"	"	"	"	Rutledge adm. amot. of amot.	7.08½
"	"	"	"	"	Ben Gapaway on amot.	12.00
"	"	"	"	"	Jess Lincoln on his note	405.29
"	"	"	"	"	Jess Lincoln for hire of M. for the year 1829	37.50
1830	June	16			Herbet Long amot. ans. before the death	.50
"	"	"			Same for leather	56.45½

" " " Amot May Anderson amot. returned in Inventory	63.05½
" " " Jess Lincoln for him of M. In 1829	5.00
" " " Nicholas Cook amot. of his amot	15.75
To col amot Rcd. by Adm.	1857.96½
	1331.36½
Balance in hands of Adm.	526.60½

Amount of money paid by the Adm. on the claims which have been presented against the estate of Matthias Anderson Decd.

Paid	John Cook as per recent No 1	$1.65
"	Wm P. Lamson M. D. asper amt. No. 2	40.00
"	Charles N. Green as per rect. No 3	2.00
"	John Jett as per rect. No 4	5.00
"	Jno. Jett as per rect. for Taxes 1826 No 5	10.68¾
"	Jno. Jett Tax rect for 1827 No. 6	7.75
"	Lewis Bohamon as per note lifted No. 7	55.09
"	Docb Robart Johnson as per rect No 9	42.62½
"	Mathias Anderson bond to Jacob Robertson No. 8	438.96½
"	James T. Holeman for tuition as per rect No 10	$ 53.00
"	Wm Glenn as per rect No 11	27.87½
"	Noah Gibbs as per no 12	1.75
"	Wm Anderson as per No. 13 Note lifted & explained by J. H. Anderson	144.13¾
"	Andrew Burk as per rect No. 14	136.42½
"	Charles Manning per rect No. 15	72.11
"	Mclings & Oldham as per No. 16	9.50
"	John Jett Taxes 1828 No. 17	6.93¾
"	Charles Manning for Shroud /C as per no. 18	13.75
"	Jno. W. Ford as per rect. No 19	2.25
"	J. A. Lane Clerk for Rcd. No 20	5.43 1/3
"	P. Howard as per rect No. 21	6.75
"	Nicholas Cook as per No. 22	3.50
		1037.18½

P 9

By Amo. brought from Page 8		1037.18½
Paid	J. G. Mitchell as per No. 23	16.25
	Chas. S. Golden as per no 24	6.00
	Russell Maybound No. 25	1.25
	John Payne No. 26	13.52½
	Danl Mc[illegible]lan No. 27	2.82
	John Warren N. 28	.50
Paid	Duncan Wade asper No. 29	8.00
"	Glenn & Lincoln No 30	7.80
"	Fisk & Montgomary No. 31	7.00
"	Benjam. G[illegible]ay No. 32	12.00
"	Hurbat Lone hire in Tan yard on affct. J. H. Anderson	147.63
"	Same Postage on letters	.37½
"	Same 1 quire paper	.25
"	Same making enbres on land of said estate	2.35
"	Sawaying? $1 paid Burgess amot. $3.50	
"	Spence Mitchell amot. $4/50	
"	Gracy $2.35	11.35
"	Alexander Lonry Jr.	.52½
"	Charles Mayberry	2.35
"	John Shankhs	2.80½

* Joseph Nwell amot and him and Gro. W. Ledbetter Partianship 1.39⅛
the above no. 33 as per afft. /C

$1331.36⅛

We the underassigned commissioners report that after a full investigation, of the vouchers and documents submitted this to us we find the foregoing Statement, and believe that is a correct representation of the Situation of said estate thus Oct. 1830.

David Arms
R. Nelson
David Snodgrass

Recorded 15th June 1831
Test Jacob A. Lane clerk
White County court.

Inventory of the estate of George Slaughter Decd. returned on oath by William Simpson adm. at January Session A. D. 1831.

One horse 3 behairs 1 spinning wheel 1 oven half Sett knives & forks half Dozen spoons 4 plates half set Tea cups & saucers. one plow 1 weeding hoe. one pair Hames one collar. Sundry bed clothing /C November 30, 1830.

William Simpson
Administrator

Recorded 16 June A. D. 1831
Test James H. Lane clerk
White County clerk

An amount of the Sale of the property of George slaughter Decd. returned an oath by William Simpson administrator at April Session A. D. 1831

2 chairs sold to Polly Saughter for	$ .25
P 10 one totton sping wheel Do	.37½
One oxen and ad Do.	2.25
Three Knives & 2 forks	.12½
half dozen spoons	.25
Four plates & 2 saucers	.25
one plough	.12½
one bed & furniture & Bedspread	.25
one horse sold for	14.00
	17.87½

William Simpson adm.

Recorded 16 June A. D. 1831
Test Jacob A. Lane clerk
White County court.

An Inventory of the estate of Charles Carter Snr. Des. returned on oath by John Fryer and Rebekah Stipe at October Session A. D. 1830.

One mare one horse one cow Two calfs one negro woman named Jeroina one negro woman named Mary. Two negro boys vis: Benjamin and Thomas. Two small negro girls vis: Matilda & Malinda. Two oxens. Three stearts. 2 beds and furniture. Two. bedsteads. One Bureau one table. two cheirs one check Real one cotton wheel one flax wheel one glass bottle one Big Pot. one oven one skillet one Tea Kittle. 2 Piggins, one washing tub. one flat Tub. one meal Tub. one sifter, one keg. 1 pot rack one side saddle one Sett warping spools. Three slays one cross cut saw one scycle & cradle 2 Iron wedges three axes three plough two pair Traces chaines 3 old hoes one drawing Knife. Two augers one flax hackle.

John Fryer
Ribckah his x mark Stipe

Recorded 16 June A. D. 1831.
Test Jacob A. Lane clerk
White County court.

An Inventory of the estate of Abraham Conner Decd. returned on oath by Hugh Conner and John W. Simpson adms. at October Session A. D. 1830. Towit:

1 mare & colt 2 cows & bulls 3 yearlings 1 cow 1 yearling colt. 35 head of sheep. 43 head of
P 10 hogs 15 Geese 1 Loom 1 Barshear plough 2 shovel ploughs 1 Bull-tongue plough 2 pair Geers 1 bottle. 2 single-trees 4 saves 1 Lock-chain 2 oxen 1 mattock 3 hoes 1 grind-stone 1 scythe & cradle 1 salt kettle 1 man's Saddle 1 side saddle 1 Bridle 4 Beds & furniture 1 2 tables 1 clock 1 candle stand 2 cotton wheels 2 pair cards 1 check roule 8 chairs 2 water pails 1 flat stand 2 Tubs 2 smoothing iron 2 ovens & lid 3 pots 1 skillet 1 fire shovel 2 Sadles 1 flesh fork 2 pair pot hooks 3 bells 1 pair candle moulds 1 Trumpet 1 ten bucket 1 coffee pot 1 coffee mill 1 Bottle 1 Jug 1 dish 7 knives 10 forks 4 spoons 8 Tea cups & 5 saucers 1 sugar box 1 Boll 1 Jar 1 Looking glass 4 viles 2 pewter dishes 3 pewter plates. 2 pewter Basons. 6 Tea-cups 2 clupels 1 Bible 1 Rasor 1 pair Bellows 1 stackoats 2 stacks Rye 60 Bushels wheat 1 Tribbed 1 note on Joseph Burden for $25 one amount on Isaac Sharp for 50 cents a balanse on an amot. on Nathanal Burden $1.00 Balance of an amot on Gustmas Haswood for $8.38½.

Hugh Conner }
J. W. Simpson } Adm.

P 11 Recorded 16 June A. D. 1831
Test Jacob A. Lane clerk
White County court.

Account of the Sales of the property of Abraham Conner Decd. returned on oath by Hugh Conner and John W. Simpson Admr. at October Sessions A. D. 18.30

Hugh Conner 1 cow & calf at	$5.06¼
William C. Bruthans 1 cow & calf	5.93¾
Wm Conner 1 Bull	2.25
J. W. Simpson 1 Bull	.75
Simon Doyle 1 heifer yearling	.62½
Antony Debrell 10 head sheep at 81¢	8.10
John Jett 10 head sheep at 81¢	8.10
Anthoney Dibrell 10 head Sheep at 81¢	8.10
Hugh Conner 4 head sheep at 50¢	2.00
Gustonas Harwood 1 mare & colt	31.75
J. W. Simpson 6 head hogs 1 horse	19.50
J. W. Simpson 1 sow & 3 shoats	2.50
Benjam Hamlett 1 sow & 10 shoats	6.75
Benjam Hamlett 1 sow & 9 shoats	7.87½
Hugh Conner 1 sow & 3 shoats	3.00
Simon Doyle 1 sow	1.87½
Daniel Richards 1 pair Bellows	1.25
Wm Conner 15 Geese at 28½¢	4.27½
Hugh Conner 1 Loom	6¼

Wm Conner 1 cotton wheel	.87½
Hugh Conner 1 cotton wheel	.37½
Jno. W. Simpson 1 Barshear plough	1.87½
Jas. W. Simpson 1 bull-tongue plough singl & cleves	1.12½
Hugh Conner 1 shovel plough sing.t. & clevis	1. 6¼
Amot forward to page 12	$125.07½
P 12 Amot. brought from page 11	$125.07½
Isaac Plumby 1 Log chain	3.06¼
J. W. Simpson 2 plow Irons	.37½
Jacob Anderson 1 boatler ?	1.00
Isaac Dobbson 1 pair Geers	1.31¼
Hugh Conner 1 pair Geers	175
J. W. Simpson 1 mattock	1.25
Griffin Garner 3 hoes	.56¼
William Conner 1 axe	.93¾
J. W. Simpson 1 scythe & cradle	3.81¼
Gustanas Haswood 1 grind stone	.75
John Wallace 1 kettle	1.62½
Wm Conner 1 large pot	.81¼
Hugh Conner 1 oven, bed & hook	1.12½
J. W. Simpson 1 axe	.56¼
Wm Conner 1 skillet	.56¼
Hugh Conner 1 oven & lid	1.37½
Wm Conner 1 smothing Iron	.25
John Denton 1 man's saddle	13.37½
Elisa Conner 1 Bed & furniture	5.00
Elisa Conner 1 side saddle	5.00
Wm Conner 1 Bed & furniture	5.00
Hugh Conner 1 Bed & furniture	5.00
Wm Conner 1 Bed & furniture $3 1 chest $3 1 Table $1	7.00
Hugh Conner 1 Table	.62½
Terry Gellentine 1 clock	13.12½
Nany Hill 1 candle Stand	.50
Wm Conner 1 check Reels	1.56¼
Elisa Conner 2 pair cards	.25
Hugh Conner 8 chairs	.50
Nancy Hill 1 Bedstead	.75
Hugh Conner 2 pails 2 churns 2 Tubs	.50
Elizabeth Hill 1 pot	2.62½
Simon Doyle 1 pot rack	1.06¼
Hugh Conner 1 pot rack	1.50
Simon Doyle 1 shelling machine & Bell	.25
Hugh Conner 1 bucket, candle moulds and Trumpet	1.12½
Hugh Conner 1 coffee mill & coffee pot	.81¼
Jacob Crowdar 1 Bottle & Jug	.37½
Elisa Conner deeph ware knives forks, sugar box, ball Teacups & saucers	.50
Elizabeth Hill 1 jar	1.37½
J. W. Simpson 1 Lot pewter	3.18¾
Wm Pennington Lot Irons	1.00
amot forwarded to page 13	$216.55½
P 13 amot. brought from page 12	$216.55½
Elisa Conner 2 slays & Harness 25¢ 1 Looking glass 6 ned 6¼¢	.31¼
Elizabeth Hill 1 Bible	.87½

Hugh Conner Lot leather	.25
Elisa Conner Tray & Sifter	.6¼
Donl. Richards 1 still Tub	.50
Joseph Phifer 15 Bushels wheat 87¢ p	13.12½
Russell Gist 5 Bushels wheat at 89¢	4.45
Isaac Dobbson 1 stack-Rye $3.25 1 stack-Rye $2	5.25
Gustanas Harwood 1 stack Oats	4.12½
Total Amot.	$245.50½

Hugh Conner }
J. W. Simpson } Adms.

Recorded 16 June 1831
Test Jacob A. Lane clerk
White County Court.

Inventory of the estate of Joshua Porter Desd. returned on oathe by Woodrow P. White at April session A. D. 1831 who is adm. lc.

The tract on which John Porter Desd. occupied in his lifetime number of acres not known also 1 negro girl Jane 18 April 1831.
W. P. White adm.

Recorded 17 June 1831
Test Jacob A. Lane clerk
White County Court.

Inventory of the estate of Thomas Williams Desd. returned upon oath by Robert Officer Edward Elms administrator at October Session A. D. 1830.

One still one cross-cut saw one waggon and geers for hind horses one Black colored bull tree small steers-one yoke of oxens & yokes 2 small steers one red and brindle steer one white faced cow & calf two heifers & one steer one black cow one bill cow & bull one cow one yellow cow and calf one small red cow & calf and white steer one speckle heifer one large sorrell gelding one old gray mare Bellons annell and other smith tools. One negro woman named Sall. one negro boy named Aaron one negro girl named Hannah. One negro boy named Sampson one negro girl named Fanny one negro girl named Patsy one negro boy named Lige. one black horse colt. one gray mare filly one bell on grey mare one hundred pounds bacon. the hog all round one hundred fifty Do fifty one pounds midling bacon twenty five pounds midlin bacon . Ninty five pounds Do Seventy two pounds bacon Seventy two bonds bacon fifty five pounds Do. Two hogsheads and Rye in them. four graines & Rye in them 28 head same Do containing 24 heads Third Lot Do containing 13 head. Fourth Lot Do. containing 2 head. one bond and obligation on John Mitchell to deliver in a tin acre field one half of the cows raised on said field. one black one Rifle geer and implements one shot gun three beds bedsteads and furniture 2 covelets and one two trunks one bed bedstead and furniture below stairs cupboard and all thats in it.one tub
P 14 and pitcher one coffee mill one looking glass one barshear plough and Bull tongue one barshear plough & Bull tongue one barshear plough and Bull tongue one barshear plough & Bar. one kettle three axes 2 Bells foot ads reaphook carying knife 2 singletrees 2 clevis 1 parcal of leather the 2/3 of calf-hide now in the nat of Dyers one pair trace chains 2 single trees stretchers 1 c one broad axe anville stake and bull tongue leather small price one hoe one pair harnes and traces one pair traces and backband one hoe one log chain one shovel plough one saddle one lot of corn one Lot of Tolax one Keg of Tobacco one grind stone one tub wheat one tub and wheat in it on tub and salt Laddles & a sieve 9 head of sheep 3 sheep and bell spring house contents on kettle kitchen furniture above and below stairs.

deer skin. sheep skin 2 cotton wheel. flax Rod. one pair of cards shoe-makers tools and bench one bedstead and furniture one bedstead and furniture Do the same dresser & furniture Crowbar and grubbing hoe 2 kigs crow and coffee mill 1 pair sheepshears 1 reap hook 8 chairs 1 scythe & cradle 2 stacks of whear 2 stacks of Rye 2 stacks of oats all the corn growing on the same side of the road which the house stands with the exception of fifty bushels and the cotton now growing on the primeses 1 bucket 15 head stock hogs 3 head stock hogs 2 head stock cattle balance cattle. 5 head stock hogs balance of the tole of hogs geese and ducks one cow brute in possisian of Wm Gannerson on Mattox 2 plows and stocks one suttle wheel and walter plow one hand axe 1 pair of saddle Bags 1 spade 1 shovel one note on Isaac Denton and James Cox for $2.25 cents. one note on William Kinard for $14.12½ cents one note on Samuel Miller $3.50 cents one note on John Robertson to Catharine Williams for $6.39 cents A. G. Bradly constable Rect for note on G. W. Jones for $4.87 P one note on James & John Hudson for $65. one note on Frances Moore for 40 Bushels corn one note on James Hudson and E. Elms for $23. Lincoln $15.88 balance on a note from Geo. W. Ledbetter Adesse. one note on John Jett, Jacob Robinson, James Hayes & Lewis Bohanon balance amo. $146.11 cents money remaining on hand which come to the possession of Adm. $116.12½ cents 12 of August 1830.

Robert Officer } Adms.
Edward Elms }

Recorded 17 June 1831
Test Jacob H. Lane clerk
White County court.

Amount of the sale of the property of Thomas Williams Decd. returned on oath by Robert Officer and Edward Elms adms. at October Session 1830.

One still $16.75 one cross-cut saw $8 one black colored Bull $8.	$32.75
one waggon & geer for hind horses $37 three small steer $22.	59.00
One yoke steers & yoke $20 2 small steers $9.12½	29.12½
one red cor & brindle steer $4.37½ one white face cow & calf $10.12½	14.50
2 heifers & steers $7.12½ one black cow $6 Bell cow & bell $6.62½	19.75
one yellow cow & calf $5.68¾ one red cow & calf $6.25	11.93¾
Sow $1.50 one speckle heifer $3.75	10.87½
one Sorrel Gilding $54.25 one cow $6.25 one Grey mare $30.	90.50
P 15 Bellows Anvell and other smith tools	$20.75
Negro Woman named Sall $251.12½ Negro boy named Aaron $315.	566.12½
Negro girl named Hannah $267. Negro boy named Sampson $300.12½	567.12½
Negro girl named Fanny $203,50 negro girl named Patsy $200.	403.50
Negro boy named Lige $150. 25 one black horse colt $16.25	166.50
One grey mare filly $50. one bell on gray mare $.62½	50.62½
one hundred pounds bacon $8.75 one hundred fifty pounds do $11.25	20.00
fifty pounds Bacon $5.06¼ Ninety four pounds bacon $8.	13.06¼
Ninety-five pounds bacon $7.12½ seventy-two pounds Do. $5.12½	12.25
Seventy-two pounds Bacon $5. fifty pounds bacon $4.	9.00
One hogshead & Rye $3.12½ one green & Rye in it $3.75	6.87½
one gune & wheat in it $6.93¾ one grene & Rye in it $3.	9.93¾
one gum & Rye in it $2.50 one Hogshead & Rye in it $1.	3.50
135 W corn $7.37½ 1st Lot hogs 28 head $63	70.37½
2nd Lot hogs 24 head $81. 3rd Lot 13 head $10.62½ 4th Lot Do. 2 head $4	95.62½
Bond & obligation on John Mitchell for half corn in 10 acre field	17.00
one clock $12.06¼ Rifle gun and implements $18.37½	30.43¾
One short gun $4.12½ 1 Bedstead & furniture $11.12½	15.25
2 Bedsteads & furniture $26.50 2 coverlets 1 quilt 1 candle pan $10.87	37.37

1 Trunk $2.50 1 Trunk $1.75 1 Bedstead & f furniture $12 16.25
Cupboard and all in it $10. Tobb & pitcher $2.50 coffee mill
25 cents 12.75
1 looking glass .25 1 Barshear plough & Bull tongue $.1
1 Barshear plow $1.75 3.00
tools $5 Loom & Geer $5. 11.75
5 Beegums $7.75 1 Kittle 2 axes $5.25 2 Bells. foot ads Reap hook
& knife $3.25 16.25
2 Single tree 2 cleves $2.00 1 axe $1 parcel leather $1.37 P 4.37½
2/3 Beef hide in nat dyers $1. 1 pair trace chains $2. 1 Broad ax
$1.06¼ 4.06¼
2 single & streachers $3.31¼ anvelle stake & Bull tongue $2 5.31¼
Leather small pea $1. 1 hoe 56¼ 1 pair Names & Traces $1 2.56¼
1 pair Traces & Back band $1.75 1 hoe 18¾ 1 Log chain $2. 3.93¾
1 shovel plow 56¼ 1 saddle $3.1 Lot corn $12.12% - Lot Tlax .50 16.18¾
1 Keg Tobacco $1. grind stone .50 1 Tub wheat .87% 1 Tub wheat
$2.37% 4.75
2 Riddles 1 sive .56¼ 1 gune & salt .81¼ 9 head sheep $6.56¼ 7.93¾
Amo. carried to page 16 $2506.37½

P 16 amount brought from page 15 2506.37½

3 Lamps & Bell $1.50 - Spring house & conterets $10. Kittle 1.68¾ 13.18¾
Kitchen furniture above and below stairs $20 deer skin & sheep
skin .50 20.50
1 cotton wheel .31¼ 1 cotton wheel, flax, reel & pair cards $3. 3.31¼
Shoe maker tools & Beech $1.12% Bedstead & furniture .83¾ 1.96¼
1 Bedstead & furniture $3.93¾ Do the Same .31¼ Dresser & contents
$1.31¼ 5.56¼
crow bar & grubbing hoe $1.68¾ 2 Kegs 1 oven & coffee mill .89% 2.58¼
1 pair sheepshears .56¼ 1 Reap hook .31¼ 8 chairs $1 1.87½
1 scythe & cradle $1.25 2 stacks wheat $6.91¾ 2 stacks Rye $2.25 10.41¾
2 stacks oats 3.37½
all the corn growing on the side of the creek on which the house stands (except 50 bushels to be paid the widow) and the cotton growing 20.00
1 buckle $1.50 15 head stock hogs $3 7.50
3 head stock hogs $3
2 head stock cattle $5.62½ balance
cattle $1.12% 5 head stock hogs $4.56¼ 11.31¼
Balance of lots hogs $35. geese & ducks $1 cow in hands W. Gannonas
$3.25 39.25
1 Mattox $1.50 2 plow & stacks 2.56¼ 1 Little wheel $3.12% 7.18¾
1 hand axe & cotton plow $2.1 hand axe .75 1 pair saddle bags 2.31¼ 5.06¼
1 spade .62½ 1 shovel 12% note of Isaac Hunter & Jas. Cord $2.25 3.00
1 note from Wm Kinnard for $14.12% 1 note from Samuel Miller $3.50 17.62½
1 note from Jas. Robinson to Catharine Williams 6.39
A. G. Bradly con. Rect for note on G. W. Jones 4.87%
Note on Jno & James Hudson & Edward Elms for $23 88.00
Bal. note on Jno. Jett, Jacob Roberson, James J. Hayes Lewis
Bohannon 146.11
Money on hand which came to possession of adm. 116.12½
$3057.46¼

Robert Officer
Edward Elmes

Recorded 17 June 1831
Test Jacob A. Lane clerk
White County court

An Inventory of the estate of Benjamin Sewell Decd returned upon oath by Sarah Sewell Adm. at January Session A. D. 1831.

6 head of cattle one hog one Rifle gun a quanity of working tools two feather beds and furniture two pots one kettle one skillet eight plates one jar. two crocks one pitcher one boll one set teacups & saucers one bottle four chairs one churn one tub one fat tub smoothing iron one set knives & forks. one chest one tool box one bedstead one table one cotton wheel and cards one breadtray 2 water pails one piggin one coffee mill one coffee pot some leather four table spoons one set tea spoon one fire shovel. Some writing paper. Razor & Strap looking glass 2 books one tea cup one pair knitting needles.

his
Sarah x Sewell
mark Admx.

Recorded 17 June 1831.
Test. J. A. Lane clerk
White County Court.

An Inventory of the estate of William Anderson Decd. returned into court by John H. Anderson and John W. Roberts Adm. on oath at October Session A. D. 1830 To Wit:
one half of a wheat fan one pair smoothing irons one pair sheep shears one frying pan 2 plough & one cuttaaler one barshear plow one plow one bull tongue plow one log chain one swingletree chains & grind stone. one swingletree & clevis one Singletree & clevis and swingletree sprouting hoe 1 mattock 3 weeding hoes 3 weeding hoes 3 spades 1 pair hames & traces collar bridle & line 1 pair traces bridle collar and line 1 chain line collar & pair of Hames 3 pole axes 1 meat axe 2 iron wedges 1 broken iron wedge. 1 Tro 3 auginers 1 hand saw 1 drawing knife 1 Bureau 1 Desk 2 looking glass 1 small table. 1 large falling leaf Table 1 large family bible 9 volumes of misllaneous ? works 1 Lot of Fragments of books life of Washington in one volumn 2 volumn Misallanious Bucks Theological Dictionary 2 vol (2 chairs 1 large arm chair 2 arm more chairs
P 17 2 sets silver spoons 3 setts plates 1 small Table 1 Bedstead & furniture 1 cupboard 35 hogs 13 shoats 16 sheep 2 pair dog irons 1 large waggon 1 Rifle gun 1 shot gun 1 grind stone set Black Smith tools 1 woman saddle 1 large wheel & cards small spinning wheel scythe & cradle mowing scythe 15 bushels thrisher wheat cutting box 3 hives bee 50 empty gums Grid iron Pa hooks Ladle washing pan large iron 1 keeler set shoemaker tools Lot leather 1 side of upper leather side sole leather side sole leather tub of tools Trout ads. 1 axe 1 Lot of iron 1 flesh knife 2 tobs 1 churn 2 keeler two water pails 2 pails 2 trays 2 meal bags kitchen table Homony mortar 1 Teakettle 1 Kugrs 1 skillet small pot and pot hooks 1 pair broker Grid iron & shovel 1 oven & lid 1 Tobbot 1 oven & lid 1 large kittle 1 large wheel & cards 1 title wheel 1 yoke oxen & yokes 1 red & white steer 1 heifer 1 Dit 1 red & white steer 1 Bull 1 young yoke oxen & yoke 1 steer 1 small steer 2 steers 1 heifer 1 small cow 1 red cow 5 yearlings 1 small black heifer 2 heifers 5 steers 2 cows & calves 1 Gray horse 1 Sorrel mare colt of the above mare 1 sorrel mare & colt 1 yearling colt 1 two year old filly A Bedsteads beds & furniture 1 Bureau 1 small table 1 large chest 1 small looking glass 1 Trunk 1 small Do 2 pitchers 2 setts knifes & forks 2 small Boll cups saucers 3 dishes 1 set plates 6 Teacups 5 small cups 1 large tumblar 2 Bolls candle stick and snaffers 1 candle stick forks & forks & spoons 6 glass tumblers 3 Bolls 3 Bolls & plates 2 pitchers 1 cream ring & sugar bo 1 Bottle 1 coffee pot 1 salt cellar 2 pepper boxes tea pot sugar Boll vinegar anyell & Bottles Jug of honey 1 pair snfers 1 jar honey paral bed cloth

2 table cloths parol of toillets 1 pr. scissors Terkin Hogs lard 1 ferkin ditto 1 pair steel yards 1 pair old saddle bags 1 hammer Tar stand 1 C chair Loom & geer shuttles Timples 3 weaving slays 2 pair weaving Braces 1 weaving slay 6 Dozens candles 1 man's saddle much worn 1 side saddle 1 Boys Ditto 1 can 1 Bridle 1 Dozen fowl 1 side upper leather 85 pounds bacon A jarr 2 coffeepots 1 Jar 3 crocks Bread Basket one pair candle moulds Coffee well Grin lock mounting 18¼ lb. wool 2 Butcher knives & steel case Rasors box strap 1 C 1 jar vinegar 1 Flower barrel 1 poplar table 16 weaving spools 1 pot rack one note on Wm Ussury for $175 to be discharged in saddle a fair and reasonable trade prior dates 3rd Novr. 1829

P 18 payable 9 months after dates following a date Recd 3rd Nov 1829 one saddle at $20.7 Nov. 1829 on Woman Saddle $25. January 14 1830 one saddle $20 Recd. Feby 20 1830 one horse $27.50 Recd. May 1st 1830 one saddle $20 making in all $112.50 caring a balance of $62.50 doubtful one note on Hannah Anderson (a free woman of color) for $50 executed 9 January 1830 payable 12 months after date with a cut it of $5. carring a balance of $45 doubtful.

One Note on W. Marllow for 10 Barrels corn excuted 27 March 1830 payable 15 March 1830 doubtful one note on John & Charles winet for $20.15 due 1st Oct. 1830 doubtful one note on William Ussury for $40. due 10 May 1830 with a credit their of $20 doubtful one note on Walker Bennett for $2 werth of cotton due 1st Nov. 1829 Bad one note on Morgan Duncan executed to Isaac Taylor (not (tranfeered) for $3.61¼ due on apptication with a credit of twenty five cents the other bad one note on James B. Robinson for $6 executed to Wm & Mattheas Ande son due in Jan 1822 bad one note on David Davis for $6.83 executed to Wm & Mattheas Anderson due 22nd Jany 1822 with a credit of $2.24 out the other bad one note on Isaiah Cole for twenty five barrels good sound corn due 1st Nov 1830 doubtful One note on Jacob A. Lane for $10 due 29th Oct. 1827 with a credit of $5. indenised theiron good one note on Isaiah Cole for $32.50 to be discharged in corn at one dollar per barrel due 1st Nov 1830 bad one note on William Ussury executed to Wm & Mattheas Anderson balance due on said not $15 all of wheel Wm Anderson Decd. untitled to the Adm. of M. Anderson Decd. having recd. one half of the note 1 c. doubtful one on James Bergerson for $1. bad one on James W. Glene for $1.56 doubtful one on Duncan Wade for $23.64¼ good. The following and amounts created pending the partianship between William Anderson Decd. and Morgan Duncan all of which belong exclusendy to the estate of said William Anderson Decd by contract between him and said Duncan Towit:

One on Charles Debrell Snr. for $1.50

Doubtful one on Emey Burnnett $ .50bad

One one	Rubard Indson	$ .62½	doubtful
" "	Wm List	2.22¼	good
" "	Henry Alkerson	1.25	doubtful
" "	Asa Certain	.31	good
" "	Joseph Knowles	.35	D
" "	Walker Bennett	3.77½	Bad
" "	Washington Isham	.62½	doubtful
" "	James W. Gann	.50	Do
One on	Wm Price Ser.	$1.00	Do
" "	Wm Anderson M. G.	4.20	good
" "	Wm Williams	1.00	doubtful
" "	Wm Irwin	3.03¾	Do
" "	Jas Jones	2.37	bad
" "	Earl Carroll	.70	bad
" "	Robr. McCewm	2.50	doubtful

"	"	Susamiah Byern	.75 bad
"	"	John Rose	.62½ good
"	"	Josiah Williams	.87½ doubtful
"	"	Thomas Gibbons	$ .40 doubtful
"	"	William Rogers	.20 Do
"	"	James Baker	.50 Do
"	"	David Andrews	.93 Do
"	"	Jestha Lirst	.50 Do
"	"	Ganys Hutson	$ .35 doubtful
"	"	Tho's Sperry	1.12½ Do
"	"	Wm Baker	.25 Do
"	"	Jestha Yarbrough	.75 Do

one negro man named Amos. one negro woman named Lydia one negro boy named Niche one other Negro boy named Same. one negro girl named Peggy—and additional Inventory will be returned when we shall be able to acertain the balance of the property 18th October 1830.

P 19

John H. Andrews
John W. Roberts

Recorded 17th June 1831
Test Jacob A. Lane clerk
White County court.

An amount of the sale of the property of William Anderson Decd. returned an oath by John H. Ande son and John W. Roberts Admrs. at October Session A. D. 1830 Towit:

John Walker one half of a wheat fan	$9.00
Jno. Jno. Anderson 1 pair smoothing Iron	.93¾
Daniel Clark 1 pair sheep shears	.25
John W. Roberts 1 Frying pan	.68¾
Joseph Kerr 2 purvles & 1 Cullvates	1.56¼
William J. Bennett 1 Barshear plough	1.00
John Gibson 1 plough	.62½
Joseph Kerr 1 Bull tongue plough 68¾ 1 Log chain 3.37½ 1 swing table chain & grindstone 56¼ 2 swingletree & 2 clocks $1.55 1 swingletree .38 Wm J. Bennett 1 sprouting hoe .38	6.93
John Gibson 1 Mattock 76 1 Fro .50 1 pot rack .75	
Joseph Kerr 3 weeding hoe .70 2 spades .75	
1 pair traces bridle, collar and leire 3	
1 Ditto $1.25 1 meat axe .20	5.90
James Cooper Snr. 3 weeding hoes	.30
Jestha Yarbrough 1 spade	.25
John A Carrick 1 pair Harmes Traces collar dridle line	2.81
Wm J. Bennett Chain lenes, collar 1 pair Hames	.56¼
Joseph James two pole axes	2.13
Wm J. Bennett 1 Iron Wedge	.57½
John H. Anderson 1 Iron wedge	.68¾
Jestha Yarbrough 1 broken Iron wedge	.12½
Chawey Newcomb 2 auger	.50
Joseph Jones 1 handsaw	1.00
Chamay Newcomb 1 auger	.50
James Bradly 1 drawing knife	.62½
Forward to page 20	$38.97½
Amount brought from page 19	$38.97½
Elisa Anderwon 1 Bureau $14. 1 Desk $12 2 looking glasses 3.18¾	29.18¾

James Carrick 1 small Table	1.00
John D. Anderson 1 layor folling leaf table	5.25
Eliza Anderson 1 layer family table $4 $inn Vol. Miscellanious works $2.43¾ 1 lot of Fragment of books .25	6.68¾
William Rodgers life of Washington 1 Vol.	.50
John Brown 2 volumes Miscellaney	1.00
Levi Obern, Buck Theorogecal Ditconary 2 vol.	$2.25
Jas Kerr 6 chairs	2.04
George Davis 6 Do	1.74
Levi Oburn 1 Loyd Arm chair	.51
Jas. Jones 2 common chairs	.62½
Eliza Anderson 2 set silver Tea spoons	7.75
William Rodgers 1 set plates	.37½
James Cooper Jr. 1 Do	.37½
Levi Oburn 1 Deo.	.37½
Jesetha Yarbrough 1 small Table	2.00
Eliza Anderson 1 Bedstead bed & furniture $18 2 pair grid irons 3.93¾	21.93¾
Samuel Ussrey 1 cupboard	16.25
Henry Lydia 5 hogs	11.06¼
Russell Gist 5 Do	7.81¼
Anrelew Radley 5 Doo	9.25
Jas Kerr 13 shoats $8.12½ 10 shoats $7.10 shoats $6.75 1 waggon $.72	93.87½
James M. Nelson 16 sheep	10.25
Hugh Gracy 1 Rifle gun	8.00
Chancy Newcomb 1 shot gun	5.00
Anthony Dibrell 1 grind stone $2.75 Set Black Smith tools $4.50	48.25
Isam Cook one new Mans saddle	10.25
Eliza Anderson 1 layd wheel & oids	2.00
May Anderson Small spinning wheel	2.31¼
John Brown scythe & cradle	1.55
Jas Kerr mowing scythe	
Chancy Newcomb 5 Bushels thrished wheat	3.75
Wm J. Bennet 5 Do $3.805 bu Do. $3.75	7.55
William Little cutting hoe	3.31¼
George W. Jones 1 hive bees 2 empty gums	2.25
Jno. Jett 2 Bee hives & 3 empty gums	4.75
Chancy Newcomb Grid iron 50 c pot hook & Ladle 50 c	1.00
John W. Roberts washing bason	.18¾
James Swift large ovem	1.37½
James Carrick 1 Keeler	.12½
George Davis set shoe making tools	1.12½
amo. carried to page 21	$373.46½
P 21 Amot. brought from page 20	$373.46½
Joseph Jones Lot Leather	1.25
Benjam McClain	1.25
Levi Oburm Side Lot leather	.37½
Jas. Jones Do	1.37½
David Heffiner Lot tools	.87½
Joseph Jones foot adz	.50
Jno. W. Roberts 1 axe	.37½
Jas. Herd 1 Lot of Iron	.62½
Danl Clark 1 fash knife	.25
Wm J. Bennett 2 Tubs	.63
Jno. H. Anderson 1 churn	.37½

Nicholas Overton 2 Keelers	.37 ½
Anthony Dibrell 2 water pails	.38
Nicholas Overton 2 pails	.50
Benjamin McClain 2 Trays	.50
Chaney Newcomb 2 meal bags	1.75
Richard Nelson Kitchen Table	.75
John H. Anderson 1 Homany mortar	.12½
Eliza Anderson 1 Tea Kittle	.37½
John W. Roberts 1 Keeler	.14
George Davis 1 skillet	.50
Nicholas Overton 1 small pot & pot hooks	.62½
Wm J. Bennett 1 pair broken grid iron & shovel	.64
Levi Oliver 1 oven & Lid	1.18¾
Chaney Newcomb 1 Tribbet	.12½
John W. Roberts 1 oven & lid	.75
Chaney Newcomb 1 llard kittle	1.50
James Carrick 1 layer wheel & cards	1.50
Berry Harmatt 1 little wheel	.25
Elisha Swift 1 yoke of oxens & yoke	26.25
John Jett 1 Red and white steer	3.75
Hays Arnold 1 heifer	4.00
Anthony Dibrell 1 heifer $4.75 1 red & white steer $4.	8.75
John Jett 1 Bull $4. 1 red cow $7.25	11.25
Jas. Herd 1 young yoke oxen & yoke	12.50
Anthony Debrell 1 steer $4. 2 steer $10 Samuel Duskell 1 heifer	5.25
Nicholas Overton 1 small cow	4.00
James Bradly 5 yearlings	11.00
Jas Kurr 1 black heifer $3.25 1 heifer $2 1 steer $3	8.25
George W. Isam 1 heifer	3.62½
Amot. forwarded to page 22	$518.86½
P 22	
Amot frought from Page 21	$518.86½
John Jett 1 cow & calf	8.87½
Jas Kerr 1 cow & calf	7.56¼
Saml. Druskell 1 Gray horse	40.75
James H. Jenkins 1 sorel mare $32.50 1 colt of above mare $17.	49.50
John L. Prior 1 sorrel mare	40.00
William Buster 1 colt of above mare	25.00
James H. Jenkins 1 yealing colt	20.00
Eliza Anderson one 2 year old filly $40 bed, bedstead & furniture $20.	60.00
Wm Bunker Bed stead, bed & furniture	22.00
Rubard Nelson Do.	25.00
Jno. L. Price Do.	20.00
James Crowder 1 Bureau 13.50	13.50
Rubard Nelson 1 small table	1.00
Eliza Anderson 1 large chest	3.12½
Wm Brown small looking glass	.25
George W. Jones 1 Trunk	.75
Eliza Anderson 1 Trunk 6½c 2 pitchers 25¢	.31½
Jno. L. Price 1 Sett knives & forks	2.25
Joseph Kerr 1 Do.	.87½
Jno. W. Roberts 2 small balls	.68¾
Eliza Anderson cups & saucers	.25
Russell Gist 2 dishes	.91

Samuel Ussery 1 Do.	.25
Jno. W. Robarts 1 Sett plates	.60
Nicholas Overton 6 tea cups 5 saucers	.26¾
James Cooper cups	.18¾
Levi Oliver 1 large Tumbler	.50
Russell Gist 2 bolls	.54
David Hiffner candle stick and snuffers	.60
Joseph Jones Candlestick	.45
Rub. Indsaw forks & spooner	.18¾
Jnos. Kur 6 Glass Tumblers	.37½
Danl. Clark 2 Bottles	.25
Daml. Ussury 1 Dol	.40
Nicholas Overton 3 Bolls & plates	.50
Richard Indsaw 2 pitchers	.25
Jas. Kerr cream ring, sugar Boll	.25
William Kerr 1 Bottle	.43
Wm Rodgers 1 coffe pot	.58
Sharp Whitty 1 salt cellar 2 pepper boxes Tea pot & sugar boll	.25
Jno Kerr Vinegar Armlet & Bottle	.25
Arch Bowman 1 jug & honey	3.25
Amot forwarded to page 23	$871.83

P 23 amot. brought from page 22	$871.83
Nicholas Overton 1 pair sapors	.31
John H. Anderson 1 jar Honey	2.00
Eliza Anderson parol bed clothing	.50
Levi Oliver 2 Table cloth	.75
Eliza Anderson parol Tarteles	.50
Jno. L. Price 1 Ferkin Hogs lard	6.00
Levi Oliver 1 Ditto	2.12½
Sam Ussry 1 pair sailyards $1.12½ 1 pair old saddle bags 25¢	1.37½
Jno. Kerr 1 banner Tar stand 1 ¢	.37½
John L Price 1 chair	.50
Jno. W. Roberts Loom & jar $7 shuttles & timples 50¢ the weaving slays $1.25 2 pair weaving carmass $1.04	9.79
James Bradly 1 weaving slay	.50
Jno. H. Anderson 6 Dozen Candles	.75
Wm J. Bennett 1 man saddle much worn	4.50
Eliza Anderson 1 side saddle $6.25 Boys Saddle $2.	8.25
John H. Anderson 1 can	.25
Eliza Anderson 1 Bridle 2¢ 1 Dox foul 50¢	.76
Jas Jones 1 side upper leather 2.25	2.25
Jno. H. Anderson 35 pounds bacon	3.85
Russell Gist 39¢ bacon	4.09½
Geo. W. Jones 11 Bacon	1.32
David Hiffner 1 jar	.37½
John L. Price 1 Do	1.00
Benj Hammott 2 Do $1 1 coffee pot & hook .25	1.25
John Young 1 jar	.25
John W. Roberts 2 crocks	.12½
John Young 1 coffee pot	.43
John W. Roberts bread basket, 1 pair candle moulds 25¢	.25
Wm Rodgers 1 coffee mill	.51
Jno. Young Grid lock & mounting $2.12½ 2 Butcher knives & steel 69¢	2.81½
Wm Rodgers case Razor box & strap 1 ¢	1.31¼
Jno. W. Robarts 1 Jug vinegar	.64
Benj McClain 1 FlourBarrel	.25

Jno. H. Anderson 1 poplar Table .60
Levi Oliver 13½# wool 5.11
Jno. W. Roberts 16 weaving spools .25
$938.49¼

John Anderson
John W. Roberts

Recorded 17th June 1831
Test Jacob A. Lane clerk
White County caurt

P 24 His additional Inventory of the estate of William Anderson Dcd. returned upon oath by John H. Anderson one of the administrator at April Session A. D. 1831 To wit:
Two Barrels 1 young horse a small quanity sod cotton 1 Log chain 15 Bushels wheat 20 Bushels Rye 1 meal trough 1 vinegar cask 2 salt Barrels 2 flour Barrels 1 Jug 3 Barrels 1 large box 1 wheat trough 1 curryimg knife 1 half Bushel measure 1 wire sifter 1 meal chest 1 soap trough 1 pail 1 Lot old iron 8 stacks strow small quanity of unbroken flax 100 barrels corn 36 Bushels corn 46 Bushels rottan corn & crobbin small quanity cabbage 22½ Bushels irish potatoes 22½ Bushels potatoes 800 Bundle fodder 17½ Bushels rye 4¼ Bushels wheat one amot. on Anthony Dibrell for $38.38¼ good one amo. on Duncan Wade $13.11 good
One on Jno Newman for $25.00 good
one on John Cranin 5.31½ bad
" " A. Gamble .12½ good
one claim filed with the Tucker.
The following property is in the possession of the adms. balance unsold one wooden clock Two Saddles recd. of Conn Ussey a States an preceeding paper 14 sides leather not quite Tammed 1 undiffant bed without any furniture.
Hired the negroes belonging to the estate as follows Towit:

Amos for	$56.00
Lydia Amos's wife for	25.00
Peggy for	11.25
Same for	46.00
Hired for 12 months 4 Nov. 1830	
Total	$138.25

Negro boy Miles returned by a former Inventory had been Hired to John Newman by Wm Anderson in his fifetime. Said boy never came to our possession of said Newman prior to the expiration of the term of time of our aid.

John H. Anderson

Recorded and examined 17 June 1831
Test Jacon A. Lane clerk
White County court.

An additional amo. of the property of William Anderson Dcsd. returned on oath by John H. Anderson adm. at April Session 1831.

John H. Anderson 2 Barrels	.50
John W. Roberts 1 young horse	26.25
Eliza Anderson Small quanity seed cotton	2.00
John H. Anderson 1 Log chain 1.75 5 Bushels wheat $4.	5.75
Joseph Burden 5 Budhels wheat	4.05
Amot carried to page 25	$38.55
P 25 Amot. forwarded from page 24	$38.55
Thomas Duncan 5 Bushels wheat	4.00
Joseph Burdin 5 Bushels Rye	1.87½
John H. Anderson 5 Bushels Rye.	1.50

Thomas Duncan 5 Bushels Rye	1.45
John H. Anderson 5 Bushels Rye	1.45
Same 1 meat trough	.30
David Hiffan vinegar cask	.60
Thomas Duncan 2 Salt Barrels	.25
Jno. H. Anderson 2 Flour barrels	.32½
John Gibson 1 Jug	.62½
John H. Anderson 3 barrels	.14
John Gibson 1 large box 25¢ 1 wheat trough 6¼¢	.31¼
Richd Judson 1 currying knife	.25
John Gibson 1 half bushel measure	.25
Jsac Bennett 1 wire sifter	.41
Jno. H. Anderson 1 meal chest 46¢ 1 soap trough 12½¢ 1 pail 30¢	.88½
Richd. Judson 1 Lot old iron	.12½
John H. Jenkins 8 stacks strow	2.92
Eliza Anderson small qunity unbroken Flax.	.25
Gustanas Howard 10 Barrels corn	12.10
John H. Anderson 40 Do	49.60
Richd Nelson 5 Do	6.25
Alexdr. B. Lane 10 Do	12.50
Joseph Collins 20 Do	25.00
Samuel V. Carrick 15 Do	18.25
John H. Anderson 36 Bushels corn $9 46 Bushels rotten corn and nebbins $5.12½ small quanity of cabbage $1.00 22½ Bushels Irish potatoes $4.95	20.07½
John W. Roberts 22½ Bushels potatoes Irish	4.95
John H. Anderson 800 bundles fodder $8.--17½ Bushels Rye $4.17½ 4¾ Bushels wheat 3.56¼	15.73¾
Recd of William Marlowon his note heretofore wintnessed 10 Barrels corn and sold the same on a credit of 12 months for Rend of Isarah Bole 14½ Barrels corn in part of his note for 25 barrels her to fore witness and sold this same as above for	28.8.½
Recd. of Camn Wm Ussury $62.50 in three mens daddle at a fair trade price as spacefor in his note heretofore witnessed and sold on as above for	20.00
	$269.74½

John A. Anderson

Recorded 17th June 1831
Test Jacon A. Lane clerk
White County Court.

P 26 In the name of God Amen. J. John Porter of White County State of Tennessee being weak of body, but of sound and disposing mind and memory blessed be almighty God for the same Do make and publish this my last will and testament in manner and form following this is to say: First I give and bequeath unto my son Joshua Porter one negro girl named Jane, also I further give and divide to my said Son Joshia his heirs assigns all the lands and tenements that I possess in WhiteCounty and lastly as to my personal estate and chattels of what kind and resation sowereI give and bequeath to the balance of my children, to be equally divided amongst them or as near as the value of the case will admit of and do hereby appoint my said son Joshua Porter my sole executor of this my last will and testament hereby regoking all former wills by me made. In witness whereas of I have hereunto Set my hand and Seal this 10th day of February 1831.
Signed Sealed and declared by the above named John Porter to be his last will and testament in presence of as who have hereunto subscribed our names

as witness in presence in presence of the Testator.

Woodson P. White
John Graham

State of Tennessee ⌶
White County ⌶ April Session
⌶ A. D. 1831

This day was provided in open court opposite will bring the last wil and Testament of John Porter Des. and the due executor thereof as such person by the oath of Woodson P. White and John Graham subscribing witness thereto for the purpose and things therein witnessed and that the said Joh Porter was at the execution and publication thereof sound and disposing mi and memory where upon came Woodson P. White into open court and undertook execution thereof and took the oath of an executor and with Jacob Anderson entered into and acknowledged here in the sum of three thousand dollars co tioned as can requires. Which is ordered to be recorded. Given at office April 11th to be recorded.
Test Jacob A. Lane clerk
White County court.
Recorded and examined 20th June 1831
Test Jacon A. Lane clerk
White County court.

Inventory of the estate of John Porter Desd. returned on oath by Woo son P. White Administrator at April Session A. D. 1831 Towit: 2 small stil 1 cupboard 1 clock & case 1 Bedstead & bord 1 Grind stone 1 still Tub & sw ing bag small quanity of powder meal Tub and small Keg. 1 salt keg and whi barrel 2 crocks 1 washing tub 2 pails 1 churn 1 Tray 1 sifter 2 ovens and 2 skillets without lids 1 set grid irons 1 pot 2 pair pot hooks 2 mens sad 1 Bridle 1 womans saddle 1 Lock chain 1 cutting knife and box 1 Flake stan 1 Barrel with some brandy quanity not kown 1 cow hide 1 sheep skin
P 27 1 water table 1 pair shoes 3 home made blankets 1 small blanket thr sheets 1 great coat & some wearing clothes 2 feather beds & Blankets 3 sla & 1 Bag 1 flax wheel 1 cotton wheel 3 Bee gums 1 cart 1 pair of geers 1 De 1 chest 12 peaces bacon a small quanity of hogs lard 1 sorrel mare 1 young horse 2 cows & yearlings 8 hogs a few chickens and geese 5 chairs 1 churn handsaw auger drawing knife 2 Barshear plough 3 Bull tongue 1 clevis 2 iro wedges 2 peaces iron 1 mattock 3 axes 1 broad axe 1 bell & collar 1 pot ra four Tongs 1 pair saddle Bags 3 peaces leather 1 flax hackle 1 Em bullar a small quanity of cotton 2 hogsheads & small keg 2 waggon check reel 2 co pots 4 Tea cups 1 coffee mill 2 small pewter cardes 2 pitchers 8 cups & saucers 8 spoons 5 Earthern Bolls 1 chanber pot 5 Earthen plates 4 pewter plates 2 pewter dishes 3 knives 2 forks 1 pair cloth shears 1 pint bottle 1 churn 1 piggin 1 old scythe & Hangings 1 Rifle gun and shot pouch 1 half Bushel 1 pair steelyards 1 cotton receipt 218 lb Lud cotto n 1 cotton nap 67th Lud cotton 14 gallon cagg 1 small tin box & candle moulds. Rend. $10. cash in hand one note on Francis Johnston $6. One note on Jacob Anderson $ which is to be discharged in Rye one note on John Nearly John S. Moody for $4. one note on David Bradford for about $2.80 one note on R. C. Poteet fo 125 bushel corn due next fare One note John Seals & William Graham one the same for $325 on for $2.75 1 note for 20 on J. A. Jenkins to be dischared in cash notes one note on John Seals for $2.25 one note on Isham Hale for $3. one note on M. & J Webb for $4 one note on James Gramthan for $9 one note one Levi & Thomas Hood for $2.62½ one note on George Miller for $2 one note on John Terry for $14 due 1811.

A. B. There fourth amount of the above debts and doubtful April 18th 1831.

Recorded 20th June 1831

Test Jacob A. Lane clerk
White County court.

J, Thomas Scott of the County of White and State of Tennessee being old and infirm in body but of perfect mind and recollection viewing the uncertainty of life. Do make and ordain this my last will and testament 1st I do this day by a bill of sale given to my two children Jonathan Scott and Hanniah Broyles and her heirs slaves named in this said bills of sale bearing with date here with it is my will and desire that the remander of my slaves Towit: Harny Jane & Billy at my death be freed from the bonds of slavery theof are old and have been faithful servants towit. It is my will and desired that all the remander of the property which I have both real and personal which I may have after keeping the afoward slaves be equally divided
P 28 between my son and daughter Jonathan Scott & Hannah Broyles and their heirs forward. I have made and signed this my will in presence of this 6th of Sept. 1829.

his
Thomas x Scott (Seal)
mark

Attest
Samuel Turney
Joseph Kerr Jur.

State of Tennessee
White County October Session of the county court A. D. 1830
This day the last will and testament of Thomas Scott Desd. was provided in open court and the admr. executor and pregtecatior thereof provided by the oath of Samuel Terney and Joseph Kerr Jenr subscribing witness thereto for the purposes and things therein witnessed and that the said Thomas Scott was to the best of their knowledge of sound and disposing mind and memory which is asked to be recorded. Given at office 11th October 1830.
Recorded 20 June 1831
Test Jacob Al Lane clerk
White County Court.

Test Jacob A Lane clerk
White County court.

Inventory of the estate Thomas Scott Ded. returned on oath by Jonathan Scott admr. with the will of the Desd marked at October Session 1830. 1 negro woman Jenny Snr. 1 negro man William 4 head of Horses 12 head cattle 17 head hogs 35 head of cows 2 stacks oats quanity not known 1 stack flax do 1 old set waggon irons 3 pairs of geers 3 ploughs 4 hoes 6 falling axes 1 Broad axe 1 Log chain 1 Iron pitchfork 1 Dying fork 2 mattocks 2 cluepols 1 fool adz 1 drawing knife 1 flax broken 2 Bells 1 Gun banco 1 side leather 1 old saddle and bridle 1 fire shovel and tongs 1 copper tea kettle 3 pots 1 oven 4 pewter dishes 16 pewter plates 3 pewter Basins 1 great coat 2 chests & wearing clothes 1 Looking glass 2 feather beds and furniture 1 Bedstead 1 Iron wedge one note on Aaron England $73 date 16th Dec. 1823 with a credit of $15.14 March 1829 also credited with $11 Jany 17th 1830 one amout on John Smith for $3 good one amont on John England for $1 good one note on Jacob Robinson date 20th January 1823 for $68 balance by credits to $32.16 cents carrying interest from 8th August 1830.

his
Jonathan x Scott
mark

Recorded 20 June 1831
Test Jacob A. Lane clerk
White County Court.

2 Willis Winfree of the county of White and State of Tennessee, being of sound mind and disposing memory do hereby make my last will and testament in manner and form following that is to say I devise that all my present debts shall be paid and after the discharged of these debts. I bequeath into my beloved wife Sarah Winefree all my real and personal property during her natural life or widowhood for the purpose of raising my children and her support and at the experation or death of beloved wife Sarah or marriage. it is my desire that my property both real and personal shall b equally divided amongst my children that is to say Elexander Winfree now bearing the name of Elexander Gridsom Banks Winefree Susan Mattock Lythea B. Winfree, Rhoda J. Winfree, Joseph S. Winefree and lastly I do hereby constitute and appoint my beloved son Banks Winefree my sole executor of this my last will and testament this 27th day of October A. D. 1829.

Willis Winfree (Seal)

Signed and acknowledged in presence of Wamen Leftwich
Jacob Kuhn Spoonur
Jonathan F. Farrington.

State of Tennessee
White County

January Session of the County A. D. 1830. This day was provided in open court the last will and Testament of Willis Winefree Decd. whereupon the adm. executor thereof was presented in open court

P 29 by the oath of Wamon Liftwich and Jacob Kuhn Spooner two subscribing witness thereto for the purpose and things thereon witnessed and that the said Willis Winefree was at the execution thereof of sound and disposing mind and memory. Whereupon it is asked to be recorded. Given at office 11 January 1830.
Test Jacob A. Lane clerk
White County court.
Recorded 20th June 1831
Test Jacob A. Lane clerk
White County Court.

In the name of God Amen. I William Fisher being weak and Sickly in body but of strong mind and perfect memory Do make and ordain this my last will and Testament: First and in the first place. I give my soul to Almighty God and my body to the dust from which it came to be buried in good decent christian burial at the discrition of my executors Second I give and bequeath unto my beloved wife one negro girl named Catharine as long as she remaines a widow one cow and calf the peck of my block one goo feather bed and furniture my daughter Masse Moore has got her portion of this title white 2 give unto my daughter Elizabeth a good feather bed and furniture a cow and calf called Bute I give my oldest son John one young man bridle and saddle. I give my son William one young horse colt I also give unto my wife one horse called Florince and my mare called Nance and thirteen head of hogs the balance of my persheation property to be given up to my executors for them to sell and all the loose plunder, my waggon forming tools that is on my plantation which I now live to be sold and the money to be equally divided between my wife and all the children two stell and a set of still tubs to be sold with the rest of the property. I want my wife to have the use of my plantation where I now live to raise her children on as long as she remains a widow and the balance of my lands to be rented out and the rest to be applied to the use of raising family. and four large barrels of brandy to be sold with rest of plunder. I wished one yoke of steers and cart the house hold and kitchen furniture for the u of my family. In confermation whereof I appoint

P 30 my friends Daniel Walling and Isaac Tailor my Sole executor this 19 day of February one thousand eight hundred and thirty one.

Wm Fisher

Wilson Upchurch
Samuel A. his X Moore
mark

State of Tennessee }
White County } April Session County Court A. D. 1831.

This day the last will and testament of William Fisher Decd. was provided in open court and the adm. executor and publication thereof was provided in open court by the oath of Wilson Upchurch and Samuel A. Moore subscribing witness thereto for the purposes and things therein witnessed and that the said William Fisher was at the execution thereof of sound and disposing mind and memory whereupon Isaac Taylor and Daniel Walling named executor therein appeard in court and undertook the oath prescribed by law and with Thomas Robinson and James Randols entered into and acknowledged bond conditioned as the law requires which is asked to be recorded.
Given at office 11 April 1831.

Test Jacob A. Lane clerk
White County court

Recorded 20 June 1831
Test Jacob H. Lane clerk
White County Court.

Amont of the sales of the property of the estate of Gilly Geer Decd. returned on oath by James Cooper & Sanuel Ussury at January Session 1830.

1 cow & yearling $7.12½ Loom & Shuttle $3.25 3 slays & Harness $1.12½	11.50
1 iron wedge .50¢ 4 chairs 50¢ 1 mare $3	
1 set plates 81¼¢ 2 dishes 37½	5.18¾
1 crock & cups 6¼¢ 1 Box 56¼¢ 2 pairs & horse shoes 25¢ 1 chest 50¢ 1 Tub 25¢	1.62½
Wheel & cards 37½¢ 1 Brindle 12½¢ cotton 1.31¼ Bed and stead 500¢ hoe 25¢	7.06¼
1 side leather 275¢ 1 field corn 15.00 1 Lot hogs 5.68¾ 1½ Bus Rye 50¢	23.93¾
	$49.31¼

Recorded 20th June 1831
Test - Jacob A. Lane clerk
White County court.

James Cooper
Samuel Ussery
Administrator

A list of the sale of the property of John Pass Decd. returned on oath by James H. adm. at April Session 1829.

Martha Pistole 3 cutting knives	$3.50
Martha Pistole	
Alfred G. Bradly 1 stack Fodder	2.00
Thomas Williams 1 stack Fodder	2.00
William Warriner 1 stack Do	1.04¼
Thomas Williams 50 Bushels corn	8.12½
Martha Pistole 1 saw	2.06¼
William Akendge 1 stack fodder	1.25
James H. Pass 1 stack fodder	1.62½
Jacob Robinson 1st Lot of 1st choice of pork 575th	14.32½
James H. Pass 2/2 choice lots at $2 6/8 per c. wt 1100 lb	30.25
Wm Akridge 1 lot at $2 7/8 per C wt 575 lb.	16.52½
Alfred G. Bradly last lot at $2 7/8 per c. wt 606 lb.	17.30
Josiah Burgess 20 Barrels corn at 6 per Barrel	20.00
James H. Pass 28 Barrels & 3 Bur at 6/ per Barrel	28.60

Thomas Williams 50 Bushels corn at 7/6 per Barrel 12.
P 31 Martha Pistole 1 cow & yearling 6.
Thomas Pistole 50 Bushels corn at 6/ p. Barrel 10.
Martha Pestole 25 Bushels corn at 6/ per Barrel 5.
Benjamin Welhite 25 Bushels corn at 6/ per Barrel 5.
$187.

James H. Pass Admr.

Recorded 20th June 1831
Test Jacob A. Lane clerk
White county court.

An additional Inventory of the estate of John Pistole Decd. returned on oath by James H. Pass admr. at April Session 1829.
one note on Telford for $30.96 due 4 March 1824 bad debt $30.
note on Jared C. Pucket for $10 good 10.
Receipt on P. Williams for the collection of a debt on Abner Vaughn for $115 bad and hopeless 115.
Note on John Dean for $13 bad debt 15.
Amont on Charles Manning 17.
A list of the hire of the negroes belonging to the estate of John Pistole Decd after the widow ahd off her Thirds.- Sale of 1827.
James H. Pass to per boy Jeffy 37.
James H. Pass to P boy Simon 39.
Benjamin Wilhite to P. Girl May 31.
Robert Howard to P Boy Charles 50.

Amot forwarded to page 32 $345.4

P 32 Amount brought from page 31 $345.4
proceedings for 1828.
James H. Pass to per Girl May 8.
Jess England to P. boy Charles 76.
John H. Anderson to P. Boy Simon 52.
James H. Pass to P. Boy Jeffy 52.
William Rutledge to 70 Bushels corn $14 John Rutledge to 70 Bus. corn $14 which was for wet extra of the widows thirds 28.
$561.

James H. Pass Adm.

Recorded 20th June 1831
Test Jacob A. Lane clerk
White County court.

Report of the settlement by commissioners, with James H. Pass admr. of John Pistole Decd. returned at July session A. D. 1829.

State of Tennessee }
White County } Pursuant to an order issued from the worshipped cou of please and quarter session for White County and to us the undersigned directed to settle with James H. Pass adminstrator of John Pistole Decd. u to the 1st day of January 1829 by leave to report as follows Towit:— It appears from the records furnished us that the said pass in Chargeable and indebted to said estate for the amount of sales of property negro here /c to the amount of $1776.77 cents and the said pass exhitels his amount as here with filed and allowed him against said estate to the amount of $1263.31 cents and that these was purchased by the widow Martha at the sal of the property of the Decd to the amount of $344.61¼ cents and by Thomas J. Pistole one of the heirs to the amount of $183.91 cents and also by Ben

Wilhite one other of the heirs to the amount of $153.37½ cents which several sum have not been by him collected as he states and which amount he claimes a credit for in addition to his account aganst said estate which when added to his account makes in all the sum of $1945.20¾ cents which after deducting the amount he is chargeable with would leave the estate indebted to him the sum of $168.23¾ cents up to 1st January 1829. Given into our hands and seals this 13th day of July 1829.

David Snodgrass (Seal)
Anthony Dibrell (Seal)
William Simpson (Seal)

Recorded 20th June A. D. 1831
Test Jacon A. Lane clerk
White County court.

Inventory of the estate of Martha Pistole Desd returned upon oath by James H. Pass administrator at July Session A. D. 1829 1 Dish 1 Bason 1 earthen dish 1 Sett cups & saucer 2 Tea cups 1 coffee pot 1 sett knives & forks 2 preserve pots 3 earthen plates 9 pewter plates 1 pair sheep shears 1 candle stick 2 Basons 1 spoon & funnel 1 salt cellar and sugar comnister P 33 1 pair cotton cards 1 cotton wheel 1 yoke of oxen 1 Waggon 1 oven & lid 1 pot & hooks 1 pot & Bail 1 kettle 1 pot rack 1 water vessel churn and half bushel 1 Loom 1 plough & swingletree 1 coulter and flock of Geese 2 head of sheep 24 head of hogs 12 head of cattle 1 sorrel mare 1 Gray mare 1 sorrel colt 1 yearling filly 2 crocks 1 Tin bucket 1 jug 1 Tea kettle 1 Jug 1 jar 1 fire shovel 1 scythe & cradle 3 Tubs 1 Grind stone 1 sifter and meal Tub 1 dresser 1 pair warping bars 1 Table 1 axe 2 jugs 2 Beds & bedsteads 1 chest 1 Book case 1 Bible 11 chairs 1 mattock 1 pair fire dogs 1 side saddle 1 flat iron 2 Bee stands 1 Big pot 2 hoes 3 cutting knives 2 pitchers 1 Tumbler 1 cloth brush 1 flax wheel 1 Looking glass 2 Raw hides.

James H. Pass Admr.

Recorded 20 June 1831
Test Jacob A. Lane clerk
White County court.

An Inventory of the estate of John Anderson Desd returned on oath by Robert Anderson snr. admr. at October session 1828 Towit:
3 beds and furniture of sound quality, 1 common cupboard plain walnutl small book case small and rough a terporary one 1 Table and 9 chairs table nearly worn out 1 large pot 1 small pot 1 small oven 1 kettle small 1 skillet (small also) 1 cotten wheel worth scarely anything 1 flax wheel Unclap 1 pair cotton cards half worn 1 washing Tub 2 piggins 1 sifter for meal 1 mare 1. 2 year old colt (a mare) & 2 young colts 1 smothing iron 1 looking glass (a small one) 1 old man saddle 1 snoffer bit bridle 1 small fire shovel 1 sett of plow gears iron Traces 3 cows 3 yearlings and 2 calves 20 head of sheep there are some hogs not yet reduces to possession so as to know exacty the number a quality 1 axe partly worn 1 mattock partly worn 1 hoe 1 iron wedge 2 shovel ploughs Towit: 1 old & 1 new 1 Bull Tongue plough 1 coutle 1 common panned loom 1 hackle for flax 1 cutting knife for straw 1 pair sheep shears 1 auger 2 Seperate small swingletrees 1 part worn handsaw 20 Geese there is a crop of cotton on the farm of the Desd. also of corn yet to be used or disposed of one fourth John Franklin is entitled to 2 small pewter dishes 4 pewter plates partly 5 earthen plates 5 Bowls small common ones 1 Broken set knives and forks a few spoons 1 coffee pot 1 Broken set teacups and saucers.

Robert Anderson Adm.

Recorded 20th June 1831.

Test - Jacob A. Lane clerk
White County Court.

Return of Barnett King Guardian to the heirs of Asa Mott Desd. made on oath at April session 1829 Towit:

April Court 1829 after settling all expences I find a balance remaining of three dollars and sixty nine and a half cents due by.

B. King Guardian

Recorded 20th June 1831
Test Jacob A. Lane clerk
White County Court.

Return of George W. Ledbetter Guardian to Polly Simpson made on oath at January Session 1829 Towit:

To amount record $10.00
2 cow & calf and 4 head of hogs

George W. Ledbetter

Recorded 20th June 1831.
Test Jacob A. Lane clerk
White County Court.

Return of John Walker Guardian to the heirs of Kindall Savage Desd. made on oath at January Term 1829 Towit:
No alteration in the estate of the heirs of Kindoll Savage since the Last years return.

John Walker

Recorded 20 June 1831
Test - Jacob A. Lane clerk
White County Court.

Return of John Walker Guardian to the heirs of Alexander Kerr Desd. made on oath at January Session 1829. Towit:
No alteration in the estate of the heirs of Alexander Kerr sinee the last years return.

John Walker

Recorded 20th June 1831
Test - Jacob A. Lane clerk
White County Court.

Return of Hannah Broyles Guardian to Solina & Abraham Broyles made on oath at April Session A. D. 1829 Towit:
She states that since her return made in 1828. Solina has arrived at the age of 21 years and that she has paid Solina the sum of forty dollars part of her estate, that there has been no alteration as to the money of Abraham Broyles except the addition thereto of the simple interest on the money his part of the nut of land is worth say three dollars a year.

Hannah his X mark Broyles

Recorded 20th June 1831
Test - Jacob A. Lane clerk
White County Court.

Return of William Hill Guardian to William H. Cluxorn seviving heir to Elijah Cluxon Jur. Desd made on oath at January Session A. D. 1829.
There came into my hands as Guardian to said tifnut the sum of $500.
Increase thereof up to 11th January 1829. 243.

Amont paid out for said ward as fully appear by my report to January Term 1828 $51.25
Paid to said Ward a horse at 80.00
and cash $30 all for unessary equipage and support 30.00
F 35 paid to the clerk for this report .62½
paid for trustee for said ward the sum of 8.70
170.57½
$573.36¼

Which leaves in my hands of the wards money the above sum of five hundred and seventy three dollars thirty six and a fourth cents including the original debt and interest said Guardian farthis states that a farm desended to said Ward whereas Richard Brown now lives that a settlement for improvements /c has taken place, that said Brown is to have the plantation or the use of some until the sum of ninety three dollars is discharged by rents /c said Brown having occupied said farm one year Say 41 acres at one dollar and fifty cents per acre leaving dew said Brown in like manner thirty one dollars and fifty cents which is to be paid in rents of said farm or property - as part of the amount paid the further sum of fifty dollars for unlessaries which will then leave in my hands the sum of $523.36¼
January 18, 1829

Wm Hill Guardian

Recorded 20th June 1831
Test Jacob A. Lane clerk
White County court.

Return of James Anderson joint Guardian with James W. Copeland of the heirs of John Anderson Desd. makes oath that he has no money in his hands sworn to in open court 13th Oct. 1829.

J. A. Lane clerk

Test Jacob A. Lane clerk
White County court.

Return of Joseph Herd Guardian for Morgan & Susanah Bryan infact heirs of Morgan & John Bryon Desd made on oath at January Session 1829.
To Susanniah Bryan for rents of the year 1827 the sum of $20.45
Cr. By cash paid as Guardian 5.24
As to Morgan there is nothing dew to him nor four him yet.
Recorded 20th June 1831
Test J. A. Lane clerk
White County Court.

Return of Isaac Taylor Guardian to Eliza D. Gleeson made on oath at January Session 1831. Towit:

Isaac Taylor Guardian of Eliza D. Gluson reports to court that he has laid out and expended for the use and crufet of his work Eliza D. Gluson for various wares and merchandies since his last report of the 19th January 1828.

The said Isaac Taylor Guardin as above reports to court that he has received of the money of his ward Eliza D. Gleeson since his last report of the 19th January 1828. Viz:

By cash received from John W. Gluson adm. of Edward Glusom8 $55.06
By two notes for the heir of two negroes Henry & Emily not yet dew 45.00
12 January1829. $100.06

Isaas Taylor Guardian
of Eliza D. Gleeson

Recorded 20th June 1831
Test Jacob A. Lane clerk
White County court.

P 36 Return of Anthony Dibrell Guardian to the minor heirs of Matthas Anderson Dead made on oath at January Session 1829. Towit:
I do hereby report that no funds has as yet come to my hands as guardian of said infant children.

Anthony Dibrell Guardian

Recorded 20th June 1831
Test Jacob A. Lane clerk
White County Court.

Return of John W. Gleeson Guardian to Frances Gleeson made on oath at January Session A. D. 1829 Towit:
I John W. Gleeson Guardian to Frances Gleeson Do hereby report the following account for the year 1828 Hired one negro boy called boy called Henry to Thomas Green for which I hold his note for the sum of $15 dew 13th February 1829.
Hired one negro boy named William to Juleus Sanders for which I now hold his note with Archibold Conner Securetery for the sum of $20.25 due 13th February 1829.

John W. Gleeson Guardian
of F. Gleeson

Recorded 20th June 1831
Test Jacob A. Lane clerk
White County court.

Return of Anthony Dibrell Guardian to the heirs of Wm Gracy Dead. made on oath at January Term 1831.- Reports and says he has no funds as yet come to his hands as guardian to said infant heirs.

H. D. Dibrell Guardian

Recorded 20 June 1831.
Test J. A. Lane clerk

Return of George W. Ledbetter Guardian to Polly Simpson an infant made on oath at January Session 1830. Towit:
That since the last return to this court he has not received any additional part of the estate of said child He is now living on, and cultivating part of the land divided to said Polly Simpson Do theirs.

George W. Ledbetter

Recorded 20th June 1831
Test Jacob A. Lane clerk
White County Court.

Return to Thomas Hill Guardian to the heirs of James Hill Dead. made upon oath at January Session 1830.
The amount of money in hands of
P 37 Guardian is $240.00
Expendition for Taxes of 1829 $.34½
clerk fee on Return of Guardian .62½
bought the widows part of the land for the heirs 5.00 5.97
234.03

Recorded 20th June 1831 Tho. Hill Guardian
Test Jacob A. Lane clerk
White County Court.

Return of Barnett Kemp Guardian of Asa Moot Decd made on oath at January Term 1830 Towit:

The amount due the heirs of Asa Moot Decd after all parts credits is given is four and a half cents.

B. Kemp

Recorded 20th June 1831
Test Jacob A. Lane clerk
White County court.

Return of Robert Cooke Guardian to the heirs of Elijah Sayer Decd. made on oath of January Session 1830 Towit

The amount as settled by Major Isaac Taylor & Eli Sims Esqs. then return being \$161.70¼ — of which sum was paid for schooling books and clerks Janr. 1828 \$7.50 — In the year 1829 paid for schooling Books & to Jess H. Vermillion for teaching Bartlett and Peggy Sayers 5 months \$6. For shhool Books and paper \$.87½ for clerks for on last January return .62½.

Robert Cooke

Recorded 20th June 1831
Test Jacob A. Lane clerk
White County court.

Return of Hannah Broyles Guardian of Abraham Broyles made on oath at January Term 1830 Towit:

That there has been no alternation in the estate of his word madeby her since her last return — January 11th 1830.

her
Hannah x Broyles
mark

Test Jacob A. Lane clerk
White County court.

Return of Joseph Herd Guardian to Susannah Broyles made on oath at Jannuary 1830.
Towit:

Dr. to cash received for rents	\$17.50
Cr. By cash paid for repairs & Taxes \$11.03½	
By cash for shhooling 4.00	15.03½
January 11th 1830	\$ 2.46½

Joseph Herd Guardian

Recorded 20th June 1831
Test Jacon A. Lane clerk
White County court.

P 38 Return of Joseph Herd Guardian to Susanah Bryan made of oath at January Session 1830 towit:

Makes the following return for 1829.

Drs. To cash received for rents	\$17.50
Or By cash for repairs & Taxes \$11.03½	
By Cash for shhooling 4.00	15.03½
	\$ 2.46½

Joseph Herd Guardian

Recorded 20th June 1831
Test — Jacob A. Lane clerk
White County court

Return made by William Hill Guardian to William H. Cluxon, heir to

Elijah Cluxon Jur Decd. made on oath at January Term 1830.
Amot remaining in my hands 1st. January 1829 belonging to said infant $523.
Insterest occonrg thereon to 1st January 1830 31.

$554.7

Amont paid out for said ward as P. receipt from R. Brown for unessine $38.75
Interest on this payment from 1st October 1829 to 1st January in the year 1830. .57 39.3
$515.42

Which leaves in my hands of said words money the sum of five hundred fifteen dollars forty two and a fourth cents including the original debt and interest. I have also received from Richard Brown the sum of Twenty five dollars in property it being in part of the amount due from said Brown for rents upon the property of said Ward after said Brown keeping said farm the year 1829. deduct out of the above sum the sum of sixty two and a half cents for making this report 9th January 1830.

Wm Hill Guardian

Recorded 20th June 1831
Test Jacob A. Lane clerk
of White County court.

Return made by Alexander Glenn Guardian to Layton Hitton made on oath January Term 1831.

I have money in my hands and possession the sum of one hundred and te dollars and twenty three cents includes principal and interest thereon from 1st January 1829 to the 1st January 1830 amounts to the sum of six dollars sixty one and three fourth cents — Principal and interest $16.8

Alexander Glenn

Recorded 20th June 1831
Test Jacob A. Lane clerk
of White County court.

Return of George W. Ledbetter Guardian to Polly Simpson made on oath at April Session 1831. being an amount for expences /c.

For clothing, washing, boarding and lodging said infant from the Octob Term 1827. of White County Court up to the present day viz: the 12th April 1830. at 20 dollars per year $50.00

George W. Ledbetter

Recorded 20th June 1831.
Test — Jacob A. Lane clerk
White County Court.

Return of Isaac Taylor Guardian of Eliza D. Gleeson made on oath at January Session 1830.

Guardian has laid out and exBendence in purchasing goods, wares and merchandise for the use and benefit of his word Eliza D. Gleeson since his last report 12th January 1829.

and that he has received notes executed to him as Guardian to Eliza D. Gleeson for the hire of a negro woman and negro girl for the hire of a negro woman and negro girl for the year 1829. but not yet due for $42.43½
P 39 15th January 1831.

Isaac Tayler Guardian
of Eliza D. Gleeson

Recorded 20 June 1831.

Test — J. A. Lane clerk

Return of John Walker Guardian to heirs of Kindall Savage Desd made on oath at January Term 1830 Towit:

No alteration in the estate of the heirs of Kindall Savage since years return.

John Walker Guardian

Recorded 20th June 1831.
Test - Jacob A. Lane clerk
White County court.

Return of John Walker Guardian to heirs of Alexander Kerr Desd. made on oath at January Term 1831.

On alteration made in the estate of the heirs of Alexander Kerr since last year return.

John Walker Guardian

Recorded 20th June 1831
Test Jacob A. Lane clerk
White County Court.

Return of Anthony Dibrell Guardian to the heirs of Mattheas Anderson Desd. made on oath at January Term 1831.

Guardian Reports that none of the estate of his words have come to his hands.

Anthony Dibrell Guardian

Recorded 20 June 1831
Test Jacob A. Lane clerk
White County court.

Return of Anthony Dibrell Guardian to the heirs of William Gracy made on oath at January Tern 1830 Towit:

That none of the estate has come to his hands and possession.

Anthony Dibrell Guardian

Recorded 20th June 1831
Test Jacob A. Lane clerk
White County court.

Return of John Walker Guardian to the heirs of Kindall Savage Desd. made on oath at January Term 1831.

No alteration in the estate of the heirs of Kindall Savage since last years return.

John Walker Guardian

Recorded 20th June 1831
Test Jacob A. Lane clerk
White County Court.

P 40 Return of John Walker Guardian to the heirs of Alexander Kerr Desd. made on oath at January session 1831.

No alteration in the estate except 2 have with mahats the oldest heir and paid her one hundred and eleven dollars and forty centsApril 17th 1830. this 10th January 1831.

John Walker Guardian

Recorded 20th June 1831
Test Jacob A. Lane clerk
White County court.

Return of Thomas Hill Guardian to the heirs of James Hill Decd. made on oath at January Term 1831.

Paid to Clabcern Hill one of the heirs he being Forety one years of age $63.00

The balance remaining in my hands is $189. January 10th. 1831

Thomas Hill Guardian

Recorded 20th June 1831
Test Jacob A. Lane clerk
White County court.

Return of George W. Ledbetter Guardian to Polly Simpson made on oath at January Session 1831.

That he has received for rent of land	30.
Bushels corn	$ 6.00
also oats to the amount of	2.00
	8.00

Recorded 20 June 1831 George W. Ledbetter
Jacob A. Lane clerk
White County court.

Return of 2 quatans Howard Guardian to heirs of James Howard Decd. made on oath at January Term 1831. amount in my hands $163.43½ Interest on sum from 22nd Decr. 1829 to 22nd Decr. 1830 $9.78 alowed not by worn irrepair. $10.

Now in my hands as Guardian 10 January 1831 $163.21½

Recorded 20th June 1831
Test J. A. Lane clerk

Jqa. Howard Guardian

P 41

Return of Anthony Dibrell Guardian to the minor heirs of Mattheas Anderson Decd. made on oath at January Term 1831.

That he has no money in his hands as Guardian.

A Dibrell

Test - Jacob A. Lne clerk
White County court.

Return of Anthony Dibrell Guardian to the heirs of Wm Gracy Decd. made on oath at January Term 1831.

That he has no money in his hands as Guardian.

A. Dibrell

Recorded 20th June 1831
Test Jacob A. Lane clerk
White County Court.

Return of Alexander Glenn Guardian to Laton Hutton made on oath at January Term 1831.

That he has in his hands $123.85 cents in cahh being the principal and interest from the 1st day of January 1830 up to the 1st day of January 1831.

Alexander Glenn Snr.

Recorded 20 June 1831
Test - Jacon A. Lane clerk
White County Court.

Return made by James W. Copeland Guardian to the heirs of John Anderson Decd. made on oath at January Session 1831.

One note on John Payne for one 1st January 1831 $47.50
cash recorded for cotton 13.50
61.00

Paid to John Franklin $43.00
H aggards rect for muneas cornal in such Wm Charten Jno Anderson
Representative 7.50
Larus recept paid to Robt Anderson 15.25
To Service rendered by me as Guardian in 1830 6.00 71.75
minor Estate 61.00
Balance due me $10.75
James W. Copland

Recorded 20th June 1831
Test - Jacob A. Lane clerk
White County court.

Inventory of the estate of William Gracy Decd. (one part) returned on oath by Anthony Dibrell Executor at January Session 1829. Which due to his hands since the former return Towit:

1 note on D. L. Mitchell balance due 21th nov. 1825	$26.64½
1 note on John N. Allstadh due May 1827	5.00
1 Receipt D. L. Mitchell for note on S. D. Hill which is doubtful	20.00
1 note on S. D. Hill due 13th August 1826 — bad	2.00
1 note on Anthony Dibrell due 15th March 1827	53.00
forwarded topage 42	$106.64½

P 42 Amount brought from page 41	$106.64½
1 note on Anthony Dibrell due 10th Jan. 1826	43.00
1 note on Same due 21 April 1826	30.00
1 note on D. L. Mitchell due 9th March 1826	27.37½
1 note on Hugh Gracy	75.00
	$319.52

Anthony Dibrell Executor

Recorded 20th June 1831
Test - Jacob A. Lane clerk
White County court.

An Inventory of the estate of Jacob Robinson Decd. returned on oath by Anthony Dibrell and David Ames Executors at October Session 1828. Towit:
13 head horses Towit: 2 Gildings 4 mares 5 yearlings colt 2 spring colts 13 head cattle Towit: 4 cows 2 oxen 3 heifers 4 calves 70 head sheep 18 head geese 1 set smith tools consisting of annil vice 4 harmnars bellows 1 saddle & saddle bags 1 pack saddle 4 kettles 4 ovens 2 lids 2 pair pot hooks 2 set of knives and forks 2 Razors & Box 1 pitcher 4 crocks 1 jar 3 dishes 6 plates 1 set cups & saucers 2 Bottles 1 set salt cellars 1 pair candle sticks 6 Bee stands 1 set spools 10 Books 1 smoothing iron 2 kegs 1 cutting box 1 coffee mill 1 pair cleves & Traces 1 swingle tree 1 clevis 5 sides of leather 1 scythe and cradle 1 Rifle gun 1 milk stand 1 Tin box 2 Tea cups 1 common cupboard 1 Desk 1 chest 5 tables 1 Loom 3 large wheels 2 little wheels 1 check Reel 4 sleighs 1 washing Tub 3 water pails 3 peggins 1 half bushel 6 beds and furniture some wheat quanity not known small balance on a note on Thomas Eastland.
Recorded 21th June 1831.
Test Jacob A. Lane clerk
White County Court.

Amont of the sales of the property of Jacob Robertson Decd. returned by Anthony Dibrell one of his Executors on oath at January Session 1829 To wit:

James T. Holeman 1 Bed & furniture	$13.00
Frederick Lyda 1 Dito	14.25
Robert Huett 1 Dito	14.50
Henry Lyda Halling leaf table	4.43¾
Anthony Dibrell 1 Bedstead	1.50
William Brown 1 Dito	.75
Amot forwarded to page 43	$48.43¾

P 43 Amount brought from page 42	$48.43¾
Joshia Hicky 1 Bedstead	1.62½
William Bohannon 1 lot stock hogs 29 head	15.00
James Thomas 1 cow & calf	4.50
Samuel Madewell 1 cow & calf	6.75
Jno. W. Dismakes 1 calf	1.25
Henry Eller 1 cow and calf	5.75
James Thomas 1 heifer	5.75
John Dismakes 1 cow and calf	4.75
Benjam Gipson 1 yearling	2.75
Hurry Lyda 1 work steer	18.06¼
Robert H. Hewet 1 work Bull & yokew	9.12½
Maderson Fisk 1 sorrel mare	55.00
Jno. Warren 1 Bay horse	30.00
George Long 1 Bay mare	38.63
Wm Brown 1 Bay Colt	24.00
James H. Pass 1 set smith tools	37.00
William Brown 1 sorrel yearling colt	13.50
James Eastland 1 Bay mare & colt	40.62½
James Thomas 1 Bay colt	30.25
Joshia Hickey 1 sorrel leyed mare	21.31¼
Solomon Robinson 1 sorrel filly	23.25
Robert Hewett 1 colt	19.25
Henry Eller 1 colt	7.00
Brea Bevers 1 Bay filly	20.00
Wm Matlock 1 Bed & furniture	10.50
	$494.06¼

The foregoing certains the amount of property sold 28th October 1828 the balance of the property unrestated in the Inventory is not sold bur remains upon the premises.

Anthony Dibrell Executor

Recorded 21st June 1831
Test - Jacob A. Lane clerk
of White County court.

In the name of God Amen I John Johnston Cezr. Of White County and State of Tennessee being of sound mind and memory but adnanud in years and knowing the uncertainty of life do make constitute and publish this my last will and Testament First I reccommend my sole to God that gave it and my body to the earth in favorable hopes at the general reserucction of being recorded in the glory when trouble is no more and as to what it has pleased God to Bless me with in this world I dispose of in the following manner Towit:

1 This my will and desire is that all my just debts shall be paid from the sails of some of my stock.

2 This I give my son Buttar Johnston one dollar to him and his heirs for-

ever.
This 3rd I give my son Meajah Johnston one dollars also to him and his heirs forever.
4 This I give to my daughter May Brown one dollar also to her and her heirs forever.
5 I give my son Allen Johnston one dollar to him and his heirs forever,
This 6 I give to my grandson John Johnston son of Meajah Johnston my tract of land where I now live on and tis my will and desire that my wife Poly shall have a pat of the said tract land to live on as long as she lives single. This 7 I give my wife Polly one bay horse now by the name of Jack also two cows and calf and all my household furniture, also tis my will and desire after my debts is paid from the sale of some of my hogs that they shall be equally divided between my wife and the aforsad John Johnston.
This 8. I also give John Johnston two cows and calves This 9. It is also my will and desire that John Ward son of my wife Polly shall have two cows calves and my bay mare to him and his heirs forever.
This 10th I give to my grand daughter Simthmy Whitely daughter of Isack Whitely one bay colt ot her and her heirs forever. I also my friends Samuel H. Allen and George Allen my executor to this my last will and Testament. Give unto my hand and seal this twenty fifth day of January in the year of our Lord eighteen hundred and 28.

John Johnston

Witness Re. Cox
Isack his X mark Whitely

State of Tennessee()
White County) January Session 1830. This day the foregoing and opposets will-the lastwill and Testament of John Johnston Decd was produced in open court and the due execution thereof proven by the oath of Robert Cox and Isaac Whitely Subscribing witness thereto for the purpose and things therein witnessed. and that the said John Johnston was at the execution thereof
P 44 of Sound and disposing memory whenupon it is ordered to be recorded Given at office 11th January A. D. 1839.

Test Jacob A. Lane Clerk

Recorded 23rd June A. D. 1830. White County Court

Test Jacob A. Lane Clerk.
White County Court.

b c1750

In the name of God Amen, I WILLIAM STEWART of the county of White Laberor--Being very sick and weak and low in body but in my perfect since and Sound mind and menory (aged about nearly 79 years) and calling to mind that I have to die. Think proper to make a will and Do hereby make adain and constitute this my last will and testament. and do give and bequeath as followth: 1st I give my Soul to god the giver, hoping he will pardon and forgive my Sins and receive my Soul to rest.
2nd I give my body to the earth to be decently buried at the discressing of my executors hereafter named.
3rd. I give and bequeath to John Stewart my Grand Son twelve and a half cents to be
45 raised out of my property and paid over to him in due time.
Fourthly I give and bequeath to my granddaughter Jane Dalton my bed and furniture also one cow and calf. the cow called Sany also one man Saddle also I give and bequeath her the said Jane my grand daughter Dalton after dedcting any uncessary expenses for my burial such as coffin Sheet 16 the balance of a note that I put into the hands of William Sims constable

for collection on the widow Margaret Taylor and Lee Taylor
5th I give and bequeath to my grand daughter my daughter Dalton one cow and calf and Yearling the cow called spike horn 6th I give and bequeath Benjamin Dalton one yoke of Steers formely the property of Tobert Dalton Decd. 7th I give and bequeath to my Grand daughter Elizabeth Dalton one bed and furniture formely the porperty of Tobert Dalton Decd. This the above will I do and have made is my last will and testament revoking all other wills regacies 1 c by me heretofore made and I do hereby nominate constitute and appoint James Taylor and Thomas Jones my true and lawful executor to act and attend the business above mentioned. In T Testimony whereof I have here unto Set my hand and Seal this 16th May. 1829.

his
William X Stewart
mark

Attest J. M. C. Taylor
Thomas Jones.
State of Tennessee
White County } July Session A. D. 1829. This day was produced in open court the last will and testament of William Stewart and the due execution and Publication thereof provided in open court by the oath of James M. C. Taylor and Thomas Jones the Subscribing witness thereto for the purpose and things therein witnessed and that the said William Stewart was at the execution thereof of Sound and disposing mind and memory. Whereupon it is ordered to be recorded. Given at Office the 13th day of July A. D. 1829. Recorded 23nd June 1831.

Test Jacob A. Lane Clerk
White County Court.

Test Jacob A. Lane
White County Court.

In the name of God amen, I MATHAS PENNEGRASS of the County of White and State of Tennessee. being weak of body but of Saound mind and disposing memory for which I think God, and calling to mind the uncertainty of human life and being desires to dispose of all my worldly Substance as it hath pleased God to Bless me with I give and bequeath the Same in manner following, That is to say I give and bequeath unto Samuel Tilinchin of the County of White and State aforesaid at the desease of my self and wife Margaret the land whereon I now live. Containing Seventy acres lyaing and being in White County and State of Tennessee in two Surveys one of fifty acres the other containing Twenty acres. also all the Stock of cattle, Sheep hogs &C together with their increase that is now in my possession to be his the aforesaid Tlenchen's at my desease and the desease of my wife Margaret also all the farming tools to be Said Tlinchen's

P 46 I give and bequeath my oldest daughter Elizabeth to my oldest son John to my Second son Peter to my third Son William to My to my fourth Son James and to my youngest Son Matthew each an equal part of my household furniture the balance of all my part of a portion or estate that I may be entitled to in the State of Virginia at the diseased of my wife Margaret's Step Mother. I will and bequeath to my wife Should I die first and other wise her my loving wife to dispose of the same at her pleasure and last of all I nominate and appoint my truly friend Eli Sims to take care of this my last will and testament untill my diseas and the desease of my wife Margaret at which time he will have the Same recorded. In Testamony whereof I have hereunto Set my hand Seal this 19th July 1830.

His
Mathas X Pennegrass
mark

In person of Aaron Hailly
Eli Sims

State of Tennessee }
White County } October Session A. D. 1830.

This day was provided in open court the last will and testament of Mattheas Penniegrass Desd. whereupon the due execution thereof was duly provided in open court in open court by the oath of Eli Sims and Aaron Hailly Subscribing witness thereof, for the purposes and things thereon mentioned, and that the same was duly published as the last will and Testament of the said Mattheas Pennegrass Desd and at the execution therof he was of Sound mind and disposing memory whereupon it is orded to be recorded. Given at office 18th October 1831

Test Jacob A. Lane Clerk
White County Court.

Recorded 23nd June A. D. 1831.
Test Jacob A. Lane clerk White County Court.

In the name of God Amen, I JAMES CHARLES OF the County of White and State of Tennessee being of Sound mind and memory do make this my last will and Testament and do bequeath as followeth—First I give my daughter Smitha Miller one dollar, Secondly I give my son James Charles one dollar, Thirdly I give my son Alina Charles one dollar
P 47 Fourthly I give my daughter Susannah May one dollar Fifthly I give my daughter Leroy Young one dollar, Sixthly I give my Son Stephen Charles one dollar, Seventhly I give to my Son Hiyram Charles one dollar. Ninthly I give to my daughter Elizabeth Woodlen one dollar, Tenth I give to my son Solemon Charles one dollar Eleventhly I give to my Son Joel Charles one dollar Twelfthly I give to my daughter Tobetha Charles one dollar the above Sum to be paid out of my personal estate and the residence of my estate both real and personal. I give to my beloved wife Tobetha Charles to have and enjoy during her natural life or widowhood and for her to dispose of the same as She may think proper between my children. Given into my hand and Seal this 16th March 1816.

Signed Sealed and Acknowledged in presence of
John Armstrong

his
James X Charles
mark (Seal)

State of Tennessee }
White County } October Session A. D. 1830.

This day was provided in open court the within the last will and testament of James Charles Desd. and the name of John Armstrong thereto as a witness whereupon came Anthony Dibrell Nathan Haggard and John B. McCormich into open court who being first Sworn in due form of law make the following Statement To wit:— Nathan Haggard States that was acquainted with the hand writing of said John Armstrong in his lifetime and thinks it is the hand writing of Said John Armstrong the witness to said will Anthony Dibrell says he was acquainted with the hand writing of Said John Armstrong but cannot Say posetively that it is his. John McCormick says he was well acquainted with the hand writing of Said John Armstrong and Says he believes Said will and altercation therto be be the hand writing of Said John Armstrong all of Said Witnesses Say that Said John Armstrong has departed this life, whereupon it is adised by the court that said will which is well proven be recorded. Given at office 18th October A. D. 1830.

Test Jacob A. Lane Clerk of
White County Court.

Recorded 23nd June A. D. 1831.

Test Jacob A. Lane Clerk of White County Court.
State of Tennessee
White County } Pursuant to a named order of order of the worshipful Court of Said County made at the April Session of Said Court appointing in the undersigned commissioners to Settle with the John Walker Guardian of Mahala Kerr and Levi Kerr the infant heirs of Alexander Kerr Desd We Inch at Sparta on the 17 day of April 1830 and after examining the papers and vouchers which was to us produced we thereupon make the following Report Towit:

The amount received by the said Guardian on the 10 March 1821		$185.00
Interest thereon 9 years after proper deduction		59.97
Amot. of the estate in Guardian hands		$244.97
Paid Clerk of White County Court		$ .87½
Paid Alto Lane for Declaration		4.50
Paid M. Parkerman for certifing papers		.12½
Paid M. Dibrell for drawing money		2.37½
Paid County Court Clerk for Services		7.25
Paid Dito Deto for copies &C		1.75
Paid Deto Do Return for 1830		.62½
P 48 Paid William Duncan for schooling Mahala		3.50
Paid for boarding Mahala & Schooling		16.00
To Charges for Senaces traveling &C	62.00	25.00
		$182.97
There on 2 Distribution a Share is		$122.48½
The Share of Mahala who named Joel Whitley is		122.48½
From which deduct her share of charges		40.75
		$81.73½
The Guardian has paid Joel Whitty as appears from 3 Recepts		$106.00
due for Share of Mahala Joel Whittey's wife		81.73½
Over paid by the Guardian to Joel Whittey		$ 24.26½
This Sum the Guardian Credits with half the Sum due from the administrator		10.17
Due from Joe Whittey to the Guardian		14.09½
The Sh are of Levi Kerr is		$122.4[illegible]
Deduct his Share of the charges		21.2[illegible]
		$101.2[illegible]
Due to him from the administrator		10.1[illegible]
Due to Levi Kerr		$111.4[illegible]

Given unto our hands and Seals and Seals the day and year above

Turner Lane (Seal)
David Mitchell (Seal)
A. Dibrell (Seal)

Recorded 27 June 1831.
Test Jacob A. Lane clerk White County Court.

Return of JAMES W. COPELAND Guardian to the heirs of John Anderson Desd. returned on oath at January Session A. D. 1830.
State of Tennessee
White County } To the worshipful court of Pleas and Quarter Session, January Session 1830. James W, Copeland being the Guardian of Elizabeth Anderson, Nancy Anderson, Patsy Anderson, James Anderson & Noah Anderson Children of John Anderson Desd respectfully tenders his amount as Guardian for the year 1829 which is or follows:- Following notes executor to Said Copland as
P 49 Guardian all due the 25th August 1830.

One note on Stephen K. Charles for	$10.10
One note on John C. Turner for	50.55
One on A. Johnston for	2.00
	$62.65

out of which Said Copeland is entitled services rendered $2000
Paid at Sale .37½
Paid to County Court .62½
3.00
$59.65

Recorded 27th June 1831 James W. Copeland
Test Jacob A. Lane Clerk White County Court.

Return of WILLIAM HILL Guardian to WILLIAM H. CHRISTEN made oath at January Session A. D. 1831.

State of Tennessee
White County
To the worshipful court of pleas and quarter Session!— I WILLIAM HILL Guardian to William A. Christen Do hereby report to your worships that the time for which I was appointed Guardian aforesaid has expired he the said William H. Christen having arrived to the age of twenty one years and upwards I have come to a final Settlement with the Said William and here Subjoin a true copy of his receipt. Recorded 8 November 1830, from William Hill five hundred and forty dollars 16 cents in full of all the money coming to me from my father Elijah Christen's Jr. Estate the Said William Hill having been appointed my true and lawful Guardian Attest

John Parker William H Christen

Given into my hands and seal the 10th day of January 1831
William Hill Guardian
(Seal)

Recorded 27 June 1831. Test Jacob A. Lane Clerk White County Court.

List of Sales of the property of John Anderson Decd. returned on oath by Robert Anderson Senr. Admr. at January Session A. D. 1829.

1 Skillet 18¾ Shoe Hammer &pincers 1.00 c	$1.56¼
1 curry comb 25¢ 1 hand saw 75¢	
1 Basket & Spools 37½¢ 2 pairpot hooks 37½	1.75
Forwarded to page 50	$3.31¼
P 50 Amount brought from page 49	$3.31¼
John Franklin 1 pair pot hooks 25¢ 1 sifter 75¢	1.00
Stephen Holland 1 Scythe & Cradle	1.75
Lynan Sabern 1 Slate	.25
James Miller 1 pair cards	.18¾
Anderson Johnston 1 deto	.50
John Halterman 1 cows hide	2.25
John Franklin 1 kettle & lid	2.62½
Francis Vaunerman 1 churn	.37½
James Miller 1 mattock	1.37½
James Miller 1 auger	.62½
John Franklin 1 Shovel 50¢ Flax Hackle 181¼¢	2.31¼
Anderson Johnston 1 Iron Wedge 62½¢ 1 piggin & hooks 50¢	1.12½
John Frankin 1 half Bushel	.40
Alvin Rickman 1 weeding hoe	.70
Andrew Johnston 1 Bedstead	1.50
Henry Oramly 1 Bridle bit	.12½
Washington D. Cosby 1 Swingle tree & clevis	.75
Stephen Richman 1 Swingletree & cleves	.62½
Alvan Rickman 1 mans saddle 725¢ 1 Blanket 181¼ 1 Bridle 50¢	9.56¼
P 50 John Franklin 1 check Reel 112½¢ 1 Box 12½¢	1.25
Lyman Saburn 1 Bag wool 24¼ at 40¢ 970¢ 1 meal bag 81¼¢	10.51¼

Anderson Johnston 1 Tray .12½
John Franklin 1 Smoothing Iron .62½
James Miller 1 Brass Candlestick & Shairs .56¼
Henry Crowsby 1 Razor & Shaving box 1.00
James Miller 1 Tin Canster 56¼¢ 1 Slay 93¾ 2 pair weaving harness25 1.75
Henry Owens 1 coffee pot 62½ 1 Stone pitcher 31¼ .93¾
Isaac Williams 1 Small keg 1.25
Washington D. Cosby 1 Loom & Temples 4.00
John Halterman 1 Bee gum 1.50
James Copland 1 cutting knife 1 Box 2.25
John Franklin lot wild hogs 4.00
James Miller Lot hogs 4 Sows 4 shoats 1 pig 7.31¼
Saphen Holland 485 pound end cotten 8.39
Albert G. Vannesan (?) 1 washing tub 62½ 10 Barrels corn 12.20 12.82½
Andmwson Johnston 10 Barrels corn at 112½¢ p. Barrel 11.25
Charles Cheak 10 Barrels corn at 112½¢ pr Barrel 11.25
Albert G. Vaunersan 1 Lot corn 14 Barrels 4½ Bushels 16.39
Lynan Saburn 3 Gleese (?) 1.00
James Miller 1Lot flax .43¾
James Copland 1 Bookcase 1.62½
$131.91¼

Amount brought from Page 50 $131.91¼
p. 51 Henry Owens 1 Looking Glass .10
William Anderson 1 Bible 50¢ 5 other Books 1.50¢ 2.00
Lyman Sayborn 1 Vol. Fletcher's Appeals .50
Robt. Anderson Jr. 1 pot rack 1.00
1 pot 2.50¢ coner cupboard 9.93¾ 13.43¾
Jas. Copland 1 broken Set plates 7 small bolls 2 pewter dishes
3 pewter plates broken set knives & forks 6 table Spoons 1 bread basket
1 crook 4.00
James Copland 1 Small bed & furniture 6.12
Anthony Dibrell 1 Bed & furniture 15.00
Stephen Holland 1 Dl Do. 15.00
Jabes Anderson 1 Side & piece Seal leather 1.62½
$189.69⅛

Robt. Anderson Adm.

Recorded June 27th 1831.
Test Jacob A. Lane Clerk White County Court.
Return of Alexander Glenn Guardian of Laten Heltar made an oath January Session 1829.

Alexander Glenn Ser. Guardian to Laten Heltar Do hereby report to Said Court the manner in which I have disposed of the property and effict of Said Heltar for the year 1828.
Come to hand in the year 1817. $94. of this amount principal and interest after deduction all unessay expences the remained in my hands on the first day of January county court. for the year 1828. $108. the interest on this amount for twelve months is $6.48 which being added to $108. makes $ $114.48 cents paid of this amount for Schooling and for return for 1828 $4.25 having a balance in my hands up to this oath 12th January 1829. $110.23

Alexd. Glenn Guardian

Recorded 27th June 1831. Test Jacob A. Lane Clerk White County Court.

Report of Comm appointed to Settle with Robert Anderson Adm. of John Anderson Decd returned upon oath at April Session A. D. 1830.

State of Tennessee
White County We the undersigned being appointed commissioners at January Session of the county court 1830 to Settle with the adm. of John Anderson Decd

We report and Say that the Administrator Stands charged with the Sales of the property belonging to Said Estate, the amount of one hundred and eighty eight dollars ninety Seven and one half cents $188.97½
We also report that the Administrator proceeded receipts $ to the following amount

To May Fitsgerald to proven amount $10.00
Carried to page 52 10.00 188.97½
P 51 To amot brought from page 51 188.97½
By amount brought form page 51 10.00
By expense traveling to Earl Tennessee & returning 18.00
By funeral charges paid to George Rodgers for Diseased 6.25
By Payning Doct. Montgomery needed (?) bill for diseased 6.00
By paying Charles Whittey amot of note 7.00
By paying Charles Whittey amot. of note 15.80
By paying Stephen Holland amot of note 11.75
By paying Joseph Cummings full amot of a Judgement that Stephen Holland obtained against the Adm. 13.90
By paying John Franklin for picking cotton of the Decd. 3.25
By paying Isaac Drake in full of a Judgement against the Decd in the circuit court White County as Security for Ralph Matthews 88.72
By paying Anthony Dibrell for cost in above cause 2.15
By paying J. A. Lane Clerk for fees an adm. of estate 5.12½
By paying previous amot to David Certain 5.60
By amount allowed to Robert Anderson the Administrater as a compensation for his trouble, Service and attention in administration of Said estate 10.00
$203.54½ 188.97½

We therefore report and say that the estate of the Deseased is fu fully administered and the administrator has over paid the Sum of $14.57
Given into our hands and Seals this 26th March 1830.

Turner Lane (Seal)
John Byor (Seal)
Recorded 27th 1831 Test Jacob A. Lane Simon Doyle (Seal)
Clerk White County Court.

Inventory of the estate of ALFRED G. BRADLEY Decd. returned upon oath by Jess England adm. at October Session A. D. 1829 To wit: 2 Bedsteads 1 Table 1 chest 1 flax wheel 1 cotton do 1 cards 6 chairs 1 pot 1 oven 2 Skillets 1 pair hooks 1 wooden clock 1 Looking glass 1 coffee mill 2 pitchers 14 plates 1 Set cups & saucers 1 pepper box 4 knives & forks 3 Spoons 3 jars 2 crocks 2 Jugs 1 churn 2 pails 1 trumpet 1 milk Strainer 2 smoothing irons 1 pair Gears 1 meal Sifter 2 ploughs 2 Swingletrees 2 cleves 1 key 1 drawing knife 1 Bell 2 hoes 1 writing disk 2 head cows 1 axe 3 head horses 1 Rifle gun a Small crop of corn quanity not known.

Recorded 28th June 1831. Test Jacob A. Lane Clerk White County Court.

List of Sales of the property of Alfred G. Bradley Decd. returned upon oath by Jess England adm. at January Sessions 1830. To Wit:

William Bullock 1 Smoothing Iron .87½
Robert Ward 1 Table .26¼

Lewis Bohamon 1 plough & Stokk 1.50
Edward Bullock 1 plough& Stock 1.06¼
J. D. Bosvelts 1 pair chains 1.50
Jess England 1 Sorrel mare 20.00
Thomas Lovelady 1 Skillet .75
John Anderson 1 Gun & shot bag 27.31¼
John D. Boseth 1 Wash Tub .56¼
Barsheba Bradly 1 Glass knives & forks Spoons .56¼
Thomas Lovelady 1 Coffee pot .37½
Duke A. Bradley 1 mans Saddle 6.12½
Thomas Lovelady 1 Gugg .25
Aaron England Senr. 1 axe 1.00
John England 1 Sorrel mare 28.00
John Boseth 1 hoe .31¼
Aaron England 1 chest 1.37½
Abarshealy Bradles 1 cotton wheel 50 ¢ parel plates 106¼
flax wheel 50¢ 2.06¼
John Dyer 2 chairs 1.75
Thomas J. Pistoll 1 Dick 1.06¼
Joseph Bartlett 1 Jar .75
P 53 John Dyer 1 Stone Jug .68¾
Jgreasheas Howard 1 Skillet .50
Aaron England 1 pair pot hooks .31¼
Josaph Bartlett 1 pitcher .25
William Warriner 1 meal Seive .50
Joseph Bartlett 2 crocks 1 Gar .37½
Joseph England 1 Trumpet .25
William Bullock 1 oven & 1 1.81¼
Jessee Clark 1 coffee Mill 1.56
Robert Ward 1 Bedstead & cord 1.12½
Same 1 Beadstead 25¢ 1 churn 12pc .37½
Lewis Bohanon 3 pails 1 Bag .75
Elijah M. Ganegam 1 clock 5.12½
Jess England 1 Bible 1.00 1 Slay 43¾ 1.43¾
Mathew England 1 mitchany book .25
Danl. Bartlett 1 Slay .31¼
James Ward 1 coat, plane & Bitt 14.00
Mathew England 1 Martingable & Spurs .81¼
Duke A. Bradles 1 hat 1.00
John Dyer 1 packet Book .86¾

Amot forwarded to page 54 $129.75¾

Amot brought from page 53 129.75¾
P 54 Jess England 1 cradle 1.00
Matthew England 2 geese .37½
William Warrner 1 mare 31.50
Bushela Bradles 1 Loom .75
Matthew England 1 Razor & Box .75½
Thomas Bohamon 1 note of land .56¼
Aaron England 1 drawing knife .43¾
James Ward 1 curry comb .12
William Warriner 1 kettle 2.37½
Barthsheba Bradles 1 bead 3.68¾
Duke A. Bradles 1 cow 11.00
Joseph England for wheat .50
Aaron England for fodder 1.12

Joseph England for fodder	2.25
Aaron England Jr. for Cotton $2.01 for flax 12¢	2.13
John Farley 1 Bell 37½¢ 1 hammar 31¼	.683/4
Joseph England 1 Deanter	.56¼
Amount	$189.56 3/4

Jess England Adm.

Recorded 28th A. D. 1831
Test--Jacob A. Lane Clerk
White County Court.

Inventory of the estate of Timothy Harris Decd. returned upon oath by John Taylor Adm. at October Session A. D. 1828. Towit: 2 mares 14 head cattle 25 or 30 head of hogs 1 Rufle gum 1 large kettle 1 oven 2 pots 1 skillet 2 ladles 1 bridle 1 Bed & furniture 1 plough Gears & cleves 4 hoes 3 axes 1 Grindstone 1 Loom (proven away) 2 Bedsteads 2 Tables 1 Bell 1 handsaw 1 drawing Knife 1 auger 1 pair Spoon molds Ladle L Sett plates 2 large dishes 1 Set Knives and forks 1 Lot Spoons 1 pair Steeleyards 3 Stone Jugs 1 Bottle 2 hides of leather. One Side Charges for tanning Same Cooper Ward 1 howell 1 cotton wheel 1 Iron wedge

John Taylor Adm.

Record 28th June 1831
Test-Jacob A. Land Clerk
White County Court

Amount of the Sale of the property of Timothy Harris Decd. returned on oath by John Taylor Adm. at October two 1828.

Anten Cooker 1 Sorrel Mare	$23.00
James Harris 1 two year old filly 1500¢	
10 head hogs A 50¢	19.50
John Barr 17 head hogs	9.62
James Harris 12 head small hogs 1.18 3/4 1 cow yearling & Bull 5.37½	6.56¼
John Tayler 1 large Kettle & hooks 400C 1 Bull 487½	8.87½
Rebekah Tayler 1 cow & calf	8.87½
Amot carried to page 55	$76.43 3/4
Amont. brought from page 54	$76.43 3/4
James Harris 1 pot & pot hooks 312½--1 how 37½ 1 axe 1.81¼¢ 1 Tone hank 25 Knives forks plates & dishes 50¢ 1 Table 100¢ 1 Bedstead 25¢	7.31 ¼
James Sperry 1 white Steer	8.50
Jess Angel 1 Steer	5.00
Martin B. Angel 1 cow & calf	6.75
John Young 1 cow & calf	5.37½
Same 1 cow & calf	8.18 3/4
William Baker 1 yearling heifer	1.62½
Lee Roy Taylor 1 Side Leather	3.50
John Taylor 1 Deto	3.75
Samel Brasby 1 Deto	3.62½
William Irwin 1 mans Saddle	3.04
John Taylor 1 womans Deto	1.12½
John Acuff 1 Rifle Gun	6.00
Wm Pretchett 1 small pot	1.00
Wm Baker 1 how	1.06¼
John Taylor 2 hoes	1.00

Samel Brasby 1 Deto 3.62½
William Irwin 1 mans Saddle 3.04
John Taylor 1 womans Deto 1.12½
John Acuff 1 Rifle Gun 6.00
Wm Protchett 1 small pot 1.00
Wm Baker 1 how 1.06¼
John Taylor 2 hoes 1.00
P 55 Same 1 axe .62½
Wm Baker 1 pair chains Hammer & ball ax 1.62½
John Taylor drawing Knife & hand Saw 275¢ 1 dish Some plates
& knives 1.25 1 cotton wheel 12% 1 Jug 31½¢ 1 Bed & furniture 162½
Spoon mould & ladle 31 1 plough and Clevis 75¢ 7.12½
Wm Pritchett 1 Grindstone .87½
Samel Laffrity iron wedge auger & Steely aids 2.75
John Young 1 Jug .56¼
John Sullivan 1 Jug .13½
Saml. Laffnty 1 Bottle .25
Ruban Pearm 1 homell .18¾
Peter Peneyar 1 Bell .62½
Jesse Elrod 1 Table .06¼
Amt. $158.45½

Record 28th June 1831 Test--Jacob A. Lane Clerk White County Court
John Taylor Adm.

The estate of Timothy Harris Decd. to John Taylor Adm. Nov.
24th 1829. Cash paid J. A. Lane Clerk $3 Cash pd. Doct. Fish 75¢ 3.75
Apl. 17 1830. Cash Jas. Townsc and for Grant $4. Cash paid for
Taxes 45¢ 4.45½
To cash paid W. Pritchett Coffin 600¢ cash paid Isaac Taylor amt.
100¢ 7.00
To cash paid Hny Burton cryer at Sale 1.00¢ cash due by estate to
Jno Taylor 500¢ 6.00
To Service as administrator rendered in Selling the Estate of the
Decd. Subject to allowance by court 1¢ 10.00
At July Session 1830 allowed by court
Recorded 28th June 1831 $31.20½
Test--J. A. Lane Clerk Jno Taylor Adm.

Inventory of the estate Gilby Geer Desd. returned upon oath by Samuel Usury and James Cooper Adm. at October Term 1829.

Left a tract of land and Six acres of corn, 1 mare 1 cow & calf 7 hogs 1 Bed and furniture 1 Bedstead 1 loom 4 chairs 1 Sugar Box 8 plates 1 crock 3 Tin cups Some Talax (?) 1 cotton wheel 1 weeding hoe 1 chest 4 slay 1 pair cotton cards 1 Tub 2 piggins 1 Iron wedge a cotton patch a potatoe patch.
Recorded 29th June 1831 Test--Jacob A. Lane Clerk
P 56 White County Court

Inventory of the Estate of John Rutledge Decd. returned on oath by William Rutledge & Herbert Long Admns. at October Term 1828.
6 Bedsteads & furniture. 1 cupboard 5 tables 1 Bureau 1 Loom 1 Trunk 1 chest 1 disk 3 Sugar Boxes 7 Earthen plates 2 dishes 4½ yards drab cloth 2 Sets dog irons 3 Kettles 3 pots 3 Skillets 3 ovens 1 Lid 2 Sets Knives & forks. 2 Sets large Spoons 1 Set Tea Spoons 2 looking Glasses

1 Set Cups & Saucers 2 pitchers 2 Smoothing irons 1 Decunter 12 chairs 2 wheels 2 coffee mills 6 axes 4 hoes 1 Mattock 3 plough 3 pair Gears 3 Swingletree 1 Reel 2 saddls 2 Grindstones 2 plows a number of books 12 pewter plates 4 Screw Augers 3 Clenpels 1 Iron square 1 Box old irons 1 Barn box of grain 15 hogs 1 Coopers Ads 1 Rummy crib 2 cythes 1 cradle 3 bells 1½ cross-cut Saw 1 Clevis 2 pipe Augers 1 Tea Kettle 1 funnel 1 Home, Razor & case 1 Ink Stand 2 Showels 4 Barrels 2 Short pieces of iron 2 pails 1 piggin 1 Brass Candlestick 1 Cutting Knife & Steel 1 Hackle 2 wash pans 12 sheep 1 cow & hearling 1 drawing Knife 1 Log chain 2 ox yokesrings and Staples 10 head hogs 2 large negroes 1 named Will and the other Delphy 1 note on Mathew G. Moore for 31½ Barrels corn balance of a note on John Mattock $2.00 one note on John Brown for $3.75 one note on Charles Rutledge for $53.00 one trade note on Thomas Roberts for $1.95 balance of a note on Charles Rutledge for $46.50 one note on Mathew G. Moore for $12.00 1 note on Nathan & William Holland for 9 Barrels & 2 bushels corn 1 corn note on Johnston Carlin for 40 Barrels 1 Note on J. W. G Goff & John Lyon for 5 Bushels Salt 1 note on Samuel D. Davis $2. One note on Thomas Roberts for 58 Bushels Salt credit for the Same note for $30.50 1 note on Wm Smith for $1.
Recorded 29th June 1831 Test--Jacob A. Lane Clerk White County Court

Amount of the Sale of the property of JOHN RUTLEDGE Decd. returned on oath by William Rutledge Admr. at April Session A. D. 1829 To wit:

William Rutledge 1 Saddle $5 1 lot Tools $1.00	$6.00
James Rutledge 1 hand Saw	.13
John Dyer 1 Keg	.25
Amot. carried to page 57	$6.38
P 57 Amot. brought from page 56	$6.38
Wm Rutledge 1 pair Smoothing irons 87½¢ cupboard & furniture $14.00 folding table $5.	19.87½
Saml. Turney 1 Club axe	2.37½
Richd Brown 1 Delto	.87½
John W. Dismaker 2 axes	1.25
Wm Simpson 1 Staple & Ring	1.00
William Rutledge 2 weeding hoe	1.50
William Misdow 1 drawing Knife	1.25
Jas. Hunter 1 cutting Knife	2.12½
William Simpson 2 Grubbing hoes	2.00
John Gilpatrick 1 Lot old irons	1.25
Rubd. Brown 1 large pot	3.87½
Jguatens Howard 2 large ovens	5.00
Wm. Rutledge 2 Skillets 112½ 1 oven & gridiron 112½	2.25
James Snodgrass 1 Small oven	1.00
Herbert Long Pot & Hooks $1. 2 Sugar boxes $1.25--1 Lot Kitchen furniture $3.12½	5.37
Solomon Wilhite 1 popular table	.37½
Wm Wisdon Scythe & cradle 81¼ 1 Tar bucket 18 3/4	1.00
Wm Rutledge 2 pot hooks 50¢ large plough & hoe $3.87½ Shovel Plough 1.12½	5.50
Wm Rutledge 1 showel plough 75¢ Ring & Saple 1.06¼ 1 large Bell 93 3/4 1 cotton wheel 2.00¢ 1 Delto 100.¢ 1 check Reel 50¢ 1 looking glass 75¢	7.00
Herbert Long 1 pair hames & traces	4.00

William Simpson Delto Delto 3.12½
Sams 1 Small bell .87½
John Gelpatrick (?) 1 Ditto .37½
Solomon Wilhite 1 iron wedge .56¼
John Gilpatrick (?) 2 screw augers 1.62½
Hewey Rutledge 1 hackle 2. 31¼
Jesemiah Wilhite 1 Bar iron 4.62½
Thoma s A. Lea 1 bed & furniture 26.06 ¼
Russell Gist 1 Ditto 15.00
Rubard Brown 1 Bureau $9.25 1 clock $22.50 31.75
John W. Dishmaker 1 chest & Tin plate 1.50
Wm Rutledge 1 trunk $2. 1 Side Saddle $10. 1 Loom & Slays $9
350 acres of land with a reserve of Rods Square at Graves $1450-1471.00
Rubard Brown 1 Bed & furniture 32.50
Herbert Long 1 Ditto 27.00
Russell Gist 1 Ditto 12.00
Chas. Amie Rutledge 1 Ditto 11.50

Amot. Carried to Page 58 $1725.19½
Amot. brought from page 57 $1725.19½
Gilbert Williams 1 Side Leather 2.06¼
William Rutledge Snr. 1 Ditto 2.31¼
P 58 John W. ishmaker 1 chest .12½
Herbert Long 1 piece cloth 15.50
William Glenn 1 Small Table 1.25
William Rutledge 40 Barrels corn $30 1 Lot tools $5.81¼ Single-
tree 25¢ 2 planes 1.31 ¼ 1 Tin pan 25¢ 1 Lot copper $3.50
4 deer Skins $ 1.25 42.37½
Herbert Long 1 pipe auger 3.06¼ 1 Tin pan 12½ 3.18
Joseph Junter 1 Box iron 7.06¼
Jno W. Desmaker 15 Sheep $15.50 1 coffee mill 1.12½ 1 axe 56¼ 17.183/4
Larkin Misdow 1 kettle 62½¢ Iron Bar 1.50¢ 2.12½
William Letter 1 large kettle 2.62½
William Rutledge 1 flax wheel 1.25¢ ½ Dozen chairs 200.¢ 3.25
Jno W. Dismaker 4 chairs 1.00¢ 1 Razor & glass 87½ 1.87½
Solmon Wilhite 4 chairs .87½
Larkin Misdom 1 Lot Tim tubes 200¢ 2 Books 875¢ 10.75
Wm Rutledge 1 lot Books 5.11
David Snodgrass 1 small Table .933/4
Henry McKinny 1 small skillet .50
Matthew ngland 1 Slate .25
James Snodgrass 1 Lot Books 175
Herbert Long 2 Books 1.81¼
Ben. Wilhite 1 Book 56¼ 1 pot & wheel 31¼¢ .87½
Jno. W. Dismaker 1 Lot Books 81½ 1 heifer 4.75¢ 1 cow $4 9.56
Wm Rutledge 1 pistole 1.87½ 1 pr fire irons 3.12½ 1 Disk 1.81¼
1 Kettle 3.87½ 1 Table 56¼ 1 meal tub .50 1 Basket 50¢ 1 churn 25 12.50
William Misdon 1 pr fire irons 3.25
Geog. M Glenn 1 meal tub 1.12½
Jno Gilpatrick 1 Tub. .31¼
Dempsy Lambeth 1 chain trace .62½
Wm Rutledge 1 Grindstone 1.62½
James Snodgrass 1 Ditto .62½
Matthew England 1 hemel 1.18 3/4 1 keg 81¼ 2.00

William Rutledge 1 Log Chain	3.12½
Same 1 Lot hogs	5.00
Same 1 Note for corn 9 Barrels	6.50
Amot.	$1898.36½

Recorded 29th June 1831 Test--Jacob A. Lane Clerk White County Court.

In the name of God Amen. I THOMAS URUEY of White County and State of Tennessee being in Slow Condition in body. but of a sound mind but being reminded of the unsertainty of life, in the world and have a dessireto dispose of what property it has please God to bless me with in a way that may be for the Satisfaction of my family this my will I humble request that my beloved wife Sarah Usrey Shall have all my property after my just debts are paid as long as she lives in this world but when she desesed what is left I do hereunto affix my hand and Seal the Sixteenth of June in the year one thousand eight hundred and twenty nine.

his
Thomas X Usrey (Seal)
mark

Test--Samuel Usrey Sarah Manefee Frances his X mark Cooley

State of Tennessee)
White County)
) October Session A. D. 1830

This day was provided in open Court the last will and testament of THOMAS USREY Decd. and the same was proven in open court by the oath of Samuel Usrey, Sarah Manafee, and Frances Cooley. Suberibing Witness thereto for the purposes and things therein mentioned as the last will and Testament of Thomas Usrey Desd. and that he was at the execution and publishing thereof of Sound and disposing mind and memory. Whereupon it is ordered to be recorded. Given at office 11th October A. D. 1830.

Test--Jacob A. Lane Clerk
of White County Court

Recorded June 30th A. D. 1831 Test Jacob A. Lane Clerk White County Court.

State of Tennessee)
White County) I JACOB ROBINSON of Said County and State aforesaid knowing the uncertainty of life and now being of Sound body and mind do make this my last will and testment in manner following Towit:
First I give and bequeath unto my Son James Robinson all the notes, bonds, and accounts which I hold on him and have paid as
P 60 his Security amount about Seven hundred dollars. I also give to my Son James Robinson Twenty shillings. I do also give and bequeath to my Son Ruben Robinson all the notes, bonds 1¢ which I have paid for my Said Son to the amount of about three hundred dollars. I also give to my said Son Ruben twenty Shillings. My having given my Son Ruobin Robinson property heretofore reocwlar the rightful possession. I also give and bequeath unto my grand daughter Margaret Dyer during her life time one negro girl named Rachel about eleven years old and at her death to be given to her son Jefferson Dyer Together with the increase of Said negro girl. I give and bequeath unto my beloved daughter Lady, one negro boy named Arch about nine years old. I give and bequeath unto my beloved daughter Lucy one negro boy Anthony age about Seven years old. I give and bequeath to my beloved daughter Betsy one negro boy named Elic about five years old.

I also give and bequeath unto my beloved daughter Polly one negro boy about four years old named Abaham. I also give and bequeath unto my be-lovedbeloved daughter Sally one negro girl about two years old named Mosiah. I desire unto my three named children Andrew, Manuel and Sally the tract of land on which I now live that is the Balance of the tract of land I now live on after I lay off to my Son William Rovinson a certain piece of said tract of land. I desire unto my Said Son William the number of acres not yet known. I also desire unto my said three children Andrew, Manuel & Sally all my lands attached to and connected with my salt well, together with my interest in Said Salt well to my Said three children, Andrew, Manuel and Sally. I also request that my four children William Andrew, Sally Manuel and Sally. I also request that my four Children, William, Andrew, Sally Manuel pay unto my beloved son Solomon one thousand dollars at the expiration of twelve months after they shall have the possession of Said property. I also request and desire that my wife shall have a Saffcimay of the farm and the possession of the house where I now reside also have Gorden and his wife Mary. Also two horses worth Sisty dollars each. And four &calves together with farming utensils sufficient to carry on a small farm during her lifetime. I further give and bequeath unto my Son Manuel at the death of my wife, Gordon and his wife Mary and their increase from this day. I request that Abfaham Sam Agness and Jacob together with all my Stock of horses cattle to be Sold and the proceeds thereof be applied to the payment of my just debts and the balance after paying Said Debts to be equally divided between my four children Lucy Betsy Polly and John. request that my negro woman Dolly be Mancepated and lastly I do nominate and appoint my executor to this my last will and testament. In Testimony where of I have here unto Set my hand and Seal this 6th day of January A. D. eighteen hundred and twenty four.

Witness his
Anthony Dibrell Jacobm X Robinson
David Ames mark

August the 16th A. D. 1826. I JACOB ROBINSON do by way of alteration make the following on account of a change of property first I will unto my daughter Eady Six negroes namely Jenny about twenty four years old, her daughter Susan aged two years Lucinda about eight years Martha Six years of age and a boy two years old named Jefferson all the the children of Jenny also one other negro boy thirteen years of age called Archibald. To my said daughter Eady and to her bodly heirs and in the event of no heirs to be divided between her brother and Sisters equal and in the event of her having heirs and them dying before the children becomes of age, it is my request that said negroes be hired out and the proceeds go to my grand-children until they become of age. and I do give and bequeath unto my dauthter Lucy, Agness and her child Ellis, this is in place of a negro boy Anthony which I have sold since writing this will which Said negro I give to my said daughter Lucy. And her bodily heirs. together with the negro heretofore named in the forgoing will to her and her bodily heirs forever. And it is my will that in the event of my daughter Lucy having no heirs that all the property so willed at her death be equally divided. So willed at her death be equally divided between her brothers and Sisters and request that if my Said daughter Lucy has heirs and dies before they become of age. that Said negroes be hired out and the proceeds go to Said heirs and I do further give unto my children, Solomon Andrew Manuel and Sally that

Portion of property which was allotted to my son John. I having given to my Said John his portion Since making the foregoing will and I do further give to my Son Solomon a negro boy named Samuel and I do release my children heretofore assigned from the payment of my son Solomon one thousand dollars except my Son William. I will that he pays my Son Solomon two hundred dollars. I do further request and will that my Son Andrew and Manuel pay to my daughter Sally two hundred dollars each in consequence of the land he etofore given her. Which is now taken from her and given to my Sons, william, Andrew and Manuel. It is my desire that my negro Samuel be emancpated. he having bought himself and paid the Same to me with the exception of about one hundred dollars

Witness:
Anthony Dibrell
David Amos

his
Jacob X Robinson (Seal)
mark

I Jacob Robinson in consequence of the death of my son William to whom I had given a portion of the land included in the foregoing will. I give and bequeath that part and all other lands which I am possessed of to my two youngest Sons Andrew and Manuel to be equally divided between the two boys yet deserving my wife to have her Support of the land and plantation as before mentioned in this will. And I further will and request that my five negroes Towitt:
Abraham, Jacob Gordon May & Agness be set free at the expiration of Seven years from the first day of February next and that Said negroes remain until that time in the possession of my three Sons Ruben, Andrew, and Manuel and the hire or labor of Said Negroes and to be applied to the payment of my just debts and Should Said debts be extingushed before theexpiration of Said Seven years from the first of February next it is my request that Said negroes be freed as soon as Said Debys are paid & I do herein revoke all parts of this will which gives those negroes or disposes of them in anyother way this 26th day of July A. D. 1828 It is my further desires and request that the increase of Agness up to the first of February 1835. Should go to my beloved daughter Lucy in the Same manner as before Stated. And it is further my desire that the increas of Mary up to the first Feby. 1835 be given to my son Manuel and lastly I request my executers heretofore named to give out of my estate to James Dalton a Saddle worth Twenty five dollars. And thirty head of Stock hogs
P62 when called for and request that should there be any Suplus property, horses, cattle or hogs at the death of my wife the Same I will and bequeath to my daughter S lly and household furniture of my description the date above written.

his
Jacob X Robinson (Seal)
mark

Witness: Maderson Fish Jas T Holeman

State of Tennessee }
White County } October Session A. D. 1828.

This day was provided in open court the last will and Testament of Jacob Robinson Decd. tate of the county of White and the due exe cution thereof as Such was duly proven in open Court by the oath of Maderson Fish and James T Holeman Subscribing Witness thereto for the purpose and things therein mentioned. and ordered to be Recorded.

Given at office 13th October A. D. 1828.

Test-- Jacob A. Lane Clerk

Re corded 29th June 1831
Test---Jacob A. Lane Clerk, White County Court

Inventory of the estate of FREDRICK COATS Desd. returned upon oath by Lewis Bohannon Admr. at January Session A. D. 1830. Towit: Six head of cattle, Two pots, Some Chairs & Table. S ome hogs amount not yet known.
Lewis Bohannon adm.

Recorded 1st July A. D. 1831
Test---Jacob A. Lane Clerk White Coun ty Court.

Report of comms. returned on oath of the Settlement of the account of ROSIA JARVIS Adimr. of estate of ALEXDR KERRDecd. returned at January Term 1829.

The estate of Alexander Kerr Desd.
To Rosia Jarvis Adm. Dr.

	To cash paid Adam Huntsman as on Attorny at Law	$5.00
	To paid the Clerk White County Court for Letters Administration	.35
	To fur for returning Inventory	.35
	To 3 days Service in Colleting and Selling Property	6.00
P 63	To finding Widow & Children in provisions one year	30.00
	To fee annexing county Seal to Letter of Admr.	.75
		$43.45

State of Tennessee
White County   Purscrant to the written order of White County Court We have met and examined and considered of the justness lc of the above account is reasonable and ought to be allowed le January 12th 1829.
William Simpson W. C. Brittain John Rose
Recorded 1st July A. D. 1831
Test---Jacob A. Lane Clerk White Couny Court.

An Account of the SAles of the property of HENRY DODSON Desd. returned on oath by Jess Dodson Admr. at October Session A. D. 1828. Towit:

1 By Coat	$8.00
1 pair boots & 1 pair Shoes	3.00
1 parcelof wearing Clothes	5.00
1 Suit of broad Cloth	15.00
1 other Suit broad Cloth	12.00
1 Fine ha t	5.00
1 Umbrella	1.50
1 pair Saddle bags	3.87½
2 pocket Knives & Gloves	.50
1 pocket Book & Razor	.50
Amt.	$54.37½

Jesse Dodson Adm.
Recorded 1st. July 1831 Test---Jacob A. Land Clerk White County Court.

Account of the Sales of the property of JOHN SMALLMAN Desd. returned upon oath by Joseph Cummings Jr. Adm. at April Session A. D. 1830.

Isaac Plumles 1 horn	$45.00
Elijah Mays 1 chest & madoxe (?)	2.87½

Wm Dodson 1 negro woman named Lydia & her child 420.00
Edmond Godard 1 negro boy named Isaac 170.00
James M. Smallman filly, bedstead and cotton Wheel 13.00
Andrew Bryan 1 Loom 1.75 1.75
Bryan Sparkman 1 Check Reel .75
Danl. Holingsworth 1 pair Geers $2.50 1 pot rack 1.18 3/4 3.68 3/4
James Godard 7 head hogs 6.62½
Mos es Godard Sr. 1 cow & calf 7.75
Wm. Carter 1 bedstead .50
Geog. Yates 1 Looking Glass 75¢ 1 Slate 37¼ 1.12½
James Randals 2 hoes 25¢ 2 ploughScrews & axe $1.37½ 1.62½
Recorded 1st. July 1831. $674. 68 3/4
Test—J. A. Lane Clerk Jas. Cummings Just Admr.
White County Court With Will Annexed

Return on estate of ELIJAH SAWYERS Decd. made on oath by Robert Cooke at January Session A. D. 1829 To wit:
Return of the amount of the balance of the estate of Elijah Sawyers Dcd. as Settled by Major Taylor and Eli Sims Esq. being appointed by court to se ttle with Sarah Sawyer Administration of Elijah Sawyer Decd. the said commissioners Settled with the executor and her husband Robert Cooke and the Said Commissioners found in the hands of Said executor the Sum of one hundred and Sixty one dollars Seventy and one fourth cents agreeable to them return made to court the 14th April 1828.
The necessary expenditures of Said estate of cash paid to Jacob A. Lane as a Balance due him for Said return .50
Cash paid Jesse H. Vermellion for Schooling Tobias and Bartlett Sawyer 4 months each 6.00
For School books and writing paper 1.00 7.50
$154.20¼

Recorded 1st. July A. D. 1831 Test. Jacob A. Lane Clerk
White County Court Robert X Cooke
his Mark

List of the Sale of the property of FREDRICK COOK Decd. returned upon oath by Lewis Bohannon at April Session A. D. 1830 To wit:
Washington G. Hayes 6 head hogs 10.25
John Potts 7 head hogs 11.00
Same 7 head hogs $6. 1 Barrell 25¢ Lewis Bohannon 13 hogs $9.25 3 chairs 81¼ 1vessel $1.00 pots, baskets 10 31¼¢
1 Box 12½ bread Tray 6¼ 11.56¼
P 65John Henry 3 head hogs $4.25 2 cows $5.75 10.00
Thomas Cooper 5 head hogs 14.06¼
Wm Jay 3 head hogs $10.06¼ 1 Bedstead 6¼¢ 1 churn 6¼ 10.18 3/4
Wm. Boyd 1 wheel .56¼
William Griffith 1 hog 2.12½
Richard Moore 2 cows 17.12½
James E Robinson 1 cow 6.56¼
Jno. Stamps 1 Sheep 81¼ 1 pot $3.93 3/4 4.75
William Bohannon 1 Sow .68 3/4
James Hutson 1 pot 1.06¼
Andrew L. Smith 1 Table to Hutson ..12½

John Robinson 1 Bull 4.25
Marlin Southard 1 Riffle Gun $1.25 1 hog $4.50 5.75
Robt Officer busky a pple trees 1.00
Loban Walker 1 hog 1.75
Saml. Williams 1 hog 2.00
Richard G. Jay 1 hog 2.25
Lewis Bohannon 4 hogs 6.00
Amot. $129.31¼
Recorded 1st July 1831 Test--Jacob A. Lane Clerk White County Court.

Account of the Sales of the property of FRANCES B. THOMAS returned on oath by William Hunter Admr. at July Session A. D. 1828. Towit: William Thomas 1 cow & calf $9 1 white cow $6.25--1 heifer $2.50--1 spinning wheel $3.12½ 1 churn 37½c 1 skillet $1.12½ 1 coffee pot basket 1C 1.25¢ plates 1C $2.00 1 chest $ 1.56¼ 1 pot rack $1.56¼ 1 axe & hoe $2.62 one Bureau $25.31¼ 1 Bed & Stead $16.50 1 BedStead $1.87½ 1 Diper 25¢ $75.31¼
Jonathon Simmon 1 white yearling $5.50 1 Table 100C 1 coffee mill and two crocks 1.18 3/4¢ 1 flax wheel 2.56 ¼¢ 10.25
Newell Thomas yoke Steers $20.50 1 horse $26.50 1 glass 75¢ one hackle $5.25 53.00
William Hunter 5 head hogs $6.81¼ 4 glasses 68 3/4¢ 1 pot 56¼¢ 8.06
Amot. forwarded p 66 $146.62½
Amot. brought from page 65 $146. 62½
Jess Thomas 1 womans Saddle $6.50 1 Bail Bucket 100C Tea cups Knives and
P 66 forks 4.31¼ fire Shovel & Tongs 2.18 3/4¢ Small pot 25¢
2 pair pot hooks 56¼ 1 large table 1.18 3/4¢ 50 bu. corn $13.12 29.12½
Joseph Newill 1 check Reel 62½¢ .62½
Joseph Thomas Fire Dogs $4.00 6 chairs $2.26 6.88
Amt. $183.26
Recorded 4th July 1831 Test--J A. Lane clerk White County Court
Wm. Hunter

Amot. of the Sales of the property of HENRY HITCHCOCK Decd. returned at April Session 1829. On oath of William Hitchcock Admr. Towit;
Rosewell Pool note $80.00
Kmany Pool 39.00
Sqeiw Leftwich 35.00
John Rutledge 20.00
John Prior 25.00
Epliam Perkins 18.00
John Garvis 10.00
William Mathews 3.87½
Cash in hand 10.00
Leather & Rasor 15.00
1 man Saddle 16.00
William Hitchcock 23.00
Amot. $294.87½
Recorded 4th July A. D. 1831,
Test--J. A. Land Clerk White County Court.

Report of a Settlement made by Comrs. with the Adm. of HENRY HITCHCOCK Decd. at July Session A. D. 1829. Towit:

We Mannow Leftwitch and John W. Ford, having been appointed, (together with David Snodgrass Esq. who is not present) to Settle with William Hitchcock Esq. administrator of the estate of Henry Hitchcock diseased have this day proceeded to Said Settlement and give the following Statement To wit:

The estate amounted as appear from the end of the Inventory to $294.87½	
To making coffin paid to Samuel Cassway	10.00
To buying Clothes to Wm. Glenn	15.37½
For medical Attention to Wm. C. Thinkuston	45.25
For boarding nursing an attention to WammonLeftwitch white	30.00
To welding Tomb to Phillip Mallory	25.00
For Corn Set to Isaac J. Leftwitch Esq.	5.00
To Geo. Absworth for Amt. duly authur treated	2.77
Amot. forwarded to page 67-- $294.87½	136.39¼
Amot. brought from page 66--$294.87½	136.39¼
Paid to Nicholas Cook	3.00
For MineWhite Sick to Cobr. W. H. Smith	.75
For Ruben White sick	.75½
Paid Simon a barber for Shaving	.37½
Clerks fees in all	2.10
Paid Wm. Collin for making Shroud	1.00
$294.87½	144.37

The Commissioners deem it necessary to State the different items of which said estate consisted as they are presumed to be all certained in the Inventory which has been returned to court they however think proper to remark t at there are two debts yet uncollected one on James Russell of $16. Which it is probable will be collected and one on Epheam Purkins which is considered doubtful $18. Amounting $34. This $34. last mentioned together with the amount payments above set forth long ducted from the
P 67aggregate amount of Said estate leaves in the hands of Said Administrator the Sum yet indisposed of the Sum of $116.50½

Year commissioners respectfully report that from their own observation and information on which they say they believe Said Admistrator for his trouble and the proformance of the verious duties developing on him as Such ought be allowed, the Sum of $40.00
They further State that for a considerable part of the payments above mentioned Satisfactory vouchers have been provided and for all of them. Such evidince on is Satisfactory to the wards of year Commissioners all of which is respectfully Submitted this 10th day of July 1829.

Wamon Leftwich (Seal)
John W Ford (Seal)

Recorded 4th July A. D. 1831
Test--Jacob A. Lane Clerk
White County Court.

An Amot. of the Sales of the property of ELI DODSON Desd. which was made liable to Sale by the last will and Testament of the Ded. which has come to the hands of Joseph Cummings and William Dodson Executor--returned
1 mans Saddle $2.06¼ weeding hoe & plough 1.81¼ $3.87½
1 Rufle Gum $20. ½ of a Mare Colt $20. 1 churn 12½ 40.12½

12½ Bushels corn $2.60/ 50 Bushels Dito $7.56¼ 10.16½

$54.16¼

Recorded 4th July 1831 Test-Jacob A. Lane Clerk
White County Court

Jos. Cummings Jr } Exr.
William Dodson J. }

Inventory of the Estate of ELIJAH ENGLAND Decd. returned upon oath by Ayelsy England Admt. and John England Adm. At July Session 1828. 150 Acres of land nine negroes $100 in Cash 1 Cash Note on Joseph & William Kerr and Jonathon C. Davies doubtful due November 1st. 1828 One Note on Robert Johnsoan due Dec 25th 1828 for $35 doubtful 9 head of horses 41 head cattle 200 head hogs 33 head of Sheep 12 head of geese 5 featherbeds bedsteads and furniture. 1 Table & chest 2 cotton Wheels 1 pair Cards 2 flax Wheels 2 kittles 1 pot 3 ovens 1 pot Eramoal 1 loom 1 Looking glass 1 pair fire dogs 10 chairs 1 Set Knives & Forks 3 dishes 8 platess 3 Jars 2 pitchers 4 crocks 1 sture pot 1 Set Table Spoons Tea cups & Saucers 3 bowls 1 Set Tea Spoons 1 Coffee Mill 1 Coffee pot 1 Tin trunck 1 pepper box 1 Salt Sellerquanity of books 5 pails 1 Churn 1 Chedk Rul 1 half Bushel 2 Riddlers 1 Seine 2 Smoothing irons 2 Saddles & Bridles 1 Rifle Gun 1 Shot pouch 1 Whip Saw cross Cut Saw tin partnersip 1 hand Saw 1 vessel 2 augers 1 drawing Knife 1 Broad Axe 5 fallin Axes 1 froe 5 ploughes 2 hoes 2 Mattocks 2 pair Geers 2 clocks 1 pair Streach 1 Log chain 1 Iron Wedge 1 Scythe & Cradle 2 Sickles 1 cutting box and Knife. 9 Bee Stand s & hides in Tan 2 pair pot hooks 1 flax brake 1 Grind Stone amont on Mathew England for thirty dollars in trade doubtful.

Ayelsy X England Adm.
His mark
John England

Recorded 4th July 1831
Test--Jacob A Lane Clerk White County Court.

Report by [Snr] Commissioners of a Settlement made with the Executors of ELIJAH CHRISUM Decd returned on oath at October Session A. D. 1828 Towit:

Pursuant to an order of the worshipful Court of Pleasad Quarter Session A. D. 1828, appointing us whose names are hereunto Subscribed, Commissioners, to Settle with James Chrisum and John Chrisum, Executors of the last will and Testament of Elijah Chrisum Senr. Dece ased, late of the County of White concerning the amount of the Estate of the Testator which came to their hands as Executors, Report and Say as follows, Towit: First, that the amount of the Sales of the property of Said Testator, and names by them received upon notes executed to him in his lifetime, is, as appeard from an account current returned by said $2276.24½ Executors on oath, at the July Session A. D. 1819 of White County Court

To amount of part of lands bequeathed to the heirs of Elijah Chisum Snr. Decd. as evidenced by Report of Commissioners made at $1000.00 January County Court A. D. 1822.

To amount of Sales of three Small tracts of land, one toDANIEL SNODGRASS and two to William Hill, on the 2.st July 1828---- 302.00

Total amount of Estate Real and personal $8578.24½

Said Executors Distributed

To Nimrod Dodson, who intermarried with Elizabeth Chrisum daughter of the Testator, Towit:

On the 19 January 1820 the Sum of $1000.00

On the 17 July 1820 the sum of 100.00
On the 15 August 1822 the sum of 269.00
On the 8 March 1823 the sum of 50.00
On the 11 December 1823 the sum of 50.00
On the 14 April 1824 the sum of 150.00

Amount $1619.00

Dr.

To total amount of Estate brought Forward $8578.24½

By amount paid Nimrod Dodson As legatee

Cr.

P 69 $1619.00

The heirs of Elijah Chisum Jern. Dead. Son of Testator By amount of lands bequeathed to them by their Testator for which See Report of Commissionrs herein before refered to made at January Court 1822 $1000.00 for the County of White.
By Receipt of William Hiol Guardian to Wm H. Chrisum, Surviving heir to Elijah Chrisum Jur. Decd.

Heirs of WILLIAM CHRISUM Decd. a Son of the Testator, By paying Seth Cason, who married with Elizabeth Shisum daughter Decd. paid 14 August 1822--$150. By paying Seth Cason, above, 15th August 1824 50 200.00

SALLY CHISUM, daughter of William Chisum, Decd By Amount of Bill at Lincoln's 21st January 1825 $8.27¼ By cash paid 26th & 28th March 1825--$121.18 3/4¢ By amount Bill at Lincoln Store, 20 May 1826 $9.56¼ by amount Bill at McClong & Oldham 16 Septr. 1826 $4.28 3/4¢
By a mount Bill at Lincoln Store in 1826 $3.81¼
By amount Bill in Store McClung 1C 1826 17 1834 amount paid Sally Chisum $164.21

8 578.24½ $2983.21

The following is the SIMMS disbursed for the heirs of William Chisum Decd. to their joint use Towit:
By cash advanced for support of (s ee forward) children December 4th 1818 $20.00
By paying fee to Thos. H. Fletcher for attending to Lawsuit 30 Sept 1825 10.00

Drs. carried forward

amount brought forward $8578.24½ 2983.21
By paying Fee to James Campbell and F. Jones Mltos. for Lawsuits 20 th July 1826 20.00
By paying Judgement for heirs against their Interse state, in favor of Thomas Simpson 31st Octr. 1827 16.71
By paying costs against hiers in Warren County Court 2nd Nov. 1827 18.00

84.71

By amount paid to HOHN CHISUM Guardian to the heirs of William Chisum of William Chisum Decd. July 1821
P 70
By amount retained by JOHN CHISUM Executor and one of the heirs of the

Testator.

The following Items were disbursed for debts against the Estate of ELIJAH CHISUM Snr. Decd. the Testator for funeral expences, expences in making Sales Managing the Estate lC To paying A. Huntsman his fee

Sept. 16 1822	$10.00
To paying John Carpenter debt 11 August 1819	3.50
To pa ing Henry Deweerse 14 Aug. 1819	1.25
Paying Note to Isaac Farley 25 Dec 1818	30.00
Paying Saml Weaver 3rd Dec. 1818	1.00
	45.75
	45.75
	~~$8578.24½~~
	3113.67

To paying WM. GLENN'S Bill 8 Aug 1818	$24.25
To paying Isaac Robinson's Acct. 18th Jany 19th 1819	1.25
To Thomas Williams Acct. March 10th	1.00
To Taxes 1818 paid John Taylor	6.39
To Isham Farley's acct. 18 Jany. 1819	1.00
To Samuel Weaver 3rd Dec. 1818	2.00
To amount paid on Coffin, plank funeral Service Charles McQuire	21. 37½
Crying at Sale 3rd Dec. 1818 paying A. Lance for work 3rd Dec. 1818	1.00
Paid W. Farley debt due from Estate	5.00
J. B. Hancock Acct. Nov 28th 1818 1.62½	1.62½

carried forward

Feb 11 1836

P 71 Paying big Sam for Isaac Robinson	$1.00
paying Ira Bedwell for Estate	0.75
T Spirits for Sale lC and while the deceased and his wife Lucy lay sick	22.25
To paying B. Lee for Coffin	2.87½
To paying Ira Bedwell Smith work	1.75
	$93.5

By amount of Insolvent debts arising out of the Sales of the Estate not yet received

By debt on John Pratt	$5.56¼
By debt on David Davis	56.23
By debt on Levi L. McBee	13.06¼
By bal. debt on Saml Thomas	100.50
By debt on Dewy Smith	225.75
	$401.10

For fees Services and Expences

By amot. paid Jacob A. Lane	$25.00
By amot. paid N Haggard	50.00
By amot allowed Executors by Comrs. for Services in Selling Said Estate, exclusive of clerks and Attorneys	300.00
	$375.00

	\$8578.24½	\$3983.29
Debts of Testator, funeral expences etc.		
By debts paid funeral expences, and for Supplies at Sale etc.		139.26½
Disbursements and Distributions		
By paying Nimrod Dodson	1619.00	
By land to heirs of E. Chisum Jr. Decd.	1000.00	
By paying Seth Cason	200.00	
By paying Sally Shisum	164.00	
By paying for joint use of Wm Chisum's heirs	84.71	
	\$8276.24½	\$3983.29

To amount of estate as Set out in the Recaptretation	\$8276.24½
By amount for Insolvances, fees etc. funeral expenses, Service etc	915. 37
Nett amount against Executor	7360.87½

Distributers respective Shares	
To Nimrod Dodson in right of wife	\$1472.17½
To heirs of William Chisum Decd.	1472. 17½
To Willaim H. Chisum Heirs of Elijah Chisum Jr. P 72	1472.17½
To James Chisum 1472.17½	1472.17½
To John Chisum	1472.17½
Amount of Shares	\$7360.87½

Sales of land in Recapitutation mentioned is to be divided among the above named persons;the executors retaining therefrom, the amount of expenses incured, in enclosing the Graves of Elijah Chisum Ser.and Lucy Chisum Decd. the father and mother of Said executors, when Said Expences are ascertained.

Interest Account	
To amount Interest due Nimrod Dodson on his Share	\$69.63
To Interest due Seth Cason	44.20
To Interest Due Sally Chisum	76.62
To Interest due W. H. Chisum	237.05
To Interst due five Minor heirs of Wm. Chisum Decd	520.00
	947.77

It will be seen that the amount of each Distributive Share is \$1472.17½ cents, which will Stand amoungst the heirs of WILLIAM CHISUM as follows, there being seven of them, and the Executors having paid and advanced money for the joint benefit of Said heirs, to the amount of \$84.07 cents would leave their Share amounting to the Sum of \$1387.46

Each Share amounting to the Sum of 198.20

besides the Sum mentioned in the Interest account above--Therefore

There is due to the heirs of WILLIAM CHISUM as follows, Towit:

To Sath Cason, principal and interest	67.83
To Sally Chisum principal and interest	110.61
To five other minor heirs of Said William principal and interest	1511.27

To william H. Chisum Son of Elijah Jernr Bal. principal and interest 709.22½

The amount of the Shares of Nimrod Dodson
Principa 1 and Interest being 1541.80½
and the Said executor having paid to him of 1619.00
therefore they have paid to him an excess, over and abo a bove his Share to the amount of the Sum of 77.20
which Said last mentioned Sum Should be by him refunded to Said Executor.

It being represented to the Commissioners that there remained in the hands of ELIJAH CHISUM Ser. the Testator, the Sum of fifteen dollars 6¼¢ due to William Hill, Adm. of Elijah Chisum Jr. Decd. unaccounted for, and for which Said execution are bound to account The Commrs therefore direct that that Sum with interest from the time it fell due until paid, be paid by Said executors, out of the land last Sold by them, and herein before refered to. when the money for the Same be Collected Also, one dollar for one day to Turner Lane, one Commissioners.

The commissioners, therefore, having fully examined all the papers, records and documents relating to the Estate of the Said Elijah Chisum Ser. Decd. Report and Say, that the Said acount and report as before herein Stated, Shews a true, full, and perfect Statement of the amount of ea ch Distributive of the Said Elijah Chisum Decd. Senerally--John Chisum his father and Mother, prepared at Nashville, and holling same $23. and further, that the price for putting up the Mason work as herein before expressed round Said Graves, thr further Sum of $25.--all of which is allowed him out of Said Estate, by Said commissioners.

All of which is most respectfully Submitted to the worshipful Court. Given under our hands and Seals 18th Sept. 1828
Turner Lane (Seal) Anthony Dibrell (Seal) Jacob A. Lane (Seal)
Recorded 5th July A. D. 1831
Test--Jacob A. Lane Clerk White County Court

Report of the Assignment of provisions by Commissioners to the widow of THOMAS WILLIAMS Decd. returned at October Session 1830. Towit:
State of Tennessee }
White County } Pursuant to a Commissioner to us directed from the worshipful Court of pleasant Quarter Session for the County of White. We David Snodgrass, William McKinney and Samuel Johnston this day at the house of the late Thomas Williams Desd. After being duly Sworn to act fairly and unpartially to the best of our abitation do assign and Set apart the following provisions for the widow of the Said Thomas Williams Decd. in the manner following.:

1. We Set Apart in the first plan all the the Sweet potatoes and Irish potatoes now growing on the primeses of the Said Thomas Williams Desd.
2. All and everything now growing in the Garden on Said primeses.
3. All the Chicken now on the place of the Same.
4. 20 Bushels of wheat.
5. One hundred Bushels of corn.

P 74

6. Twenty-five pounds of coffee, forty pounds sugar which shall be furnished by the adminstrators
7. Four hundred pounds good pork

8. One hundred pounds Bacon.
9. two pounds Spices two pounds pepper two pounds Gingar

All of the above articles and things Shall be furnished by Robt. Officer and Edward Elms Administrators of Said estate. they taking all th crop and anything in their possession and furnsting the foregoing out of the same, to be paid by them to the widow, whenever She shall use the Same Given into our hands and Seals this 12th day of August. 1830.

David Snodgrass (Seal) Wm. McKinney (Seal) Saml. Johnson (Seal)
Recorded 6th July 1831 Test-Jacob A. Lane Clerk White County Court

Report of the Settlement by Commissioners made with Jonathan Howard administrator of James Howard Decd. returned at January Session 1830

State of Tennessee }
White County } To the worshipful Court of pleasant Quarter Session. January Session 1830. James H. Pass & Elijah ward Comm ssioners humbay (? by leave to tender their teport as commissioners appointed by Said Court to Settle with Jonathus Howard Adm. of James Howard Decd. Having fully examined all the papers and accounts that came to our hands relative to Said Administration of the estate. we found upon Settlement that the Said Jonathus Howard is acountable as administrator to Said estate for the Sum of two hundred and Seventy Seven dollars to which Sum he is Chargeable a s money and effects that he have not disposed of an paid out. There are two notes in Said Howards hands on George Dawson the one for $24.88 c the other $74.75 cents which we have dharged him with. and the collections of which is doubtful. We would further report to your worships that
P 75 we have allowed Said Howard the Sum of Six dollars 75cents on his Services as Admr. and to which he is entitle to Credit. Given unto our hands and Seals the 15th Jany. 1830.

James A. Pass (Seal)
Elijah Ward (Seal)
Commissioners

Recorded 6th July 1831 Test-Jacob A. Lane Clerk White County Court

Inventory and Sales of the property of DAVIE EVANS Decd. returned on oath of James Randals and Eli Sims Admrs. at October Session 1828. James Randals and Eli Sims Administrator of the estate of David Evans Decd. In amount with Said estate.
By return of Inventory to one negro woman named Susan. one negro boy named Jackson one named Clayburn and one guirl child together with one horse and some cattle and Kitchen furniture some of which property has never come to our hands, except the negro boy Jackson which was sold by order of court. The amount of Sale was one hundred & Sixty Six dollars fifty cents. 166.50

There is one horse Some cattle and Kitchen furniture which was in the hands of Andrew Townsend at the time of one administration Which he the Said Townsend refuses to give up. and which we cannot get in our possession.

The negro woman Susan and two children is now and was at the time of Administration in the State of Kentucky one of which we learn is now dead and the others is put out of our reach So that it is doubtful Whether they will never come within our reach. The above is a true Statement.

James Randals } Adm.
Eli S[1]ms }

Recorded 6th July A. D. 1831
TEst- Jacob A. Lane Clerk White County Court

Account of the Sale of the property of ~~MARTHA PISTOLE~~ Decd. returned on oath by James A. Pass Adm. at January Session A. D. 1831

James H. Pass 1 cotton wheel	1.25
William Belcher 1 Flax wheal	2.18 3/4
John Pistole 4 pewter plates	.56¼
Randolph Ramsey 1 Set plates ~~pewter~~	1.87½
Thomas Bohanon 1 Earthen Dish	.25
Same 5 Earthen Plates	.37½
Randolph Ramsy 1 Set knives forks and Spoons	1.56¼
James H. Pass 1 Lot of plates 4 Basins & 1 dish	3.75
George Ramsy 2 Pitchers	.37½
Amot. forwarded to page 76	$12.18 3/4
Amot. brought from page 75	12.18 3/4
Samuel Ussuy 1 pair Cotton Cards	.06¼
Hohn Dryer 1 jug	.12½
Ditto 1 jug	.06¼
William Pryer 1 coffee pot	.12½
John Pistole 1 coffee pot	.37½
Judale Stone 1 pair Sheep Sheers	.62½
George McGlen 1 pair old cards	.12½
John Pistole 1 Lot crocks 3	.25
William Mason 1 Lot pickle pots 2	.12½
P 76 James H. Pass 1 Large Jar	.75
John Sligo 1 copper tea Kettle	.12½
William Rutledge 1 Lot pitchers & jugs	.50
John Pistole 1 Oven lid and hooks	1.81¼
J. D. Bosorth 1 fire Shovel	.37½
James H. Pass 1 oven and lid	1.50
James H. Pass 1 pot rack 1.00 1 Salt Collar 18 3/4	1.18 3/4
Aaron England 1 hoghead	.16¼
Saml. Dyer 1 barrel	.31¼
John Pistole 1 fat tub	.18 3/4
Enoch Menphew 1 large pot 3.62	3.62½
John Mason 1 large pot	2.00
James H. Pass 1 Grindstone	1.50
Randolph Ramsy 1 Scyth U Hangins	.56¼
John Pistole ~~1~~ weeding hoe	.43 3/4
James H. Pass 1 axe	.75
Saml. Dyer 1 mattock	.87½
Saml Usrey 1 Lot Teacups U Saucers	.25
John Pistole one half Bushel & two pails	.25
J. D. Bosorth 1 pail 1 piggin	.25
Saml. Ussey 1 Loom	2.50
James H. Pass 1 pair weaning bars	.06¼
Same 1 churn	.12½
John Pistole 1 Sifter tub and tray	.18 3/4
Benjamin Wilhite 1 Sugar Box	.25
Andrew Robinson 5 hogs first choice	7.25
Aaron England Jr. 1 Sow & Seven pigs	1.68 3/4
Andrew Robinson 17 head hogs last choice	9.00

	James H. Pass Steer yearling	1.75
	Andrew Robinson 1 red cow & calf white face	7.12½
	John Sellers 1 red heifer yearling	1.00
	John Pistole 1 brindle cow and calf-	4.12½
	Benjamin Wilhite 1 red cow and calf	5.31¼
	Amot forwarded to page 76	$71.75 3/4
	Amot brought from page 75	71.75 3/4
	William Rutledge 1 Barren cow	4.25
	John Sellers 1 Black heifer-	1.50
	Nathan Holland 1 cow red Sides white back	3.06¼
	John England 1 bell and collar	1.25
P 77	Jonathon Howard 1 waggon	41.75
	Jno. Pistole 1 set cutting Knives 2.18 3/4 1 Clevis 31¼	2.50
	William C. Bounds 1 cow hide	2.06¼
	Joseph England 1 cow hide	1.50
	Elizabeth Ward 1 meal bag	1.18 3/4
	Saml. Usery 1 Dito	.50
	David Snodgrass 1 Gray mare	12.62½
	Solemon Duncan 1 Gray filly	26.25
	James H. Pass 1 Sorrel Mare	22.75
	John Pistole 1 Samll bell collar	.37½
	James H. Pass 1 Side S^a^ddle	15.12½
	Stanford Brickin Half Dozen Chairs	1.56¼
	William Bullock 4 chairs	.25
	James H. Pass 1 Morgin Bible	6.00
	Joseph England 1 Trumel Bedstead bed and furniture	5.50
	Thomas Bohannon bed & furniture & bedstead	13.18 3/4
	James H. Pass 1 Red Steer	1.31¼
	J. D. Bosorth 1 Looking glass	.56¼
	Robert Howard Jr. 1 chest	5.00
	John Pistole 1 Table	2.37½
	Larkin Ramsy 9 head Geese	1.56¼
	John Rogers 1 flat iron	.75
	James H. Pass 1 Shovel Plough & collar	.62½
	William Pryor 2 head Sheep	2.06 3/4
	William Broyles 1 Candle Stick	.06¼
	Corn to my hands one yoke of oxen in the winter of 1829 Which I charged to myself after going the legatus a refusal	
	James H. Pass 1 yoke of oxen	20.00
	came to my hands in the winter of 1830.	
	One hog the property of Martha Pistole Decd. which I put up and made pork of charged to James H. Pass weighing after fattened 129 lb at 18/prC	3.87
	Total amount	$275.58¼

James H. Pass Admr.

Recorded 7th July 1831 Test--Jacob A. Lane Clerk White County Court

In the name of God Amen. I JOHN TERRY of the County of White and State of Tennessee being sick and weak in body, but of Sound mind disposing memory for which I thank God. And calling to mind the uncertainty of human life and being desirous to dispose of all Such worldly substance as it has pleased God to Bless me with I Hohn Terry first I give to my

wife Betty Rerry during her life time all my real and personal property and after her decease then I give to my Grandson John Graham one negro girl named Jude by his paying all of his brothers and Sisters and equal part with himself after two disinterested men values the negro girl Jude and then it is to be understood that I John Terry paid Six hundred and four dollars for part of the land that I now live on and I give the Same together with the land to my Son Joseph Terry. And then I give to my daughter Sally Durgin one negro girl named Harriette or to Said Sally Durigin heirs. And then I give to my grandson Jesse B. Terry one mo- la tto boy named Ben and also one young SorrelMMare with white in her
P 78forehead then at the desease of my wife Betty Terry I want the balance of property sold, and after all my just debts and burial expences paid and then I want Seven dollars given to my daughter Magy Graham. And then one third of the balance given to my daughter Sally Dorgin or her heirs and one third to be equally divided between Magy Graham heirs and lastly I do hereby Constitute and appoint William Hill and Sammuel Brown my executors this being my last will and Testament hereby revoking all other or former wills or testament by me heretofore made. In witness whereof I have here-unto Set my hand and Seal this the twenty Sixth day of October one thousand eight hundred and thirty. John Terry (Seal)
Signed, Sealed, published and dictated to be the last will and Testament of the above named John Terry in presence of us, who at his request and in his presence have here unto Subscribed our names as witness to the Same
Thomas Bounds (Seal) John B. Bounds (Seal)

State ofTennessee }
White County } July Session A. D. 1831 of the Court of Pleasant and quarter Session for White County

This day was provided in open Court the foregoing and above last will and Testament of John Terry Desd. whereupon the due exectution and publications thereof was proven by the oath of Thomas Bounds and John B. Bounds Subscribing witness think for the purposes and things therein mentioned and that the Said John Terry was at the date thereof of Sound and disposing mind and memory whereupon it is ordered to be recorded. Given at office 11th July A. D. 1831.

Test--Jacob A. Lane Clerk of
White County Court

Recorded and examined 18th August A. D. 1831
Test--Ja cob A. Lane Clerk White County Court

P 79 Agreement of provisions etc. by Comrs. to MAY SLAUGTELE Decd. out of the estate of the Decd. for the support of herself and children for one year returned at July Session A. D. 1831, Towit;

We the undersigned commissioners ixpressed in the within order the house of May Slaugtele on the 9th of this Instant and Set apart forty Bushels of corn. Six hundred pounds pork and two Bushels of Salt, for the Support of Said May and family for one year Given into our hands and Seals this 9th July 1831.

David Whitaker (Seal)
John Bohannon (Seal)
Nathan Bartlet (Seal)

Record examined 18th August 1831 Test--Jacob A. Lane Clerk
White County Court.

Report of a Settlement by commissioners with JAMES H PASS Adm. of JOHN PISTOLE Desd. returned on oath at July Session A. D. 1831.
State of Tennessee
White County Pursuant to an order of Court made at April Term of County Court of White County and to us directed etc. we have proceeded to e xmmine the Situation of the Witness of the estate of John Pistole Desd. in the hands of James H. Pass Administration to Said estate and find that since a former Settlement made with Said Pass by David Snodgrass Anthony Dobrell and William Simpson Com. up to the 1st January 1829. That Said pass has Since that time paid and provided good vouchers to the Sum of one hundred and fifty nine dollars nine & %cents and that we have allowed him for his Services the Sum of eight dollars making in all one hundred and Sixty seven dollars nine and a half cents.
Given unto our hands and Seals this 16th day of July 1831

David Snodgrass (Seal)
Wm. Hill (Seal)
William Simpson (Seal)

Recorded 23rd Dec. 1831 Test-Jacob A. Lane Clerk White County Court.

Report of a Settlement of Commissioners with JAMES H PASS Adm. of MARTHA PISTOLE Decd. returned on oath at July Session 1831.
S tate of Tennessee
White County Pursuant to an order of Court made at April Term of County Court of White County and to us directed. We have provided to Settled with James H. Pass administ rator to the estate to the estate of Martha Pistole Decd. and find that from the list of Sales of Said estate that he became indebted to the estate to the amount of two hundred and Seventy five dollars 38$\frac{1}{4}$ cents and that he has paid and provided good voucher and allowance for his Service etc. which we have allowed him the Sum of forty Seven dollars 22$\frac{1}{2}$ cents which Sum when deducted from the amount of of Sales would have Said pass indebted to Said estate two hundred and twen eight dollars and 15 3/4 cents. Given unto our hands and Seals this 16th day of July 1831.

P 80 David Snodgrass (Seal) William Hill (Seal) William Simpson (Seal)
Recorded December 23rd 1831 Test-Jacob A. Lane Clerk White County Court

The estate of JAMES MCCLARN Decd.
In Act with Isaac Tayler Adm. Desd.

August 7 1828

To 2 days going and returning from McMinnville to attend to a suit in Chancery T. Hopkins vs. J. Tayler Adm. Ap	2.
To cash for Expences	1.75
July 26, 1829	
To 2 days going and returning from McMinnville and attending the Sale of Mr. Hopkins land at my instance as Adm. of Said Estate	2
To cash for expenses during Said trip	1.75
For Services trouble etc in attending Said Estate	50.00
	57.50

The amount of the personal estate, Debts due and owing the Same and by me collected is $1837.66 nearly the whole of which I have had to contend forwhich has greatly delayed beyond any reasonable calculation and my wish the final Settlement of the Business of Said estate but I have recently finally succeeded in obtaining all the debts due the estate and are prepared to Settle with each of the Legatees of the same I would now Submit to your Worships and ask whether it would be right, that an

a dditional allowance be made me for my trouble and Services as Administrator to the one heretofore made and the Acct.a s above Stated.
9 July 1832 Isaac Taylor Adm.
Recorded 5 October 1832 Test-J. A. Lane Clerk White County Court
by N. Oldham D. C.

P 81 State of Tennessee]
White County Court] Pursuant to an order from the worshipful court of pleasant Qua rter Session to us directed for the things and purpose therein mentioned all being present do lay off and Set apart the following things (Diz) pork two thousand pound, eight Bushels and half of Salt. Five hundred Bushels of corn Five milchcows, the crop of Flax, the crop of Cotton , the fleece of wool, the present crop of wheat For sugar, coffee, Blacksmith work and Shoeing family and all other contingent expences that the necessity of the family may require, one hundred and fifty Dollars we the undersigned beg leave to Submit the following report--Given our hands this 8th July 1831 James H Pass]
Thomas Bounds]] commissioners
John Pennington]

The above is the report of the Commissioners who were appointed to Set Apart. Such part of the estate of John Dyer Decd. as would be Sufficient for the maintainance of the widow and her family
Recorded 5 October 1832
Test--J. A. Lane Clerk W.C.C. by N. Oldham D.C.

Return of Joseph Cummings Guardian to Eli Dotson heir of Eli Dotson Decd. made on oath at July term 1832.
Return the the following as the amt in his hands belonging to his Said word Towit: The Sum of $ 38.52½ July 14, 1832 Joseph Cummings Guardian for the heirs of Eli Dotson Decd.
Test J. A. Lane Clerk W.C.C. by N. Oldham D.C. Recorded 5 October 1832.

Return of Alexander Glenn Senr. Guardian for Laton Helton made on oath at Jany. term 1832.
State of Tennessee]
White County] To The worshipful Court of pleasant Quarter Session January term 1832. I Alexander Glenn Ser. Guardian of Laton Helton do hereby report to Said Court and Say that I have in my hand and possession the Sum of One hundred and Twenty Three dollars Eighty five cents in cash the 9th day of January 1832 which Stand good for Alexander Glenn Ser.
Recorded 5 October 1832 Test J. A. Lane Clerk W.C.C. by N. Oldham D.C.

P 82 Report of the asignment of provissions by commissioners to the widow of Benjamin Sewell deceased returned at Jany. Term 1832 towit: Two Steers at $8 one cow at five dollars one heifer at Eight dollars one Rifle Gun at Sixteen dollars one handsaw at two Dollars one drawing Knife one Inshave (?) one chisel one George One axe the whole at two dollars Seventy five cents two Beds, and furniture one bed stead at 20. dollars one churn and Dresser furniture at two dollars Castings two dolla rs fifty cents one Jar at one dollar one table one chest one shaving glass, one flat iron one tray at one dollar Secenty five cents--The above Articles was valued by the Com. the 31 October 1831.

Jonathon Short
Bussel Short
Robert Watson

Recorded 5 Oct. 1832 Test J. A. Lane Clk. W.C.C. by N. Oldham D.C.

Report of Moses Goddard Guardian for the Infant heirs of John Smallmon deseased upon oath at January Term 1832
State of Tennessee }
White County } ,Moses Goddard makes the following account and report of the estate of his wards James M. Smallman, Elizabeth Smallman, Sally Smallman & Mary Smallman Infant Heirs of John Smallman deseased In Cash on hand Received 19 November last not loan out $520.
Tract of land of one hundred and fifty acres not yet rented
Recorded 5 Oct. 1832 Moses Goddard
Test J. A. Lane Clerk W.C.C. by N. Oldham D. C.

Report of Ja mes W. Copeland Guardian to the Heirs of John Anderson Dcd. April Term 1832.

James W. Copelannd Guardian of the Heirs of John Anderson Decd . Returns to court as follows: NeHolas and Buman Harden & Abr. Hardin a note for money due 25 December 1832 this Sum $30. 30.00
Received from Abr. Harden for cotton being Rent 1.25
He has disbursed and paid out $31.25
as Guardian aforesaid and to E Webb on the 12 Sept. 1831 13.08
To J. A. Lane for Appt and two provisions returns to this his Sum 1.87½
To Nathan Haggard Atto at Law for defending suit by Scifa brought Martin 5.00
19.95½

P 83 This a ccount execlusive of services of Guardian Given Since the last return.
James W. Copeland Guardian
Recorded 5 Octr. 1832 Test Jas Land Clerk W.C.C. by N. Oldhan D.C.

Return of Thomas Hill Ser Guardian to the heirs of James Hill deseased yupon oath at January Term 1832.

An Account of Thomas Hill Ser. Guardianship to the heirs of James Hill Deceased No expence in in the year 1831 The a mt in my hands is one hundred and Eighty nine dollars Janny. 9. 1832
Thoma s Hill Sern.
Recorded 5 Oct. 1832. Test---J.A. Lane Clerk W.C.C. by N. Oldham D.C.

Report of Anthony Debrell one of the Executors of Jacob Robinson deceased upon oath at January Term 1832
State of Tennessee }
White County } To the worshipful court of pleasant Quarter Sessions now in Session Anthony Debrell one of the Executors of the last will and testament of Jacob Robinson Des. Beg leave to repesent to your worship, that they have exhausted all the personal estate except the Slaves of their Testator in paying just Debts against him and there yet remains unpaid Debts which made it necessary to sell one of the Slaves since last term of this Court Ner. Abraham to a certain Joseph Hunter for the Sum of

four hundred dollars being a fair price. But your petition had not previously applied to this court for privilege to make Sale of said Slave. They now ask your worship to Sanction said Sale and mow to make an order accordingly and they wil l ever pray etc. Anthhny Debrill
Recorded 5 Oct. 1832 Test- J. A. Lane Clerk W.C.C. by N. Oldhan D.C.

Report of John B. McCormick Adms. etc. of James Peakdeceased upon oath at April Term 1832.
State of Tennessee }
White County } The petition of Jacob R. Peak and James Peak by their Guardians John B. McCormick and John B. McCormick Adms. of all and Singular the goods and Charity rights and credits of James Peak deceased to the Worshipful County Court for the County of White Your potition or Begs
P 84 leave most respectfuly to State to your worship that the personal estate of the Said James Peak is exhausted that then there Judgements one in favor of Charles Manning for the Sum of $130.37 with Costs one in favor of Felix Robinson amounting to 686.96 with costs one in favor of Woodrow P White $189.77 There are some others but it is believed that sufficant can be made out of Some Debts still owing the estate of doubtful character to meet them. They are of small account Your petition states that he believes it is to the interest of the estate that such Sales should be made. He further States t at he has proceeded the indulgence of the Creditors and consent Your petitioner prays the order of this court authorising him to make sale of such parts of the Real E tate as May be most advantagious, according to a Law passed at the last Session of the General Assembly for the benefit of the heirs of James Peak deceased and as in duty bound will ever pray etc.

John B. McCormick
Adm. & Guardian

Recorded 5 October 1832 Test J. A. Lane Ck. W.C.C. by N. Oldhan D.C.

Report of John Fryer one of the Executor of Charles Carter Deceased upon oath at April Term 1831.
State of Tennessee }
White County } April Term 1831 of White County Court.
The petition of John Fryer one of the Executors of Charles Carter Ded. Beg leave to state to your worship that one the 24th day of December la st he was under the necessity of Selling a negro Boy named Benjamin. then about ten years old to a certain Woodson P. White for the Sum of Three hundred Dollars this he was obliged to do to pay a debt owing by said Charled Carter payable in negro property on the 25 of last December forfour hundred Dollars The sale of said negro leaves yet a Balance on that note unpaid Your petition therefore prays yours worships to Santion said sale by an order of this Court and to allow the Executors of said Carter to make a Bill of Sale of the negro boy Benjamin to Said White and as in duty bound etc the negro boy was taken by and Sold to Said white at a full and fair price

John Fryer
his
Rebecca X Carter
mark

Recorded 5 Oct. 1832 Test-J. A. Lane Clerk W.C.C. by N.Oldham D.C.

P 85 Report of the assignment of provisions by the Commissioners to the widow & children of William Fisher Decsd. at Ocr. Term 1831

State of Tennessee ⟩
White County ⟩ In obedience to an order of the worshipful Court of pleas & Quarter Sessions forSaid County we the undersigned have this day met at the late residence of William Fisher Deceased to set apart a years provision for the Widow and children of the Deceased do find the effects of Said Estate all sold by the Executor--we are therefore of opinion that the widow should be allowed a credit on her note forththe Support of the children as She had to furnish the prowision--Given under our hands this 3rd day Oct. 1831. Thomas Robinson & Joseph Herd

Recorded 6 Oct 1832 Test J. A. Lane Clerk W.C.C. by N. Oldham D.C.

Return of Robert Cooke Guardian to the Heirs of Elijah Sawyers Deceased upon oath at April term 1832 to wit:

My Return of the expenditures of the estate of Elijah Sawyers Deceased Since my return of April Session 1831. April 11 1831 paid Jacob A. Lane one dollar and twenty five cents his fees of office as Receipt doth appear $1.25

Nov 5. 1831 Bought for the use of said children onequire of paper at twenty five Cents .25

April 3. 1832 paid Joseph W. Little School master for Tuition of said Ward in last Six months by the days they went to school Four Dollars and Thirty one cents as Rectd. 4.31¼

P 85 E.E. $5.81¼

Robert Cook

Recorded 6 Oct. 1832 Test J. A. Lane Clerk W.C.C. by N. Oldham D.C.

Return of George Dong Guardian of Stephen Pistole upon oath at April Session 1831. Towit:

State of Tennessee ⟩
White County ⟩ To the worshipful court of Pleas and Quarter Sessions, April Session 1831. I George Long Guardian of Stephen Pistole make the following Report of my Guardianship one Note on William Simpson & Anthony Debrell for fifty dollars due 26th febry 1831--One note on Jesse England forfifty dollars due 22nd febry 1831 One do on Benjamin Wilhite for$50. due 8th March 1832 Two negro Slaves Charles &
P 86 Annaia hired for the above Sums. One horse and Saddle--credits to which I am entitled--By cash George W. Gibbs as Stephen Pistoles part of a fee to Said Givvs in the Case George Long Guardian & others vs James H. Pass a nd wife 12.50

By cash paid for the Said Stephen past for Searching Records postage and copying Records paid Wisdom for pork 6.69 money lost by said Stephen .50¢ 7.19

By cash paid Daniel Kelly for Schooling 10.00

whole amount paid out $36.44

I do hereby certify the above to be a just & true Report

April 1831. George Long Guardian

Recorded 5 October 1832 Test J. A. Lane Clerk W.C.C. by N. Oldham D.C.

Account Sales of the property of DAVID &JANE EVANS DECEASED returned upon oath by Eli Sims & James Randals Adms. at Oct. term 1830.

State of Tennessee }
White County } We the undersigned having heretofore been appointed administrators of David & Jane Evans Decd. do hereby report and say that since the aforesaid appointment as administrator that there has come to our hands one Small negro boy a Slave named Jackson aged about Six years old which negro Boy we advertised and Sold the same and Henry Lyda become the purchaser of Said Boy at Said Sale and bid the sum of one Hundred and Sixty five Dollars and fifty cents--- And no other property of Said estate has come to our hands. Given under our hands this 18 Oct. 1830.

Eli Sims (sl.)
James Randall(sl.)

Recorded 6 Oct. 1832 Test J. A. Lane Clerk W.C.C. by N. Oldham D.C.

Account of the Sale of the property of DAVID EVANS deceased returned upon Oath by E. Sims & J. Randals Adms. at January Term 1832.

We the undersigned Admrs. of the goods & chattles, rights & credits of David Evans decd on the day of August 1827 proceeded expose to sale one negro Boy called Jackson about six years old on a credit of Twelve months when Henry lyda became the purchaser at the price of $165.50 No other property has as yet come to our hands. Witness our hands this 9 day Janry. 1832.

Eli Sims } Adms.
James Randall }

Recorded 6 Oct. 1832 Test Jacob A. Lane Clerk W.C.C. by N. Oldham D.C.

P 87 Account of Sales of the balance of the property of William Anderson des. Returned upon oath by John W. Roberts & John Anderson Adms. at Oct. term 1831 We return the following as the Sale of the Balance of the property belonging to the Estate of William Anderson Deceasd. Returned in the Inventory heretofore returned by us sold on a credit

of 12 months Too men's saddles for	$25.43 3/4
Thirteen Sides of upper & stool leather	37.15¼
One old clock & old Bed without furniture	1.00
Total	$63.59

Recorded 6 Oct. 1832
Test J. A. Lane Clk. W.C.C.
by N. Oldham. D.C.

John W. Roberts } Adms.
John H. Anderson }

Account of the sales of the property of John Porter Decd returned by Woodson P. White Adm. upon oath at July Term 1831 towit:
Sale on the 14 day of May 12 months credit:

William L. Mitchell To 1 cutting Box	.37½
George Ledbetter 1 Sorel Mare	20.25
G. Yates 1 Bay horse $13. failed to give surety & sold to James Graham	14.25
Dan Griffeth 1 cow & calf	8.12½
Noah Dotson 1 cow & calf & 1 Bell	8.12½
Dan Griffeth 1 Steer	3.75
John Brock 1 red yearling	1.25
G Yates 1 Blk Heifer $3.75 Resold to John Miller	5.12½
William L. Mitchell 7 head of Geese	1.25
Henry Dotson 8 head of Hogs	12.00

Robert Davis 1 Cotton Wheel 1.25
G. Yates 1 old Saddle & 1 Sheepskin 1.62½ resold to S. Dotson 1.06¼
James Graham 2 Hids 2.75
John H. Dale 1 Large pot 2.50
Dan Griffith 1 pr. chains, hammer & Swingletree 2.00
John Dale 2 waggon wheels & tires 3.00
John Brook 1 Barrel & Sifter 1.00
Robert Davis 1 Check Rul .95
Dan Griffith 1 waggon Body 1.00
John H. Graham 1 Bedstead .25
W.M. Young 1 plow & hoe 1.37½
John Dale 1 Barrel pails churn etc 36¼
John Brock 5 chairs 1.25
John H. Graham whiskey Barrels etc 2.00
John Dole 1 Table .75
William M. Young 1 pail .50
Noah Dotson 1 Bedstead & cord .26
W. L. Mitchell 1 wheel 1.06¼
Jesse Worley Small quanity of cotton .12½
P 88 Sales of Porter's property continued
John Brock 1 skillet .81
Samuel Dotson Saw drawing knife etc. 1.25
James Simmons Kegs etc .50
George Yates o pr Steelyards 1.57 Resold to John Mitchell 1.12½
Isaac Dotson 1 pair fire Dogs 1.75
John Brock 1 oven 2.06¼
James Simmons 3 ovens etc 2.06½
George Yates 1 large oven pothooks shoes & umbrella 1.75
William Denny 1 pr. Saddle Bags 1.87½
Sammel Dotson 1 axe 1.37
John Yates 1 Barrel .13
Danl. Griffith 1 plow 1.68
John W. Riddles 1 Flax Hackle 1.45
James Simmonss a few peices of Leather 2.12½
Robert Davis 1 a xo& Mattock 1.25
John W. Riddles 1 piece of Iron ..95
John Graham 1 counter & Clevis .75
Lemus Sparkman 1 pot Rack .87½
Dan Griffith 2 Bull tongues & old axe 1.00
John H Dall 1 Bull tongue & 2 wedges 2.00
Samuel Miller 1 Set Spools etc .75
John White Senr. 1 pr. fire tongs & shovel 1.12½
John Brock 1 log chain 3.06¼
L. Miller 1 Barrel Broad axe etc 3.62½
John Yates 4 Bee Stands 8.00
G Yates 1 Still & worm $51. Resold to D. Wallis for 28.75
John Dale 1 Still & worm 34.25
Jacob Kuner 1 Side Saddle 12.00
James Simmons 1 piece of leather .25
Jacob Kuner 1 Bed and furniture 10.00
John Brock 1 Bed & furniture 1.56¼
Jess Holland 1 Man's Saddle 17.00
Jacob Kuner 1 pr. cotton cards .37

John Felton 1 Bureau 4.00
John Brock 1 Stay .18 3/4
James Dotson 1 do .18 3/4
Dan Griffith Small quanity gunpowder & slay berry hanes
1 chest 1 Bible & testament 6.00
Dan Griffith 1 Gun 6.00
Clyton Nichol 1 Glass .75
John Kiner Sundry Earthrn ware & coffee pots 5.18 3/4
John Brock 1 crock .50
John Yates 1 do .50
P 69 Porters sale continued
Jacob Kuner 1 crock .25
John Yatez 1 pr Shears .43 3/4
George Yates Sundry of pewter $6.00 resold to John Brock 3.75
Robert Davis meal Bag .06¼
Jess Scoggin 1 clock 10.00
Jacob Kuner 1 Side Saddle 12.50
John Yates 1 hogshead .25
Hugh Gasting 1 old Scythe .12½
Clifton Nichols 1 pad Lock .31¼
John Yates 1 Grindstone .25
Bacon purchased by various persons 15.37½
John Yates chickens 1.00
W.L. Mitchell 1 Tubb .12½
John Dotson 1 half barrel Brandy .06
Noah Dotson 1 Sale& Sla te .12½
Jas. /Simmons 1 Goard off at 3/9 resold to Jno Yates .37½
John Kiner 1 Big coat 2.18 3/4
Solomon Reese 1 cart 5.91½
John Payne 1 Bridle .75
$333.06¼

o Woodrow P White Adm.
of John Porter Dcd.
Re corded 6 Oct. 1832 Test J. A. Lane Clk. W.C.C. by N. Oldham D.C.

Account of the Sale ofof the prpperty of Joshua Porter Dcd. Returned upon oath by Woodrow P. White Adm. at July term 1831.Towit: The amct. of the Sale of Joshua Porter Decd. on the 14th day of May 1831, on 12 Months credit towit: Uriah York to nigro Girl Jane 387.00
W. P. White Adm. of Joshua Porter decd.
Recorded 6 Oct. 1832 Test J.A. Lane Clk W.C.C. by N. Oldham D.C.

Account of the sale of the property of William Kitchen Dcd. returned upon oath by Richard Judson Adm. at July term 1831. The amount of the sale of William Kitchen Dcd. sold on May 28th 1831. Agreeable to advertisement total amt 23.80
All the personal property being Sold except one man which was taken by virture of an execution at the instance of ----now in the hands of D. L.M Mitchell Slief(?) Witness my hand this 28 day May 1831.
Recorded 6 Oct. 1832 Richard Judson Adm.
Test J. A. Lane Clerk. W.C.C. by N. Oldham D. C.

P 90 Account of the Sale of ofthe property of William Fisher dcd. returned by Daniel Walling & Isaac Taylor Executors at Term 1831.

The proceeds of the sails of the property of the Estate of William Fisher Decd. as Will the rights & credits of the said deceaseds estate so far as the same hath come to the bonds or Knowledge of the said decease or Executors**

To Sundry plow hoes. 11 Bee hives fourteen head hogs all sold for 29.70 3/
To Two Stills, still tubb some Barrels etc six Hogs all scrst for 83.50
To 4 barrels Brandy 1 waggon 1 Mare & colt & 28 head sheep all sold for 248.33½
To 1 Bull 4 heifers 3 Steers one cow and yearling all sold for 45.38
To cash on hand .75
To Bryan Cook, claw hammer 1 froe 1 Broad axe 1 Bar Iron & Log chain 5.68 3/4
To 3 axe 1 Xcut saw 2 pr. chain 1 steel Trap all sold for 9.12½
To 1 Tobacco Barrel 2 Guns & Shot Bags 2 Ox Yoke some Bacon & corn sold for 28.62
To 1 Barrel tar 4 cotton Receipts for 50.77 seed cotton 77.06½
To 1 Saddle 1 pr. Saddle Bags 1 Rye stack 1 oat Stock 13.38½
To 1 cow & calf 26 Geese 2 Reaphooks 1 auger and 2 chisels 8.18 3/
To 1 note for 18$ payable in lumber, some Lumber & 2 lot of hogs 18.95
Total amount of the proceeds $569.25¼
of the sales of the property of the Estate of William Fisher Ded. including the Cash on hand which came to the hands of his executors sold the 6 & 7th of May 183 is five hundred & sixty nine Dollars Twenty and one fourth cents as above stated.

Inventory The following shows the amount of the Debts due the Estate of William Fisher Ded. by notes. The makes of all of are said I believed to be insolvent or a t least nothing can be collected from them by coersine measures unless they possessed a willingness to pay. Some of which have left the county to us unknown where

One note on I Black for 15$ due 1 Nov. 1829
One on G.W. Rector for 6.50 21.50
Alexander Morre constable Receipt for Reubin Ross & Jno.Chisum 50.00
One note on Thos & Charles Mayberry for Balance 17.77½
One note on Morgan & Jno. Elledge for Balance 6.68 3/
Two Notes on Lewis & Charles Franks for $75 each 150.00
One note on Jas Saxton for 10$ one notes on Hugh Caperton for 115. 125.
One note on David Telford for 2. One on George W. Recton for Balance 3.50 5.50
The total amt of Debts due the estate 376.46

William Fisher by notes so far as hascome to the hands or Knowledge of his Executors is three hundred and seventy six Dollars and forty six cents no part of which is believed by said executors can be collected There seems to be some unsettled book accounts due the Estate of the Deceased but to what amount at this time we are not prepared to say, but we will reserve to ourselves and claim the priviledge of disclosing this fact when the same shall hereafter be of certained u
P 91 up in a supplemental Inventory or report. 12 July 1831

Daniel Walling } Adms. of
Is aac Taylor }

Recorded 6 Oct. 1832 William Fisher Decd. Test J. A. Lane Clerk W.C.C.
by H. Oldha m D.C.

Account of the Sales of the property of the property of Archibald Warren dcd. returned upon oath by James Davis Adm. at Term towit:

1 Yoke of oxen to Brittian Johnson 13 August 1831 12 mos credit for	26.00
1 plow and Gears sold to Levi Bozarth	1.75
1 Sorrel Horse sold to Joshua Hickey for	50.00
1 Dutch oven 1 lid sold to Mrs. Bozarth	1.75
2 hoes and 2 sheep sold to James Walker	2.37½
1 Mattock and 1 Lapring to S. Strong	1.00
1 Large wheel sold to John Brown	2/00
1 pr. Cotton cards to J. Garret	.75
1 woman's Saddle to Levi Bozarth	12.75
1 slay to Delila Stell	1.00
1 Bell to L Bozarth	.75
1 plow to James Walker 1.00 1 mans Saddle to John Warren 8.00	8.00
1 loom to Jas Smith 1.00 1 Dresser to S. STrong .75	1.75
1 pot to Sally Warren 1.25 1 cow & 2 calves to E. Lefever 8.5	9.75
3 chirs to Wm Thompson 1.50 ½ Iron wedge to Jas. String 37½	1.87½
1 looking Gla ss sold to James Smith	.50
1 feather Bed & furniture sold to Sally Warren	1.00
All the above sold at Publick sale at 12 months	$126.12½

Credit on the 13th August 1831. There has also come to my hands One note of hand on Credar Fills for five Dollars due 17 Nov. 1830 5.00 Also one on Wesley Green for Seven Bushels of corn which is subject to a credit.

Recorded 6 Oct. 1832 Test J. A. Lane Clk. W.C.C. by N. Oldham D.C.

Inventory of the estate of JOHN TERRY DECD. returned upon oath by William C. Bounds Adm. at October Session 1831. Towit:

1 Bay mare 1 yearling colt 6 head of cattle 1 yoke of work Steers 1 pr cart Wheels 13 head of hogs 3 head of Sheep one scythe & cradle 1 Bee Stand Three Beds & Furniture 3 Bed steads Brunk some cupboard furniture 1 Ba rrel 1 pr. hames Sundry Irons 3 prs. pot hooks 2 common Tables 2 shovel ploughs 2 smoothing Irons 1 flax wheel 3 chairs 1 chick Rul 1 pr. fire tongs 1 fire Shovel 1 pr Dog Irons 1 Cupboards

P 92 1 large kettle 1 Frying pan 1 oven 1 oven lid 1 skillet 1 pot chain 1 churn 3 piggins 2 pickling Tubs 1 half Bushel 1 cotton Wheel 2 sides leather 1 Mattick 1 axe 1 Large 1 jug five old Barrels 1 keg 1 jug Bottle Flax crop. Crop. Crop of corn in the field say 30 acres crop of cotton say between 2 & 3 acres some unthrashed wheat

William C. Brown Adm.

Recorded 6 Oct. 1832 Test-Ja A. Lane Clk. W.C.C. by N. Oldham D.C.

Inventory of the Est of JOHN DYER DECD. returned by Samuel Brown one of the Adm. upon oath at July Term 1831 exclusive of support set apart by commissioners for widow and children towit:

3 beds and furniture 3 bedsteads 1 clock 1 chest 1 cupboard & furniture 1 Big Wheel 1 Settle wheel 1 Rul 6 chairws 2 tables 1 Looking glass 3 stone Jars 2 pots 2 ovens 1 oven lid 2 kettles 1 Handsaw 1 cutting Knife & Box 2 augers 1 chisel 1 drawing knife four stays 1 Loom 5 salt Barrels 1 washing tub 3 pails 5 crocks 2 Breadtrays 1 pr cotton cards 1 pr candle moulds 1 coffee mill 1 coffee pot 1 set Knives of forks

1 Bull tongue 2 pr Gears 2 shuck collars 1 log chain e axes t weedin hoe 1 Mattuck 1 Riddle & seive 1 half Bushel 1 Man's Saddle 1 woman's Saddle 1lpr Saddle Bags 1 Ridding Bridle wood work of Waggon 158 lb. Iron wagg tire 1 Black mare 7 year old 1 sorrel mare 11years 1 sorrel mare 9 years old & her colt 1 sorrel filly 2 years old 1 Roan filly 3 years old 2 wor steers 9 three years old steers 12 head of young cattle, 1 Grindstone 50 head of hogs of different sizes 13 head of wild hogs 12 head sheep 1 Scythe & cradle 1 negro womans a slave named Ann about 33 years old 1 negro Boy a sla ve named Rovert about 13 years old 1 negro Girl a slave named Katy about 10 years old 1 negro woman a slave named Cady about 18 years old 1 negro boy a slave named William 8 years old This la named woman (is Eady) was sent by Sally Dyer's father to John Dyer in his lifetime But no title was made by the father of said Sally wife of John Dyer Ded. for Said Negro woman
7 hides of common size taken from cattle that died with disease these are at Rose 's to tanned on the shares 4 Beef hides at myer's to tan on the Shares. 3 sides of leather tanned at Myer's one half of them bel-longing to Myer's for Tanning.

One note on Edward Bullock due 1 Sept 1829 for $10.00 one on Adam Massa due 27 Nov. 1829 for 1.81¼ an acct against Adam Massa for $ 3.80 One note on George Sifers due 1 Sept 1829 Bad for $ 10.00 one note on Joseph Hunter due 19 April 1831 for 20.00 One note on Daniel Wilhite due 13 Jany. 1830 for 20$. One note on Zacarich Sullers for Sixteen dollars due 8 July 1828. Credit 10 Nov 1829 for $10.s on said note le a Balance besides Interest of 6.00$ Bad

P 93 One Note on Isaac Hayten due 1 Sept 1829 for 16.75 credited 1 August 1830 with 15.00 leaves a balance of bad 1.75
One note on Walker Bennett due 1 Sept. 1823 of bad 20.25
One note on Same 19 Oct. 1821 of bad 17.00
One note on Same 1 Sept 1816 of bad 16.00
One note on Matthew England due 1 Nov 1827 due 15.00
credit on Said note dated 30. March 1829 of 6.00
leaves a balance of 9.00
One note on John Shepherd and James Taylor due 1 Mar 1831 $1.98
credited with $18 Dec. 3 1830 leaves a balance of 180.00
One note on John Perrow payable to pinckney McCarven due 5 July 1828
Bal .87½
One note on Aaron England due 1 Sept 1829
for 3.00 credited 12 Sept 1829 by 1.50$ balance 1.50
One note on Jesse B Clark due 25 Dec. 1830 1.70
One note on James Ward due 25 Decr. 1829 1.75
One note on Samuel Brown due 4 febry 1830 for 9.00
an account against same 3.25 12.25
One note on John Rutledge given to James Peak due 25 Decr. 1820
for $45 assigned by Jno Brown to John Dyer 5 June 1821 bad 45.00
An account against John Rutledge bad 23.25
One note on Shadrack Price due 1 may 1830 for 15$ credited by
$8.17 July 1830 leaves bal doubtful 7.00
An obligation on Shadrick Price due 15 Decr. 1830 do 6.50
One note on John Gooch payable to Wm. Dyer due 25 Dec. 1829 12.50
One note on Solomon Wilhite due 9 Aug 1829 doubtful 50.00
One note on Solomon & Benja. Wilhite due 18 may 1830 50.00

One note on Wm. Dyer to Jesse Lincoln due 1 May 1829 Doubtful	11.00
One note on Rice & Hidkox due 1 Sept 1829	23.33 1/3
One note on John Tawson due 25 Decr. 1824 bad	31.00
One Note on William Anderson due 17 July 1830	200.00
On acct. against Same Doubtful	10.00
One note on Elijah Ward due 1 May 1830 for 100$ credited 5 Nov. 1829 ($21.83)	21.83
One note on Jacob Robinson & Elijah Ward due 25 Decr. 1821	25.00
One note on Ruebin Robinson due 17 febry. 1828 Doubtful	10.71
One note on Same due 9 May 1828 for $5.55 credited by 50$ on 14 August 1830 Dobtful	5.55
One note on Samuel W Carrick due 1 June 1830	29.40
One note on Jesse Lincoln due first June 1830 for $183.56 Credited 15 July 1830 for45$ Bal	138.56
One note on Jesse Lincoln due 28 Decr. 1831	78.00
One Note on Alfred G. Beedles due 14 April 1829 payable to H. McFarland Bad	1.25
P 94 forwarded	
One note on Joseph Cumming & J. Whittley due 1 Jany. 1828 for 19.00 credited with $13. Doubtful	6.00
One note on Robert Johnson & Noah Philips balance being Interest	1.65
One note on Larkins Wisdom due 19 feby 1830	6.62
One note on Bassel Beedles & John Franklin due 1 Oct 1820 for $11.00 credited 16 March 1821 with 6.50 Bad	4.50
One Receipt on Alfred G. Beedles for the Collection of a note on Matthew G. Moore & Patrick Potts due 1 mos 1827 doubtful	9.00
One Receipt on Alfred G. Beedles for the collection of a note of W William Rutledge	2.66 2/3
One order to John Dyer by William Dyer by William Dyer on Jesse Lincoln and Protished by Jesse Lincoln and protished by Jesse Lincoln on the 4th June 1831 Doubtful	1.50
One Judgement in Esq Pennington office against John & Jesse Bounds for 70$ interest 6.75 obtained 16 May 1820 and credited with 35$ about March 1831	41.75
An account on S. Price Doubtful	.50
An account against Joseph England do.	1.00
An account " James Ward d0	1.00
An account against Thomas Bohanon do	.50
An account against Jas. Kerr for Bacon in 1830	10.00
An acct do John Gooch payable in cattle	10.00
An acct. do Wm. Matlock	1.50
One note on Samuel Dyer to William Bullock due 25 Decr 1832 Bearing interest from 22nd [illegible] 1831 for	100.00
One note on William Bullock due 25 Decr. 1831 payable to Sarah Dyer	19.50
One Note on John England payable to Adm. of John Dyer due 24 April 1831	8.00
The four last mentioned notes were taken since the death of said John Dyer	
One note of Samuel Dyer due 25 Dcr. 1831	50.00
An Acct. against the Estate of J. Robinson decd. filed	115.00
One claim against Nancy Bedwell do	22.00
One acct. on William Bullock do	37.65½

There has been some increase in stock since John Dyers death which is included in this Inventory

Samuel Brown Adm.

Recorded 6 Oct. 1832 Test J. A. Lane Clk. W.C.C. by N. Oldham D.C.

P 95

Return of Jqutines Howard Guardian to James & Ann Howard heirs of James Howard deceased returned upon oath at July term 1832.

Jqustines Howard Guardian to James and Ann Howard children of James Howard deceased Reports as follows towit:

Amount of funds in my hands as reported as January term 1831 is 163.21½

Interest on the Same 12 months or up to January 1832 9.78

Cash received belonging to said Estate 26 October 1831 70.00

Interest on the same to January County Court 1832 1.05

Recorded 26 Oct 1832 This 11 July 1832 244.04½

Account of the Sales of the property of John W. Gleeson deceased returned upon oath by Edward Gleeson adm. and Polly R. Gleeson Admr. at April term A. D. 1832 Towit:

1 Bareshare plow to Robert Anderson Ser.	1.00
L Shove plow to Thomas Robinson	1.37½
1 Shovel plow to Rovert Wilson	.25
1 axe to Edward Gleeson	.62½
1 Iron wedge & 1 curry comb to Isaac Taylor	.75
1 parcel of Black smith tools John Tisk	30.00
1 yoke of oxen John Taylor	23.00
1 cow and calf Blanton Denton	7.56¼
3 head of cattle same	7.18 3/4
1 waggon John Taylor	43.25
1 axr Alexander Glenn Jr.	.75
1 do Joseph B. Glenn	.37½
1 shovel plough Elijah Hill paid	1.00
1 pr. of chains Joseph B glenn	1.37½
1 pr do John Young paid	.56¼
2 Hoes Obadiah Harling	.37½
1 Gun, pouch and Horn Joel Smith	14.37½
1 handsaw Avery Norris paid	.56¼
1 Bedstead Indemore B. Moore.	.43 3/4
1 Box and other articles Oscar Denton	1.87½
1 pr. Spurs & jug Edward Gleeson	.75
1 Drawing Knife Alex. Glenn Jr.	.75
1 Bedstead & furniture John Vaughn	7.81¼
1 wheel and Reel, auger etc Robert Anderson	1.93 3/4
1 Grindstone Isaac Taylor	4.00
1 Big wheel and Hammer G. Templeton	.50
1 Loom Joseph Clark	4.87½
1 Bell Joseph B. Glenn	.37½
2 slays 2 shuttles andLafuth Isaac Taylor	1.62½
1 kettle Alexander Glenn Jr.	5.12
1 oven & lid Joseph B. Glenn	2.28
1 do Wilson Upchurch	1.00
P 96 continued	
1 washing Tub to Berry Hamblet	.50
1 pot to Wilson Upchurch	1.25

2 Jars, Jug & Bucket to James Holton Paid	.50
1 Tub 1 crock one Jar, Berry Hamblet	1.62½
1 pot Trammul to Obadiah Harlow	1.62½
1 shovel & waffle Irons Robert Anderson	1.25
3 pr cotton cards to William Baker	.37
1 man's Saddle to Oliver A. Swift	17.93 3/4
6 chairs Obadiah Harlow	1.75
1 Fall leaf table, Joseph B Glenn	5.43 3/4
1 Looking Glass C Swindle Jr. paid	.37½
1 cupboard & furniture Johathon B. Glenn	18.37½
1 clock Thomas Walling	16.25
1 wash bowl & pitcher Olicer A. Swift	1.25
1 Bureau James Dillon	12.62½
1 Hone Edward Gleeson	.87½
1 Tub Oliver A. Swift	.56½
1 Beef hide Indimon B. Moore	2.06¼
1 Rawhide Edward Gleeson	1.50
1 Trough and 2 tubs Joseph Clark	.18 3/4
1 Scythe and craddle Black charles paid	.87½
1 Table James Randols Jr.	.37½
1 do Docia Randals	.31¼
1 coffee Kettle and pitcher conteiss James	.75
1 Keg Edward Gleeson	.25
a variety of Books James Randals Jr.	3.00
1 case of Razrs and strap Ed Glesson	.75
Land and primises united to Darius Clark Jr.	21.31¼
His interest to the undivided tract rented one year E. Glesson	3.50
1 Cutting Knife John Taylor	.81¼
1 side saddle Mary R. Glesson	5.00
1 Bed and furniture Alexander Glesson Jr.	12.12½
1 Bed & dito Mary R. Gleeson	5.00
1 Sorrel Mare Madison Fisk	31.00
1 Foot Adze William White	.62½
1 Bay mare John Rascoe	20.12½
1 Bull John Harlow by Charles Hensley	4.00
1 negro man Adison John W. Simpson	601.00
1 negro Woman & child Indemon B. Moore	376.37½
1 negro Boy named Carrol Mary R. Gleeson	230.00
1 negro Girl do	191.00
1 negro Girl Dochia Randols	200.00
1 pr. fire dogs Tinias B. White paid	1.62½
P 97 continued	
1 Lot of Article Kitchen ware Joseph Clark Surl.	.43 3/4
1 pile of corn Edward Gleeson	23.00
A quanity of corn Ten Barrels reserved for the Widow E. Gleeson	40.80
2 Sheep Indimon B. Moore	1.37½
1 Hog Edward Gleeson	.87½
1 Fodder stack James Randal	1.12½
1 peice Leather Thomas Cann	1.81¼
1 do do R. B. Perkins	.87½
1 Fodder Stack William Chuster	1.31¼
1 Book James Randals	1.75
2 Books one slay dO	.75
	$1937.82½

Recorded 30 Oct. 1832 H. Oldham D. C. Of J. A. Lane Clerk.

Account of the Sales of part of the property of the Estate of John Terry Deceased returned upon oath by William C. Bounds admr. at January term A. D. 1832 Towit:

1 Flax wheel to John Gram	2.75
1 Flax do Joseph Terry	.50
1 cotton wheel Joseph Terry	.62½
1 Reel M. Wallis	.81¼
1 Dining table I Isham	.50
1 " " Jas. Pearson	1.25
4 chairs Joseph Terry	.12½
Shovel & tongs to J. Whitson	.75
1 pr. fire dogs W. C. Bounds	1.50
1 tea Kittle J. Whitson	.43 3/4
1 pr. Steel yard J. Terry	1.06¼
1 pr candle moles do	.12½
1 coffee mill Jas. Graham	.43 3/4
1 Serve do	.50
5 pr. Dilph I Isham	.62½
9 Dilph plates Jno B. Terry	.37½
3 pewter Basins J. Whitson	3.00
3 " plates W. C. Bounds	.75
Ink Bottles Thos Bounds	.06¼
2 Glass Tumblers & salt cellar J. Terry	.31¼
1 Candle stick S. Price	.12½
1 Lot Table ware Jno. Moore	.75
Knives & forks to S. Price	1.00
1 cupboard Benj. Mackey	.81¼
1 Trunk Jno. Isham	1.31¼
1 Bed & furniture & Bedstead I. B. Clark	6.12½
1 do do Jos. B. Terry	10.12½
1 do do Polly Goforth	5.75
1 Oven and lid John B. Terry	1.68 3/4
1 Skillet S. Richardson	06¼
3 watter Piggins Jas. Pearson	.25
pot rack Jno. Moore	.56¼
1 pot & Lid Eliza Pearson	1.12½
1 flat Iron Jesse B. Clark	.62½
1 do do	.50
2 churns & Jug W. H. Barnes	.37½
1 Frying pan to Mat. Mathis	.37½
Leather to John B. Terry	1.25
1 side do I Lovelady fer	1.74
1 Bee Gum J. Pearson	.12½
1 Bull tongs plough E. Elmore	.25
1 ploughshear Jo. Graham	.56¼
1 pr. hames & Chains Thos. Barnes	2.12½
Barrel & scraps of Iron W. C. Bounds	4.75
1 axe Philip Whiteson	.37
1 Bill James Mills	.25
2 hoes & etc John Crook	.50
1 pr. strechers Jnel Moore	1.75
1 mattock P. Whataker	1.00
1 pot T. J. Lovelady	.50
1 sprouting hoe E. Elmore	.18 3/4

1 Scythe Blade John Crook	.50
2 Barrels Joseph Terry	.31¼
Barrel John Crook	.43 3/
1 axe Jeremiah Whitson	1.06¼
1 plate & tub Wm. Kirby	.25
1 yoke of Steers J. C. Dewey	25.00
1 cow h. Hughs	7.00
1 do Isaac Mills	6.25
1 White Heifer J^oseph Terry	4.00
1 cow Wm. Kirby	12.25
1 plow Elijah Elmore	1.31¼
1 do Ul. Kirby	.50
1 cow & culd John Moore	10.87½
8 head of hog do	16.25
7 do Matthew Wallis	12.12½
1 crib corn Joseph Terry	36.37½
1 Mare Jesse B. Terry	34.37½
1 colt Benjamin Harris	17.06¼
1 Serves B. Mackey	.12½
3 Sheep James Mills	2.06¼
Some flax B. Mackey	.56¼
Some wheat Wm. K. Bradford	.37½
cart wheels Reuben Whitson	5.12½
1 meal tub John Crook	.18 3/
1 pr. scythe Blades Wm. Kerby	.06¼
Hired Negro Girl to Thomas	3.00
Bounds 6 mos. for 1 Hog Benja Mackey	1.50

William C. Bounds Admr.
Recorded 30 Oct. 1832 H. Oldham D.C. Of J. A. Lane Clerk

Account of the Sales of the property of the estate of John Dyer deceased returned upon oath by Samuel Brown Adm. & Sarah Dyer Adm. at January term A.D. 1832. Towit:

Sarah Dyer

To 1 bed & furniture & Bedstead	5.00
To 1 bed & do do	12.00
" 1 " do do	12.50
To 1 " do	13.50
To 1 cupboard & Some furniture	4.35
To 1 chest	3.00
To 1 pr. Saddle Bags	2.00
To 1 man Saddle	7.00
To 1 Side Saddle	8.00
To 1 cotton Wheel	.50
To 1 flax do	.75
To 1 Real	.62½
To 6 chairs	.37½
To 1 Looking glass	.37½
To 3 piggins	.62½
To 2 Ovens & lids & pr pot hooks	2.12½
To 2 pots 2.25 2 Skillets & lids 1.37½	3.62½
To 2 Kittles 2.50 1 Handsaw 75	3.75

1 Drawing Knife & chisel	.31½
4 Slays 1.00 3 crocks & 2 Bread trays .50	1.50
1 pr cotton cards candle moles 1 coffee mill	1.00
John Herny 2 augers	.18 3/4
Knives & forks & coffee pott S. Dyer	1.00
Sarah Dyer 1 Loom & Harness	1.75
5 Salt Barrels	.63½
1 Mattock 31¼ 3 axes 1.75	2.06¼
Thomas Roberson 1 Gun & pouch	15.00
Sarah Dyer 1 patent Clock	13.50
2 tubs 1 wash tub & ½ bus. measure	1.00
2 Shovel plows 1 Bull tongue & t hoes	2.18 3/4
1 log chain	3.25
1 Grindstone	.37½
1 Bridle	.75
2 pr. chains 2 pr. hames 2 collars and backbands	2.00
1 Riddle & Seine	.18 3/4
Paul chapin 150 Iron	10.
John B. Terry wood work wagon	16.
Sarah Dyer	
1 Scythe Blade & cradle	1.50
11 head Sheep	10.25
1 cutting Knife & Box	1.25
26 head hogs	25.12½
Jonanthan Scoot 1 Sorrel mare	57.50
William Price 1 Brown mare	32.00
Sarah Dyer 1 Sorrel mare 11 yrs old 1 Sring colt 12years old	
Sorrel Filly 1 roan filly 8 years old Sorrel	60.00
Paul Chapin 1 yoke & steers	30.62½
T. Lovelady 1 small bull	4.56¼
Ul. Daniel 1 red cow	8.00
G. Cardswell 1 pided steer	5.50
J. Robinson 1 red Steer	8.06¼
T. Lovelady 1 pided year old steer	3.00
S. Dyer 3 first choice Bee stands	1.50
Saml. Dyer 1 Bee stand 5 chairs	.25
S. Brown 1 do 6 do	.31½
Jp. Hunter 1 do 4 do	.25
Sarah Dyer 10 head Geese	1.25
Shepherd & Taylor 9 head cattle	72.00
S. Brown 1 side upper Leather	1.87
A England 1 do	1.06¼
J. Pennington 1 do	2.00
Saml. Dyer 7½ harrow teeth	1.00
Sarah Dyer 1 Bull yearling	1.50
" " 1 Steer	5.00
" " Some Leather at tanyard	2.3½
" " 2/3 of 2 sides leather	3.25
" " 5 sides upper do damaged	2.75
" " 2 tables	.50
" " 13 wild hogs	7.00
one note on James Ward	3.50

Adm. knew not about this claim in making former Inventory therefore was not there included etc.

Account of the Sales of the property of the estate of James Davis De ceased returned upon oath by Ephian Davis Adm. at Aprol term 1832. Towit:

Ul. Davis 1 year old cow brute		3.00
J. Dotson 2 Bells		.87½
do	2 cow hides	2.50
E. McLauglin	1 man Saddle	.50
I. Graham	1 Halter chain	.81¼
E. McLaughlin	1 man Saddle	.62½
Martha Davis	1 Side Saddle	1.62½
Ul. Davis	6 Turkeys	1.50
James Davis	10 Ducks	1.00
S. Dotson	1 Grindstone paid	.50
Jno Davis	1 horse (tobe sold again)	30.00
James Davis	1 Bay mare	35.06¼
Ul. Davis	1 Rifle Gun & Pouch(this is to be sold again)	7.50
Wesley Davis	1 Bridle	.25
Ar. Davis	1 cattle note fer 30$ at	16.51
Ul. Davis	1 cow	7.00
George Miller	1 year old cow	3.06¼
W. Davis	1 year old cow brute	3.00
E. Davis	1 Sorrel mare (tobe sold again	58.44
John Graham	1 Bridle	.62½
Marthag Davis	2 head of Sheep	1.07½
do	1 Lot Short corn	1.62½
Alexd Miller	1 Lot corn	4.50
Eph Davis	1 do	4.56¼
do	1 do	4.62½
do	33 bush. corn at 11p Bo	6.60
El Davis	1 Lot tobacco	.12½
F. Johanson 2$ worth Deerskins		1.12½
John Davis 1 mans Saddle this saddle is to be sold again		15.75
	Total	$24.37½

Recorded 31 October 1832 N. Oldham D.C. J. A. Lane Clerk

Account of the sales of the property of the estate of WILLIAM KITCHEN Ded. returned upon oath by R. Judson Adm. at Oct term 1832 towit:

Aug 4th 1831 Sold an old mare	7.37½
July 28 1832 Sold a parcel of oats. 0 mos. cr.	4.81¼
	$12.18 3/4

Recorded 31 Oct 1832 N. Oldham D.C. of J. A. Lane Clerk
Richard Judson Adm.

P 100 Inventory of the property of the estate of THOMAS DUNCAN deceased returned upon oath by William & George Duncan Admrs. at October term A. D. 1832 towit:

One waton one man 7 head of cattle 13 head of Sheep 32 head of Hogs 3 plows 2 hoes 1 mattock 1 pr Gears 3 saddles, a crop of Rye and oats and fodder & 2 Bee stands 1 Loom some flooring plank 2 9 Geese 1 Rifle Gun 1 Lock chain 3 Beds and furniture 1 Bureau 7 chairs 1 Big wheel 1 little Wh

1 Re ol 2 pots & hooks 1 oven 1 Skillet 1 frying pan 1 Set of Dog Irons 1 pot rack 1 pail 2 piggings 1 churn 2 tables 10 delph plates 6 pewter plates set of tea cups and saucers 1 Basin 1 Dish 2 Jars 1 Coffee pot 1 shovel 2 Bells 3 books 1 Grindstone 1 Slate 1 Smoothing Iron 1 Iron wedge 4 Baskets 1 knige Box 823 feet of Sheeting plank 400 ft. Weather boarding plank on A. Dibrell also 40 fts. flooring plank on the Same one note on B. F. Sanders bad debt $6.25 on James Telferd bad debt one note on John Adkins fer 12.50 One account on the County transrered from John Adkins transfered from John Adkins transfer not assigned fer Seventeen dollars both bad debts. One account on Daniel Clark fer $33. One Account on William Duncan fer Eighteen Dollars 91 cents. $2.75 on Peter Howard by order bad one account on Charles Certain fer 4.45 in Shoe making one account on David Glenn fer $1.00 in coopering one Dollar fifty cents on James Crowder. One account on Isaac Bennett in trade for three dollars and Seventy five cents one account on Archibald Hawks fer $5.12½ in trade on account on Joseph Hawks fer 9.25 bad one note on Joseph Bullard fer 0.25 bad debt. One judgement against William Green and John Green fer 13$ bad. One Account on Rachel Bennet fer $1.84

William Duncan

Recorded 1 November 1832 G. W. Duncan N. Oldham D.C. of J. A. Lane Clerk.

Inventory of the property of the Estate of ROBERT HOWARD deceased returned upon oath by Jguatine Howard ADm. at Oct. Term A. D. 1832 towit: 2 Horses 10 head of cattle 2 Rifle Guns 4 head Sheep 25 or 30 head of hogs 1 Bellows vise and anville r hammers and Screw plate 1 Set of or part of a Set of old wagon Irons 1 cross cut Saw 1 hand Saw 3 Drawing Knives 3 augers 2 plains 6 pr Drawing chairs 2 Horse Collars 2 Shovel plow hoes 2 Bull tongue hoes 4 weeding hoes 2 long hoes 1 Mattuck 2 Bearshere plows in part 2 large Kettles 1 Large pot 2ovens and Lid 1 Stew Kettle 1 Skillet 2 pr. pot hocks 1 pot rack 2 side Saddles 3 Bridles old 1 Log chain 1 frow 1 hand adze 3 falling axes 2 Iron wedges 4 clevis 2 or 3 Swingletrees. 2 Sets fire Irons 1 Smoothing Iron 1 pr. Stretcher 1 cutting knife & Box 3 chisels 2 guages 1 round shave 1 box containing shoe tools 1 Grindstone 1 Small Bar Iron 1 loom 3 setts pewter plates 4 basins 1 Dish 1 Keg 1 lard stand 1 pail 1 Bucket 1 half Bushel 2 jugs 2 Jars 1 Bedsted 2 Beds and furniture 1 Table 1 looking glass 1 folio Bible 1 common ditto 1 set Knives and forks 1 Set spoons 4 chairs 2 cotton wheels 1 Flas wheel 4 sides leather 1 Jackscrew 1 pr sheep shears 1 coffee mill 20 lb wool 6 weaving slays 4 pr. weaving harness.

Ign Howard Adm.

Recorded 1st Nov. 1832 N. Oldham D.C. of Jacob A. Lane Clerk

Report by commissioners of a settlement made with the administration of Gilly Gear dcd. upon oath at July term A. D. 1832.

DR.		CR.	
To 1 cow & yearling	7.12½	By expense of making coffin	.62½
1 loom & shuttles		one note paid	.81¼
3 Slays & 1 pr frames	1.12½	Taxes acct. & Smith act.	3.12½
1 Iron wedge	.50	A. Dibrell acct	2.75
4 chairs	.50	William Simpson do	1.00
1 mare	3.00	proven act of Fred Gear	10.00
1 Set Delph plates	.81¼	Sims Dearing acct.	1.00
2 Delph Dishes	.37½	Jacob A. Lane Clerk's fee	4.75

1 Box	.56¼	Expenced by Commissioners	1.37½
1 crock & cup	6¼	Jas. Cooper one of the adms.	
2 pails & horse shoes	.25	7 days settlin g said estate	4.37½
1 chest & one tub	.75	do 1 day Settling with com.	.62½
1 wheel & cards & 1 briddle	.50	amt paid coms. fee	2.00
to cotton 1 bed & stead	6.31¼	By Balance remaining in Adms.	
1 side Leather & 1 H'o	3.00	hand at Settlement	16.12½
1 Field of corn 15.00	15.00		
1 Lot of H gs	5.68¼		
½ Bushels Rye	.50		
	$49.31¼		$49.31¼

We John Walker and Eli Sums being appointed commissioners at April Sessions A. D. 1831 to settle with and make report thereof to this
P 101court with James Cooper and Samuel Usrey Adms. of the estate of Gilly Gear dcd. in obedience to Said order have as we believe made a thorough examination of all the business of said estate and find there within as by us stated to be true report.
Given unto our hands this 11 day of July 1831

John Walker }
Eli Simms } comms.

Recorded 1st nov. 1832 N. Oldham D.C. of Jacob A. Lane Clerk of W. C.C

P 102 Report by commissioners of a Settlement made with administrator of john Johnson deceased upon oath at July term A. D. 1831 Towit:Dr.
To amt of the Sales of the property that come to my hands $68.89¼

	Cr.
By this same paid Barthenia Brown	1.00
" " " " ELiz Johnson Shroud	7.82½
" Isaac Whittys proven acct	2.06¼
" Dot Robert cox for attendande	10.00
" Jess Allen p Note	5.00
" Henry Burton crying property	1.00
" for whiskey at Sale	1.50
" B. Johnson his Legaccy	1.00
" J. Allen Fr. Making coffin	3.00
" M. Cambrell by reqt. of Johnson	2.00
" expences attending 3 years count &tc.	25.00
By Bal in adm. hands	9. 56
	68.89¼

George Allen Executor
of John Johnson Decd.
A true report of receipts and accounts given us by George Allen Executor of John Johnson Dcd.

William Irwin }
James Russell } coms.

Recorded 1s t Nov. 1832 N. Oldham D.C. of J. A. Lane clerk of W. C. C.

Report by commissioners of a settlement made with the Executer of the estate of Eli Dotson decd. upon oath at April term 1832 Towit:
We the underwigned having been appointed commissioners by the worshipful court of pleas and Quarter Sessions for White County now

in session to settle with Joseph Cummings Jr. Executer of Eli Dotson De and make report to the present term beg leave to State that we have performed the duties assigned to us a nd report as follows towit:

Dr.	Dr.
[illegible] property of E. Dotson Decd.	54.16½
Rcd. from A. Brown on act	.50
" " A. Moore on note	15.50
" " John Bell Act & note	3.50
" " Polly Dotson act.	9.50
	$83.16½
By this Same paid Jno Bell	2.64 34
By this same paid E. Donalson	3.12½
By this same paid Henry Brown	1.00
By this same paid U. York	2.60
By this same paid D. L. Mitchell taxes	3.10
By this same paid A. Bryan note	2.25
By this same paid J. A. Lane Clerk fees	4.87½
Joseph Cummings Jr. and William Dotson Exr. for Services	.25
this amt in hands of the Executor	38.52½
	$83.16½

From the foregoing Receipts and vouchers witnessed before us it appears that there is sti ll a balance in the hands of
[illegible] the executors amounting to the sum of $38.52½ after discharging the debts against said estate all of which is respectfully submitted to your worships. Given under our hands and Seals 16 April 1832

John W. Ford
Wammon Leftwich

Recorded 2nd Nov. 1832 Jacob A. Lane Clerk W.C.C. by N. Oldham D.C.

Report by commissioners of a settlement made with the Administrators of JOHN RUTLEDGE deceased upon oath at Oct term 1831.

We the undersigned having been appointed by the court of pleas and Quarter Sessions for White County commissioners to settle with William Rutledge & Herbert Long Administraters of the Estate of John Rutledge decd. beg leave to report as follows towit:

We find said Rutledge U Herbert Long administraters of the Estate of John Rutledge decd. beg leave to report as follows towit:

We find said Rutledge & Long chargeabel with this Sum on acct of the

Sales of the personal property.	Dr.	448.30½
To Sale of Real estate		1450.00
By amt A. Dibrell receipt forcosts in Suit Cr.		
J Rutledge is Wm worm		25.46
Mathas Andersons Administraters		7.08½
Paid Joseph Hunter		20.00
" Thomas Rice		4.00
" John Jett past Ext. John Chisum vs John Rutledge		53.63
" William Glerm		4.25
" Woodrow P. White		520.
" Andrew Burke		152.00
John Brown		29.12½
James H. Pass		3.38
do		14.00
do		14.04 23
do		72.00
Jguatons Howard		7.00
Willia m Russell		9.50

John Dunn	6.00
Larkin Wisden	6.62½
R. Henderson	2.50
William Hester	.55½
do	.50
John L. Smith	15.00
Leftwich & Alstead	1.00
William A. Sheilds	40.00
Ma thew Watson	30.12½
H. C. Davis	1.50
Richard D. Crowder	1.12½
Robert Baxter	10.00
Thomas Gibbons	1.50
	1398.36½

	Cr.	Dr.
		1398.36½
P 104 Amt. Brought over		
By amt. paid William & John Ridge	81.40	
Henry McKinney	50.00	
James H. Jenkins	12.18 3/4	
John W. Ford	5.00	
William Hes ter	43.00	
James Rutledge	2.50	
Edw ard Elms	1.40½	
Samuel Dickson	50.00	
A. Skidmore	15.40	
Benjamin Gassaway	10.00	
Madison Fish	51.25	
James Webb adm. etc.	241.13½	
By a mt paid D. Snodgrass etc	18.00	
D. Snodgrass	32.29	
Johhua Fox	21.75	
Joel Yeager	9.00	
86 amt. paid Jasm M. Carver 1.25 paid		
John Wallis $44.00	45.25	
Ja s. T. Holman 50 Glover Randell 17.33 1/3	67.33 1/3	
James & John Chisum Executors etc.	25.00	
Wm Glenn $155.88 paid mason & Beadles $5.00	160.88	
John Jett 5.00 paid Ul. Usry $25.12½	30.12½	
S. Turney $10.25 Wm. Wisdom $29.50	39.43 3/4	
J. Snodgrass 26.43 3/4 W. Mason 10.	36.43 3/4	
Jesse England 1.00 Aquilla R. Macley 31	32.00	
George McGhee 4.68 3/4 Jas Miller 2.00	6.68 3/4	
Charles McQuire	4.00	
Jesse Lincoln	42.21	
William Simpson	.50	
Fennel Peck Co. 19.25	19.25	
Thomas Roberts	10.00	
Jesse Lincoln	4.43 3/4	
Charles Mannings	9.25	
Russel Gist	14.12½	
James Peaks representatives	70.62½	
James Powlr representative on note 864.56¼		
Given by John Rudge & W. Rutledge	164.31¼	

Francis Pride 1.00
By amt. paid Uniah York 52.86
" " " J. Lincoln Lns. Vincent 16.00
" " " W. Rutledge act Services Rend.
& Money expenced in Settling said Estate. 200.00
To amount due William Rutledge
over paid 650. 12½
$2548.483/4 2548. 48 3/4

P 105 After having examined the accouhh of the Sales of Property both real and personal belonging to the estate of John Rutledge Deceased as well as the vouchers proceeded before us by William Rutledge one of the administraters of said estate. We find a balance in favor of said William Rutledge of $650.12½ all of which is respectfully submitted
Oct 14th 1831 David Snodgrass }
Ulaman Leftwich } coms.
John Ul. Ford }
Recorded 2nd Nov. 1832 Jacob A. Lane Clerk W.C.C. by N. Oldham D.C.

Report by commissioners of a Settlement made with the administrator of JOHN SMALLMAN Ded. upon oath at Oct. term 1831.

We undersigned having been appointed by the court of pleas and Quarter Sessions fer White County Commissioners to settle with Joseph Cummings Jr. as administrater with the will annexed of the estate of John Sma llman deceased report as follows towit:

To total amount for which Joseph Cummings stands changeable
674.68 3/4

By Sherriff re ceipt for takes for year 1830 2.98½
By A. G. Summerson acct. 19.75
By amt. paid Jacob A. Lane 3.37½
By amt. paid D. S. Mitchell 2.00
By amt. paid Joseph Cummings acct for
Services rendered in settling the estate - 35.00 63.11
Bal 611.57 3/4

From the foregoing settlement there appears to be a balance in the hands of the administrater of $611.57 3/4 all of which is respectfully submitted Oct. 17, 1831
Recorded 2nd Nov. 1832 John W. Ford }
Wa mon Leftwich } coms.
N. Oldham D.C. of
J. A. Lane Clerk.

Report by commissioners of Settlement made with the Adms. of ALFRED G BEEDLES Ded. upon oath at April term 1832.

State of Tennessee }
White County } In an obedience to an order from The County Court of White County at April Session 1832 appointing us the undersigned Commissioners to Settle with Jesse England adm. of the Estate of A. G. Beedles decd. we find the admt. chargeabde with $189.56 3/4 as per Inventory $149.06¼ of diff. 40.50½ & we find the Adm. owes to said Estate 1.17¼ and is allowed for his Services $12. Given under our hand this 13 April 1832.

Recorded 2nd Nov. 1832 James H. Fass }
N. Oldham D.C. of Lewis Dearing } coms
J. A. Lane Clerk W.C.C. D. Snodgrass }

P 106 Report by commissioners of a Settlement made with the adm. of JOHN LONG Decd. upon oath at October Term A. D. 1830

State of Tennessee }
White County } Pursuant to an order of the co rt made at July Session of White Cty. Court A. D. 1830 appointing us Anthony Dibrell and Wamon Leftwich commissioners to settle with George long Admr. of John Long decd. we have this day gone into a full fair and impartial settlement with the said George Long admr. investigating all matters of the estate of the said John Long decd. which we find to be as follows towit:

Came unto the hands of the administrators as appear from the clerk certificate 77.68
Said Adms. has paid the taxes on said 186 acres of Land 13 years 20.74½
we also find that the Deceased owed to the administrator at the time of his death $135. in good trade and we think the above Sum of $99.68 3/4 in cash is sufficient to discharge said note of $135. in trade 99.68
The said administrator produced an act for cash paid to John Carow attorney at law for defending a suit brought against the heirs of John Long ded. $38 amt. allowed said administrator for his Services $5. whic Leaves a bal in favor of the Admr. of ($63.74¼) Sixty three dollars weventy four and one fourth cents which sum is due from the estate of said Jno Long ded. to the said Adms. as appears from the accounts etc. herein the filed this 31 July 1830

A. Dibrell
Wamon Leftwich

Recorded 2nd Nov. 1832 N. Oldham D. Clerk.

Report by commissioners of a settlement made with the administrato of JAMES PEAK ded. upon oath at April term A. D. 1830.

Jacob Peak & John Rutledge Adms.

To amt of the Sales returned in all		
Cr.	Cr.	Dr.
By amt. of account paid William Hunter	11.	3069.56¼
By amt of account paid James T. Holmans order	10.	
By cash paid Jiram Allen	85.00	
" Peter Howard	20.87½	
Amt act paid Robert Cox	26.37½	
Amt Act paid Charles Manning	70.57	
Amt. " Doct. Lawrence Crowder	19.87½	
Note David Ames	5.00	
" M. Guise	4.00	
Act J. Pistole	5.00	
P 107 Amt up		3069.56¼
By amount Act paid Stephen Mann	4.00	
By " " " William Gracy Jr.-	7.12½	
" " " " Allen	100.56½	
" " " " Dibrells recpt for Debt due Alexander	266.00	
By amount th. Rights note	17	
Acct paid Gussaway	12.00	
William B. Roses Receipt	11.62½	
Cash paid Peak	20.00	
Cash George Broyles note	100.00	

White County } Pausuant to an order
P 108 made at the January Session of our County Court 1830 We William 87
Glenn, James F. Holman & James Snodgrass proceeded on the day of
January 1830 to settle with the Administrators of James Peak deceased
and certify that the foregoing herein contaied to be a just and true
report of the said estate to the best of knowledge and beleif April
Sessions 1830.
By amount Act. paid Mitchell pself 4.50
Recorded 2nd Nov. 1832 there Receipts from Jete William Glenn
N. OLdham D.Clerk Sheriff for money owing James Snodgrass
" " " " owing White Chisum for taxes 874.65 F. Holman

Amt. note paid Gibbs 15.00
" " paid Kercundole 150.00
" " " " W. P. White receipt 30.00
" " McCormick receipts Sundry note for which Adm. are entitled to
a credit on note on A. B. Land 150/00
By amt one note on Isaac Abshire 2.06¼
" Several other small notes contained in rect. 63.42½
another receipt for small notes from McCormidk 242.53 3/4
By do do do do 272.89
By do do do do 27.
The following paid by William Rutledge Jetts recpt
118.60
By amt of Whites receipt 320.00
" " Burkes Receipts 152.00
" " Glenn receipt 4.25
To Two promisory notes returned in
Inventory on various person 716. 31
By amt. articles purchased by Mrs. Peak
at the Sale 480.00
By amo of two notes held by William M. Bryan
Aur. on J. Peak for $1-0. cash and interest on the same
$30.00 230.00
By amt to Bal act. 51.30 3/4
3785.87½ 3785. 87½

To tha t the said Adm. have in thier hands money which they have not
applied to the payment of the debts of the entestate Fifty one Dollars
thirty one and a half cents January 1830.

State of Tennessee }
White County } Peusuant to an order
P 108 made at the January Session of our County Court 1830 We William
Glenn, James F. Holman & James Snodgrass proceeded on the day of
January 1830 to settle with the Administrators of James Peak deceased
and certify that the foregoing herein contaied to be a just and true
report of the said estate to the best of knowledge and beleif April
Sessions 1830.

Recorded 2nd Nov. 1832 William Glenn
N. OLdham D.Clerk James Snodgrass
James F. Holman

Report by commissioners of a Settlement made with the Executors of
ELI DOTSON ded. upon oath at January Sessions A. D. 1830.

To 1 Rifle Gun 20$ ½ mule colt 20$	40.00
To 1 Bed and furniture	20.00
To 1 parcel of Hags	10.00
To 3 Beestands 6.00$ 3 head Sheep 6.00	12.00
To 7 head Geese 2.33 1/3 1 Saddle 2.06¼	4.40
To 50 Bushels corn at Robert Mayes	7.56¼
To 12½ Bushels do at Alexn Moore	2.60
To 1 plow 1.34¼ 1 H e 50 1 churn 12½	1.93 3/4
To 1 washing tub 2 Piggins 1 keeler	1.25
To 1 Ster kettle & 1 skillet	1.50

To 1 Big Wheel & Cotton Cards		2.00
To 2 Bedsteads and one card		2.00
To6 Earthen plates		.37½
To 4. Knives and 4 forks		.75
To 4 Iron Spoons 25 1 chair 25		.50
To 1 note on Alexander Moore		15.80
To 1 note on Reuben Ross		12.00
To 1 note on " "		22.25
To 1 note on Solomon Charles		14.45
To 1 " " John Bell		1.25
To 1 note do		2.25
By amt of Rosses 2 notes which cannot be collected		34.25
By amt paid the wife of Eli Dotson ded.		52.25
By amt act. filed by Solomon Charles		14.35
By amt do " " Elizabeth Donelson		3.25
By amt " " " Uriah York		2.60
By amt " " " Adrian Bryan		2.45
By amt " " " John Bell		2.68
By amt " " " Henry Bowen		1.00
By Jas. Cummings paid Clerks fees	2.12½	
By Do " Taxes 1828	1.68¼	3.74
By cash paid commissioners owe due each		2.00
	174.57	118.95 3/
P 169		
To amt brought up being amt of said estate	174.57	
By amot. up		1118.!
By amt allowed Executors for services		20.00
By amt paid Lane Clerks fees		.62½
By amt paid taxes for 1829		2.47½
Total amt paid out encluding Rosses 2 November		$142.04 3/
By this Sum to Balance executors act		32.52½
	174.57	174.57

To amt now remaining in the hands of the Executor
for which they are responsible to daid estate January 2nd 1830 32.52½

David L. M tchell }
Robert Gamble } coms.

Recorded 3rd Nov. 1832 N. Oldham D.C. of Jacob A. Lane Clerk W.C.C.

Report of Edward Gleeson Adms. and Polly R. Gleeson Adms. of the Estate of John W. Gleeson deceased upon oath at Oct. term 1831.

STate of Tennessee }
White County } Petition

To the worshipful County Court now in session fore the county aforesaid the petition of Edward Gleeson and Polly R. Gleeson administraters of John W. Gleeson ded. Your petitioners beg leave to State to your worship that since the death of Said John they have been appointed and duly qualified in this Court as administrators of his estate. They would furthe rstate that the principal part of the estate of the said John Consists in negro property that is to say, one negro woman POlly Supposed to be between 35 and38 years of age one negro man named Adison aged a bout 22 years, one negro boy named Carrol aged some where about Ten years one negro Girl name

Louinda aged seven or eight years one Negro girl name Julia aged about three years one negro girl not named aged abott one yaer the other personal property it is believed would not exceed three hundred dollars in value, if that amount-- the Estate is indebted to an amount considera bly more than the value of all the personal property besides or exclusive of the negroes. Your Petitioners Polly Gleeson widow of said John, is, under the Laws of Tennessee as she is advised entitled to half the peesonal property of her title husband after his just debts and habitities are paid, her said husband having died without any lawful issue--Your petitioners further state that the other distributier or pe sons entitled to a distributive shore of Said estate are Ma jr. Isaac Taylor in
P 110 right of his wife Margarette, Edward Gleeson, James Gleeson, William Gleeson, George F. Gleeson Doct. Madison Fisk in right of his wife Eliza D.-- Mary Jane Smith daughter of Ama Smith now deceased. Your petioners represent to your worship that theirs only being Six negroes in all at this time and Eight distributier, seven of whom, only being entitled to half the personal estate after payment of debts it will be impossible or extremely inconvient to distribute the personal estate after payment of debts of said John without selling said negroes as well as the other personal estate--They therefore pray your worship to make an order to authorise your petition to sell the slaves on the usua l credit as they have no doubt they cannot do their duty to themselves and the others concerned in anyother way.
Recorded 3rd Nov. 1832 N. O$_1$dham D.C. of Jacob A. Lane Clerk W.C.C.
Edward Gleeson Adms.
Polly R. Gleeson Adms.

Report of the Sales of the property of the estate of John Pistole Decd. by Enoch Murphy adms. upon oath at July Term 1832. towit:-
Nancy Pistole Dr.

To 1 Skillet and Lid	.31½
To 1 pot & Lid to same	.43 3/4
To 1 Oven & Lid & Hooks	.31¼
" 1 Oven & Lid	.50
" 1 pot and hooks	1.62½
" 1 Kkillet and Lid	.06¼
" 1 half Bushel	.06¼
" 1 Flat Iron	.31¼
" 1 Tub	.06¼
" 1 pail 12½ pr chains & backband 12½	
" 1 plow Singletree & clevis 31½	.93 3/4
" 1 Hoe 12½ 1 axe 12½	.25
" 2 piggins 25 Lad.e & fork 12½	.37½
" 1 Shovel 25 1 pot rack 100	1.25
" 1 Sifter .37½ pitcher, jar & crock 12½	.50
" 3 Bottles 31½ 1 Large Wheel 31½	.62½
" 1 Reel 37¼ 1 washing tub	.43 3/4
" 1 Loom 25 2 Slays 31¼	.56¼
" 6 chairs 37½ 1 Srainer 12½	.50
" 1 Lot of Dresser Ware	.50
" 1 churn	.12½
" 6 vials 12½ 1 Chest 100	1.12½
" 1 clock $10. 1 Table 87½	10.87½

To 1 Bedstead & furniture	4.50
To 1 do do	2.00

Nancy Pistole Dr.

To 1 set Spools	.43 3/
To 1 Bed Stead	.50
To 1 Lot corn	3.00
To 1 Chest	.37½
To 2 pr Cotton Cards	.25
Thos Stone 1 coffee mill	.18 3/
Nancy Pistole 1 pr Shears	.12½
A. McGhee 1 pr. Harness	.06¼
Nancy Pistole 1 Table	1.37½
To Black mare & Saddle	50.00
Tho Snodgrass 15 hogs	16.25
Nancy P,stole 7 Sheep	4.37½
To 1 Brindle cow & calf	6.50
Enoch Murphy To 1 cow & calf	5.25
L. Murphy 4 cattle	11.00
To 9 shoats	1.62½
Tea ste Massa 3 prs U Leather	3.19
Nancy pistolr 1 Basket	.18 3/
John McGhee to 1 cutting machine	3.50
Nancy Pistole to 1 Lot Bacon	11.00
L. S. Murphy to 1 3 year old filly	21.00
Jgreatine Howard 1 two years old filly	27.25
Nancy Pistole to 2 Hinds 3.25 1 pr pot hooks 12½	3.37½

P 111

Recorded 3rd Nov. 1832 N. Oldham D.C. of J. A. Lane Clerk W.C.C.

Enoch Murphy Adm. of the
Estate of John H. Pistole decd.

I JOHN VANDIVER a citizen of White County and State of Tennessee do hereby make this my last will and testament being at this time in m right mind and proper Sinces. I do hereby first will that all my just debts shall be paid out of my property that after this is done, that Secondly my wife Sally Vandiver shall be entitled to the one third of the remainder of my estate both real and personal--then the remaining two thirds, shall be placed in the hands of Ephraim Berry (own brothe to my said wife Sally) for the especial purpose of raising and educati my four children whose names are as follows (towit) James Vandiver Elihugh Vandiver, Rachel Vandiver and Thomas E. Vandiver and when my son Thos. the last menhioned child of mine by wife the said Sally, sha arrive at the age of twenty one years, then whatever property either personal or real that may then be remaining on hand shall be sold on credit of one year and the Neet proceeds thereof equally divided between my said four children herein before named. And it is further my will that James Scarbrough and the Said Ephraim Berry herein before named act. as my executors to this my last will and Testament. In testimony whereof I here unto affix my hand and Seal this Sixth day of October in the year of our Lord 1827.

Signed Sealed and Acknowledged in presence of us

John Vandiver (Seal)

Joseph his X Williams mark

Purnina X Williams mark

Thos. Eastland

State of Tennessee ◊
White County ◊ April Sessions of the County Court A. D. 182\
This day the last will and testament of John Vandever was produced in open court and the due execution sand publication thereof as suxh was proven in due form of law by the oath of Thomas Eastland and Joseph Williams two subscribing witness thereto for the purposes and things therin mentioned and ordered to be recorded. Given at office the 13 day of April A. D. 1829.
Recorded 3rd day Nov. 1832 N. Oldham D.C. J. A. Lane Clerk W.C.C.

P 118 In the name of God Amen--I JAMES DAVIS of the County of White and State of Tennessee being in perfect health of body and of perfect mind and memory thanks be given unto God Calling unto mind the morality of body and knowing that it is appointed for men once to die: Do make and ordain this my last will and testament, that is to say principally and first of all I give and recommend my Soul into the hands of Almighty God, that gave it and my body I recommend to the Earth to be buried in Decent Christian burial at the desoreetion of my Executors nothing doubting but at the General resurrection I shall receive the same again by the Mighty power of God. And as touching such worldly estate wherwith it hath pleased God. to bless me in this life, I give devise and dispose of the same in the following manner and form--First I give and bequeath to my wife Martha Davis one certain pat of the tract of land. I now live on to include the Dwelling house and to a Certain ditch that runs across my plantation to keep in possession until her decease also the house hold furniture with all the working tools, also I give to my son Ephrain Davis the balance of the Said Tract from the ditch above mentioned also I give to my son Ephrain Davis the balance of the Said Tract from the ditch above mentioned also I give to my son Ephraim Davis the balance of my tract of Land at my wife Martha Davis's decease likewise I constitute and ordain my son Ephraim Davis and woodson White the Sole Executors of this my last will and testament--also I give to my Son-in-law William Burks one dollar--I also give to my Son-in-law Archibald Welch one Dollar, I also give to my daughter Priscella Davis one dollar also the balance of my Estate to be equally divided between the balance of my sons and Daughters by them freely to be possessed. And enjoyed. I do hereby utterly disallow, revoke and disown all and every other former, testaments, wills Legacies, bequests, executors by me in any ways before named willed and bequeathed ratifying and confirming this and no other to be my last will & testament in witness whereof I have hereunto set my hand and Seal this Twelfth day of August Eighteen hundred and thirty one.

James X Davis (Seal)
his mark

Signed, Sealed, Published, pronounced and delivered by the Said James Davis as his last will and Testament, in the presance of us who in the presance and in the presence of each other have hereunto subscribed our names. Attest.

State of Tennessee ◊
White County ◊ October Sessions A. D. 1831

This day the last will and Testament of JAMES DAVIS deceased was produced in open Court and the due execution and

P 113 publication thereof by the Deposition of John Davis regularly taken in the County of Wayne and State of Kentuckey and returned unto this court that Said James Da vis was of Sound and disposing mind and memory at the execution thereof Whereupon Came Ephriam Davis named as Executor in Said last will and Testament and took upon him self the burden of the executinn thereof and took the oath prescribed by Law and with James Davis and John Davis entered into and acknowledged bond in the Sum of five hundred Dollars conditioned as the law requires. Given at office the 17th October A. D. 1831. Test Jacob A. Lane Clerk by N. Oldham D. Recorded 25 Nov. 1832 Jacob A. Lane Clerk by N. Oldham D. C. of W. C. Court

Be it remembered that I THOMAS SCOTT of the County of White and State of Tennessee being of Sound mind and perfect memory though weak of body and knowing that all men are born to die. Do make and ordain this my last will and testament in Manner and form as followeth: that is to say, I will and bequeath unto my beloved children Jonathan Scott and Hannah Broiles wife of Abraham Broiles and their heirs forever all the personal property of every discribtion, negroes etc., whil I am possed of at my death to be equally divided between my said children Jonathon & Ha nnah they being my lawful heirs and I do further give and bequeath unto Rebecca Scott formerly my wife, but not recognis ed as such at this time three dollars and to her Children three dollars each, which She has had since I married her which Children is not recognised as my bodily heir and all the money, debts due and I give and bequeath unto my two Children namely Jonathan and Hannah and their heirs etc. forever. In testamony whereof I do hereunto Set my hand and Seal but lastly I do cromemorate and appoint Abraham Broiles and Jonathan Scott my executors to this my last will and Testament dated this 15th day of January A. D. 1822 his

Jonathan X Scott
mark

Test Anthony Dibrell
Manuel Parkison

S tate of Tennessee }
White County } July Session A. D. 1830

This day the within last will and testament of THOMAS SCOTT Decd. was provided in open Court and the due execution and publicationthereof proven in open Court in due form of law by the oath of Anthony Dibrell, to be the act and deed of the Said Thomas Scott Deceased and that he was at the exectuion thereof of Sound and disposing mind and memory. Whereupon came Jonathan Scott (Jonathan Scott Executor) in Said last will and testament mentioned and undertook the exectuine thereof , and with Jquathus Howard and Elijah Ward entered into and acknowledged bond in the Sum of five thousand dollars conditioned as the law requires who took the oath prescribed by law which is order to be Recorded. Given at office 12th day July A. D.183

Jacob A. Lane Clerk
White County Court

Recorded 12th January 1833 J. A. Lane Clerk White County Court.

P 114 Return of James W. Copeland Guardian to the heirs of John Anderson Ded. upon oath at January term A. D. 1833. Report to court that the amount of the funds of his wards in his hands is the same as it was at the last report be made, except one dollar 12½ cents fer fees and disburtions be made on said Estate

James W. Copeland
Recorded 1 February 1833 Jacob A. Lane Clerk by N. Oldham D.C.

Return of Alexander Glenn Senr. Guardian to Lughton Helton made upon oath at January Term A. D. 1833.
Reports and says that I a m in possession of one hundred and thirty dollars and twenty five cents cash principle with Interest from the 9th day of January 1832 up to the present date. Given under my hand this 19 day Jany. 1833.
Redorded 1st February 1833. Ja cob A. Lane Clerk by N. Oldham D.C.

Return of Thomas Hill Guardian to the heirs of James Hill Deceased upon oat at ~~January~~ Session A. D. 1833. Reports t at he has paid to two of the heirs which of age sixty three dollars fifty cents each, and that there now remains in my hands for the two heirs which are under age one hundred and Twenty seven dollars this the 18th day of Janua ry 1833.
Recorded 1st Febgruary 1833 Thomas Hill Jacob A. Lane Clerk by N. Oldham D. C.

Return of moses Goddard Guardian to the infant heirs of Jno Smallmn Ded. upon oath at January Term A.D.A1833.
Says that he has in his hands as Guardian to the aforesaid infant heirs the Sum of $427.00
Recorded 1 February 1833 Moses his X mark Goddard
Ja cob A. Lane Clerk by N. Oldham D.C.

Return of John Walker Guardian to the heirs of Alexander Kerr Ded. upon oath at January term A. D. 1833.
Reports no alteration in Said Estate since last years returns January 14th 1833.
Recorded 1 Befruary 1833. John Walker
Jacob A. Lane Clerk by N. Oldham D.C.

Return of George Long Guardian of Stephen Pistole upon oath at January Term A. D. 1833.
Reports that he received from his wards part of the negroe 33.95
One note on Jesse England due 12 April 1833
One Mare and SAddle the above is the only accumulation of money to the estate of my ward and the only alteration therein since my last return as Guardian January 14th 1833.
Recorded 1 Bebruary 1833 George Long Guardian
Jacob A. Lane Clerk by N. Oldham D. Clekk.

Return of John Walker Guardian to the heirs of Kendel Savage Deceased upon oath at January Term 1833.
Reports no alteration in said Estate since last years return 14 January 1833
Jacob A. Lane Clerk by N. Oldham D.C. John Walker

Account of the Sales of the property of the Estate of Elijah England Adms. and Elija England Adms. at January term A. D. 1833. Eliza England as follows towit:
Fine Beds and furniture 20.00
One dresser dresser furniture and table

One chest 7 chairs & 1 looking glass 1.00
Two cotton Wheels & 2 Flax Wheels 2 Kettles 1 pot three ovens one pot Frammel & pr. fire dogs 1.00
P 115 1 Loom 1 Stew pot 1 lot Books 1 chesk rule
one half bushel 2 Riddles 1 Seine 2 Smoothing Irons 1.00
1 Saddle 2 Bridles 4 apils churn 1 handsaw 2 augers one Drawing knife 1 board axe 5 falling axeq 5 ploughs 2 hoes 2 mattocks
2 pr.Stretchers 1 Log chain 1 Iron Wedge 1 Scythe & cradle
2 Syoles 1 cutting box & knife 8 Raw hides 2 pr pots hooks 1 flax bark 5.00

½ of a Xcut saw	1.00
0 Bee stands	2.00
1 wripsaw	4.75
50 head of Hogs for	10.00
13 head of cattle for	20.00
28 hogs	10.00
34 head of sheep	17.00
Flock of Geese	1.00
4 head of Horses	100.00
1 Steer	4.25
28 head of hogs	29.37½
5 head of hogs	9.62½
H. England 1 Rifle Gun	11.50
A England 1 Steer	5.50
Tho Cooper 1 do	4.81¼
" " 1 do	5.00
Tho Rice 1 cow & calf	6.50
John S. Price 1 cows & calf	6.50
Tho. Rice 1 steer	2.00
John S. Price 1 cows & calf	6.50
" " 1 steer	2.61¼
Red Moore 1 do	3.00
M. England 1 Steer	2.87½
do 2 do	10.75
do 2d0	9.00
P 116 Willaim McKinney 2 steers	8.50
do 1 steer	2.50
Alfred G. Beedles 1 do	2.12½
Do 10 hogs 4th chhice	10.00
Berry Hamlet 1 Steer	4.43 3/
Moses Turney 1 cow	7.12½
Jno Weaver 5 hogs 1st choice	16.50
Robert Cox 5 do 2nd do	12.50
Thos Little 2 Steers	12.56¼
Daniel Bartlett 1 Filly	38.00
Tachariah Anderson d0	37.00
Joseph England 1 horse	22.50
Richard England 1 do	26.37½
John England 1 colt	11.75
Used by Eliza England after Sale	
2 Stee rs	14.00
8 head of Hogs	30.00
Amount of Sales	$565.92½

John England Adms. of
Elijah England Dcd.
Recorded 4th February 1833 Jacob A. Lane Clerk by N. Oldham D.C.

Report of commissioners of a Settlement made with Richard Judson Administrator of William Kitchen Deceased at January Session A. D. 1833
State of Tennessee ⎫
White County ⎭ In pursuance to an order of the county court of White County appointing us the undersigned commissioners to Settle with Richard Judson Adm. of William Kitchen Decd. find the Administrator Chargeable in his two returns towit:

	Dr.
In his first return the sum of	23.50
In his 2nd do do	12.18 3/4
" " 3rd cow sold not returned to court	5.26
1 3 Bushels corn owing by Said Adms.	2.60
Corn at Sale	3.37½
	46.92½

paid Judgth to Sheriff	8.95
paid note Adms.	6.25
paid part Debts to Lincoln	7.37½
paid John Anderson	5.00
paid Howard Cost	.50
paid Sheriff Lawson & Kitchen	8.85
paid Joel Whitley acct.	1.00
paid Farley act.	.50
paid clerk J. A. Lane	2.50
paid Attorney fee	5.62½
paid for coffin	4.00
	51.30
To Debts Recorded by adms.	46.92½
For which the administrator is entitle to a credit	4.37½

Four Dollars for monies advanced by him to said Est. 15 Jan. 1833.
Recorded 7 February 1833 A. Dibrell
J. A. Lane Clerk by Jesse Lincoln N. Oldham D.C.

Account of the Sales of the property of theestate of THOMAS DUNCAN Decd. by G. W. Duncan adm. upon oath at January term 1833.

Ten head of Sheep	10.00
one man's Saddle	3.37½
one log chain	3.50
one Dagon plow	1.00
one Grindstone & plow	.87½
1 Lot Hoes and Chairs. 1.06¼	1.06¼
1 Axe & Wedge	.75
1 Saw Collar & Swingletree	.50
2 Beds 100 1 saddle & Bridle 131½	2.31¼
1 Rifle Gun	8.31¼
1 Sett of fire Dogs	1.37½
1 Basket and chains	.56¼
one pot	2.12½
1 B ee Gum	2.18
1 pot & oven	.75
1 Skillet	.75
1 axe	.56½

1 Check ful 25 1 Lot Books 75		1.00
2 Wheels 25 one waggon $49		49.25
1 Frying pan		.12½
1 mare 30.25 1 Loom 50		30.75
plank 3.00 9 Head Hogs		16.62½
1 Hog 1.51¼ 10 Hogs 6.01		7.52¼
635 feet plank		4.77
1 Mattock 75 1 Bereau $10		10.75
1 Bed & furniture		9.00
2 do		5.00
3 chairs 2 yearlings 5.06¼		5.81¼
1 cow 7.75 1 Heifer 5.12½		12.87½
1 Heifer 3.00 52 Bls. Corn	$52	55.00
1 cow 6.12½ 1 cow 3.00		9.12½
1 Lot of oats		10.06¼
13 Bushels of Rye		4.16
20 head of Geese		5.40
9 " do		2.43
5 Barrels of corn		5.00
4½ Barrels corn		4.50

Recorded 7 February 1833. George W. Duncan Adm.
J. A. Lane Clerk by N. Oldham D.C.

In the name of God Amen. I EDWARD HOLMES of the County of White & state of Tennessee being of a sound mind and memeory do make this my à last will and Testament hereby revoking and disowning all wills of codi-cials by me heretofore made in promise my will and desire is that all debts now due me or shall hereafter become due be collected and out of such monies my will & desires is that all my just debts be paid & con-tract be complied with & if there be not money enough thus collected to answered the purpose above named my will and desire is that so much of my perishable property be sold as will answer it and no more, Items my will and desire is that my dearly beloved wife Nancy Holmes have the use and benefit of the possession on which I now live & the tenenents per-taining thereto during her natural life & at her death to be equaly divided between my two children Alfonzo S. Holmes & Manisa Holmes and their heirs forever should they have any, should one of them die without a lawful heir, all the property shall descend to the other and his or her heirs as the case maybe, should they botha die with out a lawful heir shall all descend to my brother & sisters children--Item my will a nd desire is that my four young negroes Eliza, John, Caro-line & Jefferson and all the rest of the property with the exception of the two horses one of which is a Gray & the other a Sorrel, the sorrel I bequeath to my dearly beloved wife, Nancy Holmesm The Gray I give and bequeath to my beloved sister Mary Baker--The beformentioned property be kept and remain to her for the purpose of supporting my beloved wife and children likewise for the Education of my two children during her widow hood or
P 118 natural life unless she should live and remain a widow longer than the children should become of age & whenever she marries or dies or the children become of age whichever of cercumstances occurs first the negroes their increase & property shall be equally divided between my two chil-dren Alphonze & Maniesa Holmes to therein and to their heirs forever should they have any and if not my will and desire is at their death that the negroes and property descend to my brother and sisters children,

Item--My will and desire is that my negro woman Lydia be freed--Lastly I appoint Rovert S. Mitchell and Willaim Baker Executors of this my last will & Testament. In Witness whereof I have hereunto set my hand & affixed my seal this the 14th day of one thousand eight hundred and thir three Signed Sealed published and delivered to be the last will & testament of Edward Holmes.

In presence of Attest.

Thomas Williams — Edw. Holmes. (Seal)

William Glenn

Joseph Nolen

State of Tennessee }
White County } April Session A. D. 1833

This day the death of Edward Holmes deceased last of White County sugges ed where upon Robert L. Mitchell & William Baker his Executors produced here in open Court a writing purporting to be the last will and testamen of the deceased whereupon the same was proven as such by the oath of Thomas Williams and William Glenn two suvscribing witness thereto for the purpose and things therein mentioned and that the said Edward Holmes was at the date and publication thereof of Soujd disposing mind and memory and at the Same day came the Said Robert L. Mitchell & William Baker appointed as executors by said last will and testament and took upon themselves the execution thereof the oath prescribed by law and together with Asa Certain and Elmers Jones entered into and acknowledged bond conditioned as the law requires. Given at office the 8th day of April A.D. 1833

Recorded 23 May 1833 Test Jacob A. Lane Clerk of W.C.C.

N. Oldham D.C. — By N. Oldham D.C.

In the name of God Amen I ROBERT McEWING of White County and State of Tennessee being weak of body, but of sound and perfect mind and memor blessed be godfer the same do make and publish this my last will and testament in Manner and form following that is to say-first I give and bequeath unto my beloved wife Ane McEwin a certain Chestnut sorrel mare two cows and calf, such as she may dhoose upon two sows and pigs also ho Bacon that has to do her this year also what corn is here also what hogs will make her meat for the next years also all her household pluuder I wish the said Anne McEwin to have the use and benefit of --the clock exception and put to

P 119 sale also two plows and two Hoes, this is all left for the benefit of raising my children and also I wish my beloved wife to have the use and benefit of all this property so long as the remains my widow otherwise to be sole and put to the use and benefit of my chilain also my wish is for the said Anne McEwin to have the use and benefit of the plantation where I now live on until my youngest child bedomes of of age, then I wish my son Madison McEwin to have it but he is bound at that time to support his Mother decently while she lives if alive at that time--Also I give and bequeath a certain tract of lands containing one hundred and fifty acres to my daughter, Elizabeth and Amea McEwin and all the rest of personal property. I wish to be sold for the purpose of paying my just devts. With cash notes which may be collected an lastly at the deceased of my beloved wife Anne McEwin. I wish equal divide made of all the personal property which may be hers at that time at that time or when the youngest child becomes of age--Also I give and bequeath unto my beloved wife Ann McEwin all the money that may arrive from this sale after paying all my just debts to raise and school my children and what ever sum may be collected of my father's estate from Flemming. I wish my two Daughters Elizabeth and Anna McEwen to have the same also my Step-daughter , Sarah McGarrah I wish her to have a bed also my stepson Elijah if he lives at home until he is of age and puts all the benefit of his labor to the use of my ~~family I wish him to have a~~ horse worth Sixty dollars in trade--Hereby I appoint Ebenere Jones to be one of my executors and also Isaac Hutton I hereby appoint as my other executor of this my last will and testament hereby revoke all other former wills by me made--In witness wherof I have hereunto set my hand and Seal this 9th day of August in the year of our Lord 1832. Signed sealed published and delivered by the above named Robert McEwin to be his last will and testament in the presence of us who have hereunto Subscribed our names as Witness in the presence of the testators.

his Richard X Cole mark — his Caleb X Tollison mark — Robert McEwin (Seal)

State of Tennessee }
White County } April Sessions A. D. 1833

This day the death of Robert McEwin tate of the County of White was suggested whereupon Ebenere Jones and Isaac Hutson his Executors produced here in open Court a writing purporting to be the last will and Testament of the deceased Whereupon the same was proven as such by the oath Richard Cole and Cubb Tollison two Subscribing witnesses thereto for the purposes and things therein contained that the said Robert McEwin was at the date and publication thereof of sound disposing mind and memory and at the same day came come the said Ebenezer Jones and Isaac Hutson appointed
P 120 as executors in said last will and testament and took upon themselves the execution thereof who took the oath prescribed by law and together with Robert S. Mitchell and Richard Judson entered into an acknowledged Bond contained as the law requires---Given at office the 8th day of April A.D. 1833.

Recorded 20 June 1833 Test Jacob A. Lane Clerk
J. A. Lane Ck by White County Court
N.O. By N. Oldham D.C.

I WILLIAM STAMPS being of sound and perfect mind and memory do make and publish this my las t will and testament in manner and form following--firts I give and bequeath unto my beloved wife Sarah Stamps one bay mare also two cows and yearlings also five head of Sheep and all the hogs now in my possession and all the beds and all the household furniture also one side saddle also his farming tools belonging to sd premises also all my turning tools and black Smith tools and all the corn and bacon now on hand
and one dollar to Sandford Stamps is heirs besides the land that was divided to his heirs by Edmodn Stamps by the request of myself--also one dollar to Edmond Stamps also one dollar to John B. Cherney and all the rest of the heirs to have all the rest of the prpperty to be divided amongst them except the Tract of Land whereon I now live containing fourteen acres and three fourth which land I purchased of Thomas Hoon which tract or parcel of land I give and bequeath and give unto John B. Cherrey (my-son-in-law) which land he shall hawe no control

over until the death of myself and my wife Sarah Stamps, except forthe benefit of myself & wife aforesaid and such part as maybe necessary for the comfort and convenience of his own family by the consent of myself and wife Sarah Stamps etc. and I do hereby appoint Constitute, my son Edmond Stamps my executor in fact that he may see and to attend to the faithful preformance of this my last will. Signed sealed and published the day and date above witness before us.

William Stamps (Seal)

Dennis Hargis
Samuel Johnson

State of Tennessee
White County } April Sessions A. D. 1833

This day was exhibeted here in open Court a writing purporting to be the last will and testament of William Stamps deceased tate of the County of the County of White and the due execution and publication thereof as the last will and testerment of the said William Stamps deceased by the oath of Samuel Johnson one subscribing witness therto for the purposes and things thereof of sound and disposing mind and memory which is ordered to be recorded.
Given at office the 15th Apl. 1833. Jacob A. Lane Clerk. W.C.C.
by N. Oldham D.C.

State of Tennessee
White County } July Session A.D. 1833

This day was exhibited here in open court a writing purporting to be the last willand testament of William Stamps deceased late of the county of white and the due execution and publication thereof as the last will and testament of the said William Stamps deceased was proven by the oath of Cowen Hargis one other Subxeribing witness thereto for the purposes and things therein mentioned and that he was at the date thereof Sound and disposing mind and memory which having in the manner been proven at April term of said court 1833 by the oath of Samuel Johnson the other subscribing witness thereto for the purpose therein contained where upon it is ordered by the court to be admitted to record. Given at office the 8th day of July A. D. 1833.
Recorded 18 August 1833 By N. Oldham D.C. Test Jacob A. Lane Clerk W.C.
J. A. Lane Clerk
By N. Oldham D.C.

Inventory of the Estate of EDWARD HOLMES returned by Robert L. Mitchell and William Baker Exr. upon oath at April term 1833 Infact One note of hand executed by N. A. Long Nov. 27 18 32 for Eighteen Dollars to Edward Holmes due Six Months after date--One due bill on Julius Sanders for three dollars given March the Eight 1830. not good-- One note of bond executed by N. A. Long July the Ninth 1832 for Eighteen dollars to Edward Holmes and it is Credited Eleven dollars and fifty cents which leaves a balance of Six dollars and fifty cents--four notes hand executed by B. T. Baker the 6 th day of January 1832 for twenty five dollars each to Edward Holmes one of shich is to be paid in 1833 another 1834 another 1835 and another in 1836-- Also another note of hand executed by R. T. Baked for fifty dollars the sixth day of January 1832 due the first day of November 1832 and then are credits on this note to the ammount of thirty dollars which leaves a balance of twenty dollars--

One sorrel Filly 2 years old nine head of Cattle the most of them small Eleven head of Sheep fifty Seven head of hogs the most of which are pigs. The wood work of one Waggon--three plows two pair of Gears--one axe one endifferent chest--one Mattock, one Loom, six chairs one table one spinning wheel one bot one man's saddle three Bedstead three Beds and furniture one cupboard about one hundred weight of Tobacco in the hand two sets of fire dogs, one oven one Brass Kettle one large pot two small pots one side saddle one good briddâ 4 two indifferent one's Mardh 22, 1833
Recorded 13 August 1833 Robert L. Mitchell
J. A. Lane Clerk William Baker
by N. Oldham D.C. Ex. of Edward Holmes ded.

P 122 Inventory of part of the Estate of Edward Holmes deceased.
Return upon oath by R. L. Mitchell & William Baker EX^{rs}. at July term 1833.
Four negroes one set of Knives and forks and two sets of plates Eight bowles, two pitchers two sets of Teacups & Saucers four Glass bottles one sugar Dish, one Tea pot, six Jars two coffee pots one Bible & testament, one Dictionary three Glasses one large pitcher one Butter pot, three crocks one copy book one japaned Box, some corn some Bacon & some fodder.
Recorded 13 August 1833 Robert L. Mitchell
J. A. Lane clerk William Baker
by N. Oldham D.C. Executors of Edw. Holmes ded.

Report of assignement of provision by commissioners to the widow of John W. Gleeson at January Term 1832.
State of Tennessee }
White County } We the undersigned commissioners being appointed by the worshipful county court of said county at October term 1831 forthe purpose of assingning one years provision for the support of Mrs. Polly R. Gleeson Widow of John M. Gleeson deceased do assign Ten Barrels of corn and twenty dollars to be paid out of first money collected from the sale of the property of the estate to purchased her pork, Salt and coffee Witness our hand and Seal this 18th November 1831 John Jett (Seal)
Recorded 13th August 1833 Thomas Robinson (Seal)
J. A. Lane ck by Joseph Hord (Seal)
N. Oldham D.C.

Report of assignment of provisions by commissioners to the widow & the children of William Mooner deceased at July Session A.D. 1833
We the commissioners in obedence to an order of the worshipful Court of pleas and Quarter Sessions of the White county January Session 1833 to lay off one years support for the widow Weaver of White County do report and say that she be allowed what corn there is in the crib and pickles pork is on hand and three Barrows in the pen and the milk of two cows
Joshua Hickey (Seal)
Ebenezer Jones (Seal)
Joanthan C. Davis (Seal)
Recorded 13th August 1833 J. A. Lane Clerk by N. Oldham D.C.

Report of assignment of provisions by commissioners to thewidow and children Benjamin Bowman deceas ed at July term 1833.

State of Tennessee ◊
White County ◊ To the worshipful court of pleas and Quarter Session for said county

We whose names are hereunto subscribed being appointed commissioners to allot and set aside one years provision
P 123 of the estate of Benjamin Bowman deceased for his widow do report that we have set apart the following a rticles, towit: 200 bushels of corn this quanity is Juded to be in the crib on the premises of the said Bowman--1000 pounds of Bacon 550 of which is supposed to be on hand in possession of the widow--18 bushels of wheat, about6 bushels of this quanity suppose to be on hand 96 pounds of Sugar and 48 lb of coffee, no part of this is on hand two dollars worth of Salt money of the above articles not being in possesson of the widow, we order that she the widow of the said Benja. Bowman be entitled to the Sum of seventy five dollars the value of the article lucking which are set apart by us for her support and maintainanse and that the administrator pay to the widow the said sum of $75 out of the first money collected all of which is respectfully submitted may the 3rd 1833.

Recorded 13th August 1833 David Walling (Seal)
J. A. Lane Clerk by N. Oldham D.C. Thomas Robertson (Seal)
Andrew Cope (Seal)

Report by commisiioners of a settlement with the Adms. of DAVID & JANE EVANS Deceased at April Term A. D. 1833.

State of Tennessee ◊
White County ◊ In pursuance of an order of court appointing us David S. Mitchell and Joseph Herd Commissioners to settle with Eli Sims & and Ja mes Randals administrators of the estate of David & Jane Evans deceased. We have this 15th day of April 1833 proceeded to Said Duty and are production of the exhibits and accounts of receipts and disbursements it appears they are chargeable with what appears on the Debit side and entitled to credits for what appears on the credit side

Debits

To one negro boy slave named Jackson sold for	165.50

Credits

By one Receipts for compromise of Suit ferqa fee paid to an att. in Kentuckey by the name of Squire Turner	25.00
By Cash preoupt of Daniel Brick for compromise of suit for negro boy Jackson	25.00
By cash paid David Irwin clerk	1.07
By cash paid Sheriff concerning said suit of negro	.62½
By cash paid clerk White County Court for copy 2 orders	.50
By cash paid Richard Crowder acct filed with Admr.	2.56¼
By cash paid Lucretia Huston preceipt	1.50
By act. for 50lb pork at 2½¢ psf	1.25
By amt of Funeral expences and cloth etc	10.00
By cash paid for boarding for childsen, washing and lodging four weeks at fifty cents a week	8.00
By amt paid for boarding Lodging & washing for one woman and two children 4 weeks and addition to bcack woman in child bed	12.00
P 124 To amount Debits brought over	165.50
By amount 19 days of said administrators traveling to and returning from Kintuckey on business of said Estate for Services of selfs & horses etc	76.00

By one other trip to the Same place by one of the Adms. 13 days at the rate of $2 per day 26.00
By amt. paid expences bringing negro boy Jackson from Kintuckey to Sparta 5.00
By amt. apid postages on letters of the EState business .37½
$195.88 3/4

We do hereby certify that we have examined the aforesaid Accounts and receipts and that we have made a just and true Statement of the amounts etc. of such claim as filed with us by the aforesaid administrators--We witness our hands andSeals this day & year above written.

Recorded 13th August 1833 David S. Mitchell (Seal)
Jacob A. Lane Clerk Joseph Herd (Seal)
by N. Oldham D.C.

Account of Sales of the estate of William Weaver Deceased. Returned by Joseph Kerr. & Jesse Davis ADms. an Fanny Weaver ADms. at July Term A. D. 1833.

Thomas Sherrel to 1 cow		7.00
Elum Sherrel two Steers 2 yr old		8.00
William Brewster	1 cow Brute	3.25
	1 Steer blidd	10.12½
	1 heifer	5.00
Fanny Weaver	15 Hogs	15.00
	1 cupboard	5.25
	1 do	2.50
2 Beds & furniture		10.00
10 old Chairs		1.00
1 Table & old trunk		3.50
2 Wheels 1 chest & 1 Reel		3.50
3 Bedstead beds. & Furniture		16.50
1 set Castings		1.00
2 Looms		1.00
1 mare		22.00
Witthew Cordell 1 Table		3.00
Sq. M Stephen 1 Broad AXe		2.75
John Saylors 4 head hogs		2.50
Caffenery Martin 1 Calf		2.00
Robert Martin	1 cow	7.31¼
J. C. Dew	1 sow & 3 pigs	1.31¼
Joshua Heckey 16 head hogs		16.62½
Travis Elmore	1 Skillet 1 Lid	1.56¼
Joel Garret 1 pot		1.00
Simpson cash 1 old pot		.37½
Ridley Jones 1 do		.37½
Richd. Tayler 1 Rifle Gun		14/75
James C. Mitchell 1 plough		1.00
Jared C. Pucket 1 Scythe & cradle		2.68 3/4
Will Campbell 1 plough		1.00
Simpson Cash 1 Rug & Steeple		.50
David Clark 1 Iron Wedge		.56¼
John Campbell	1 do	.43 3/4
Tho C. Martin 1 Screw auger		.43 3/4
Will Mills 1 coffee Mill		.37½

Fanny Weaver 4 Geese	1.00
Carths Whitfield 1 Hoe	.31¼
Zachariah Usrey 1 man's Saddle	2.50
Tobacco sold on 2nd March	4.50
Tobacco Sold on 2nd March	4.50
Henry Collin 10 head hogs	4.06¼
Thomas Sherrel 1 sow	1.75
Abraham Sailey 3 shoats	1.50
P 125 Caffey Martin 3 shoats	1.37½
J. C. Dew 1 do	.25
Aaron England 1 Mail Swing	1.81¼
Jess Davis 1 Bell	.25
Joel Garret 1 Table	.50
Fanny Weaver 1 plow and gear	.75
2 pails & 2 pans	.25
1 pot rack 1 side Saddle tree	.81½
1 Bed and some other old articles	.31¼
1 Bed Stead 1 Looking glass	.50
1 Axe	1.00
Ca sh i hand of Fanny Weaver	40.87½
Cash in hand of Jo. Kerr Adms.	9.62½
	$265.00

Inventory of Notes which came to Adms. & Adms. hands

Account against Jefferson J. Shaw	4.25
1 note on James Mills	2.00
1 " Isaac Mills due Nov. next	4.50
1 " John Massey sevr.	.12½
1 Account on William Rutherford	.25
1 note on William Smith	1.06¼
1 " Andrew Lyner	.37½
1 " Richd. Judson & Tach. Jones	9.25
1 Acct on William Brown	1.37½
	$22.18 3/4
	287.18 3/4

This appears to contain all the personal estate of William Weaved deceased that came into the hands of the administrators of said estate— there is some other unsettled insolvent accounts which is not worth notice they not being in a Situation to be collected. There is likewise a book account with some unsettled accounts on which we have tried to make Settlement and collections without success they being small and generally disputed no further return can be made at this time. No correct account of the amo nt of debts against the estate can be obtained. Although we have tried to obrain it. the demands against the estate we think not to be less than from Seven to Eight hundred dollars which will leave after applying the present amount of something like five hundred dollars which defect must be supplied out of the real estate.

Given under our hands and Seals

Recorded 13 Aug. 1833
J. A. Lane Clerk by
N. Oldham D.C.

Joseph Kerr }
Jesse Davis } Admr.
Fanny Weaver Adms. of William Weaver Deceased

P 126 In the name of God Amen I John Dale of the County of White and of the State of Tennessee being weak in body but of sound and perfect mind and Memory do make and publish this my last will and Testament in Manner and form following (tha t is to say) first I give and bequeath unto my beloved wife Lucy Dale the house and farm I now occupy, one bay mare 1 woman's saddle one bed and furniture one cow & calf & Ten dollars in cash which she is to enjoy during her natural life or widowhood, as she is to be at the expence of raising & schooling of the two youngest Daughters towit:
Julian Eliza & Polly Melinda which the said three children is to have all the household furniture after their mothers death or as they become of age, they are to have their propertional part of Said Furniture-I also give unto the said Julian one certain sorrel mare three years old filly with Saddle & Bridle rated at $125.00 one cow & calf two head of sheep one Sow & pigs at $15. and one third of the above Land--I also give and bequeath unto my two youngest daughters Eliza & Polly Melinda Elizas is to have a certain sorrel mare with white legs 3 years old bridle & Saddle rated at $125. one cow & calf two sheep & one sow & pigs $15 and one third part of the aforesaid Land--I give and bequeath unto Polly one black filly saddle & Bridle rated at $125. one cow & calf two head of sheep one Sow & pigs $15.00 and one third part of the aforesaid land. And in case any of the avove children should die without leaving a lawful heir, then and in that case the said property is to revert back to the balance of the heirs to be equally divided--I also give and bequeath to Thomas Servis forty two and one half acres of Land where he now lives $10. per acre for which he has a Deed for the same. Also one horse bridle and Saddle at $150. one bed and furniture rated at $20. one chest & wheel $9. one chair 31 one set of plates, spoons & pitcher $2.00 cow & calf 10.00 one two year old heifer $6.00 and one sheep $1.25 which property he received and has been in full possession of the same and converted it to his own use--I also give unto Benjamin Mays one mare S ddle and Bridle $100. one bed & furniture $20. one cow & yearling $12.00 One Trunk $5. one crock & sett of spoons $1.12½ & one big wheel $3. two horses and one hoke oxen rated at $290. which property the said Mays has previously received from me.--I also give and bequeath unto my son John Dale the tract of Land he now lives on situated in the North West corner of my claim in the Hickory Valley and bounded agreeable to the lines made by Woodrow P White except on the southern boundary line It is to run from the post oak corner running across the Said Southern boundary a direct line to
P127 Doyles line in a Sink near the old field, running thence round West Doyle's line to John White's and with his line to the aforesaid Marked lines rated at $250. One horse saddle & B idle at $95. one cow & calf and one cow rated $15. one bed, coverled $20 one sheep $1.50--$4 worth of hogs one chain 31. shich he has previously received and is in possession of the same--I also give and bequeath unto Pleasant White one horse & saddle $95. Bed & furniture $20. one cow $10.00 one sheep $1.50 4 head of hogs $12. one tract of Land Mitchell place $225. Household furniture & calico $5.00 your receipt for Mill $600. half the price of mill Irons and one Lock chain $7.50which amount he has previously received. I also give and bequeath unto my son Daniel Dale to year receipts for the mill $600. O e cow tract of land adjoining my farm $250. One mare Saddle & Bridle $100." one cow & calf $10. one bed & furniture $20.one sheep $1.50 $4.00 worth of Hogs your part of the chain & mill Irons $7.50 all of which he has previously received I also give and bequeath unto David

Molley as per Receipt $129.50 in property which amount he has received I further give devise to my four Grand children William J Malley the wife of Henry Riddles their heirs and assign all the land I hold in Jackson County on the waters of Russells Mill seatcontaining by estimation 470 acres more or less to hold to them their heirs and assign forever. I further give and divise to my son John Dale his heirs and assign the following tracts of Land towit: 130 acres of Land adjoining Joel Moonyhans land on Cumberland Mountain also one other tract of Land on Cumberland Mountain on Rosses Road known as the Sorrel's place containing 10 acres. One other tract of Land on the brick of Cumberland mountain above Jesse Dodson south side of the Main Caney fork containing 25 acres of Land also one other tract of Land near the pine mountain containing 50 acres known by the name of Sorrel's place rated in all $400. I also give unto him one bay horse e year old $50. one black cow & calf $10. O e Rifle Gun $10.00 & the gollaher Tools $16. I also further give and devise to my son-in-law Benjamin Mayes and his heirs 120 acres of Land on the South side of the main Caney Fork adjoining Dan Giffith Esq. rated at $480. and one Gray horse three years old $50. I further give and bequeath to my son-in-law Thomas Lewis my horse Nohn rated $228 Alsoone motley cow & calf $15. this amount is express by understood to be for the benefit of said Lewis children--I hereby retain for my own use and benefit the house & land t at I now occupy & one bed & furniture during my natural life--revoking all former wills by me made. In witness Whereof I have hereunto set my hand & seal this 24th day of August 1833.

Test W.P.White — John Dale (Seal)
John White Jr.

P 128 State of Tennessee) October Session A. D. 1833
White County)

This day the death of John Dale late of the county of White deceased was suggested in open Court when upon was produced the last will andtestament of the said John Dale deceased and the due executin thereof as such was proven in open court by the oath of Woodson P White and John White Jr. two subscribing witness thereto for the purposes and things therein mentioned and that the said John Dale a t the date of the execution and publication thereof was of sound and disposing mind and memory. Whereupon it is ordered that the same be recorded-- Given at office the 14th day of October A. D. 1833.

Jacob A. Lane Clerk of the County C.
of White County

By N. Oldham Dep. Clerk
Recorded the 25th Nov. 1833. J. A. Lane Clerk By N. Oldham Dep. Clk.

In the name of God Amen, I THOMAS SPERRY of the County of White and State of Tennessee being of Sound mind and in the full enjoyment of my intellectual faculties but somewhat afflected in body, and remembering that is appointed unto all men once to die, and being deserves so to arrange my worldly affairs as to leave no just ground of complaint with any of the human family, do make and ordain this my last will and Testament, 1st my desire is that my body be intered in a decent and Christian manner, and I give my soul to that God from whom it was derived and moreover feel a firm abiding faith that my body will be raised at the reserection of the just Item. My will and desire is that all my just debts be first paid. I give and bequeath to beloved wife Sally all my household and Kitchen furniture during her natural life, and at her death to be divided in equal porportions amongst my children Charles R. Sperry Elizabath Long. John M. Sperry and Nancy Mark. Item: my will and desire is that that house and lot on which I now live in Soarta with all its appertananoes, and all my personal property of every description (with th exception of the household and Kitchen furniture above disposed of) be s sold without reserve to the highest bidder on a twelve months credit with bonds and approved Security and that the proceeds of said Sale when collected be applied in equal propertions to the above named heirs my wife Sally Sperry , and that the same be equally divided between them and paid over to them by executors herein after named-- Item Whereas Alexander Lowery is justly indebted to me in the sum of Sixty five P 129 dollars--and whereas Charles Meek is likewise justly indebted to me in the Sum of two hundred and twenty two dollars: now I will and desire is that these debts together with all others that may be owing me be thrown into a common fund with the proceeds of the sale of my personal property as above provided for and such arrangement made as will secure due equal and just division of the entire amount or aggregate sum between my wife and children named above. Item--What actual cash I may have on hand at my death I wish excepted out of the above general disposition of my personal property and desposed as follows. I wish my executor to pay over immmediately on third of it to my wife and equally divede the balance between my children above named.

I hereby niminate, constitute and appoint my friend Alexander B. Lane Esq. sole Executor of this last will and testament with full p8wer to act in that Character in such manner as he may deem legal and right

In testimony whereof ' have hereunto set my hand and seal this 18th day of September 1833. Thomas Sperry (Seal)
Signed & sealed in presence of Richard Nelson John Warren W. E. Morton

State of Tennessee }
White County } October Session A. D. 1833

This day the last will and testament of Thomas Sperry deceased late of the County of White was produced herein open court and the same day came Richard Nelson and Willaim C Thoskmorton two of the subscribing witness thereto who being first sworn in due form of Law upon their oath do say they saw the said Thomas Sperry sign and Seal the said last will and testament and publish and proclaim the same as such, that they subscribed their names as Witness in his presence at the date and publication thereof and that the said Thomas Sperry was of sound and disposing mind and memory--and the same day also appeared in open court Alexander B. Lane, who is appointed to be executor to said said Thomas Sperry by said last will and testament, and undertook the execution thereof and for the faithful performance of the execution of th the said will entered into and acknowledged bond with Jesse Lincoln and Anthony Di rell in the Sum of Three thousand dollars condition as the law required and took the oath prescribed by law. Whereupon it is ordered to be Recorded. Given at office the 21 day of Oct A. D. 1833.
Recorded 28th Nov 1833 Jacob A. Lane Clerk of theCounty Court of White County

J. A. Lane Clerk by N, OldhamD.C.

P 130 A Settlement made by commissioners with Samuel Brown ADmr. and Sarah Dyer Admr of the Estate of John Dyer decd. upon oath at October term A. D. 1833.

State of Tennessee }
White County } We the undersigned being appointed by the county Court of White County to settle with Samuel Brown and Sarah Dyer Administrators and administrater of John Dyer ded. do make the following report that is

We find said Admr. chargeable as contained in his Inventory returned at January term of the County Court 1832 Marked A. 506.60
Interest on that sum up to this time 33.
Amt contained in Inventory mark B returned January term 1831 & good Debts 1498.54
Interest upon the same 278.04¼
Amount come into hands of Admr. since return of his Inventory 10.50
All of which is set out in Statement Marked C
2326.68¼

Cr.

By D d Debts returned a s set out in said Statement marked C. not enclosed in the above charge of $1498.54 193.39
By amount paid out as pr Statement marked D. 225.66 3/4
By amount in the hands of Wm. Dyer pr. Rect. 147.15
By amount paid Commissioners 6.00 378.21
1947.86½
8.00
1955.86½

The above Sum of nineteen hundred and fifty five dollars eighty six and one half cents we find now remaining in the Admr. hands .
This 21st October 1833.

Recorded 26th Nov. 1833. Anthony Dibrell
Jacob A. Lane Clk. John Jett
by N. Oldhan D.C. Charles Reeves

Report of a Settlement made by Comr with John W. Simpson and Hugh Comer Administrators of the estate of Abraham Cormer deceased at October Session 1833.

Puesuant to an order of the Worshipful court of White County granted at their July Session in the year of our Lord 1833. We the undersigned coms. appointed to settle with Genl. John W. Simpson and Hugh Cormnor Adms. of Abraham Cornor deceased met at the dwelling house of General John W. Simpson on the [illegible] day of September A. D. 1833. After examining the accounts and vouchers of Said Administrators, Report and say that the amount of Sales of the said estate was 255.15½
P 131 Out of which Sum they have paid to Sundry persons for which they produced proper vouchers 113.09½
Tha t then an yet outs tanding debts in the hands of the heirs 112.83 3/4
is 225.93
which taken from amt. sales leaves a balance in the hands of Admr. 29.22½
The Admr. J. W. Simpson brings in a charge against the estate for his troubde 10.00
The Comrs. now attending Charges 2.50 12.50
16.72½

All of which is respectfully Submitted
Recorded 26th Nov. 1833 Turner Lane Senr. }
Simon Doyle } Coms.
Joseph Cummings Jr. }

Inventory of the Estate of BENJAMIN BOWMAN deceased returned upon oahh by Joseph Herd Admr. at October term 1833.
1 note on Thomas Stipe due 26th day of December 1832 for $97.50 with a credit thereon stated January 22nd 1833. $11.00--Good.
1 note on said Stipes due 1 Nov. 1832 for 500 lv. of Tobacco with a credit thereon for 310 lb. of Tobacco Good-- 1 note on John Chapman for 300$ in horses due 25th December 1825 credit on the within note the 15th day of February 1826 $280.00 do the 23rd day of June 1832 for $14.00 Doubtful--One note on William Flinn for 1600 lb. of good merchantable leaf Tobacco due the 1 Nov. 1832 with a Credit thereon for 600 lb of tobacco one note on John Bussel due 1 day of May 1833 for $15.00--One ree ceipt on Nathan Haggard atto. for a note on William C. Brittain for $200. 24th febry 1823 20.00$ to come out for atto fee one judgement on Joseph Kerr for $80.00.

The avobe is a just and true return of the debts due said estate so far as have come to my Knowledge this 5th day of August 1833.
Recorded 26 Nov. 1833. Joseph Herd
Jacob A. Lane Clerk Administrator
White County Court by N. Oldham Dep. Clerk.

P 132 Account of the Sales of the estate of Benjamin Bowman deced. returned upon oath by Jas. Herd Admr. at October term 1833.

1 Barshear plow sold to Robert Anderson	2.00
1 Dager plow sold to James Walling	.50
1 Kittle do Osian Denton	1.00
1 Bell do John G. Jones	.56½
1 Curry comb do Edward Gleeson	.25
1 broad axe do L. B. Faris	2.12½
1 Falling axe do do	.68½
1 Lot of Tool do Winkfield Hill	2.06¼
1 wedge & tools do Jas. Walling	.81¼
1 pr. Waffle Irons do Jno Haltiman	.75
1 Log chain ring & Steeple do Lewis Fittel	4.00
1 pitch fork & 2 Bridles do R. Anderson	.31¼
½ of a cross out saw do Jas Anderson	1.62½
1 Cast Dish do Winkfield Hill	.43 3/4
1 Lot old barrels do Wm. Templeton	.37½
2 Dry Hides do John Halliman	2.50
1 Wheel & REel dO W. Hill	.25
1 Loom do Blanton Denton	3.12½
1 Lot Tobacco 15lb 12½ do Tho. Crawley	1.87½
1 do 20lb 12½ do J. G. Jones	2.50
1 do 20 lb 10¢ do	2.00
1 do 20 10 J. Dillefield	2.20
1 clock do Nancy Bowman	20.00
1 Bureau do do do	5.00
1 Bed & furniture do do	5.00
1 Bed & furniture do do	3.00
2 Bed Steds do do do	2.00
1 looking Glass & books do	5.00
1 Table & lot of furniture do	3.00

1 lot of Farming tools do	8.00
1 Lot of Plunder	5.00
6 Iron Bands do Wm. Earles	3.00
1 Lot of Tobacco 20 lb 10½ Jas Knowles	2.10
1 Lot do 44 10½ do N. Bowman	4.62
1 Rifle Gun do Jesse Walling	18.00
1 Waggon & Gear do Jno Stipe	60.00
1 Lot Ware & Steelyards do N. Bowman	4.00
1 Cupboard do J. Stipe	7.75
1 Bay Colt 2 years old do J. Sparkman	58.00
1 " do 1 year do do Tho Stipe	33.00
1 Sorrel do do	33.75
1 do horse do S. Holland	60.06¼
1 Bay Mare & colt to Nancy Bowman	83.00
1 sorrel do do do	54.00
1 do horse do Jas. Cason	36.06¼
1 mans Saddle do N. Bowman	3.00
5 head of Cattle do G. D. Howard	12.56¼
1 2 year old Steer do L. B. Faris	5.00
1 Bull do Benton Denton	6.31¼
1 Heifer do do	5.18 3/4
1 do do Michael Henderson	4.25
1 cow do Jas. Anderson	8.62½
1 Heifer & calf do Nancy Bowman	4.00
1 Brindle cow do do	7.50
1 cow & calf do do	8.00
1 cow do do	8.50
1 Lot Rasers & con do Jno Stipe	3.31¼
1 Hog do C. Dranes	2.50
4 do do John Fisher	9162½
5 do do W. E. Jutson	8.93 3/4
18 do do William Flinn	10.75
2 Bee Stands do Nancy Bowman	.50
1 Wheal & 6 Chairs do	2.00
500 Buls. oats 88½ do J. G. Wilhite	4.42½
250 Binds do 90½ do Th. E. Hutson	2.26¼
250 " do 96½ do J. Haltman	2.41¼
9 Sheep do N. Bowman	9.00
10 do do E. Henderson	9.06¼
1 Grindstone do N. Bowman	.50
1 Feed trough do J. Stipe	.06 ¼
1 Keg of Tobacco sold to William Simpson	27.75
	$749.94 3/4

The above is a just and true return of account sales of the Estate of Benjamin Bowman dcd. this 5th day August 1833

Joseph Herd Adm.

Recorded 28 Nov. 1833.

P 158 Amount of the 1st Sale of the property of Charles Carter Sur. Deceased made by John Fryer Admr. returned on oath at January Term A. D. 1834.

Edward Anderson 1 F ce 50¢ Melford Cay 1 Auger 56¼¢ 1.06¼
John Stepo 1 Barshear plough 81¼ James H Doyle 1 Iron Wheel 50¢
1.31 ¼

Edward Anderson 1 pair Geer 100¢ John Stepe 1 pair Gear 1.18 3/4 2.18 3/4
Robert Love 1 Axe 2.00½ Joel Smith 1 axe 62½
Jno Mitchell axe 212¢ 4.75
Stephen Holland 1 shovel Plough 125¢ 2.37½
Joel Smith 2 hoes 62¢ Jno Fryer 1 Table 4.37¢ 5.00
Edward Anderson 1 Tub 82¢ Wm Pennington1 oven 1.00¢ 1.82½
Saml. Thomas 1 mare $17.62¢ Wm. Kerr 2 chairs 75¢ 18.37½
John Stipe 1 colt 18.00
$54.68 3/4
Recorded 17th January 1834 Test. J.A. Lane Clerk John Fryer Admr.

Return of 2nd Sale of the property of CHARLES CARTER Senr. Decd, returned by John Fryer Adm. at January Term 1834.
to tract land sold to Rebecca Hogan by direction of Taxes for $405.
Recd. for Rents $40. 445.00
John Fryer 1 cow $3.25 James H. Doyle 1 Scythe 2.00 5.25
Simon Doyle 1 Cross cut saw 3.87¢ 1 wedge 50¢ 4.37½
James Randals 1 cow 450¢ Jeptha West 1 mare $30.50 35.00
Hosea Letter 1 horse $48. 48.00
Hugh Gracy 1 negro woman sold 29th May 1830 186.00
John Fryer 1 negro boy Sold to Woodson P White 24. Dec. 300.00
$1023.62½
Recorded 17th January 1834 John Fryer Admr. Test J. A. Lane Clerk.

Report Thomas Burgis Guardian to the heirs of John Hicks dcd. made upon oath at the January Sessions A. D. 1834.

That no money has come to his hands of their estate.
But he has paid for their Schooling $1.66 2/3

Thomas Burgess

Recorded 30 January 1834 Test J. A. Lane Clerk by N. Oldham D.C.

Report of John Walker Guardian to the heirs of Alexander Kerr dcd. made upon oath at the January Sessions A. D. 1834.

No Alteration in the estate of the heir of Alexander Kerr Since last years return January 13th 1834.

John Walker Guardian

Recorded 30 Jany 1834 J. A. Land Clerk

P 134 Report of Moses Goddard Guardian to the heirs of John Smallman dcd. made upon oath at January Sessions A. D. 1834.

That he has in his hands three hundred and twenty five dollars of their money in his hands not yet loaned out 15 January 1834.

Moses X Goddard Guardian
his mark

Recorded 30 Jany 1834
Jacob A. Lane Clerk.

Report of Wamon Leftwitch Guardian to Malinda Rowland and Tennessee Rowland now Tennessee Shaw Miner heirs of John Rowland decd made upon oath at January Sessions A. D. 1834.

Respectfully Submits to the worshipful county Court of White County the following Statement which will Show the condition of the Estate of his Wards 1st The amount of the estate of each as will appear from Documents and vouchers in my hands and which has come to my hands as as Guardian is $680. 17½ making an aggregate of $1360.35. He further shows that the Said Tennessee Shaw has received from him the entire amount nt of her part of the estate as will appear from a full and clear receipt. Now in his possession Signed by her husband Jesse W. Shaw being $680.17½ He further shows that he has expended for necessary colthing for the said Malinda suitable to her condition $107.03¼ Leaving in my hands a balance of $573. 14¼ all of which is Respectfully submitted this 13th day of January 1834.

Wamon Leftwich Guardian

Recorded 30 January 1834 Jacob A. Lane Clerk.

Report of John Walker Guardian to the heirs of Kindle Savage made upon oath at the January Sessions A. D. 1834.
No alte4ation in the estate of the heirs of Kindel Savage since last years return January 13 1834.

John Walker Guardian

Recorded 30 January 1834 Jacob A. Lane Clerk

Report of Thomas Hill guardian to the heirs of Jas. Hill deceased. made upon oath at the January Sessions A. D. 1834. The amount of money in Thomas Hills bond is one hundred and twenty six dollars as Guardian
Recorded 30 January 1834

Jacob A. Lane Clerk.

P 135 Report of John Mason Guardian to James Howard monor heir of Joward dcd. made upon oath at January Sessions A. D. 1834.
The following is a true account of the estate of James Howard Sr. for as the same has come to my hands as Guardian. One note on Corder S one & Elizabeth Bowman amts with interest to $13.25
This Sum is Cash $20.00
Settlement with Iquationos Howard former Guradian not completed.
Recorded 30 January 1830 John Mason Guardian Jacob A. Lane Clerk.

Report of Anthony Dibrell Guardian to the Heirs of William Gracey dcd. made upon oath at January Sessions A. D. 1834.
That he has paid out for the support and maintanence education of said children while he was Guardian and begs the worship full Court to make an allowance to Susanah Roberts formerly Susanah Gracy for the Same agreeable to her receipts which said General Sums werereceived by me and collected for the hire of negroes mentioned in the will of said Gracy commencing with N. 1. and including receipt N. 9 amounting to the sum of $293.92½
paid Said S. Gracy as per receipt filed in Settlement made by the commissioners having been charged with hire negroes as administrator 101.50
Also paid as per Receipt No. 10 40.00
440.42½

I have hired the negroes and received for the same while Guardian the sum of 455.42½
Leaving in my hands the Sum of fifteen dollars which I charge for my services as Guardian 17 January 1834

A. Dibrell

Recorded 31 January 1834 J. A. Lane Clerk by N. Oldham D.C.

Inventory of part of the Estate of John Dale deceased made upon the oath of Daniel Dale one of the Admr. at January Sessions A. D. 1834 One note on John Miller due 11 May 1833 for $8.00 bad. One note on John Miller due 15 Nov. 1825 for $5.00 doubtful One note on John Baker due 1st Decemr. 1835 for $3.00 dispute--One note on George Miller due 1st Der. 1833 for $100 doubtful--One do on John & M. Seals 25 Decr. 1833 for $300 doubtful--One note on William Frazer due 1st Decr. 1833 for
P 136 $3.00 doubtful One note on John Miller due 27th Decr. 1833 for $3.00 doubtful one on John H Miller due 26 December 1833 for $3.00 doubtful. One note on John H. Miller due 25 December 1833. for $3.00 doubtful. One note on Jacob Kuner due 25 December 1833 for $4.37½ Dispute--One note on David Moore due "5 December 1833 for $10.00 One protested order on Locky Seals now Locky Gaston for $ 4.00 or Twenty Bushels of corn dispute. One note on Jacob Robertson deceased due 1st February 1830 for $ 72.00 with the following credits endorsed thereon this one of twenty five dollars not dated--One of $4.00 Decr. 22nd 1820 one of $3.00 April 14. 1822 doubtful one note on William Gist executed to Bluford Warren and by him transferred to John Dale due 1st Sept. 1820 for $22.50 with a credit endorsed thereon of $20 date of credit not given dispute--Are affidavit of a lost note on Joseph Kurnes due 10th February 1827 for $10.00 in young cattle dispute One note on Burwell Seals due 27 Decr. 1822 for 56 Bushels of corn with a credit without date of 26 Bushels corn dispute One note on William Wheeler due 13 July 1820 for 5$ with a receipt endorsed thereon of $5. 24th July 1823. Doubtful One note on Fent C. Cormer Crocket Herbert and Archibald Commer for $176. due 25 April 1834. One note on Same persons for $196. due 25 April 1836. One note on Edmond Price for $25.87½ due 20th October 1823 dispute One note on Richard Pettit for $2.50 due October 1830 dispute One note on James byers for $8.00 due 26 Decr. 1832 disperate One note on Daniel H. Busser for $8.00 due 8th September 1830 desperate One note on John Yates for 325 Bushels of corn to be paid at any time between 1st of May and 1st August inthe year 1834. One note on Stephen D. Hill for $20 disperate One note on Stephen D. Hill for five dollars desperate One sorrel mare one yoke of oxen & yoke 3 small Steers 1 red Heifer 1 pided do 1 small red calf 1 small red Heirfer 9 head of Sheep 31 head of Hogs 9 head of Goats 1 Still and worm 2 old Saddles 1 man's Saddle Blacksmith tools small Smith Irons 1 set of Harness & collar 1 plow 1 Gun one do 1 musket and shot Bag and horn one cotton Gin one hand saw one large plough small irons one auger 1froe 1set Waggon preeching 1 Broad Axe 2 augers 1 wedge Sundry small Irons sundry irons, waggon Boxes 3 plough 2 chisel Waggon Hoops 2 chairs 1 pr Stretchers 2 half chairs one axe Ring & chairs one bell & collar one Bell one dog collar, small bell & coller, one large lock 4 Ear bells 1 jack Screw 2 waggon wheels 4 Irons 2 large Waggon tire one scythe and cradle bone pr Geer and Harness, Gears and Harness one Shovel plough One iron wedge one churn 2 Grindstone one bridle & still tubbs one cross cut sas Scythe and Cradle 2 axes 2 Saws 384 Bushels corn.
P 137 The following proprety mentioned in the will of John Dale decd. was taken into possession by those named as legates in said will before the appointment of the administrators yet namely four beds & furniture 2 Bed Steads, one cupboard one Loom One clock and Case two tables one chest chest & trunk two ovens & Lids One kettle One pot one Check Rul and Some Chairs 2 Cotton wheels & one flax wheel taken in possession of Lucy without the consent of the Admr. Some other property was taken in

like manner, by John A. Dale, Thomas Lewis Benjamin Mayes etc
Recorded 31 January 1834 Daniel Dale Admr.
J. A. Lane Clerk by N. Oldham D.C.

Inventory of the estate of THOMAS BOUNDS deceased returned upon oath by Jesse A. Bounds admr. at the January Sessions A. D. 1834.

His Twelve negroes towit: two by the name of Anderson one of which is a man the other a small boy two negro men by the name of Peter, Philip and Jarrett Grown men: and Amos and Lea both boys Letty, Sophia, & denis grown women and Clara a Girl--Six head of horses (two of which are colts) twenty two head of cattle of various ages 2 yoke of oxen Sixty head of stock hogs--twenty six head of Sheep one Still fifteen Duvs, a doubling & Singling and a bucket belonging thereto one Waggon one Carryall and harness for single horse two ploughs 6 Hoes one two such auger one fine quarter auger one three quarter auger Three chisels one Waggon tongue, double and Singletree, Stay and breast chain three pair of drawing chairs & Hanes one frow one pr cast wheels one cutting Knife and box one coopers adze and drawing Knife two Log Chains--two Scythes and Craddes one Grindstone two Hammers one Hatchett two __ plains one Jack plain Nine Bedsteads one loom one set of Warping spools--Seven slays one pair spooling frames one Bureau and China press one bureau and Book case one clock and case--one table looking glass two Cotton Wheels one flax wheel Three feather beds, Bedsteads and furniture for the Same one Iron square one check rul one man's Saddle one Side Saddle eight Chairs one half Bushel one reflector two candle sticks one Rifle Gunpouch and horn five dishes thirteen plates oen Salt celler five glass Tumblers one bowl one pepper box one caster one coffee mill-- 4 pitchers one tin trunk one coffee pot four Jars two crocks 1 Jug 1 Gallon measure three Bottles one earthen pot one Kittle oue pot, one frying pan one tin pan one basin--three water pails one churn one pr Steelyards one pot rack 2 pair pot Hooks one brake P 138 iron one Iron Shovel one fire Shovel one pair hand irons Eleven teacups thn Saucers one Snoffle (?) bridle three blind bridles one bedstead 2 pr. Shares Eighty Six and a half pounds of Iron 150 feet of cherry pland 600feet poplar plank inch think three coolers one set Knives and forks--1 Set Table Spoons five Silver Tea spoons-- about 300 bushels of corn one pr. Saddle bags 1 sheep Skin for Saddle cover--one horse Whip one unbrella Staff & Ribbs upper & Sole Leather to the value of Seventy Six dollars one note payable to Jesse A. Bounds belonging to the estate of Thomas Bounds given by Carrick Lefthwick etc for one hundred and eighteen dollars forty five cents due the 3rd day of April 1834. Good- one note on Elijah ward and John Anderson for the sum of one hundred dollars payable to Margarett Bounds dated 11th October 1833 and due 25th Decr. 1833. with interest from the date this was money loaned Since the death of Thomas Bounds $100.00

One note on John Isom & John Pennington date 3 August 1833 due twelve months after date $2.25 2.25

One note on James H. Pass for $4.12½ cents due 15 Sept. 1832 by 50 cents credit 15 Sept 1832 3.62½

One note on Shadrach Price & Benjamin Harris for two dollars due 30 August 1834 2.00

One note on Ruben Bown and Solomon Wilhite for $2.56¼ due 30 August 1834 2.56¼

One note on William & Jno Bullock due 30 Aug. 1834 31.50

One note on Spivy for $21.75 due April 1828 payable in property at Bounds Mill-Dispute with

a credit thereon for $10. 7 Jany. 1833 11.75
One note on Michell Moore & Jeremiah Whitson due 30 day
1834 2.00
One note on Elijah Hooten & William K Bradford due
Aug 1834 1.50
One note on John Matthews due 20 Nov. 1835 desperate 21.00
One Note on Shedrack for $60. due 1 Sept 1831
Credited by $25.--17th Jany 1832--by $20. 15 May 1832 bal 5.00
One Receipt on Andrew J. Marchbacks for the collection
of a covenant on Thomas Hopkins which covenant bears
date 28 January 1823 on which covenant a judgment has
been obtained in the county of Warren for about doubtful 484.00
One Judgement in White Circuit Court against M Elroy and
Shropshire dated 12 June 1823 for 1002.24 their is a credit
but amount not known-desperate 1002.20
One flax hackel--two clevics two singletree--money on hand at the
death of Thomas Bounds one hundred and fifty nine dollars
(159$) Ten live hogs sold at private Sale $47.00 Fourteen
fatted hogs kolled for pork weighing 204¼ lb. two sucking Calves
F 139 Jesse A. Bounds Administrator
Recorded 31st January 1834 Jacob A. Lane Clerk.

Report of Settlement made by commissioner with administrator of the estate of William Cracy deceased return at January Sessions A. D. 1834.

We Richard Nelson and William Leftwich commisioners appointed by the County Court of White County to settle with Anthony Dibrell administrator with the will annexed of William Gracy decd. Report that we have proceeded to settle with said administrator and find and so report the following condition of the estate So far as the facts have come to our knowledge and which from the best lights we have of the Subject we believe to be correct--We find the Administrator Chargeable with the Sum of Five hundred and Ninety Nine dollars and Eighty nine and a half cents. Cr. $599.89½
Asper Receipts herewith filed from No 1 to 12 enclusive $[illegible]
$280.52½ By receipt of D. S. Mitchell fora Debt on Stephen D. Hill
not collective 20.00
By note on S. D. Hill not collected 2.00 302.52
297.37

We believe the above Statement to be correct as will appear upon Vouchers and Documents filed this 11th January 1834

Richard Nelson }
Wamon Leftwich } Coms.

Recorded 31st January 1834 Jacob A. Lane Clerk.

Report of a Settlement made by Commissioners withJohn Fryer Executor of Charles Carter decd. returned at the January Sessions A. D. 1834.

We the undersigned commissioners being appointed by the County Court of White County to Settle with John Fryer executor of the estate of Charles Carter deceased to us from the papers produced by said executor Towit:
We find executor charged with negro boy Benjamin and other property as returned at Jany Court 1834. and contained in paper Marked A.

P 140	$1023.62½
also Return made at the Same term B.	54.68 3/4
Interest upon Devts due the estate	8.00
	$1086.31
By the following Sums paid out one note executed by said Carter to said Fryer for	100.00
Interest on the Same no 1	12.00
By one other Note executed to said John Fryer	150.00
Interest on same No. 2	21.75
By his account against the estate No. 3	188.17 3/4
Pais William Green as per Rep. 4	4.75
paid Benjamin Holland do 5	4.50
paid Mitchell do 6	4.70
paid A. B. Lane Atto do 7	54.00
paid Robert Love do 8	5.00
paid Jesse Lincoln do 9	8.81½
paid J. A. Land do 10	9.64
paid Stephen Holland do 11	3.87½
paid A. Avery note 12	12.83
paid I Cain for Certificate 13	27.88
paid W. Glenn per rect 14	16.43 3/4
paid C. Hill do 15	6.72
paid W. Leftwich do 16	2.00
paid Simon Doyle do 17	4.00
paid Bigham do 18	250
paid Joseph Herd do 19	1.00
paid M. Simmons 20	3.58
paid J. A. Lane do 21	7.62½
paid do do 22	16.11
	968.83 3/4

From the above Settlement we find remaining in the hands of the executors the Sum of One hundred and twenty two dollars and forty seven and a half cents--17 Jany 1834. upon further investigation we find the executor chargeable with the following notes towit: 1 note on Henry A. freeman & Dan Custer due 25 Decr. 1833. 50.00
One 1 Ditto due 25 do 1834 on the same 50.00
One do on the Same then are Doubtful 21.43 3/4
$1207.75

Still leaves a balance in the hands of Said executor the Sum of Two hundred and forty three dollars and ninety one and one fourth Cents Given under our hands and Seals 18 January 1834 we find Said Executors has paid James W. Smith the Sum of thirty three dollars Seventy five cents which is deducted out of the Above sum of $243.91¼ cents leaving
P 141 in the hands of said Executor the Sum of $210.16 1/6 cents dated as above.

A. Dibrell
David Snodgrass
Wamon Leftwich

Recorded 31 January 1834 Jacob A. Lane Clerk by N. Oldhan D. C.

Account of Sales of the Estate of John Dale deceased made upon oath of Daniel Dale one of the admr. of said Estate at January Sessions A. D. 1834.

Sale the 15 November 1833 towit:

1 sorrel mare to William Seals 10.50

1 yoke of oxen & hoke John White Senr.	20.50
3 small Steers Samuel Miller	7.18 3/4
1 Red Heifer Simon R. Doyle	7.06 ½
1 pided do Cornileus D. Brown	5.00
1 Small red do Woodson P. White	3.25
1 Small Red calf Woodson P. White	1.31¼
9 head of Sheep George Miller	4.12½
31 head of Hogs James Simmon	16.87½
3 Goats first choice William Foster	2.25
3 do 2nd choice Abidah Crane	1.50
3 do 3rd do William Foster	1.25
1 Still & worm Dan Griffith	6.12½
2 old Saddle John Scoggin	.87½
1 Man's Saddle John Scoggin	2.50
Blacksmith Tools Daniel Dale	35.00
Small Smith Irons Woodson P White	1.00
1 Set of Harness & callars Robert Taylor	1.56¼
1 plow Jacob Stipe	.50
1 Geer John White senr.	
1 do Benjamin Mayes	3.00
1 musket Shot Bag & hour Thomas Moore	3.62½
1 Gun Rod Jesse Dotson	.25
1 Cotton Gin Daniel Dale	7.75
1 hand Saw Jesse Dotson	.87½
1 large plough John Scoggin	1.62½
1 Auger & Frow Thomas Lewis	2.06¼
1 set Waggon Breaching William Baker	1.25
1 Broad 2 augers 1 wedge Jesse Scoggin	.50
Sundry Small Irons Woodson P.White	1.87½
Sundry Irons Waggon Boxes Jesse Dotson	3.12½
P 142 Three Plough to James Graham	.87½
Small irons 2 chisels Simon R. Doyle	1.00
2 chains Simon R. Doyle	1.62½
Waggon Hoops Daniel Dale	3.00
1 pr. Strechers Benjamin Mayes	.50
2 halter chains James Graham	.43 3/4
1 ox Ring and Chain Daniel Dale	1.37½
1 Bell and Collar Solomon Dotson	1.25
1 Large Lock Thomas Moore	1.00
2 Bar Bell Woodson P White	.12½
2 # do David S. Mitchell	.37½
1 Jackscrew Jesse Scoggin	1.50
2 Waggon Wheels & Irons John Graham Jr.	2.50
2 large Waggon tire Daniel Dale	6.00
1 Scythe 1 cradle Daniel Dale	.25
1 pr Gears & Harness Thomas Lewis	.75
Gears & Harness Thomas Lewis	1.75
1 Shovel plough Russel T. Crane	.56¼
1 Iron wedge Thomas Miller	.25
1 churn Robert G. Anderson	.12½
1 Grindstone Thomas Moore	.68 3/4
1 " " Thomas Lewis	.31¼
Band Thomas Frasure	.12½
2 Still tubs Simon R. Doyle	.25

2 do Robert Anderson	.37½
2 do Daniel Dale	.62½
1 cross cut saw Daniel Dale	5.25
1 Jointer & Waggon gate Thomas Lewis	.12½
1 Scythe and cradle Russel T. Crane	.68 3/4
1 Axe William S. Mitchell	.41
1 Axe Benjamin Mayes	1.46
2 saws do do	1.51
50 Bushels of corn Thomas Lewis	18.75
50 " do Thamas Lewis	18.75
80 " do George W. Isham	30.00
50 " do Simon Bramblet	18.00
50. " do John H. Dale	18.00
54 " d0 John Yates	20.00
50 " do Noah Dotson	18.25
	$337.04¼

Recd. 3 febry 1834 J. A. Lane Ck. Daniel DAle Admr.

P 143 In the name of God Amen! I CHARLES CARTER Senr. of the County of White and State of Tennessee be in much advanced in age and very infirm-in body: but of sound and disposing mind and memory thanks be given to God for the same. Calling to mind the uncertainty of Life, and that it is appointed unto all men once to die. Do make and ordain this my last will and testament in form following namely*- I give up my immortal Soul into the hands of the omnipotent God who made me trusting in his mercy for a happy immortality and my body to be returned to the dust from whence it came and be Burried by my executors hereinafter named in a Decent Christian like manner not doubting but that at the day of the resurrection of the Dead my Soul and body will again be united.
And as to the worldly effects which it has pleased God to bestow upon me. I will devise and bequeath as follows. Namely 1st In the first place, I give and bequeath to my dearly beloved wife Rebecca Carter one negro woman named Polly and their future increase to be by my said wife held and enjoyed during her natural life--I also give and bequeath unto my dearly beloved wife Rebecca Carter all my stock of Horses, Cattle, Hogs, Sheep & and all other stock of every Kind and description whatever and all my house hold and Kitchen furniture and farming utinsils whis said stock, furniture and utinsils it is my will that my said wife Rebecca, have and enjoy forever.
2nd I give and bequeath unto my beloved Son William Carter one nigro boy named Benjamin and one Negro Girl named Malinda to him and his heirs executors or administrators forever together with all the future increase of said Negro Malinda in like Manner-- and to my son George Washington Carter I give and bequeath one negro boy named Thomas and one Negro girl named Matilda together with all the future increase of the said Matilda to him and his heirs executors or administrators forever. Provided nevertheless it is my will and desire that in case either of my two sons William or George W. Carter should die under the age of twenty one years and unmarried that his Share under this my will, shall go to the surviver and the should they both die under the said age and unmarried, then it is my will and desire that my said wife Rebecca Carter (if living) shall have the negroes hereby given to my said sons William and George W. to be by her disposed of as she or her executors or administrators may think proper.

3rd And I hereby give and I hereby give and bequeath unto my before named Sons William Carter and George W. Carter after the death of my said wife Rebecca Carter the afforesaid negro women Jemina and Polly
P 144and their future increase to be equally divided between them my said two sons share and share alike, should either of them die before he arrives at the age of Twenty one or unmarried. Then it is my will and desire that his Share in Said property shall go to and rest in the Survivor
4th I have heretofore give to the children of my first wife as much property donsisting of Land and negroes as I intend for them Namely--I gave to my Daughter Nancy wife of Henry Saddler, one negro named Sammy and a tract of Land and Some other property--I gave to James Carter one negro woman named Line and a tract of land--I gave to Staunton Carter one negro Girl named Celia and a tract of Land I gave to my Daughter Lucy wife of James Saddler two negro girls named Jane and Ulinmy--I gave to my Daughter Polly who is now dead, but who was wife of John McDanniel tow negro Girls B ick and Maria also other property was given by me to said children and they are to take nothing by this will in addition to what was given as aforesaid.
5th And Whereas Dale Carter of Jackson County has now in his possession a negro man of nine named Harry and a tract of Land containing two hundred and fifty acres in Said county of Jackson which he was to keep for three years one of which has expired and was for the use of Said Land and negro for Said three years to pay a debt of about four hundred & ten or eleven dollars and interest to Smith Suttles etc of Gainesborough.

Now it is my will and desire and I do so order that the said Dale Carter pay said Debt or that he surrender up said Land & negro immediately after my death--And I do bequeath and desire to my executors said Negro man Harry and the aforesaid tract of Land to be then sold to raise and pay all my debts and furneral expences and particularly to pay debts and interest to Joyn Freyer the Debts amounting to five hundred and fifty dollars without interest and should there be a Surplus after paying the debts and funeral expenxex then it is my wil that the Said Re Rebecca Carter have it to her own use. I hereby declare that the Tracts of land purchased from John Fryer in the name of Rebecca Carter my Said wife and William & George W. Carter is not in truxt for me but for their own proper use benefit & behalf forever.
6th I hereby will ordain and appoint John Fryer and my wife Rebecca Carte executors of this my last will and testament hereby annulling and revoking all other former will or wills by me made publishing and declare-
P 145ing this to be my last will & testament--In testimony whereof I hereunto subscribed my name and affirm my Seal this 13th day of May A. D. 1829. Charles Carter (Seal) Signed Sealed published and distained by the Said Charles Carter Snr. to be his last will & testament in our presence and in presence of each other and in presence and at the request of said testator have subscribed out names as witness thereto--The words "if living" unterlined before signed

Thomas Goen
Clabon Hill
William Fryer

State of Tennessee }
White County } April Sessions A. D. 1830
This day the last will and testaments of Charles Carter Senr. deceased was produced in open Court by John Fryer the executor and Rebecca

executrix therein named whereupon appeared Thomas Green William Fryer and Clabon Hill the attesting witness to said will. Who being duly s worn depose and say that they saw the said Charles Carter Senr. Sign, Seal, published and declare the same to be his last will and testament and that they subscribed their names as Witness there to in the presence and at the request of the Said Cahrles Carter Senr. and that he the said Charles was at the time af signing Sealing and publishing said will of Sound and disposing mind as they believe whereupon it is ordered that the same be Recorded. Given at office the 16th day of April A. D. 1830. Test J. AA Lane Clerk by N. Oldham D. C. of Said Court Recorded 21 June 1834 J. A. Lane Clerk By N. Oldham D. C.

P 146 Inventory of part of the estate of JOHN M SPERRY deceased returned up oath by Anthony Dibrell admr. at April Term 1834.
4 or 5 Bushels of Corn about 300lb pork 1 cow & calf 1 Bee stand one Bed 2 sheets 2 Blankets 1 Counterpaine 72 dos . Knives & forks 6 plates 1 Dish 1 Basin 1 pot one dutch oven 1 choping axe which property above I set apart under the Acct. of 1833 for the widow and child of Said John H. Sperry.

The fol owing property wqs sold on a credit of 12 months on the 12th Interest to the following persons for the following amounts Viz:

Sold to William Jugens one gun & Shot Bag	13.25	
Sold to Mchale Sperry one Looking glass	.50	
do one Bureau	12.00	
do 6 cups & saucers 5 spoons	.25	
do 1 Dish 6 plates 5 Knives & forks	.25	
do water pitcher & 3 Glass Tumblers	.50	
do 1 falling leaf Table	4.25	
do 1 Skillet	.50	
do 6 chairs	1.25	19.50
Sold to Alexr. B. Lane 1 Table 1.68 3/4 1 Grindstone .62½	2.31¼	
Sold to Berry Hamlet 1 Barrel Tubb & Axe	.62½	
Sold to William Huster 1 Bed & furniture & Bedstead	12.00	
Amounting to the Sum of	47.68 3/4	
Which is Secured by notes and Security unsold 1 Metal Clock Collected money from James Thomas	5.00	
do Abraham Broyles	3.75	

There are some accounts which I ingored accounting for, if they are not paid or can be collected the amount is Small Anthony Dibrell Admr.

Inventory of the Estate of WILLIAM S SONGSTRUL ded. returned upon oath by Woodson P White admr. at April term 1834. towit:

Cash on hand at the time of his death $20.31¼ balance due on his school article at the same time $103.75 but some of these debts cannot be collected also the following property three Volumes of the Children of the Abbey, Mitchell Travelers Guide through the United Steles, one pistol 1 Gold breast pin one Silver Watch one pen Knife, one umbrella one cloth Brush one tooth Brush one half pint Flask 2 pocket Books one
P 147 set of Thumb spring lancets One leather a small quanity of medium (?) & drals one trunk and wearing apparel. Given under my hand this 19th day of April 1834. Woodson P. White Admr. of William L. Longstrul ded.

Inventory & account of Sales of the Estate of THOMAS SPERRY decead. Returned upon oath by Alered B. Lane Exr. at April Term A. D. 1834. to wit:

Sold to Joseph Little one small Waggon & Gears for $81.00
Thomas Little 1 smoothing plain Jack Plain jointer &
fine plain at 3.00
1 pitch fork .37½
1 Box of Tools 3.31¼
James Carrick 1 Bridle 100 1 drawing knife .50 1.50
Ba rtlet B lcher 3 az 4 augers Scythe Box & small
articles 4.25
Richard Judson 1 pr. Saddle Ba gs 1 Spade 1.62½
James Allison 1 pr. Saddle Bags 1.06½
John Sperry 30 ps plank 3.00 1 pr Stetyards 3.00
1 Rife Gun 18$ 24.00
William Bruster 1 Steel trap 2.00
John Henry 1 Steel trap 2.00
Alexander Lowrey 1 cross cut saw 7.25 1 hand saw &
hand axe 2.12½ 9.37½
James Russel 1 Board Axe 2.00
Robert Anderson 1 Bridle 1.00
Jesse Davis 1 foot adze .75
Alexander Lowrey pr Swis 1.18 3/4
James Godwin 1 Tayaors board .75
SAlly Sperry 1 cow & calf 6.00
Thoma s Satterfield 1 man's Saddle 3.00
Alexander B. Lane 3 Barrels & 1 Box 1.50
Elijah Frost .56¼

One pr. Steelyards, one mouse trap one side of upper Leather, one piece of sole leather 1 Shend board one chopping axe Some B oom corn one Waggon bucket one Gun Lock one shaving Box One Razor & strap one horne & whitst-one 21 skeens of Sewing silk fine Sticks of twist some needles of various Sizes about Six yared of casenet in two pieces House hold furniture viz: One bureau one clock one looking Glass one Dining Table--One dressing table two beds & furniture two bedsteads one Lanthern One pr hand Irons shovel and tongs 4 chairs, coffee mill Ten eartheb plates, three Dishes candle snuffers, candle molds one ten pan five knives & five forks one Bread pan 6 Silver Tea spoons eight Saucers Seven Tea cups, one candle stick two cloth brushes, one cream pitcher 1 tin Tea pot one Strainer one Inkstand two glass Tumblers five glass bottles one Sugar chest, two Trunks
P 148 One Bible five other books two Barrels two ovens & lids two Skillet two crocks one Jug two Jars one pale one coffee pot one tin Bucket--hand bellows. One earthen pot one Basket one Bread Tray one Smoothing iron two tin cups one tea Kittle two bake pans one bench one crock one large Kittle one old coffee pot one old Pocket Book.

One note on Susan Rainey & W. C. Rainey due 25 Decr. 1833 for $200.
from information believed to be good 200.00
One note of same due 25th Decr. 1834 for $200. from information
believed to be good 200.00
One note on John Newman & Stephen Herbut for $125. in
good cash notes on solven men in White County due 21 November
1832 125.00
One note on the same same amount payable same way due
21 Nov. 1833 125.00

Receipt of Alexd. B. Lane for collection of a note on
Jno. Newman & Stephen Herbert due 21 Nov. 1829 due 2 years after date for
$125. in good cash notes on solvent men in White County Receipt dated
23 Nov. 1831 125.00
One note on Jacob A. Lane due 2nd Monday October 1833
for $15 put out for collection 15.00
One note on William R. Tucker for Sixteen Dollars due
13 August 1833 assigned to Thomas Sperry by Hohn Staples 16.00
One note on Richard Nelson for Ten Dollars due 27 February 1833
10.00
One note on John Barnhart for Twenty dollars due 25th Decr. 1833
his circumstances not known R 20.00
Receipt on James Irwin for the collection of a note for
ninety Dolars given in 1823, but the person who gave the note is
note named in the receipt dated 31 August 1833 90.00
One note on Jesse Bartlett payable to Hirams Peterson
for seven dollars due 24th July 1825 not transfered
doubtful 7.00
One note on Johnson Corbin & William Tankesly for
two ollars in good merchantable Seed Cotton delivered at
Sperry Gin due the last day of October 1828 bad 2.00
One note given by Gasper Bargar to George Long for $12.00
due 7th March 1821 and not transfered 12.00
One note on William Marlow for $750. in good Seed cotton
at the market to be delivered at Said Sperrys Gin due last
October 1828 credit by $1.75 16 March $2.00 August 25, 1829
Octob. 31 75 lb. seed cotton Nov. 18 1829 87 lb. Seed cotton supd. to be
bad.

P 149 One note on Joseph B. Glenn & Levi James for three dollars in good
cotton to be delivered at Sperry's Gin on the last of October 1828.
Credits by one dollars fifty cents also eight pounds seed cotton.
One note on Obias Green for two Dollars in good Seed Cotton at Market price
to be delivered at Sperrys Cotton Gin due last Oct. 1828 Credited by one
hundred pounds of Seed cotton Supposed to be bad. One order to Thomas
Sperry from Casington Harris for fifteen Dollars dated 10 Sept 1832. This
order on its face not directed to any person by name nor accepted by any-
one $15.00
One note on Treut C. Cornor for fifty dollars due 17 Sept 1833 put out for
collection 50.00
One claim on Jesse Lincoln for money paid him by Ebenezer Jones for
making a coat for J. W. Giff as I am informed 4.00
Rec. from Turner Lane Senr. what he said he owed
Thomas Sperry being revgually twenty this sum 20.75
Dock M. Fiske paid Sally Sperry the amount he was owing
Thamas Sperry ded. as appears from her receipt dated 9th
January 1834 3.00
Herman H. Mayborn paid on his note in full--for $2.50 due
20th Decr. 1833. As follows 18 January 1834 $1.50 3rd Feb. 1.00
Recd a N te on Samuel Driskel for $275 due 25 Decr. 1833
Ferruary 1834 2.75
Cash on hand at death of Said Sperry in Silver 62.56¼
Banknotes 20.00
Red. of William Simpson in Store on account of wood said to be owned by
John Staples Ten dollars twenty five cents which if too much I am to re-

pay said Simpson and I understand that the amount received is too much $10.25 The foregoing is believed to be correct. The article sold to Elij. Frost is not set down and it may be contained in the Inventory of an sold articles-- and these may be some other small articles in the same conditio but if mistakes can be discovered they will be correcter--I have charged myself with the money on hand as counted by Jesse Lincoln but on recounti by myself I made the sum one dollar less

Alexr. B. Lane Exr.

One receipt on P. N. Rempsey for the collection of notes amounting to $221 the receipt dated 10th Sept 1832 the balance due on this receipt except $10.00 is good from information Alex. B. Lane Exr.

P 150 report by commissioners of Assignement of prowisions to the widow & children of Edward Holmes deced. Teturned at April term 1834.

State of Tennessee)
White County) We the undersigned having been appointed and summone by the Sheriff to assign and lay off one years provision out of the estate of Edward Holmes ded. to his wife Nancy Holmes widow of said Edward Holmes deceased. We therefore have thought fit to report to your worshipful cour to allot and set apart out of Said Estate in the hands of the executors of said Edward Holmes deceased the sum of eighty dollars in money arising from the sale of the property of the deceased. Given under our hands & Seals this 10th day of April 1834. The word Eighty dollars was interlined be assigned. James Simpson (Seal)

Anthony Dibrell (Seal) Henry Lyda (Seal) James N. Nelson (Seal)
Fred Lyda (Seal)

In the name of God Amen! ISAMUEL USREY of the County of White being sick and weak in body but in perfect mind and Recollection knowing the uncertainty of human existance do make and ordain this my last will and Testament first my will is that my son "illiam Usrey have a sorrel filly three years old next spring and a man's Saddle now in the house to him forever.

2nd my Will is that my beloved Polly Usrey shall reside and hold possessio of the farm and Lands upon which I now live and keep possession of all of house and Kitchen furniture farming utensils and that she retain for her u a sufficient quantity of Sotck to support her and my four youngest childr for the purpose of raising and educating of my said youngest children which I will to her during her life or widowhood--

3rd My will is that as some of my children have heretofore received a part and portion of my property that they should receive no more until the others of my children shall be raised towit Robert Morgan Benson Samuel and William Usery have each received a portion of my estate towit About Sixty dollars each. That so soon as my youngest children shall arrive at the age of Twenty years Many that my executors hereinafter named shall pay to them the said sum in property of Sicty dollars so as to make all my children to receive equal portions of my property provided it can be done in the opinion of my executor without disfurnishing my said wife P 151 of the means of raising the balance of my said younger children agreeable to the intention here expressed. 4th my will is that should my wife marry again that shall have a childs part of all my property share and share alike and that all of the property which remains after satisfy the intention before expressed be devided amongst my children share alike and the like desposition after my children arrive at age or marry at the death of my wife. 5th I wish and will my two mares and young colt to

on the Farm with my wife and that my Executors sell such such overplus of my property as they may think necessary baning a sufficient to satisfy my intention herein expressed. My will is t at my Daughter Elizabeth arm have a bed and furniture now in my house which is her own property without deminishing her portion of my property.
6th My will is that the money arising out of the sale of such property is my executors to the payments of my just debts and what remains to be disposed of in supporting my wife and younger dhildren and in their education and t at the money be placed at lusful interest until such time as may be necessary to use. The same for Said purposes--
7th I will appoint my son Samuel Usreyand John Walker my executors to caryy into effect this my last will and testamony. In testamony Whereof I have hereinto set my hand this 6th day of April 1833.

Samuel Usrey (Seal)

Samuel Ursey
Daniel Clark
M. Fisher.

State of Tennessee }
White County } January Sessions A. D. 1834

This day was produced here in open court a writing purprting to be the last will and testament of Samuel Usrey deceased late of the County of White whereupon the due execution and publication was proven by the oathe of Madison Fike and Daniel Clark two of the subscribing witness therein mentioned. And that the said Samuel Usrey at the date and publication thereof was of sound and disposing mind and memeory whereupon it is ordered to be recorded. G9ven at office the 13 January A. D. 1834.

J. A. Lane Clerk
By N. Oldham D.C.

Recorded 1 July 1834 J. A. Lane Clerk by N. Oldhan D.C.

P 152 Inventory of the Est. of Samuel Usrey dcd. Returned by Ranson Gear admr. upon oath at July term A. D. 1834. 4 head of Horses Ten head of cattle about 40 head of Hogs 14 head of Sheep three beds, furniture and Steads 1 cupboard ½ doz. knives & forks ½ doz. cups & saucers 1 Doz. plates 1 Large dish 1 cross cut saw 1 hand Saw 1 3/4 auger 6 pewter 1 pewter dish 3 plows two pr Gears ½ doz coffee plates 1 scythe & cradle Three old axes 1 woman's 1 Loom 2 ovens 2 pots 1 old clock 1 waggon two yoke steers 2 piggens 1 churn 1 Grindstone 1 Chisel 1 pr fire Dogs 1 old chest 1 Table two bottles Ditto 2 Bibles 1 Hymen Book 1 Spinn ing wheel 2 Single trees 1 log Chain 1 Clevis 1 pr saddle Bags old 4 Salt Barrels 3 Slays 1 Ditto 2 pr. pot Hooks 1 Iron pot rack 1 coffee Boiler 2 tin pans 1 meal Barrel 4 old broken Hoes 1 pewter Basin ½ doz. spoons 1 Skillet 1 check rul 3 tin cups 1 pitcher 1 Iron wedge 1 Frow 1 Sprouting hoe 1 pr. cotton cards 1 set brass mounting for Bureau 1 account on M. W. Usrey for Sadlery of 8.98 3/4 cents 1 account on R. Gear for Bureau 1 pr Steelyards

Ransom Gear

Recorded 9 Jany 1835 J. A. Lane Clerk by N. Oldham D.C

Account of the sales of the property of the Estate of William Parker returned upon oath by Thomas Henry admr. at Oct. term 1834.

One mare	25.00
cow & yearling	12.00

4 head of Hogs	2.00
1 Set of Tools	6.00
1 Bed & furniture	2.00
1 pr Gears	2.00
1 Loom	5.00
3 ploughs	3.00
1 Man's Saddle	3.00
1 auger	.25
1 set shoe makers tools	2.00
2 axes	2.50
1 Frow	.50
2 Grindstones	3.00
1 Great Coat	13.00
1 Drawing Knife	.25
Thomas Henry Admr.	$83.50

Recorded 9 Janry 1835 J. A. Lane Cks.

P 153 Account of the Sales of the property of the Estate of Thomas Bounds decd. returned upon oath by Jesse A. Bounds adms. at July term A. 1834.

1 Rifle Gun to Margarett Bounds for	10.00
1 Table and Cupboard Furniture	4.25
3 Beds and two Bed Steads	10.00
1 Cotton & 1 Flax wheel & Reel	1.50
1 cupboard	3.25
20 first choice of Hogs	12.00
10 Hogs 5th cohice	2.00
13 Head of Cattle & 1 Bell	45.00
1 Yoke of Oxen	31.56¼
1 cow	6.25
1 Mare & colt	48.00
1 Scythe & cradle	2.00
1 horse	21.25
1 mare	15.25
1 Iron wedge	.37½
2 axes	1.12½
3 Bridles	1.56¼
3 Hoes	.50
1 Spade	.56¼
1 Frow	.25
1 pr. Steelyards	.62½
1 Grindstone	.62½
2 plows Swingletree & clevis do	1.00
3 pr. Gears	1.50
1 chisel	.12½
1 carry all	30.12½
1 Hatchel & Hammer	.25
25 head of Sheep	7.00
5 Bee Stands	5.00
1 Kettle 1 pot 1pan 1 shovel 1 Bake iron 2 pr pot hooks & 1 Pot rack do	2.00
3 coolers 3 pails 3 Jars 2 crocks 1 pan 1 churn 1 Bason	2.25
1 Gal measure 2 prs Shears & 1 coffee pot do	.25
1 Tin Trumpet	.25
1 Loom 7 Slays 1 set spools & frame	5.00

1 pr fire Dogs	.31¼
1 looking glass	1.00
1 clock and case	5.00
1 Tin trunk	.25
1 Bereau & book case	10.00
1 Side S ddle & Bridle	2.00
P 154 Account of Sales Brought over	
1 half Bushel measure & 1 Earthen pot Margarett Bounds	.12½
1 coffee mill	.25
2 cows $6	12.00
8 chairs & 1 Bedstead	.25
2 candle Sticks & 1 Reflector	.50
1 Bureau	8.00
1 cotton wheel to William Bonds	.31¼
1 Bee stand	1.37½
10 head of Hogs 4th choice	4.00
1 cow do	9.18 3/4
1 Bee stand David Nicholas	.50
10 head of Hogs 3rd choice	5.00
1 Log Chain do	3.62½
1 cooper's Adze do	.31¼
1 auger do	
150 feet cherry plank do	3.00
1 Bee Stand Samuel Madwell	2.81¼
1 Iron wedge	.25
15 head of hogs 2nd cohice Jesse A. Bounds	12.00
1 Doubletree and tongue do	5.00
1 Drawing Knife do	.75
1 axe do	.37½
1 auger do	.43 3/4
1 cutting knife & box do	.50
1 lantern do	.25
600 feet poplar plank do	3.00
1 whip	.12½
1 yoke of steers Elisha Cannon	19.50
1 cow & calf Thomas Stone	9.25
1 waggon do	70.25
1 cow & calf Albert H. Owens	10.75
1 cow Joseph Bartlett	8.50
1 cow James Korbet	7.06¼
1 Scythe & cradle William Bradford	2.37½
1 Log Chain Th mas Bohannon	2.31¼
1 Yearling Colt do	25.50
2 axes William Brown	1.56¼
1 Iron Square	.31¼
1 auger	.12½
1 axe James Judgens	.87½
2 Hoes do	.50
1 Hoe Hugh G. Huddleston	.25
1 Saw do	1.25
P 155 Account of Slaes brought up	
27 lb Iron to Jesse B. Clark	3.33
3 plain bitts & 4 Stocks Thomas Bradford	.68 3/4
3 chisels	.37½

1 cart John Moore 8.25
1 Brass clck do
1 Bee Stand Matilda England 1.00
19 3/4 lb of Iron do 2.17 3/4
Total amount $543.42 3/4

Jesse A. Bounds Recorded 10 Jany. 1835

Account of the Sales of the property of the estate of William Longstreat dcd. returned upon oath by Woodson P White Admr. at July term 1834

1 Silver Watch	3.00
1 Set of Thumb & spring Lancets & 1 Knife	.62½
3 Books (children of the Abbey)	.87½
1 map of Tennessee & Kentucky	.25
Mitchell Travellers guide through the United States /c	.62½
1 Fur Hat	2.00
1 pocket Pistol	3.50
1 Umbrella	.81¼
3 small pocket Books	.25
1 Tooth Brush Breast pin and watch Seal	.25
1 pr. Spectacles	.12½
1 cloth Brush	.06¼
1 Ca thiter and a few vials medicines	.25
2 waist Coats	2.50
weaving apparel	5.00
1 Trunk & some clothing	3.00
1 Razor strap, box and brush	.93 3/4
	$24.06¼

July 16, 1834 W. P. White Adr.
Recorded 10 January 1835 J. A. Lane Clerk by N. Oldham D. C.

P 156 Report of a Settlement made by commissioners with Alfred Merreth Admr. of the estate of Nathaniel Marlow decd. returned upon oath at Octob term A. D. 1834.

Pursuant to an order of the worshipful County Court for White County made at is July term 1834 Appointing us the undersigned commissioners to Settle with Alfred Merret and Marnel Marlow Admr. of the estate of Nathan Marlow dcd. we have proceeded to said Settlement and upon the production of proper vouchers. We find and report as follows.
That the property of said Marlow ded. sold by the administrators and boug by Alfred Merret and others as appears from a regularly certified copy of the sales made at April term 1828 amounted to $90.04. That said Alfred Merret the Admr. became indebted to the estate in the sum of Twenty dolls in cancelling a contract made between William Marlow and the dcd. in his life time in relation to a horse trade the Horse being unsound 20.00
That said merreth received of Joseph Herd a debt which he owed to said Nathaniel Marlow dcd.
Amounting to 10.00
$120.00

These two last Items are furnished by the Statement of Said Alfred Meret made before us.
We also find from a receipt of Hanil Marlow dated 20 Sept. 1834 that she had received from said Merrit in the year 1828 all the articles which she is and has applied to the support and benefit of the family of Said Nathaniel Marlow amounting to the sum of 80.553/4
That said Merrit on the 25 Sept. 1828 paid Madison Fisks account against

said Marlow as appears from the act. and receipt of Fiske amounting to 21.50
That said Merrit paid to John M. Little on the 7 April 1829 as appears from his receipt this sum 9.40
That said Merret paid to John Marlow his account which is s worh to in 1829 & in 1831 12.00
That said Merrett paid Joseph W. Little for tution of the children of said Nathaniel Marlow as appears from said Little receipts dated the 18 April 1834 this sum 6.00
That he paid to Jesse H. Vermillion for tuition as above at appears from a receipt dated 15 April 1834 this sum 8.00 137.50
17.46

We find & so report that from the shewing made before us said Alfred Merret has paid out and disbanded more of the estate than came to his hands and that not charging him with interest and crediting by the property delivered to the admr. Mariel Marlow P 157 that the estate owes him fourteen dollars 46 3/4 cents. That Mavel Marlow the Administrator received property of said estate to the amount of Eighty 55 3/4 cents.
Given under our hands this 13th day of October 1834.

Recorded 10 January 1835	William G. Sims	
Jacob A. Lane Clerk	Joseph Herd	coms.
By N. Oldham D. C.	Wm Glenn	

Account of the Sales property of the estate of Edward Holmes deceased return by Robert S. Mitchell one of the Admr.

Nancy Holmes to 6 chairs 118 3/4 one chest 361¼	4.80
" " 1 Bed & furniture 15.06¼ 1 Table 2.50	17.56¼
" " 1 Bed & furniture 12.06¼ Bed & furniture 8.37½	20.43 3/4
" " 1 side S ddle & Bridle 12.31¼ 1 coffee Mill 56¼	12.87½
" " 1 cupboard $31¼ 1 set cups & saucers.25	9.56¼
" " 5 bottles 156¼ 5 Bowles .50 1 set plates 1 Set tea plates on Search 1.56¼	3.62½
Thomas Demise 2 Tumblers	.18 3/4
Nancy Holmes 1 Salt celler 12½ 3 pitchers 1.06¼	1.18 3/4
" " 1 sugar Dish 31¼ 1 Tea pot 12½	.31¼
James Kelley 1 Tea pot	.12½
Nancy Holmes 1 Set Knives & forks 1 Loom 100	1.56¼
James Kelly 1 Dictionary	.25
Dabney C. Baker One Bible	.75
Nancy Holmes 1 spinning Wheel 1.06¼	
" " 1 check rul 56¼	1162½
" " 5 Jars.50 2 crocks 12½	.81¼
" " 1 pitchers 18 3/4	
" " 2 jugs 31¼ 1 axe 75 5 Hogs 6.56¼	7.62½
" " 5 hogs 231 ¼	2.31¼
Webster Hutchings 10 head of hogs 6.00 8 head hogs 8.00	14.00
Nancy Holmes 13 head Sheep 14.75 1 Bull tongue plow 62½	15.37½
Webster Hutchings 9 head of Hogs 5.00	5.00
Robert S. Mitchell 2 Heifer yearlings	7.00
Larkins Yates 1 young mare	21.00
John Young 1 mare	32.50
George W. Eastlane 1 Scythe & cradle	1.00
Nancy Holmes 1 Shovel plow 37½ 1 tubb 31¼	.68 3/4

Na ncy Holmes 1 pot & Skillet 1.37½ 1 pot 3.06¼ 4.43 3/4
Nancy Holmes 1 Bake oven 1.06¼ 1 pot 168 3/4 2.75
" " 1 pot & Skillet 1.37½
P 158 Account sales brought over
George W. Earthan 1 Cooper Kittle 2.12½
Larkin Yates 1 pr fire Dogs 2.81¼
William Baker 1 pr do 1.87½
Dabney Baker hames & chains .75
Nancy Holmes 1 singletree .31¼ 1 clevis . 25 .56¼
George W. Eastham 1 Mattock 1.25
Dabney Baker 1 Bee hive 1.75
Nancy Holmes 1 Singletree 31¼ 1 Shovel & trivel .50 .81¼
" " 3 Barrels 25 1 pail .62½ 1 pegging 12½ 1.00
" " cyphering book 6¼ 17 head of Geese 2.18 3/4 2.25
" " 1 Bee stand 1.18 3/4 1 Bridle 31¼ 1 do 31¼ 1.81½
" " 1 clock 10.12½ 1 Jug 37½ 1 Table 56½ 11.06½
William Lisk one blanket 1.00
Thomas Yates 1 Bell .85½
Robert S. Mitchell 1 Cow 7.75
Nancy Holmes 1 cow 7.06¼ 1 heifer 8.00 15.06¼
" " 1 Heifor 5.00 25 plank 2.31¼ 7.31¼
Robert S. Mitchell 2 steers 1850 1 ox yoke 1.00 19.50
Joyn Lisk 183 feet plank 1.25
William Lisk 1 sad Iron 1.00
Nancy Holmes 2 trays & Seines .50
Green B. Nolin 1 plow .37½
John Lisk 49 lb Dvid heals 7.00 1 Box 1.37½ 8.37½
Green Baker 1 cow Brute 3.00
Nancy Holmes for Rent of plantation for the year
1833 & 1834 20.00
Thomas Irwin one Book .75
321.59½

Nancy Holmes 1 pr hames & chains
Recorded 10 January 1835 J. A. Lane Clerk M. C. C.
By N. Oldham D. C.

Reports of John Walker Guardian to the Heirs of Kendal Lonage at January term A. D. 1835. January 12 1835. No alteration in the estate of my Wards since last return. John Walker Guardian
Recorded 23rd Jany. 1835. J. A. Lane Clerk by N. Oldham D. C.

P 159 Report of a settlement by commissioners with Edward Gleason admr. of the Estate of John W. Gleeson ded. returned at January term A. D. 1835.

Pursuant to an order of the Worshipful court of White County at July Session anno (?) Domim 1834 appointing. We undersigned commissioner to settle with Edward Gleeson administrator of John W. Gleason deceased Do hereby report that we have made the following settlement towit: Agreeable to the vouchers and papers herewith filed and numbered and clerk return.

Edward Gleeson Admr. of the estate of John W. Gleeson
dr. By the following Recipts & Vouchers No. 1 by
Obadah Harlow 11.50
No 2 Thomas Robertson 18.07½

No 3 By Thomas Robertson 16.27½
" 4 Caleb Mason .60
" 5 John McDonald 2.30
" 6 John Humphreys 1.00
" 7 Rice & Simpson 11.12½
" 8 Joseph Herd 5.60
" 9 Alvah Denton 1.93 3/4
" 10 Darius Clark 2.25
" 11 Milford Cary 3.46
" 12 Levi Jarvis 1.00
" 13 Indemon B. Moore 56.06½
" 14 Wemon Leftwich 33.75
" 15 Thomas Walling 2.57½
" 16 Indemon B. Moore 6.00
" 17 Isaac Taylor 3.52½
" 18 Alexander Glenn 2.72½
" 19 Thomas Robertson 41.56
" 20 Alexander Glenn 10.00
" 21 Isaac Taylor 73.36½
" 22 William B. Cummings 2.75
" 23 William Templeton 18.86
" 24 do do 7.00
" 25 Limas B. Farris 2.68½
" 26 Isaac Taylor 360.44
" 27 David S. Mitchell 113.62½
" 28 Oliver Swift 2.00
" 29 John Harlow 11.12½
" 30 Joseph Clark 15.45 3/4
" 31 Cornelus Jarvis 7.37½
" 32 Jesse Lincoln 20.22 3/4
P. 160 Amount of Debit brought over 1937.82½
No. 33 by Charles Hensley 2.00
" 34 William G. Sims 53.15 3/4
" 35 Barlor Gibbs .50
" 36 Ignatus Howard 8.66
" 37 William G. Sims 14.76½
" 38 do do 47.76½
" 39 Thomas Robertson 13.12½
" 40 William Carey 2.12½
" 41 John Jett 1.50
" 42 Joy Heeful 12.31 ¼
" 43 David L. Mitchell 19.08 ½
" 44 Alexander Gellings(note) 12.24
" 45 Limas B. Farris recept 9.13½
" 46 Jonathan Short 1.50
" 47 Edward Gleeson 29.04
" 48 Edward Gleeson Admr. 47.09½
" 49 John Staples a/c 4.18 3/4
" 50 Madison Fiske a/c 31.00
" 51 E. Blankenship recept 12.00
" 52 Joseph Littles recept 20.00
" 53 A receipt of J. A. Lane for fees paid by Edward Gleason Admr. filed with the papers of Edward Gleeson decd. 9.25

No 53 By Joseph W. Littles recept 132.00
" 54 Edward Gleeson a/c 200.00
" 55 Joseph W. Little & wife a/c 20.00
" This amount due the estate of Edward Gleeson deceased su our report on Settlement of that estate 105.85½ 174.16½

Balance in the hands of the administrator $193.63

Deduct the $1744.16½ the amount of credits as here allowed agreeable to all the vouchers and papers here filed and numbered from the sum of $1937.82½ and it will leave in the hands of the administrator the sum of $193.63 to be distrAbuted amongst the Legatus witness our hands and Seals this 15 January 1835.

John Jett (Seal)
David Snodgrass (Seal)
Joseph Cummings (Seal)

Recorded 23rd A. D. 1835 J. A. Lane clerk by N. Oldham D. C.

P 161 Report of a Settlement made by commissioners with Edward Gleeson Administrator Debonis-non of Edward Gleeson deceased. Returned at Januar term A. D. 1835 Pursuant to an order of the worshipful court of White Coun at July Sessions A. D. 1834 appointing we the undersigned commissioners t settle with Edward Gleeson administrator debonial-non of Edward Gleeson Snr. deceased do hereby report that we have made the following settlement towit: Agreeable to the vouchers & papers herein filed and numbered and Clerk return. John W. Gleeson Admr. of Edward Gleeson Senr. deceased as per return of his clerk of the sale of property 6713.66¼
John W. Gleeson Admr. to Isaac Taylor's receipt for a Land certificate 26 acres No. 2 50.00
Cr. By the following receipts & vouchers towit 6763.66¼

No 1	by Charles Manning	25.31¼
" 2	T. B. Rice	7.87½
" 3	John W. Gleeson Account	200.00
" 4	Isaac Taylor	783.55
" 5	by do for Eliza D. Gleeson	751.
" 6	do do do	55.06
" 7	George T. Gleeson	786.
" 8	James D. Gleeson	786.
" 9	William Gleeson	786.
" 10	Edward Gleeson	786.
" 11	David S. Mitchell tax recpt	2.98
" 12	Isaac Taylor	91.00
" 13	John W. Gleeson account	59.00
" 14	Isaac Taylor recept	6 25
" 15	Clerks fees paid by Edward Gleeson Admr.	9.00
	David Snodgrass commr. services	2.25
	Joseph Cummings do do	2.25
	John Jett do do	2.75
		$1601.01

Deducting the $5162.65¼ from the amount of the estate $6763.66¼ will leave in favor of the legates of the Sum of $1601.01 out of this last amount John W. Gleeson was entitled to his destretatived share which we find will be to each share the sum of $795.15½ deducting from that amount from the $ 1601.01 will leave a balance of $805.85½ we also find in the hands of the present administrator a note on John J. Smith for

$700 who marriedone of the Legates as a set off against the $805.35½ which will leave the sum of $105.85½ that after all the vouchers furnished P 162 us we find that the estate of of John W. Gleeson is indebted to the above mentioned estate the sum of $105.85½. Witness our hands and seals th this 15th January A. D. 1835.

John Jett Seal)
David Snodgrass (Seal) coms.
Joseph Cunningham (Seal)

Recorded 23 January 1835
J. A. Lane Clerk,
By N. Oldham D. C.

Report of a Settlement made by Commissioners with Jonathan Douglass the administrator of John H. Pistole deceased returned at January term A. D. 1835.

We the undersigned commissioners appointed by the worshipful court of pleas and Quarter Sessions of White County Court State of Tennessee at the January term holder at Sparta 1835 to Settle with Jonathon Douglas Admr. of Enoch Merphy dcd. who was administrator of John H. Pistole decd. Report as follows Towit:

To amount as pr exhibit No 1 by a certified copy from the Clerk of White County Court		$199.06½
To amount recepts to David S. Mitchell Sheriff of White County		344.55
		$543.61½
Contra		
By James Anderson for a coffin for I H. Pistole	5.00	
By Wilhite note 4	28.00	
By Levi Merrphys account 5	34.37½	
" Noah Philips account 6	2.37½	
" Fee paid Nelson & Anderson in a suit in Chancery at McMinnville Wherin James H. Pass was compdainant of John H. Pistole & others are Defendants	2.50	
" This Sum paid Stephen Pistole on a note to I. H. Pistole	6.00	
" Enoch Murphy account account for his services and expences in attending to & settling of said estate	31.00	107.25
		$436.36½
P163 To amount of interest for 9 months on day 436.36½ the balance due by Enoch Murphy decd to I. H. Pistole decd. Representatives		19.66½
		456.03

Agreeable to the above vouchers furnished to us we find report that the sum due by Enoch Murphy Admr. of John H. Pistole deceased is ($456.03) four hundred and fifty six dollars and three cents. Witness our hands and Seals this 14 January A. D. 1835.

Recorded23 January A. D. 1835
J. A. Lane Clerk
By N. Oldham D. C.

Thomas Eastland (Seal)
David Snodgrass (Seal)
Dan Griffith (Seal)

Report of a Settlement made by commissioners with John England admr. of the Estate of Elijah England deceased return at January term A. D. 1835.

We the undersigned being appointed by the County Court of White County at April Sessions 1834. to settle with Els y England Admrx and John England admr. of of Elijah England deceased met at the office of Anthony Dibrell in Sparta on the first Monday of May 1834 and proceed to examined said Settlement and find said administrators chargeable with the

following items:
1 note on Robert Johnson due Decr. 1828 30.00
Interest on the Same up to 1 May 1834 7.80 37.80
Cash on hand July 1828 100.00
Int on same to 1 May 1834 35.00 135.
1 note on J. Kerr & others things 18th July 1829 95.
Int. on Same to 1 May 1834 27.12½ 122.12
An account on W. England in trade 30.
To account of property purchased by Elmoy England admr. 30 Sept. 1828
on a credit of 12 mos. 240.00
Int. on the same from 30 Sept 1829 to 1 May 1834 66. 306.00
To amount of property sold to others as the same time on 12 mos. pay due
the 30 September 1829. 265.42½
Intrest on same to 1 May 1834 73.98 338.40
amount purchased by widow & assined to pay others 60.50
Interest on same to 1 May 1834 17.18 3/4
To amount of negro hire 1834 due on the 1 January 1835 241.25
$1288.26 3/4
On information administrator we find the administrators chargeable with
the above sum including Interest.
Cr By amount paid by John England one of the admrs.
paid Jacob A. Lane Clerk in 1828 No. $250. 250.
Int. on said payment 72.00 322.
Paid Charles McGivin for crying property 30 Sept. 1828 2.00
Int. on Same .62½ 2.62½

P 164 To amount brought over $1288.26 3/4
paid note Thomas Stone 25 Decr. 1829 No. 3 53.00
Int on the same to 1 May 1834 13.73 66.73
Paid to Charles Mannind Asser of Thomas Stone 53.34
Int. on Said payments to this time 10.26 63.55½
paid to Thomas Stone 28 April 1832 53.50
Interest on the same to this time 6.42 59.92
paid to Thomas Stone 2nd January 1833 55.00
Interest on the same to this time 4.39 59.39
Debt returned on Robert Johnson as bad
including interest 37.80
Paid to Jacob A. Lane as per recpt No. 7 .90
Paid Jesse Lincoln 7 April 1828 rect. No 8 4.31
Int on the same 1.55 5.86
Paid to Hedson & Anderson per rect. No 9 5.00
Int on the same 1.68 6.68
Paid to Elms As pr Receipt No. 10 5.00
Paid to N. G. Moore do No 11 2.50 314.23
Leaves a balance of 973.03 3/4
in the hands of the administrator.
There is now in the hands of Mrs England of the above aggreeable the sum
of 534.85 3/4
out of this sum the widow is entitled to her distribution share
amounting to 145.00
Leaves in her hands for the benefit of the children $389.85 3/4
There is now in the hands of John England admr. 439.18--the Sum of
$161.25 is included this sum (439.18) for hire of Negroes for 1834 not
due until January 1835.

Anthony Dibrell, David Snodgrass, Samuel Johnson Coms.
Recorded 23rd January A. D. 1835. J. A. Lane Clerk, by N. Oldham D.C.

Report of John Walker Guardian to the heirs of Alexander Kindle ded. returned at January term 1835.
January 12. 1835 no alteration in the estate of my wards since last years
Recorded 23 January 1835 John Walker J. A. Lane Clerk by N. Oldham D.C.

P 165 Report January term 1835 of Samuel Brown Guardian for the minor heirs of John Dyer deceased in part towit:
Robertson Alfred Claiborn Louisa and John Whister Dyer, begs leave to report and shew to the worshipful County Court that on the 13th January 1834 he and Sarah Dyer divided the notes owing to the estate of John Dyer deceased for whom they were administrator and other effects exclusive of the negroes that at t at time the share of his said wards taken together amounted to the sum of one thousand and fifty dollars. The above sum of 1050$ has been on interest up to the 1 January 1835 which principal & interest up to said time amounts $1143.42½
To one half the hire of all the negroes which are undivided for the year 1834 & due 1 January 1835. 50.76
One half of note on Ruben Robinson due 9 Aug. 1835 6.20
$ 1201.05
Crs. By Cash paid for Schooling all my wards equally 4 months 11.57½
Balance $1189.47½

The negroes an hired out for the present year and the hire will be due the 24th Decr. 1835 and the farm owned by said John Dyer was rented in the year 1834 and the rent has all been sold but as are account account cannot now be given of the amount for which it was sold, the corn not all being yet measured and it having been sold by the Barrel and on a credit till the 24th Decr. next said Guardian will not now render on account of it. The farm is rented for the present year for a third of the crop to be made. All the money of Said wards due or not in the hands of Said Guardian is a t interest. There is a small Sum of putting on interest for the benefit of Said wards. Samuel Brown
Recorded 23rd January 1835 J. A. Lane Clerk, by N. Oldham D.C.

Thomas Hill Guardian to the heirs of J. Hill deceased. Reports at January term A. D. 1835. The Amount 126.00
Thos. Hill Guardian.
Recorded 24 January 1835 J. A. Lane Clerk by N. Oldham D. C.

P 166 Wamon Leftwich Guardian to Malinda Rowland a Minor heir of John Rowland deceased returned upon oath Jany term 1835.
Begs leaves to report to the worshipful County Court for White County, that the sum of Six Hundred and eighty dollars 17½ cents which he formerly returned to this court belonging to his said ward was received by him on the 11th June 1833. And that at the same time he paid to John Rowland his former Guardian the Sum of one hundred dollars and thirty cents for necessaries furnished by him for said ward and took said Rowlands Receipts thereon of that date This item was through mistake omitted in his former report: 100.30

He paid William Usrey for necessary Wearing appearl furnished his said wards on the 22 Jany 1834 and took his receipt for the same 18.25
He furnished necessaries for his said ward from 1 January 1834 to the 1 January 1835 with Carrick Lefterwich lo of which due 1 January 1835 and their receipt is obtained amounting to 71.85½
He furnished said ward from the 1 to the 10th January 1835 and included it in the last mentioned receipt this sum 1.00
He himself furnished his said ward in the year ending 31 December 1834 with necessaries which he considered herein from the 1 January 1835 amounting to 11.00
This Sum amounting to $ $202.40½

Two hundred and two dollars forty and a half cents wherein added to the sum of one hundred and seven dollars three and a fourth cents ($309.43 3/4 which he said has xince his appointment, in all, paid out and furnished for said malinda Rowland for necessaries suitable to her condition in life all which he mosts respectfully submits.

Haman Leftwich Guardian

Recorded 24 January A. D. 1835. J. A. Lane Clk, by N. Oldham D.C.

John Fryer Guardian to Willaim Carter Legates of to Charles Carter Senr. deceased returned at January term 1835.

Begs leave to report to the worshipful County Court of White County that three little negroes which belong to said ward under said Charles Carter will towit: Malinda Matilda and Thomas have come to his hands and on the 3rd day Febrary & on the 7 February 1834 he hired out said negroes for one year for five dollars each their cloathing to be found by the herein amounting to $15.00 payable one year after date.

P 167 Up 15.00
In May 1834 he sold corn which he received as Rent for his Wards land in 1833 amounting to the sum of 37.77½
July 1834 he received Six bushels of wheat belonging to his said wards at 75 cents per Bushel 4.50
Charges of Services remand 57.27½
January Court 1834 to one days attendance in qualifying as Guardian fee 1.00
Fee paid clerk on said appointment .50
do & Febry 1834 2 days in receiving and hiring out negroes of said William Carter 2.00
Jny 1834 to cash paid for thrashing the wheat of sd ward .50
To Boarding the hand while thraching .25
May--to 2 days employed in Selling his wards corn $1. pr day 2.00
May 1834 to 1 day byself & 4 hands in jusking and measuring the corn of his said ward before stated 2.00
July To ½ days work of 4 hands boarding same & finding waggon and team in hauling oats belonging to said ward 2.00
July to cash paid J. A. Lane as fee for releasing suitier for Guardian and taking other securties .75
Amounting to the Sum of $ $11.00

The monies and means which are in his hands as the executor of Charles Carter deceased Senr. are not here reported as a settlement has not yet taken place. So as to show how much is coming to said ward and a suit

is pending against him in relation to the business. The rent received for said wards land for 1834 was in oats and wheat, and the oats are on hand ad and unsold at this time.
John Fryer Guardian
Recorded 24th January A. D. 1835 J. A. Lane Clk. by N. Oldham D.C.

Account of the Sales of the property of the Estate of William Parker ded. returned upon oath by Thomas Henry at January term A. D. 1835.

Thomas Welch to Hogs	5.00
James Jackson to one Bull	5.00
Alexander Bohanon to one Mare	33.50
Thomas Henry to one Saddle	3.25
James Bartlett to one Shovel	.56¼
Thomas Henry to One pot rack	2.00
Lewis Bohanon to 3 Shoes	.25
George Kinnard to Shoe makers tools	1.31½
P 168 Account of Sales continued	
Thomas Henry to chains plow & Hames	2.62½
Lewis Bohannon to Grind store tools	2.18
William Hudgens to Tools	2.68 3/4
Nathan Bartlett to Dishes	.81¼
Lewis Bohannon to Saddle Bags	.06¼
Alexander Bohannon to Slays	.25
John Kinnard to one axe	.62½
William Crodsey to one coat	8.50
athan Bartlett to one Hat	.50
Thomas Henry one bed	2.00
William Hudgens Shurn	.31¼
Harrison Whitson 1 oven	2.75
John Kinnard 1 pot	.50
John Kinnard 1 skillit	1.06¼
Thomas Henry 1 Wheal	2.03¼
John Kinnard poles & cray	.75
William Hudgens Horse Shoes	.18 3/4
James Yages 1 wheel	1.12½
Joseph England 1 R el	.75
John Kinnard Shears & pail	.50
John Kinnard 1 loom	4.37½
Nathan Bartlett waggon Boxes	.50
John Kinnard 1 skillet	1.75
Lewis Bohanon Apple Secoris	.12½

The estate is in debt to me for feeding of Wm. Parker ded. mare at one dollar per week for eight weeks 8.00
Seven days attnedance at one dollar per day 7.00
To money paid out 2.00
17.00

Thomas Henry Admr.
Recorded 24 January A. D. 1835 J. A. Lane Clerk by N. Oldham D. C.

P 169 Account of the Sales of part of the property of the estate of John Dale deced returned by David Dale one of the Admr. at January term A. D. 1835.
8 March 1834 Sold to William J. Malbery 2 watches 8.00

to 1 side Leather	2.56¼	10.56¼
Daniel Dale 1 side of Leather	3.00	
1 Goat Skin	.37½	
10 Bushels corn	4.10	&&7.47½
Russel T. Crane 1 Goat Skin	1.06¼	
Samuel Parker 1 do	.25	
Benjamin Mayes 10 Bushels corn	4.05	
Sold to Harmon H. Mayburn 25 do	10.00	
" James Dodson Senr. 20 do	8.20	
" Anderson Long 30 do	12.30	
" Leonard Reese 10 dO	4.10	
" John Mitchell 10 d0	4.05	
" Archbald Dodson 10 do	4.10	
" John White Senr. 10 do	8.00	
" John A. Dale 20 do	8.00	
" John Yates 25 do	10.00	
" Woodson P. White 20 do	8.00	
" William Baker 40 do	16.00	
" Jesse Dodson 25 do	10.00	
" Samuel Proter 20 do	8.00	
" Francis Hohnston 10 do	4.10	
" Irwin Carter 10 do	4.15	
20 October 1834 Thoma s Moore Millstones & mill Irons	30,00	
" Daniel Dale 40 acres 26 percher Land	10.00	
" Thomas Moore 2½ acres Land	2.50	
" Henry Rides & James Mallory 136 acres Land and one ferry boat mill stoves & Irons null saw and Irons some plank & some work to be done at the mill	526.00	
Amount	710.90	

Daniel Dale Admr.

Recorded 28th January A. D. 1835 J. A. Lane Clerk by N. Oldham D. C.

P 170 Account of the Sales of the property of the estate of Robert Howard deceased returned by Iguaterus Howard Admr. at January term A. D. 1835.

1 Set of waggon Irons sold to James H. Pass	30.00
1 Drawing Knife George Howard	.62½
1 do John Creason	.31¼
Scraps of Iron Jeremiah Wilhite	1.06¼
11 head of Hogs Geo Howard	17.25
2 Barrows William Howard	6.25
2 Sows Stephen Bedwell	3.25
48½ lb wool & Bag Mathew G. Moore	17. 83½
Lot of wool Nancy Howard	.50
Lot of Cotton Pleasant Mossa	1.18 3/4
1 Side Sole Leather Wiliam Hall	3.00
1 do John Griffith	2.87½
1 do William Matlock	3.87½
3 peices of Leather Nancy Howard	1.00
2 " Bruchor Davis Weaver	1.00

1 Drawing Knife, Robert Vanlibber .62½
3 Chessels Same 1.00
2 planes Gig Griffith 1.18 3/4
4 Augers William Mason 2.25
1 handsaw Robt. Vanlebber 2.81¼
1 X cut saw Ignatens Howard 4.75
1 Rifle Gun Clarborn Williams 15.25
1 do Harrison Whitson 15.43 3/4
2 Sing hoes Ignatens Howard .25
1 Bar Iron do .62½
1 Mattock William Hall 1.62½
1 axe Larkin Wisdom 3.00
1 Iron Wedge George Howard .75
1 Iron do George M. Glenn .43 3/4
2 axes & 3 hoes George Howard 1.56¼
1 axe Joseph England 1.87½
1 Steel trap & cutting Knife Isaac Howard 2.75
1 Barshare Plough Isham Farley 3.25
1 Plough William Howard 2.00
1 Jack Screw George Howard 4.31¼
1 cow & calf Nancy Howard 13.56¼
1 yoke of oxen William Howard 33.50
2 Steers Lewis Turner 31.12½
1 cow & calf Daniel Bartlett 8.06¼
1 Heifer George Howard 8.06¼
1 Steer Larkin Widow 6.25
P 171 1 Bay H rse sold to Jacob Anderson 56.00
1 Sorrel Horse George Howard 23.25
1 cow Larkin Widsow 6.81¼
9 Pigs Nancy Howard 1.50
1 cutting Knife John Rogers 2.00
1 Set of Black Smiths tools John Broyles Jr. 48.50
6 pewter plates George Howard 1.81¼
6 " " William Mason 2.31¼
4 pewter Basons & 6 pewter plates Nancy Howard 3.50
1 Set Table furniture Nancy Howard 1.50
3 jars do .50
2 Ovens 1 skillet 1 pot Kittle 2 pr pot hooks do 3.00
3 water vessels fo .50
1 kittle Davis Weaver 3.56¼
1 Loom & Harness Nancy Howard 4.00
1 Salt barrel 1 Tub 1 churn do .50
1 Kettle Iqvatons Howard 3.50
2 plows & 1 Swingletree Robert Howard 1.56¼
1 pr. Gears one plow & 1 false coutles
George Howard 3.06¼
1 " Hames & traces Elijah Cumson 1.18 3/4
1 Frow Daniel Bartlet 106¼
1 pr Steelyards Joseph Henry 1.00
1 " Gears Harrison Whitson 2.56¼
2 clevises & 4 Swingletrees Ignatens Howard 1.50
1 pr Gears & horse collar Henry Rutledge 2.31¼
1 " Gears Robert Howard 2.56¼

1 pr Traces Isaac Howard 1.50
1 Lot of Scraps of Iron George Howard .50
1 pr Truck Wheels & Log Chain Joshua Hickey 5.00
1 Looking Glass Isaac Howard 1.12½
1 Set shoe Makers tools Isaac Howard 3.00
1 " fire dogs Nancy Howard .50
1 Tin trunk George Howard 1.06¼
1 Razer & aHone Elisha Cannon 1.06¼
1 Table Robt. Vanlebber 1.62½
1 Jug 1 Canister, & 1 smoothing Nancy Howard .50
Buckles & needles Robert Howard .56¼
1 Bible Isaac Howard .75
1 Large Bible do 4.37½
1 Side Saddle Robert Vanlebber 10.00
1 do Isaac Howard 10.00
1 Pot Rack James Wilson 2.00
1 pr. Sheep Shears George Griffith .75
P 172 1 Mire Sifter sold to James Wilson .75
3 Bells George howard .37½
1 Round Shone Ignaleus Howard .25
1 Coffee Mill Nancy Howard .50
1 Cooper adze Thomas Bohanon .81¼
1 Blind Bridle Isaac Howard .56¼
1 Bridle George McGhee .43 3/4
2 Bridles Thomas Bohanon .50
1 Reel Robert Howard 1.12½
1 Wheel George Howard 1.25
1 half Bushel measure Thomas Snodgrass 18 3/4
1 Hackle Thomas Bohannon 1.50
1 Saddle Robert Howard 2.12½
1 Big Spinning wheel Richard Spears .62½
1 Tea Kettle John Griffith 1.62½
1 cotton Wheel Nancy Howard .25
1 Set fire Dogs Robert Howard 1.62½
1 Bull tongue plow John Rogers .81¼
1 Lanthorn Richard Spears .50
1 Bed & Stead & furniture Nancy Howard 4.00
1 Bed Sold do .50
1 Saw Set George Howard .18 3/4
4 chairs Robert Howard .57
1 chest Nancy Howard .25
1 Shovel do .25
4 head of Sheep do 2.00
1 Drawing Knife Iqvatons Howard .26
1 Grindstone do Senr. 1.69
1 Beading plane do Senr. .25
1 pr. compasses & board Adam Massa .12½
1 axe 1 shovel 1 scythe Joshua Hickey .30
1 warping mill Nancy Howard 006¼
1 Flax wheel William Howard .06¼
1 Tub & spools Nancy Howard .06¼
3 chairs do .18 3/4
Pottery 6¼ churn & tray do .12½
1 Lot of corn John McGhee 13.00

1 Lot Oats in the sheaf Robert H ward	3.00
52 Bushels corn Isaa c Howard 1.18 pbo	12.25
1 Lot Oats sold to John McGhee	3.40
1 " do Iqvqtens Howard	3.25
1 axe Isaac Howard	.40
1 Hoe Robert Howard	.25
1 Basket Geo. Howard	.37½
1 Hoe Ignatens Howard	.17
Irq Howard Admr.	542.32½

Recorded 24 Jany 1835 J. A. Lane ck. by N. Oldham D. C.

P 173 Report of Sarah Dyer and John Pennington Guardians to Nelson, Alpird Margarett and William Dyer minor heirs of John Dyer deceased returned upon oath at January term A. D. 1835.

Report that on the 13th day of January 1834. A Division took place between them and Samuel Bown, Guardian of past of the children of Said John Dyer of the notes then due or owing to the administrator of Said John Dyer deceased.

After Calculating the interest due on said notes up to that date and adding in four ninths of the hire of the negroes for the year 1834 being forty one dollars 25 centw which little Sum would be due 1 January 1835 the amount which fill to the wards was the sum of $ 881.25. This sum includes the following notes and amounts which have not been paid or received ,viz:

One note on Sarah Dyer to Samuel Brown Admr. of John Dyer ded. due 10 Sept 1832	$213.25	
Interest thereon upto 13 January 1834	17.16	230.41
One note on Sarah Dyer & John Pennington to Samuel Brown Admr. due 24 Sept. 1833	$401.00	401
One note on Sarah Dyer to Samuel Brown due 7 October 1832	22.31¼	
Interest thereon to 13 January 1834	2.00	24.31¼
One on Sarah Dyer George McGhee and Shadrock Price due 1 January 1835 for hire of negroes for 1834 payable to Saml. Brown		$660.72¼

The Balance of funds received by them on the division aforesaid and in their hands including lawful interest up to the 1st January 1835. Amounts to the Sum of 231$45

The negroes are hired for the present year the rent of the land for last year is not yet received and the land belonging to said John Deceased is rented for the present year for one third of the crop.

her
Sarah X Dyer
mark
John Pennington Guardian

Recorded 29 January A. D. 1835
J. A. Lane Clerk by N. Oldham D.C.

P 174 Samuel Brown Guardian to Robertson, Alfred, Claborn, John C. and Louss Dyer infant children of John Dyer deceased to Boarding clothing & educating Robertson Dyer three years and 3 months being up to the present time & all other expences $20.00

To Boarding clothing & educating Alfred dyer three years & 3 months up to the present time and all other expences 20.00

To Boarding clothing & Claiborn Dyer three years and 3 months being up to the present time & all other experices 60.00
To Boarding clothing and educating John Dyer, three years & 3 months being up to the precent time & all other expences65.00
To Boarding Clothing & educating Louisa Dyer three years and 3 months being up to the present time & all other expences 60.00
her $ 225.00
17 January 1835 J. A. Lane Clerk Sarah X Dyer
mark

State of Tennessee }
White County } January Sessions A. D. 1835

For reasons appearing to the satisfaction of the Court that Samuel Brown Guardian to Robertson Dyer, Claiborn, John C. Dyer Alfred Dyer and Louisa Dyer infant children of John Dyer deceased pay to Sarah Dyer widow of John Dyer Decd. the following Sums of Money out of the estate of his wards respectively Towit: Twenty dollars---out of the estate of Alfred Dyer Twenty dollars---out of the estate of Claiborn Dyer Seventy Dollars out of the estate of John C. Dyer Sixty five dollars---One of the estate of Louisa Dyer Sixty dollars agreeably to the account of Sarah Dyer Sworn to allowed by the Court in all amounting to the sum of Two hundred and twenty five dollars and that the receipt of said Sarah Dyer shall be a good voucher to him in a futend settlement of his accounts returned to said Guardianship. Given at office 17 January A. D. 1835

Jacob A. Lane Clerk
of White County Court

Recorded 29th January A. D. 1835 J. A. Lane Clerk by N. Oldham D. C.

P 175 The Estate of Nelson to Sarah Dyer her Guardian Drs.
To Boading clothing & educating him three years and three months being up to this time including all other expences. 17 Jany. 1838 35.00
The Estate of William Alexander Dyer to Sarah Dyer his Guardian Dr. To Boarding clothing & educating him three years &three months and all other expences up to the present time 17 Jany. 1835.
The Estate of Abira Dyer to Sarah Dyer her Guardian Dr. 60.00
To boarding & clothing her nd all other expences for 3 years & 3 month being up tp the present time 17 January 1835
65.00
The Estate of Margarett Dyer to Sarah Dyer her Guardian Dr.
To boarding & clothing her & all other expense for 3 years & 3 months being up to the present time 17 January 1835. 65.00
225.00

The above named Sarah Dyer most respectrully asks the worshipful court to make an allowance to her of the forgoing accouts to be paid her out of hte estate of the foregoing children respectively and to make an order on Samel Brown Guardian to part of said children to pay over to her the amount charged for the maintainance /c of his wards. The respected amount is low but the increase of their estates by interest on their money and heir of negroes & rents of Land will not justify a higher charge.
Sworn to in open Court Sarah X Dyer
17 Jnay 1835 J. A. Lane Clk. her mark

State of Tennessee }
White County } January Sessions A. D. 1835

For reasons appointing to the satisfaction of the court on the petition of Sarah Dyer one of the Guardian of Nelson Dyer, William Alexander Dyer, Abira Dyor and Margaratt Dyer that she be allowed out of the estate respectively agreeably to the accoutn the following sums Towit:
Out of the estate of Nelson Dyer thirty five dollars, out of the estate of William Alexander Dyer Sicty dollars--- Out of the estate of Abura Dyer sixty five dollars in all amounting to the sum of two hundred and twenty five dollars. Given at office 17 January A. D. 1835.

Test Jacob A. Lane Clerk of White County curt.

Recorded 29 January A. D. 1835. J. A. Lane Clerk by N. Oldham D. C.

P 176 In the name of God a men! I Aaron Cantrell of the County of White and State of Tennessee being Sick and weak in body but of perfect mind and recollection and being sensible of the uncertainity of human life do mk make and ordain this my last will and testament. First I will that at my death that god Almighty shall take charge as he will do of my Soul and that my earthly remains be deposited as is usual in my Christian country and as to my worldly Goods which Tod hath been pleased to bless my with for this short and transbiry life, I will as follows towit:
Item 1st I Will that my beloved wife Martha Cantrell shall have and enjoy in peaceable possession all my estate both real and persoanl during her natural life or widowhood. She is not to waste or dispose of said estate except for her own use.
Item 2 My will is that after the death or marriage of my Said wife Martha that all of my said estate shall be equally divided amonst my children to share and share alike.
Item 3rd I will that my just debts be paid out of such parts or portions of my property as my executor herein after named may think most expedinet to be sold for that purpose.
Item 4th My will is that in the distribution of my property assigned in the item 2nd of this my will and testament that those of my children who have heretofore received any portion of my property shall be charged with the same and after charging such property which they may have received form me into shich is turned Holch pot or putting all together then the division to be made so that no one child shall receive more than another including what they may have heretofore recieved in the distribution.
Item 5: I consider the negro girl Celah to be may property and not the property of any other person and she is included in this my will.
Item 6 My will is that my wife Martha and my son William Cantrell be executor and executrix of this my last will and that they do all things necessary to carry the true interest and meaning thereof into execution, this will make and executed in my own house on the 2nd day of October in the year of our Lord One thousand eight hundred and thirty four.

Test
Samuel Turney
Watson M. Cooke

Aaron X Cantrell (Seal)
his mark

State of Tennessee }
White County } October Sessions A. D. 1835
This day was produced in open Court a writing purporting to be the last will and Testament of Aaron Cantrell deceased late of White County

and the death of Said Cantrell. There upon suggested and proved and also came Samuel Turney and Watxon M. Cook and made with in due form of Law that they subscribed their names to said last will and testament of the P 177 Aaron Cantrell decd. in his lifetime by the request of the testator and in his presence. That he proclaimed and published the same as his last will and testament for the purpose and things thisin montioned and that the said Aaron Cantrell was at the date and publication thereof of sound and disposing mind and memory whereupon Martha Cantrell executor appointed in due form by the testator undertook and enterd into and upon the execution of said last will and testament of the deceased and in open court entered into and acknowledge bond with Samuel Turney and John Cantrell in the Sum of two Thousand dollars conditioned as the law requires and Said William Cantrell took the oath prescribed by las /c which is ordered to be recorded.
Given at office 15 Oct. A. D. 1834 J. A. Lane clerk by N. Oldham D. C.
Recorded 29th January A. D. 1835. J. A. Lane Clerk by N. Oldham D. C.

Account of William C. Bounds Admr. of the estate of John Terry Senr. deceased. against said Estate returned upon Oath at January term A. D. 1835.

1831 October 10	To 1 days	attendance & qualifying as admr.	1.00
" 14	" 1 "	making Inventory	1.00
" 17	1 "	returning same	1.00
" 20	1 "	Advertising Sale	1.00
Nov. 17	1 "	getting up the hogs	1.00
" 18	1 "	selling property	1.00
" "	1 "	Brandy furnished at Sale 3 Gals	1.50
1832 Jany 10	"	1 day returning list of Sales	1.00
		Paid fee for returning Sales	.62½
February		10 days absened in travelling to Fayetteville and back & finding horse attending to said estate	12.50
		Expences paid out on the trip	5.00
21 & 22		2 days attention to safety of said estate	2.00
		Expences paid out	1.00
		paid John B. Bounds for crying sale	1.00
		Paid J. A. Lane Clerks fee for granting admr.	1.00
		Paid Same for Inventory	.62½
Oct. 8		1 day on business of the estate	1.00
1833 Febry 9&11		2 days do	2.00
12		1 day to Sparta do	1.00
		6 days going and returning from Lincoln County Tenn and furnishing Horse $1.25 pr day	7.50
P 178		Amount of account brought over	
		To expences on the road paid	2.68 3/4
1833 Apl 1		To 1 day in going to Sparta to employ Swageeon business of the estate	1.00
22		To 1 dys in filing as adminstrator	1.00

1834	Sept 26	--1 day in preparing to take Disposing to defend the suit brought by I. D. Terry	1.00
Octr.	10	1 day in attending to obtain commission to take dispositions in said suit	1.00
	11	To four days of Self & horse to take disposition	5.00
		To expences paid out on the trip	1.12½
			$56.56¼

Amounting to the sum of which is above for services, traveling expences, fees paid the clerk of the County Court & cryer at the Sales & Brandy Willie C. Bounds Admr.
Sworn to in open court Admr. 17 Jany 1835 A. Lane Clk.
Recorded 30 January A. D. 1835. J. A. Lane Clerk by N. Oldham D. C.

I BENJAMIN HARRIS of the county of White and State of Tennessee being weak in body and on the decline but of sound mind and memory and being apprrisedof its being allotted to man once to die and being desires to dispose of my property as best suits me. Do make and ordain this my last will and testament revoking all former wills, in the manner following towit: It is my desire t at my wife continue on the tract of land upon which Lewis Jeffers now resides during her natural life and at my said wife's death, it is my desire that said Tract of Land be sold together with all the personal property which may be on hand at the time of her death and it is my will that so much of my personal estate be sold this fall as will be sufficient to pay my just debts or sooner if my wife desires and such property as she may Set apart for that purpose. And I give and bequeath unto my Son Amos Harris the tract of Land whereon my daughter Betsy Terry now lives containing by estimation about one hundred and fifteen acres all that part which lies above the Goolsby tract be the same more or less to him and his heirs forever. And it is my desirehat the tract of Land commonly called the Goolsby tract or Goolsby field tract and a 20 acres Survey adjourning said Goolsby tract or nearly so be sold at any time my wife may desire. And I further desire should my wife see property to do so before her death to cause to be sold the tract of land whereon P 179 Jeffers now lives and I give and bequeath unto my son Benjamin Harris two children, William & Benjamin Sixty dollars each--to Sterling Harris daughter Nancy An Sixty dollars --to Wooton Harris Seventy dollars and to his children Benjamin & William twenty five dollars each & give and bequeath to Betsy Harris the wife of William Harris one hundred dollars for the support and maintainance of her children by her husband William Harris I give and bequeath unto my daughter Lear Rutledge a debt on Silas Rutledge in a Judgment af about fifty dollars. I give and bequeath unto my son Amos one bed and furniture should there be any funds on hands at the death of my wife. I desire that she dispose of it as may best suit her after the Legaices before mentioned are complied with. I give Silas Harris nothing more having given to him his share of my estate. Neither do I give William Boles anything more it is my request that Should my wife marry again that she have of my estate a bed and furniture cloth /c and nothing more. I give to my Daughter Betsy Terry nothing more have given to her tract of Land this day by deed. I give to my Daughter Mary Ann nothing more. have given to her a tract of Land by deed this day. I give to William Nancy nothing more than I have already done. In testimony whereof I have hereunto set my hand & Seal the 25th day of April

1834. It is my request and desire that should there be any notes, bonds or leabilities in a ny way found in my papers or possession upon any of my papers or possession upon any of children that they be given up to them or destroyed and not collected from them except debt on William Boles I give to my daughter Betsey Terry fifty dollars to be paid at sometime when my wife may see proper. Benjamin X Harris (Seal)
Witness A. Dibrell
Jesse Stewart I nominate and appoint my wife Rutha Harris executort to this my last will and testament and Anthony Dibrell
Also Jess Stewart his
Wm. Garland Benjamin X Hariss
mark

State of Tennessee }
White County } October term A. D. 1834.

This day the death of Benjamin Harris deceased late of the County of White was suggested and proven and at the same time was proven a writing purposing to be to be the last will and testament of said Benjamin Harris deceased and the due excution thereof as such proven in open court by the oath of Anthony Dibrell and Jess Stewart subscribing witness there to who subscribed their names thereto as such at the request of the testator and in his presence at the date of the execution of said will who also made oath that the said Benjamin Harris was the date of the execution thereof of Sound and disposing mind and memory and that he published proclaimed and declared that the last will and testament for the purposes and things set forth and mentioned whereupon it is ordered to be recorded together with the proof of exectuion and publication.
Given at office 13 October 1834
J. A. Lane Clerk W.C.C. by N. Oldham D. C.
P 180
State of Tennessee }
White County } October Sessions A. D. 1834

This day was also produced in open Court on instrument and Deed in writing purposing to be a Codicil to the last will and testament of Benjamin Harris deceased late of the county of White and the due execution thereof was of sound and disposing mind and memory whereupon it is ordered that said codicil and the proof of its execution be recorded. Given at Office the 13th day of October A. D. 1831.
J. A. Lane Clerk W. C. C. by N. Oldham D. C.

State of Tennessee }
White County } October Sessions A. D. 1834

This day appeared in open court Anthony Dibrell who is appointed executor of the last will and testament of Benjamin Harris by a codicil st subjoined or annexed to said will made in writing by said Benjamin Harris deceased in his life time there upon dispent to the entering upon the execution of said last will and Testament of said Benjamin Harris, deceased and in open court renounced all rights to enter into and upon the execution of said will and testament whereupon it is ordered by the Court that said depart and renouncenation so made as aforesaid by the said Anthony Dibrell be recorded. Given at office 13th October A. D. 1834
Test. Jacob A. Lane Clerk White County Court.
Recorded 3rd February A. D. 1835. Test J. A. Lane Clerk by N. Oldham D. C.

P 181 Return of Joseph Cummings Guardian to Eli Dodson a minor heir of Eli Dodson Deceased upon oath at January term A. D. 1835. towit:
Amount in his hands belonging to his ward 38.52½
Interest on the same from the 14th July 1832 up to this time 5.93
Also one note on Daniel Dodson & Lydia Vest due 25 Decr. 1833 10.00
Also one note on Samuel & William Moore due 15 Sept. 1835 10.00
Recorded 17 February A. D. 1835. J. A. Lane Clerk
by H. Oldham D. C.

Inventory of the estate of James Rowland deceased returned upon oath by Wamon Leftwich Administrator at April term 1835. Towit: One mans saddle one bridle one pr Saddle bags one set of sadders Tools one negro boy slave for life Jackson aged about Ten years one negro boy slave for life named Harrisson aged about Twelve years one note executed by Edmondson& Smart due 1st January 1835 for $273.90 conditioned if not punctually paid them to pay Ten per cent. Good---One note on Leroy Bradley payable One note on Leroy Bradley payable to said Rowland due 1st June 1834 for $20 doubtful---One receipt on Samuel P. Howard constable for the collection of a note on Anderson Walkin for $40 due 15th Decr. 1832. Doubtful--One receipt on J. W. Rose Const. for collection of a note on Walker Wade for $600 with interest from 10th June 1833. Doubtful---One receipt of J. W. Rose Const. for the Collection of a note on George W. Scoggin for $30. due 25 Decr. 1833. Understood to be bad---One receipt of J. W. Rose Const. for one note on Samuel Olvis for $7.50 receipt is dated 23rd March 1833. Doubtful One receipt of James Scott constable for the collection of a note on James H. Jenkins for fifty dollars for fifty dollars due the 18th Febry 1834 with a credit thereon of $7. 18 3/4 leaves $42.81¼ cents good---A written acknowledgement of John Rowland that money belonging to James Rowland deceased amounting to $48.60 was in his possession.
Recorded 5 Oct. 1835. Wamon Leftwich Administrator

Report of John Mason Guardian to James Howard made upon oath at April term 1835.

That since he made a return of monies in his hands belonging to said ward he has received the additional sum one hundred and Twelve dollars 99 3/4 cents (112.99 3/4) belonging to said James Howard, which latter sum with the seventy dollars in the former return is on interest in safe hands John Mason
Recorded 5 Oct. 1835.

P 182 Report of settlement made by commissioners with Ignatius Howard admr. of Robert Howard dcd. upon oath at the April session A. D. 1835

In compliance with an order of the court of pleas and Quarter sessions at January term 1835. We the undersigned have proceeded to make the settlement with Ignatuis Howard admr. of Robert Howard deceased and find in the hands of a Amount of sales towit: $542.32½

Cr. By Receipts exhibited by admr.

No			
No	1	George Howard receipt	41.18 3/4
"	2	Isaac Howard do	37.02½
"	3	John Rogers do	18.06¼
"	4	Alexander B. Land do	5.00
"	5	David S. Mitchell do	6.47
"	6	same	7 .14½
"	7	same	7.90 3/4

No 8 Benjamin Wilhite do 5.25
" 9 George M. Ghiro do 1.50
" 10 David Snodgrass do 10.50
" 11 Robert Howard do 15.31½
" 12 John Mason do 2.00
" 13 Nancy Howard do 40.00
" 14 William Howard do 21.11
" 15 same do 41.81½
" 16 Jonathan C. Davis do 18.00
" 17 Enoch Golain do 12.00
" 18 John England do 8.00
19 Abraham M. Gille do 13.00
" 20 David S. Mitchell do 15.00
" 21 Madison Fisk do 6.00
" 22 Jacob A. Land do 2.90
Admr. a ccount allowed for settling the estate 15.00 347.62
194.70 3/4

Balance remaining in the hands of administrator amounting to the sum of one hundred and ninety four dollars seventy and three fourth cents-- The foregoing settlement we believe to be correct. So far as the matters have been brought to our aknowledge, all of which is respectfully submitte

David Snodgrass)
Recorded 5. Octr. 1835 William Hill)
Samuel Brown)(Cpms.

P 183 Report of Settlement made by commissioners with William Bounds Admr of the esta te of John Terry dcd. upon oath at April Sessions A. D. 1835. In compliance with an order of the court of pleas and Quarter sessions at the January term 1835 the undersigned Commissioners have proceeded to make the settlement with William Bounds admr. of John Terry decd.
Amt of Acct. Sales exhibited by The certificated of the Clerk Debit 234.12½
By ammunt paid out 119.55¼

CREDITS

No 1 A. B. Lane receipt 40.83⅓
" 2 same do 5.00
" 3 Jacob Lane do 1.00
" 4 John Crook do 4.25
" 5 David L. Mitchell do 2.75
" 6 Thomas Bounds do 7.12½
" 7 Saml . Brown do 2.27
" 8 Allowance made by court 56.56¼
119.58¼

We the commissioners find that amount of $114.54 cents yet in the hands of the Administratiors agreeable to the papers examined by us.
Given under our hands and seals this 13th of April 1835.

Recorded 5 October. David Snodgrass)
Isaac Buck)
Thomas Barnes) coms

Report of settlement made by commissioners with George W. & William Duncan Admrs. of Thomas Duncan dcd. upon oath at April term 1835.

We the undersigned commissioners appointed by the county court of White County at January Court 1835, to settle with George W. Duncan and William Duncan administrators of Thomas Duncan deceased makes the followi report of their settlement Towit: We find administrators charged with the following sums towit:

To amount as contained in first Inventory		289.85½
" " " " " 2nd return notes		131.38 3/4
		421.24¼
Credit for the following sums paid out		
No. 1 Paid William Marlow	20.00	
" 2 " J. C. Davis	3.87½	
" 3 " James Young	2.75	
" 4 John Walker	28.00	
Interest on the same	4.68	
" 5 JAmes Cooper	1.00	
" 6 Mitchell Sheriff	3.50	
" 7 Osburn Walker	18.02	
" 8 Mitchell Shff	10.00	
" 9 Os. Walker	2.12½	
" 10 James Anderson	1.62½	
" School Commissioners	110.00	
Amount over		421.24¼
" 11 William G. Sims PS	2.20	
" 12 A. Glenn	13.40	
" 13 Madison Sisk	10.00	
" 14 William G. Sims	2.93 3/4	
" 15 same	2.86½	
" 16 David L. Mitchell Shff.	15.00	
	247.95 3/4	
Bad note retd. towit Note on Jas Telford	6.25	
Note on Peter Howard	2.75	
" John Adkins	12.25	
" Joseph Hillard	9.25	
		30.50
No 17 Paid to J. A. Lane Clerk	3.30	
" 18 Paid to John Allen	5.71	
Allowande to William Duncan Active adms	25.00	312.46 3/1
		108.77½

Leaves in the hands of the Administrators the sum of one hundred & eight dollars 77 3/4 cents. this 13th April 1835.

A. Dibrell
John Walker

Recorded 5th Oct. 1835.

Inventory of the Estate of Dempsy Fenn Deceased returned upon oath by John White Admr. at April term A. D. 1835.
Towit: 1 Sorrel Mare 1 yoke of oxen 3 cows 1 calf 2 small Steers 1 Small heifer 16 head of Stock Hoggs 3 feather beds & furniture 1 Side Seddle 1 flax wheel, 1 bit Wheel, 1 pr Cotton Cards, 2 pots 1 Skillet, 2 pot hooks 1 fire shovel, 3 small boxes, 3 plows, 1 pr Gears, 2 briddles, 2 broad hoes 3 falling axes, 1 Tomahawks, L iron wedge, 3 Gallon Jugs, 1 coffee mill. 1 Looking glass, 2 earthen Dishes, 2 bowls, 1 set spoons, 5 Salt Barrels, 2 washing Tub 3 Pails, 2 piggings 1 Table, 1 set Knives & forks, 1 Mason trowels 1 pr Truck wheels 8 Chairs 1 Smoothing Iron, 1 Bible 1 arithmetic

2 Spillingbooks 1 English grammar 2 Hammers, 1 Howell 1 pr. pincess 2 jars, 4 crocks, 1 Razor box & brush some bar iron, 1 Debt on Cantrell Scruggs a/c 1.00 considered doubtful 1 debt on James W. Copeland for $0.62½. 1 note on Charles Crain for $2.00 doubtful 1 a/c on James Miller 0.75 1 Debt on John Payne doubtful amount unknown say $50.00 1 note on R. & R. Ross Desperate due 18 febry 1829. $37.00 1 Do. due 3rd Nov 1820 desperate, $150. I do 25 Oct. 1827 desperate 37$.
1 do 25 June 1827 desperate 100$ Cash on hand $788.70 1 Recpt. J. W. Kindrick for Ten dollars to charge 1 note on St. Holland due 30 Aug 1834. $2.94 1 Jury Tecket for 3 dys service at January term 1834 $1.50
Recorded 5th October 1835. John Witt Administrator

Report of a settlement made by commissioners with Robert Cook admr. and Sally Cook adm. of Elijah Sawyer deceased retd. at April term 1835.

Pursuant to an order of court a copy of which is hereto annexed we the undersigned having met at the house of Robert Cook Esq. on the 27th day of February 1835. have once proceeded to make the settlement therein named and find the accouts to stand as follows:

Amount of Sale in White County as pr Inventory shown	301.72½
" " money recd. for land in N. Carolina being Debt & Int	553.49½
	855.49½

The foregoing is the amt. received by Sally Cook Administratrix of Elijah Sawyer deceased and Robert Cook administrator in right of said Sally. ~~he having intermarried~~ with her.

The following were allowed as having been paid by them out of the estate of Elijah Sawyer deceased.

Henry Burton dated 26th March 1825	1.00
Jacob A. Lane dated 14 April 1828	5.42½
Same 11 " 1831	1.25
Same 18 1829	.62½
Same 20 1832	.62½
Jesse H. Vermillion 7 Jany 1831	4.00
Thomas Williams 28 Jany 1833	4.50
Joseph W. Little 3 Apl. 1832	4.31½
Joseph Upchurch 1 Apl 1828	1.00
William Watts 16 Febry 1828	1.00
Isaac Glenn 19 May 1826	1.00
Madison Fish 10 October 1824	10.00
Jesse H. Vermillion 7 Jany 1830	6.00
Same 10 Decr. 1828	6.00
William Watts 18 Aug. 1826	9.00
William C. Stone 25 Oct. 1826	4.00
John W. Goff 29 June 1830	3.50
Jesse H. Vermillion 1 April 1829	4.00
Zachariah Jones 23 Septr 1824.	3.00
By allowance for expenditures & time lost in collecting /c on said estate	195.00
	267.23 3/4

From the foregoing settlement it appears they recd. and are changeable with the that sum	855.49½
And that they have disbursed including allowances /c the sum of	267.23 3/4

It will be marked that no account has been here taken of payments to heirs as we did not conceive that a matter for our consideration.

David L. Mitchell
William G. Sims

Recorded 5 Oct. 1835

P 186 Report of Settlement by commissioners with Richd. Judson Admr. of the Estate of William Kitchen dcd. upon oath at April term 1835.

Towit: The first return	23.50
Second return	12.18 3/4
3rd com sold and not returned	5.28
13 Bushels corn owing by Admr.	3.37½
Sold Oats	3.00
Sold corn	0.37½
Rent of Farm for 1834	6.31¼
	59.01
Settlement made 16 Jany 1833	51.50
paid Nathan Haggard	10.00
paid Debt & cost to Mitchell	7.00
paid M. A. Long	10.00
paid William Kerr	.50
paid J. A. Lane	.50
Debts rcd. by Admins.	59.01
	20.29

For which the administrator is entitle to a credit of twenty dollars and twenty nine cents for money advanced by him to Said estate this date.

Recorded 5 Oct. 1835

Charles McGuire
Jonathan T Bradley
Montgomery Dibrell

Account of the Sales of the estate of Dempsey Penn dcd. returned upon oath by John Witt Admr. at April Session A. D. 1835.

James Anderson to 1 cotton receipt 250 lb. c 237½		5.93 3/4
Thomas Adair 2 Fodder Stacks		2.50
William S. Adams 1 Heifer yearling		3.44
John M Carter 1 Steer yearling		4.31¼
Allford carry 2 work Steers, yoke & truck waggin		48.39
Simion R. Doyle to Hogs	.87½	31.62½
Thomas Green 1 Frow 87½ 1 box & tools 1.00 1 hoe 18 3/4 ½ bus. measure 51.	1.69 3/4	2.57½
moses Goddard 1 cow & calf		11.50
George D. Howard 1 Steer yearling		3.75
Halterman John Iron	.64	
158 Bushels corn c 90¢ p b	28.44	29.08
Stephen Holland 1 axe	.75	
1 wedge 62½ 1 plow 150	2.12½	2.87½
Barley Holder 2 hoes 75 1 cotton wheel 188 3/4		2.63 3/4
Henry Keithley 1 sow & pigs	3.25	
Iron 77 1 hoe $100 1 pai 31¼	2.08	5.33¼
James Miller 1 Basket		.51
Lewis Philips 1 plow		2.28
Ranson B. Pinn to 2 Stacks fodder	2.25	
1 Stack oats 193 1 mare 45.00 1 axe 1.25 1 Jug ~~$ss3/Witt~~, 1 wedge lare 1.00 1 Set Gear $3.	49.41 3/4	51.66 3/4
1 Keg 13¢ 1 box tools 87½	5.00½	
1 tub	.25	5.93½

P 187 Jane Pinn To 2 cows 12.62½ 1 churn 26 122.88½
2 Tubs & 1 churn $1.00 1 Check rul .50 1.50
1 Skillet & lid 1.13½ 1 oven 1.00 2.13½
1 pot 1.00 1 Flax Wheel 3$ 4.00
3 Beds & furniture 6$ 8 chairs 2.00 8.00
1 Table 25 3 pails 25 .50
pails po 1.00 1 woman's Saddle $4 5.00
1 Side iron 12½ 1 shovel 12½ .25
1 cupboard /c 100. 1 box 50 1.50
1 Looking glass 6¼ .06¼ 35.83½
Sampson Witt 3 stacks fodder 4.18 3/4 4.18 3/4
1 axe & Howell 87½ 1 plow .50 1.37½ 5.56¼
A. W. Miller 1 Bushel potatoes .50 .50
John Holder 3 Bus do 1.50
Duhman Holder 1 do .50
John Holterman 2 do 1.00
John L. Grissom 1 Bus. do .50
The full amount 255.72
Recorded 7th Oct. 1835 John Witt Administrator

Report of Moses Goddard Guardian to the heirs of John Smallman decd. states that he has in his hands at this time three hundred and fort three in notes this 13 April 1835. Moses Goddard Guardian
Recorded 1 Oct 1835.

Report of commissioners appointed apart du allowance of provisior for one year to the widow of Dempsy Pinn dcd.

We the undersigned having been appointed by the worshipful County Court of White County to Set apart and assign one year provision for the support of Jane Penn Widow of Dempsy Pinn deceased. And her family after being duly summoned and Sworn by David S. Mitchell Sheriff. have met on the premises this day and Set apart out of the provision now on hand one hundred and fifty bushels of corn all the bacon on hand supposed to be fine hundred pounds and all the Land and soap five Bushels wheat one hundred pounds Seed Cotton and one bushel Salt. Witness our hands and seals this 14 day of February 1835.

Recorded 7 Oct. 1835

David L Mitchell (Seal)
Robert Anderson (Seal)
Joseph Cummings (Seal)

P 188 Report of a settlement made by commissioners with Woodson P. White Admr. of the estate of W. S. Longstrat at July term 1835.

Pursuant to an order of the worshipful Court White County at their April Sessions 1835 appointing us the undersigned Commissioners to Settle with Woodson P White Administratior of William S. Longstrat late said County and after examining the accounts of the said decd. we thereupon report and say--

That the amount of Sales of the property of the deceased together with amount of Debts due upon a School Article /c which came to the hands of the admr. amounted to in all 148.12½
That the said Admr. rendered his account against the estate as follows--for 2 Debts in the school article insolvent 18.75
for balance on Book acct. 5.10½
For 10 months board attendance in sickness charge for

a dministration and other contengent expences 90.00
To proven act of Carrick Lefterwich /c 10.00
To Proven act of Jenkins & Simpson 5.25
To oct. Bill William E. Throckmorton 20.00
Paid Jacob A. Lane Clerk 4.00 153.12½
5.00

Given under our hands and seals this 13 day of July A. D. 1835.
John Bryan (Seal)
Jesse Scoggin (Seal)
Recorded 7 Oct. 1835. Turner Lane Senr. (Seal)

Account of Sales of the Estate of James Rowland ded. returned by Wamin Leftwich Admr. at July term 1835.

Towit	One negro boy Harrison sold to Wm. cox for	552.00
	One do Jackson Wm. Cox	444.00
	One bay horse sold to Joshua Hickey	55.25
	One man's saddlers tools sold to S. V. Carrick	6.00
	One man's saddle sold to Hugh Gracy	19.00½

The above articles sold on credit of 12 months sold at same time for ready money Viz 1.50
1 pr. saddles Bags to Rhodum Hoyle another time at private Sale to be due 13 May 1836 1 feather bed & furniture not mentioned to R. Rowland 20.00
1107.81¼

Amounting in all to the Sum of One thousand one hundred and seven dollars eighty one and a fourth cents. 13 May 1835.
Recorded 7 October 1835 Waman Leftwich Admr.

P 180 Report of a settlement made by Commissioners with Woodson P. White Executor of John White ded and as administratior of Joshua Porter ded returned at July Sessions A. D. 1835.

Report and say that the proceeds of the sales of said estate together with the debts due to the said estate, rents of the further /c amounting in all to the sum of 828.81¼
That the sum of money due form the estate which have been disbursed and paid by the said admr. for which he produced proper vouchers toghether with an allowance of $ 50. which we have made to him for his trouble costs amounts to the sum of 222.91¼
Leaving a balance in his hand of 605.90
There in said estate nine Devises each being entitled to the sum of 67.32¼
Given under our hands and seals at Sparta this 13th day of July A. D.1835.
Recorded 7th October 1835. John Bryan (Seal)
Jesse Scoggin (Seal)
Truner Lane Senr. (Seal)

In the name of God Amen. I Jeremiah Denton of the State of Tennessee, and County of White, biong sick but of sound mind and memory I do hereby make this my last will and Testament. First I command my body to the dust. to be buried with a decent Christian burial and my Soul to God who gave it and touching my worldly estate, wherewith it has pleased God to bless me with. I bequeath and in the following manner give. 1st.—I give to my beloved wife, Sarah the one fifth part of the value of two hundred acres of land whereon I now live. Also my Sorrel mare, Saddle and bridle, also one father bed and furniture, during her natural life. 2nd--It is my will, that my four ons, Oscar, Isac, John and William have the balance of Said two hundred acres, tract of land. to be equally divided between them. 3rd-- I give unto my daughter Ann Gettings one dollar 4th--I give unto my four daughters Louichy Mc aniel, Mahala Wright, Sarah Rogers, and Goldy Couch and my five Grand Children, Clark Gettings, Jeremi Gettings, John Gettings, Martian Gettings and Oscar Gettings all of my personal property to be equally divided, So that my five grand children ge one equal Shear with one of my daughters, to be paid over to them by my executor, when they come, to the age of twenty one years-- I also give to my above named daughters, Louicy McDaniel, Mabal Wright, Sarah Rogers and Goldif Conds, and my five grand children one tract of land containgn 60½ acres lying in White County Tennessee, in the corne of gum Spring Mountain to be divided in the same proportion as my personal propecty. I wish my executor to pay my debts out of the property that I have give to my above named children and grand children. I wish him to Sell all of the above named property and land according to law--

P 190 Lastly I appoint my beloved Son Osiah Denton, my executor to this last will and testament, and I hereby disannual and disallow and revoke all former wills or wills, executors or executors . In Testamony whereof I have here unto set my hand and Seal this 8 day of August 1835.

Jeremiah Denton Senr. (Seal)

Signed Sealed and acknowledge in presents Joseph Herd Isaac Denton.

State of Tennessee }
White County } October Session A. D. 1835.

This day the death of Jeremah Denton, late of the county of White was suggested whereupon was provided in open Court. the last will and testament of the Said Jeremiah Denton Deceased, by Oscar Denton who is appointed Sole executor of said will by the deceased. And now the due executor and publication thereof was proven in open court by the oath of Joseph Herd and Isaac Denton subscribing witnesses thereto as the last will and testament of the Said Jeremiah Denton Decd. and that Said testator was at the date of the execution of Said Will of Sound and disposing mind and memory--Whereupon the court being of opinion that Said will was duly properly and well proven, to be the last will and testament of the Said Jeremiah Denton deceased. it isordered to be recorded whereupon in like manner came the Said Osiar Denton into open Court who is named and appointed Sole Executor of the last will and testament of the said Jeremia Denton Deceased, and took the oath prescribed by law, and together with John Fryer and Lewis Petit entered unto and acknowledged loud in the sam of three thousand dollars conditioned as the law requires.

Given at office 19th October A. D. 1835. Test-Jacob A. Lane Clekrk of White County Court.

Recorded 28th October A. D. 1835. Test-Jacob A. Lane Clork of White Coun Court.

State of Tennessee }
White County } May the 25th day in the year of our Lord 1835.

In the name of God Amen, I Joseph Henry of the county and State aforesaid being sick and weak of body, but of Sound mind and disposing memory for which I thank God and calling to mind the uncertainty of human life and being deserous to dispose of such worldly substance as it hath pleased God to bless me with. I give and bequeath the same in Manner following that is to say I give and bequeath to Lucinda Henry all my right, titles, Claims and interest of my goods, lands and tenenants during her widowhood to have and to rule over, and if the Lucinda Henry marries the substance to be sold and equally divided amongst my heirs and the Said Lucenda Henry to draw a childs part. In witness whereunto I have set my hand and Seal this the day and date above mentioned. igned, Sealed, published and declared to be the last will and testimony of the above named Joseph Henry P 191 in presence of an who at his request and in his presence have hereunto subscribed our names as Witness to tho Same attest.

Wm. Bartlett his
Thos. Barnes. John X Henry (Seal)
mark

State of Tennessee
White County October Session A. D. 1835.
This day was produced in open court the within writing purposing to be the last will and testament of Joseph Henry Deceased, late of the County of White and the due executor and publication thereof as the last will and testametn of the Said Joseph Henry Deceased proven in open Court by the oath of Thomas Barnes one of the Subscribing witnesses thereto for the pupposes and things thereon mentioned and that the said Joseph Henry was at the date of the execution and publication thereof of Sound and disposing mine and memory which is order to be so certified.
Given at office 12 Oxtober A. D. 1835.
Test Jacob A. Lane Clerk of White County Court.

State of Tennessee
White County July Term A. D. 1836.
This day was praduced open court the within writing purposing to be the last will and testament of Joseph Henry deceas ed late of the county of White and the due execution and publication thereof was proven in open court by the oath of William Bartlett, one other witness thereto for the purpose and things therein mentioned And that the said Joseph Henry was at the date of the execution and publication thereof of sound and disposing mind and memory which having been heretofore in like manner proven by the oath of Thomas Barnes the other subscribing witness thereto for the same purpose it is ordered to be recorded.
Given at office 4th July A. D. 1836 Test. N. Oldham Clerk of White County Court
Recorded 7th July A. D. 1836--Test. N. Oldham Clk.

In name of God Amen I JOSEPH HASTON of the County of White and State of Tennessee, being weak of bodym but of Sound mind and disposing memory for which I thank God and calling to mind the uncertainty of human life, and being desirous to dispose of all such worldly substance as it hath pleased God to bless me with after resigning my Soul to god, and my body to be buried. I do give and bequeath to my belooed wife Sarah all my worldly Substance with real and personal to make use of as She thinks proper for the use of the family and the raising of my small children. So lona as she may remain a widow and if She Should marry my will and desire is that after my wife taking one third part of all my estate the balance to be equally divided amongst my children to be enjoyed by them and their heirs forever, hereby revoking all other wills, testaments by me heretofore made. I witness of I have here unto Set my hand and Seal this 23 rd July 1827. Joseph Haston (Seal) Signed Sealed, published and delivered to be my last will and Testament in the present of William Dwery, John S. Parker, Isham Bradley

State of Tennessee }
White County } October SEssions A. D. 1835.
P 192 This day was produced in open court he within writing purposing to be the last will and testament of Joseph Haston Deceased, late of the County of White, and the due execution and publication thereof proven in open Court by the oaths of William Dwey and John S. Parker two of the Subscribing witnesses thereto for the purposes and things therein mentioned and that the said Joseph Haston was at the date of the execution and publication thereof of Sound and disposing ming and memory and that Said will is the last will and testament of the Said Joseph Haston Deceas ed which is ordered to be recorded. Given at office 12th October A. d. 1835.
Test- Jacob A. Lane Clerk of White County Court.
Recorded and examined 26th October A. D. 1835-Test Jacob A. Lane Clerk of White County Court.

Account of John Fryer-one of the Executors of Charles Carter Decd. returned on oath at October Sessions of White County Court in the year 18
Estate of Charles Carter Decd.
To John Fryer Executor Dr. 1834 Sept. 22.
To one day preparing notices in Suit Jacob 7 Rebecca Stipe against SAid Fryer as Exr. & Guardian /c in circuit Court 1.50
Octr. 22 & 23 1834 to 2 days in taking depositions in same suit 3.50
Novr. 1834 To 4 days attending court on the same suit 6.00
January 1835 To 4 days in attending to collecting of monies due the estate of Said Carter Decd. in Jackson County & praying his own expences 8 00
February11 one day attending to notifying the complaneants of the time and place of taking depositions in the before named suit1.50
March 16 To 1 days attendance on taking Report in said suit with Stype and wife 1.50
April 18 to 1 day attnedance on said Suit before the clerk 1.50
May 16 to 1 day attendance on Said Suit befor the clerk by his appointment 1.50
May 27th & 28th & 29th 1835. 3 days attendance on the same suit 4.50
To three days attendance to the business of the estate and traveling to and form Jackson County. Vis: 15th, 16th & 17th Sept. 1835 and bearing his own expences 6.00
Sept 21st. 1835. To 1 day any assed in selling business of the estate With A. Dibrell Clerk of the Circuit Court. 1.50
1834 Two days making & perfecting due to M. Hogan for land in Jackson County 3.00
Jany 18. monye paid Comrs. for estate of sd. Carter with Sd. Fryer 9.00
Paid J. A. Lane for an Report .50
May 19th Paid J. A. Lane for copy of Settlement .90
Novr. 24 paid A. Dibrell Clk. for order to Mr. Hogan .40
Recorded 26th October TEst. J. A. Lane clerk. 51.80
Sworn to in open Court 19th October 1835 J. A. Lane Clk John Fryer

P 193 Report of a Setlement made by Commissioners with Joseph Herd Administrator of Benjamin Bowman Deceased Returned at October Session A. D. 1835. Towit:

Report of a Settlement made by Commissioners with Joseph Herd Administrator of the estate of Benjamin Bowman Dedeased report and say as follows

To wit we find the Aministrator chargeable with the following Sums.

Amount of the Accounts Sales per Clerks Cirt.		750.35
To Thomas Stepes note Bal	86.50	
To Interest on Same upp to this time	20.39½	
" Do do note 190 lv. Tobacco at 2¢ pr H.		106. 89½
" William Glinns note Bal, 1000 at 2¢ pr. H.		3.80
" Judgement on Joseph Kerr		80.00
" Note on John Stipe came to hand after Sole		18.06¼
" amot of account against Robert Taylor not Account for in the Inventory		12.00
		991.10 3/4

The following debts, doubtful uncertain

The balance of Chapmans note	6.00
John Bussells note	15.00
George C. Swindle receipt 98lb of Iron	
N. Haggards receipt for Britain	200.00

Vouchers presented by Administrator to which he is entitled to a credit.

No. 1 paid adeson Fish pr. receipt	$0.00	
" 2 " George W. Anderson	2.00	
" 3 " Thomas Stipe	21.00	
" 4 " Jacob A. Lane	3.25	
" 5 paid note to David L. Mitchell pr. receipt	40.50	
" 6 " Benj. Wooton	45.75	
" 7 " Tax receipts	3.95	
By intake in addition	1.00	137.45
		853.65 3/4

We Said commissioners beg leave to report and say that we find on the hands of Said administrator the sum of eight hundred and fifty three dollars. Sixty five and three fourth cents in debts on Solvent person s, that he has paid out and disbursed the sum of one hundred and thirty Seven dollars forty five cents, that there is debts to the amount of two hundred and twenty one dollars, and a receipt for 98 lb of Iron, which debts we say are doubtful if not desperate, and that we are of the opinion, that the Services of Said Administrator an reasonably worth the Sum of thirty dollas which we recommend the Court to allow him out of Said estate. All of which is most respectfully Submitted. October 19th 1835.

Recorded 27th October A. D. 1835 — John Jett
Test Jacob A. Lane clerk. — David Snodgrass
Joseph Cummings

P 194 Additional Inventory of the estate of Benjamin Bowman Deceased which came to the hands of Joseph Herd Admrs of Said estate since making making his last return, and now returned into Court upon Oath at October Session A. D. 1835.

Wood work of Waggon Sold for	$18.06¼
An Acctl paid by Robert taylor for	12.00
Amount	$30.06¼

Recorded 27th October 1835 — Joseph Herd Aministrator
Test- Jacob A. Lane Clerk White County Court

Inventory of the estate of Samuel Usrey Deceased returned by Ransom Geer administrator with the will annexed, on oath at October Session A. D. 1835. with the receipt of the property therein named, given by Polly Usrey, the widow of Said Samuel Usrey deceased, accompanied by the certificate of Anthony Dibrell Towit:
Four head of horses 14 head of Sheeps 10 head of cattle, about 40 head of hogs 3. Beds and furniture and bed Steads. 1 Cupboard ½ dozen Knives & forks ½ dozen cups & saucers 1 Doz plates 1 large dish 1 cross cut saw 1 hand saw 1 5/4 auger ½ dozen pewter plates 3. ploughshared 2 pair Gears ½ dozen coffee plates 1 Scythe & cradle 3 old Axes 1 Womans Saddle 1 Loom 2 ovens 2 pots. 1 old clock 1 old waggon 2 yoke of Steers 2 piggins 1 Churn 1 GrindStone chissel 1 pair fire dogs o lod chest 1 table 2 bottles 1 bottle 2 Bibles 1 hymn Book 1 Spinning wheel 2 Singletrees 1 Log chain 1 clevis 1 old pair Saddle Bags 4 Salt Barrels 3 slays 1 Ditto 2 pair pot hooks 1 Iron pot rack 1 coffee boiler 2 tin panes 1 meal barrel 4 old broken hoes 1 pewter Basin ½ dozen Spoons 1 Skillet 1 check Rul 3 Tin cups 1 pitcher 1 Iron Wedge 1 Fow 1 Sporting hoe 1 pair Cotton cards 1 Set of glass mounting for Bureau 1 pair Steelyards amount of William Usrey Saddlery $8.98 3/4 cents. Account on R. Geer for Bureau. Recd. of Ramson GEEr Administrator of Samuel Usrey Dd. to the will annexed a ll the property found on the place at the time of his appointment.

her
Polly X Usrey
Widow mark of Samuel
Usrey Decd.

Attest Daniel G. Usrey.
Justify that the property left on the premeses of Samuel Usrey Decd. was not more than Sufficient to Support the widow and family. Given under my hand the 19th October 1835.
Recorded 28th October A. D. 1835 A. Dibrell.
Test-- Jacob A. Lane Clerk of White County Court.

P 195 Inventory of the property of Robert Goard Deceased upon oath by John Franklin Admr. at October Session A. D. 1835. Towit:
One mans Saddle, one cow and calf one yearlin one axe one hoe one hand saw Six knives and forks eight plates one Salt cellar and pepper bos, one chest and pot and skillet and one half, and some shoe makers tools and piggin and one chair. John Franklin
Recorded and examined 28th October A. D. 1835.
Test- Jacob A. Lane clerk White County Court

Inventory of this estate of William Carroll deceased. returned on oath at October Session A. D. 1835, by Mary Jane Carroll administratrix Towit: 1 bed and furniture, 1 Bedstead 1 Square walnut table 1 small square walnut table 1 cherry chest 1 clock 1 connor cupboard cupboard furniture 1 Toilet glass 1 churn 1 water pail 1 tim bucket 1 small pot 1 oven & lid 1 skillet, & lid 1 smoothing iron 1 pot rack 1 pair fire irons 2 stone jugs, 1 jar 1 mans saddle 1 woman saddle 2 axes 1 cow and calf 1 dark brown stud horse1 chestnut sorrel stud horse 1 four wheel carriage 1 hand saw 1 not on Wm. Austin payable to Curtis M. Dowill dated 3rd April 1835 payable one day for the sum of $2. 12½ doubtful 1 note on Thomas Givan and Sophia Givan ond for $300 1st March 1836 good.
Note on Thomas Givan and Sophia Givan for $125. in good Merchantable houses. to be valued at the rate of good second rate cows and calves at $10. due 25th December 1835. Good 1 note on David Sidhing payable to

Joseph Turney on or before the 18th Novmr. 1833, for eleven 1 Barrels of good sound vorn, with a credit thereon of ten Barrels of Corn dated 22nd of Rebruary 1834. G ood. 1 note on Fr. W. Capps due the 25th Decr. 1830 for five dollars. Bad. 1 note on Stephen H. Brady due 1st. April 1834 for five dollars Bad. 1 note on John Hall fro $200. with interest thereonfrom 2nd Jan 1832 due the 2nd Jan. 1834 with a ofedit thereon 19th Feby 1835 for the sum of $40. doubtful money recovered on a note of Joseph Dalton for $5. due 1st April 1835.

Test Jacob A. Lane Clerk White County Court.

Mary Jane her X mark Carrol Admx.

Inventory of the estate of Thomas R. Paul Deceased returned on oath by Jesse Walling Administrator at October Session A. D. 1835. Towit: 4 head of horses 1 waggon 1 pair of carriage harness 1 shot Gun pouch and horn 2 pistols 1 watch 1 small trunk with Sundry articles in if. 1 large chest of clothing 1 bed and furniture 1 clock 1 mans Saddle and two bridles and Martin Gills 1 pair of Saddle Bags 2 Boxes of Small Bells /o 1 pair P 196 of candle moulds 1 pair of Shoes 1 pair of Boots 1 Bag of clothes, part of a bolt osasburg cloth pail 1 hat 1 cap and 1 chair 1 Bag the above is just and true to the best of my Knowledge. Jesse Walling Administrator.
Recorded 28th Ocober A. D. 1835
Test--Jacob A. Lane Clerk of White County Court.

An Inventory of part of the personal property of William Roberts Deceased taken and returned by Patmer Roberts Administratix and John Griffith administrator of William Roberts Deceased on oath at October Term 1835. Towit:
4 Bed and furniture 4 Bedsteads 1 chest 2 cotton wheels 2 flax wheels 2 check Ruls 1 table 7 chairs 1 coffee mill 1 Set of delf plates 2 Earthen dishes, part of a Set of cups and Saucers. 1 Set Knives and forkes 6 tim cups 1 cofee pot 1 Fin Trumpet 3 light candle moulds 1 pair of hand Steepleyards Some Books 1 Set of Iron Spoons 2 ovens 1 Stew Kittle one large pot 2 large kittles 2 stone Jugs 1 pitcher 1 crock 1 Bread tray 1 meal Sifter 1 Razor & Shaving box 1 picken Tub 1 Lard Stand 1 Set working Spools 4 weavers reids 1 Side Saddle 1 mans saddle Some Huds--glass Seed 1 drawing Knife 1 chisel 1 auger 1 froe 2 axes 1 Scythe and Cradde 2 pair Chain traces 1 Barshear plough 3 Shovels and 2 Jumping coulters 1 Bull tongue 1 Cleves 1 Blind bridle 1 Mattock 2 hoes 1 Set gate Hinges 1 cutting Machine teeth for a harrow 1 pair Cotton cards 2 Raw hides 1 Gun barrel, moulds wipers and gun-lock 3 water vessels 1 Set or part of a Set of Halters tools. 1 palrel Gun belt 1 Bread waiter 1 mare and colt 3 head of young horses Three work Steers 10 head of stock cattle about ly haed of stock hogs 8 head of Killing hogs 18 geese about 14 head of Sheep One note on Joseph Hawks due the 15th Novr. 1829 for $3.25 in Seed Cotton to be delivered at Englands Machine balance due thereon of about 12½ cents. One note on Joseph Krapp due 15th Novr. 1828 for $1.50 in cotton to be delivered at Englands Macine bad one note on Abraham Pistole for $2.37½ due 4th Decr. 1828 bad. One note on Wesley Perkins due 16 Septr. 1830 for 75 cents. Bad. One note on Jacob Anderson due 21 June 1835. for $1.40 cents doubtful. Account and order against Elam Sherrel amounting to $9.00 doubtful. 1 pair Sheep Sheers. one cake auger 1 small pot cromb tub, old Loom Flax brake some corn, one third of of 19½ acres of corn for rent. The fourth of the oats of 25 Acres of land The rye of Ten acres -The small grain all unthrashed and the Rye yet in the shock

Recorded 28th October A. D. 1835 John X Grigfith
Test Jacob A. Lane Clerk his mark
White County Court.

Patience X Roberts
her mark

P 197 An Inventory of the personal estate of Jacob Anderson Deceased returned by ancy Anderson Administratrix on oath at October Session A. D. 1835. 1 mare and colt 2 cows 1 yearling 10 head of hogs 6 of them being Stock and the balance killing hogs 18 head of geese 30 chickens 2 Beds an furniture 2 killets 2 pots and 1 oven 1 pot rack iron 1 pair broken pot hooks 1 pair of Ditto 3 chairs 1 earthen dish 3 plates 1 Smoothing iron 1 Shovel plough and 2 pair of traces and 2 pair of Hames 2 Small weeding hoes 1 large and 1 hand axe 1 R ap hook 1 Stone Jar 2 earthhen crocks 2 earthen pitchers 1 water pail 1 stop pail 1 Loom 2 Set weaving Gear 5 tin Cups 4 Knives & forks 1 coffee pot 2 tea cups 1 Bread tray 1 meal gumm 1 L oking glass 2 Stands of Bed curtains 2 failets 1 Square table 1 Shovel Blade 1 Bolt & Clevis 1 Single tree 1 note on Zachariah Lefwise for $7. to be paid in Sound Earthen ware good a claim against Stephen D. Hill for $1 bad. A note on William Jones DEd. for $1.12½ cents good. A note on Randolph Ross for $10. with 5 or 7 years interest on the Same. Bad. About acres of corn partly raised. About 1½ acres of cotton partley raised by Decd. some sweet potatoes and Irish potatoes raised in part by Decd. 1 lar Spinning wheel and 1 pair of Cotton cards 1 small caun 1 churn 1 old pair of fire dogs 1½ Bushels of Salt 1 Pickling tub 2 Salt Barrels 1 Grind stor

Nancy X Anderson Admrx.
her mark

Recorded 28th October A. D. 1835
Test Jacob A. Lane Clerk
White county Court.

Inventory of the personal property of William Jones Deceased taker and returned by Rachel Jones Administratrix on oath at October Session A. 1835 of White ounty ourt Towit:
1 mare 15 head of hogs 2 cows and Calves wheel and cards 1 Skillet 1 Baker 3 knives 6 forks 5 plates 3 Teacups & saucers 1 Bread tray & woodan Bowl half Barrel of Salt 2 Sides of upper leather 1 side of Soal leather 1 Stone Jug 2 geese 4 hoes 1 Saddle & bridle 1 pair Womans Shoes 1 Bedstead 1 hoe 1 plough and set of iron tracrs 1 Set of Gate Hinges 2 Chairs 1 Smoothing iron 1 pail 1 crock 1 Jar 1 large family bible the life of Washington 1 volum 2 hymn bookes 1 Raqor Strap & Box 2 gun belts 1 English Reader 1 cream pitcher 1 coffee pot 4 tea Spoons 1 Stone pitcher 1 dirb pitcher 8 cents of Shoe thread 1 note due on Henry Atkinson for $4. good and account against william Irwin Esq. for $5. good but to be paid in tr An account on John Jones for $1. due intrade and cash good. One account on Prettyman Jones for $1. in trade and cash good. An account on Farmer Clouse a Minor of $1.87½ doubtful. An acount on Esq Irvim for 37½ cents and account on Washington Irven for 50 cents good Cash recovered $1.37½ an account on Rebecca Jones for 75 cents good 1 falling Axe 1 Sifter 5 p pattern of Shoe leather 1 pair shoes a crop of corn partly raised quanity of ground not known.

Rachel X Admrx.
her mark

Recorede 28th Octr. 1835
Test J. A. Lane clk.

State of Tennessee }
White County } January Sessions A. D. 1836
This day was produced in open Court a writing perposing to be the last will and Testament of Isaac Plumlee deceased whereupon the due execution and publication thereof was proven in open court by the oath of Andrew K. Parker and John Gillintine, subscribing witness there to for the purposes and things therein mentioned, that the Said Isaac Plumlee Signed, Sealed published and declared the same to be his last will and Testament in their presence and subscribed their names as Witness there to at his request and in his presence, and that he was at the date of the execution of Sound mind and memory which is recorded.
Given at office the 11th January 1836. Test. Jacob A. Lane clerk.
By N. Oldham D. C. Recorded 22nd January A. D. 1836
Test J. A. Lane Clerk by N. Oldham D. C.

Report of James Copeland Guardian to the heirs of John Anderson deceased made at January term A. D. 1836. Towit:
The note mentioned in a former report are collected.
And since his last return he paid to J. C. Davis in March 1835 (Su note) $5.50.

To Judgement in favor of Anderson Johnson 4 March 1835.	6.11¼
4 March 1835 To Judge. Alexander Moore to use	5.95
Same date To Judge A. B. Hunter to use	5.55
To Jacob A. Lane Clerk	1.50
	$24.61¼

James Copeland Guardian

P 200

Report of John H. Dale Guardian of Eliza Dale & Polly Malinda Dale infant heirs of John Dale deceased made at January Sessions A. D. 1836. ToWit:
He has nothing in his hands of theirs and the estate is in Law with the Administrators--
Eliza the mare & Saddle & Cow & Calf 2 Sheep--bed and furniture.
Polly Malinda mare Cow & Calf--2 sheep bed and furniture.
The foregoing property was bequeathed in the will to be form his death theirs.
Recorded 22 Jany 1836 J. A. Lane Clerk by N. Oldham D. C.

Report of Samuel Brown Guardian for Robinson Dyer, Alfred Dyer, Clarborn Dyer, John C. Dyer, and Louisa Dyer the infant children of John Dyer decd. made at the January Sessions A. D. 1836. Towit:
1 day January 1836 Cash on hand and Secured by notes & judgments $1079.55

Cr. By this sum paid Taxes for 1834	.48½	
" " paid Dcdt. Robertson for attendance on Robinsoy Dyer	3.00	3.48½
Leaving this balance		$1076.07½

The above sum includes the amount for which the share of my wards to the Crop of 1834. sold for on January 1st. 1835. He also States that since last report he has paid to Sarah Dyer the sum of $225 which he was ordered to do by the worshipful court. Samuel Brown
January 11th 1836.
J. Al Lane Clk. By N. Oldham D. C.

In the name of God Amen! I Isaac Plumlee of the County of White and State of Tennessee, being in feeble in body but of Sound and perfect mind thanks be given to God for the same, calling to mind the immortality of body and knowing that it is appointed for all men once to die; do mark ordain, constitute and appoint this my last will and testament and principally and first of all I give amy Soul into the hand of almighty who first gave it. and my body to the dust to be buried in decent Christian burial nothing doubting but that I shall receive the same again by the Almighty power of God, and as touching such worldy estate as it has please God to bless me with I give bequeath devise and dispose of the same in form and manner following Towit:
First it is my will and desire that all my just and lawful debts be levied raised and paid out of my moneable estate. Item 2nd I give and bequeath to my well beloved wife Margarett Plumlee, her life estate in my Message or dwelling house together with all the louds belonging to me, which which contains Fime hundred acres together with all the moveable property or estate that I my, seized and possessed of, except a certain Roan filly and Bay colt, that I have already given to my two younger Sons Isaack and Finese--Item 3rd I give and bequeath to my two oldest Sons Joel and William Plumlee each one dollar. Item 4th I give and bequeath to my son John Plumlee one dollar Item 5th I give and bequeath to my Son Denton Plymlee one dollar my reasons for giving only one dollars to the four oldest Sons isthat I have given them a reasonable heretofore.
Item 6th I give and bequeath to my Daughter Polly Turner a horse saddle and bridle to be worth Seventy five Dollars or the same amount in some other property. Item 7th I give and bequeath to my Dauthter Margaret Simmons wife of James Simmons a horse saddle and bridle to be worth seventy five dollars or the same amount in some other property.
Item 8th I give and bequeath to my Daughter Rebecca C. Williams wife of Abraham Williams a horse Saddle and bridle worth Seventy five dollars or the same amount in Some other property.
Item 9th I give and bequeath to my Daughter Elizabeth Cummings wife of Gabriel Cummings a horse SAddle and bridle to be worth seventy five dollars or the same amount in some other property.
Item 10th I give and bequeath to my Daughter NancyPlumlee two good feather beds, and furniture, 2 good cows and Calves, two Ewes and lambs, two Sows and pigs or two sows with pig also one horse SAddle and bridle worth seventy five dollars or the same amount in other good property.
Item 11th I give and bequeath to Isaac and Finese my two younger sons at the death of their mother Margarett Plumlee all my above named lands to be equally divided in quantity and quality So as to make two farms And I do hereby nominate Constitute and appoint my well beloved wife Margaret Plumlee my executor of this my last will and testament hoping that she will take the charge, upon her and I do hereby revoke, disannul, and disallow all former, wills testaments Legacis or bequests, executor or Executors by me at any time heretofore made, bequeathed or appointed. And do declare this and no other to be my last will and testament. In testimony whereof I have hereunto set my hand and affixed my Seal this the 27th day of September in the year of our Lord 1835.
Signed Sealed published and declared in prexence of us.
Andrew K. Parker Isaac Plumlee (Seal) John Gillentine

Report of John Pennington and Sarah Dyer Guardian for Culson Dyer, Alzera Dyer, Margarett Dyer and William A. Dyer infant children of John Dyer dcd. Made at January Sessions A. D. 1836.

1st January 1836. Cash on hand & secured by notes $1130.04 3/4

From which diduct this sum allowed Sarah Dyer for boarding Schooling/c. given Said children allowed at January term 1835. 225.00

Deduct also this sum being Sarah Dyer part of the hire of the negroes and rent of land 13.61½ 238.61½

891.43⅓

Credit Jany 1835 cash paid J. A. Lane for Guardian bond and former report 1.00

Paid Jacob A. Lane for order making allowance to Mrs. Dyer .25

1.25

P 201 Cr. brought up 1.25 amount on hand 891.43⅓

By cash paid Taxes on half the land .50

By Cash paid Lane & Anderson for advice /c 10.25

By cash placed in estate by making charge by John Pennington .12½

Leaving a balance of fund as in their hands $879.31

John Pennington

Sarah X Dyer

his mark

Recorded 22nd January 1836.

J. A. Lane Clk. by N. Oldham D. C.

Report, of Asa Certain Guardian to Alphonson Holmes and Marissa Holmes heirs of Edward Holmes decd. made at at January term 1836.

That no funds belonging to his Said wards have as het come to his hands Then having no settlement with the Executors of the said E. Holmes decd.

Asa Certain

Recorded 22nd January 1836 J. A. Land Clerk by N. Oldham D. C.

Report of John Fryer Guardian to William Carter Legatee of Charles Carter Senr. dcd. made at January term A. D. 1836 Towit: Cash on hand 1 day January 1836 Second by note $49.50

By cash paid Jacob A. Lane clerk for my report Jany 1835 .50

;; Kamu 1836 paid Lane & Anderson for attending to suit of Stipe & wife vs myself as Executor & Guardian of the Said ward 20.00

1835 Two days endeavoring to sell the rent oats of ward 2.00 22.50

Leaving a balance of $26.55

To which add the hire of the negroes 3rd day of February 1835 to the 3rd. day of February 1836. Secured by note 17.50

Amount in Guardian's hands $44.05

The monies which are in his hands as are executor of Charles Carter Senr. deceased are not here reported as a Settlement has not yet taken place So as to shew how much is coming to said ward. The suit mentioned as pending at the date of my last years report has been determined

and he will be able to Shew the amount above mentioned by the time he is required to report again—— The rent oats mentioned in his last report is still unsold, he offered the at public Sale but got no bid that justified their sale them is also on hand the rent corn of 1835, all which property he will indeavoer to Soll and exhibit the premises in his next annual report.
John Fryer
Recorded 22nd any 1836. J. A. Lane Clerk by N. Oldham D. C.

P 202 Report of Wamon Leftwich Guardian to Malinda Rowland a minor heir of John Rowland decd. made at January term 1836. Towit:
That since his return to the January term 1835 of this court the money then Shown to be in his hands after deducting the items of credit to which he was then entitled has since and Still is on interest. He has furnished necessaries for his Said ward form the 10th day of January 1836, at the house of Carrick & Leftwick for which their recept is taken amounting to the sum of 59. 82 3/4
He furnished his Said ward with other necessaries within the time aforesaid amounting to this sum 6.77¼
Which sum of 66.60
he claims as a credit to the amount with which he is chargeable as her Guardian taking date at this time. January 12th 1836
Wamon Leftwich Guardian
Recorded 22nd January 1836.
J. A. Lane ck. By N. Oldham D. C.

Account of the Sales of the property of the Estate of Jaber Andersnon deceased returned by Nancy Anderson admx. at January term 1836.

Nancy Anderson one Bed & loom .37½
Nancy Anderson 2 stands of Curtains and 2 Tablets .25
Nancy Anderson a lot of various articles a tubb Sheep one Tubb and fire Dogs 1 big wheel and 2 chairs .50
do 1 sow & five shoats 156¼ 1 Grindstone .25 1.81¼
do 2 pot vessels 25 1 plow & Gears hoes & reap hook .25 .50
do 1 Lot of flax 25 1 cow $9.00 1 cow & calf 1.50 10.75
do 2 axes and pot rack 25. 3 salt barrels 12½ .37½
do 1 mare and colt 37.00
$51.56¼
Nancy Anderson
Recorded 22nd January 1836. J. A. Lane Clerk by N. Oldham D. C.

Account of Saes of the property of the estate of Robert Goad dcd. returned by John Franklin adms. a January term 1836.
Sold on the 14 November 1835 at twelve months credit. Towit:
To George Wood Knives and forks 1.00
do 8 plates 37½ Skillet & pot 2.00 2.37½
Thomas Crawley 1 axe 1.00 1 hoe 60 1.60
John Franklin Shoemakers Tools 1.87½
P 203 to Pinkony Shockley yearling Heifer 3.00
" John Franklin 1 cow & calf 14.00
" Pinkony Shockly 1 handwas 1.43 3/4
" Nathan Driver 1 chest 3.00
" John Franklin 1 salt cellar & peper box .50
" Thomas Crawley 1 saddle 4.00

To Wright Lane 1 mare 26.50
Thomas Crawley 2 shoats 275 1 Hog 200 4.75
" George Wood two Hogs 7.25
" John Franklin five Hogs 5.00
" John S. Grissom Cabbage 1.25
" George Wood 1 cahir & pail .25
" Thomas Goad 2 pigs 1.06¼

The above mentioned mare, Hogs and saddle were mortgaged by Robt. Goad in his lifetime to me John Franklin--The debt remaining unpaid & the amount will be retained John Franklin Admr.
Recorded January 22nd 1836. J. A. Lane Clerk by N. Oldham D. C.

Account of Sales of the property of the estate of Zachariah Jones deceased returned upon oath by Thomas Jones Admr. at January term 1836. old the 3rd and 4th November 1835

To Benjamin Thomas 1 are & colt	$49.00
" John Jones 1 Sorrel Horse	66.00
" Alfred ones 1 sorrel Horse	75.00
" Jeremiah Webb 1 Sorrel horse	60.00
" Nancy Anderson 1 Mare & colt	71.00
" John Lisk 1 mare & cold	81.00
" Abraham Broyles 1 horse	57.25
" Rebecca Jones 1 Horse	5.00
" William Frisby 1 Filley	37.00
" David Dean 5 hogs	54.00
" do do 10 hogs	73.00
" James Cogar 5 hogs	50.50
" William Hunter 5 hogs	43.00
" John L. Price 5 hogs	40.00
" do 10 hogs	75.00
" William Hunter 5 do	32.00
" Robert Cox 5 do	30.00
" John Overly 5 hogs	2725
" Rebecca Jones [illegible]	15.00
" James Jone 1 horse	40.00
P 204 To Rebecca Jones 21 Hogs for	39.00
" John Kerr 33 do	43.00
" Hugh Gracy 1 negro manmingo	900.00
" David Dean 1 Negro woman & child	605.00
" Isaac A.codk 1 Negro boy Peter	220.00
" James Jones 1 Negro boy Jonathan	205.00
" John Gracy 1 negro boy Jefferson	361.00
" Rebecca Jones 1 negro Girl Lucinda	270.00
" Benjamin Thomas 1 negro boy Prince	600.00
" Rebecca Jones 1 cow	9.50
" William Jones 1 cow	1.75
" Isaac Firtle 1 Steer	7.43 3/4
" William Earles 1 cow & yearling	11.00
" John muman 1 Steer	4.00
" William P Lewis 1 cow	10.56¼
" Rebecca Jones 1 cow	9.00
" Nancy Anderson 2 Calves	9.75
" Thomas Eastland 1 yoke of Steers	57.00
" S. B. Arnold 1 yoke of Steers	25.00
" Joseph Almater 1 cow & Calf	10.75

To James Jones 2 Steers	21.06¼
" James Kelly 1 Steer	11.00
" Benjamin Hutchings 3 Steers	30.00
" Robert Smith 1 cow & calf	12.75
" John Newman 1 cow & calf	7.25
" Emory Bennett cow & calf	11.25
" Nancy Anderson 2 steers	10.75
" Thomas Eastland 1 cow	8.00
" James Hays 1 Bull	13.00
" George Allen 1 Heifer	8.25
" James Cantrell 2 Steers	20.25
" Thomas Hawks 1 Heifer	6.50
" Rebecca Jones 1 cow	10.68 3/4
" David Dean 1 cow	6.00
" Nancy Anderson 1 cow	10.75
" " Ditto 1 heifer	8.25
" James Russel 1 do	6.31 ¼
" Thomas Yates 1 Steer	7.25
" George Allen 1 Heifer	3.06¼
" Thomas Yates yearlings	8.62½
" Levi Bosorth 1 wagon	27.12½
" Webster Hutchings 1 Still & Tubbs	27.00
" Nancy Anderson 1 pile of Corn	12.00
" Ditto 1 do	14.00
" Rebecca Jones 1 pile of corn	62.75
" Ditto 10 Sheep	13.37½
" James Hitchcock 1 Tub of Wheat 6.50	6.50
" David Dean 1 Tub of Wheat	10.50
" Benjamin McClain 1 Tub of wheat	11.50
" Nancy Anderson 1 Tub of wheat	6.75
" William Irwin 1 Tub of Wheat	14.50
" William Baker 1 tub do	9.50
" James T. Hayes 1 Tan	12.31¼
" William Bruster 14 Sheep	18.00
" William Jones To Boxes	.25
" Lee R. Taylor Shoes	.62½
" Richard Reeves Smith Tools	19.62½
" Richard Reeves 1 Kettle	3.50
" Thomas Crowder 2 plough	.56¼
" William Baker 1 plough	.56¼
" Green B/Nolen 1 do	1.62½
" James Hitchcock 1 do	.93 3/4
" Aaron Hutchings 1 do	1.37½
" Benjamin Hutchings 1 do	.87½
" John R. Jones 1 do	.25
" David Hiefner 1 do	1.56¼
" William F. Lewis 2 wedges	1.37½
" Thomas Crouse 2 plough	1.12½
" Emory Bennett Gears	1.50
" Jonathan Price 1 pr. Gear	2.12½
" John Taylor 1 chain	3.00
" William Bosarth to Sundries	.62½
" Rebecca Jones 1 pr lf Gear	1.12½
" William Jones 1 Grindstone	1.12½
" Thomas Jones Jr. 1 pr. Gears	3.00
" John R. Jones 1 saddle	4.50

	To Washington H. Irwin 1 do	4.50
	" Rebecca Jones 1 do	6.50
	" James Jones 1axe	1.12½
	" Jesse M. Sullivan 1 do	1.12½
	" Rebecca Jones 1 do	.75
	" Nancy Anderson 1 do	1.25
	" William Irwin Spade & Horn	.62½
	" Thomas Irwin pot rack & axe	2.18 3/4
	" Rebecca Jones 1 axe	.31¼
	" do 2 hoes	1.31¼
	" William Taylor 2 do	1.31¼
	" Levi Bosorth 1 Frow	1.25
P 206	to Samuel Stoves 1 Mattock	1.00
	" James Hitchcock 2 do	1.00
	" Isaac Pirtle 4 hoes	.37½
	" Shirlvy Kirby 2 Bells	1.62½
	" James Hayes augers /c	1.00
	" Thomas Jones 1 adze	.75
	" Robert Wilson 1 auger	.56¼
	" James Hayes 1 agues	1.06¼
	" James Hitchcock ads e /c	1.06¼
	" James Cantrell Drawing Knige /c	1.00
	" David Hofern 1 Saw	.50
	" James Irwin 1 pr Steel yards	2.37½
	Levi Bozorth 1 tongue iron for cart	1.00
	" Benjamin Hutchings Shoe tools	2.12½
	" Jeremiah Bennett Leather	1.68 3/4
	" Shilby Kirby do	2.12½
	" William Baker Saddle Bags	1.00
	" James Hitchcock Scythe & Cradel	1.31¼
	" Rebecca Jones do	2.25
	" Thomas Jones Senr do	2.50
	" nancy Anderson 3 bedsteads	.75
	Benjamin Hutchings 1 cow hide Raw	2.00
	Thomas Jones Jr 1 cutting Knife	4.00
	To John Taylor 1 Tar Barrel	1.12½
	" Johathan Prints wheel & coffee mill	2.43 3/4
	" David Dean 3 pots & oven	3.62 ¼
	" William Bosorth Pott & oven	1.68 3/4
	" John Gracy Dog Irons	2.00
	" Rebecca Jones Spun Cotton /c	6.50
	" William Earles Fire Dogs	.50
	Jesse Allen 1 Gun	5.25
	To Thomas Jones Fr. 1 Saw	5.50
	" Green B. Nolen 1 Table	1.12½
	" Rebecca Jones 1 Table & press	1.00
	do do 1 loom	.50
	" do do 1 cupboard and table	3.50
	" William Jones Galss & Clock	20.00
	" Rebecca Jones Bed and furniture	18.00
	" do do	10.00
	" do 1 chest	.12½
	" James T. Crowder Slates	.37½
	" do 1 Box	.12½

To do Chest and candle Stick	.56¼
P 207 To Thomas Jones 1 pen of Oats	8.50
" Nancy Anderson 1 do	3.87½
" do 1 cutting Knife	.56¼
" William B. Jones 1 Hat & Knife	1.12½
" James Hitchcock 1 Lot of plank	.81¼
" Rebecca Jones 1 lot of Fodder	.37½
" James Jones Rye	.62½
" Rebecca Jones Shovel & Hackle	.18 3/4
" do 1 Bee Gum	.62½
" Nancy Anderson 1 Bee Gum	1.56¼
" William Baker 4 Bee gums	.75
" Emory Bennett 1 do	1.43 3/4
" Rebecca Jones 2 pr Sears	.25
do Geese & Ducks	5.00
" James Russell 33 3/4 # Bacon	3.36
" William Taylor 31½ do	3.30
" James Hitchcock 22½ do	2.37½
" Levi Bozorth 30 3/4	3.06¼
" James Cooper 84 lb do	8.40
" Ditto 84 lb	7.98
" James Taylor 5 Hogs	35.00
	$5160.52¼

Recorded 25 January A. D. 1836 Admr.
J. A. Lane Clk by N. Oldham D. C.

Account of Sales of the property of the estate of William Roberts deceased returned upon oath by Jno Griffith Admr. & Patience Roberts Admx. at January term A. D. 1836.

Sold 9th November 1835.

To Patience Roberts 1 work Steer $600 13 hogs $8.	14.00
do mare & colt $30. Draw kinfe & sheep Shares 37½	30.37½
do 1 pot 50 1 hog 1.75 1plow 50 backband & chains	3.25
do Axe 75 1 court Tub 12½ Side Saddle $4.87½	4.87½
do 1 pot 50 ingle Yoke 6¼ Ra whide 100	1.56¼
do Oats 3.00 2 Sheep 100 2 hoes 25 1 loom 6¼	4.31¼
do Wheel and Reel $1.00 Sifter & Bowl 25	1.25
do 2 Beds & Steads & furniture	6.00
do 1 Flax wheel 1504 slays 100	2.50
do 1 Auger & Chisel 25 1 oven 1 auger 25	.50
" Spools	.25
P 208 to Ptience Roberts Books 50 2 pr cards 50	1.00
" do cupboard & furniture 2 pails	4.00
" do Trumpet 25 Table 25 6 Turkeys 50	1.00
" do 3 chairs 56¼	.56¼
" Daniel Lundy Jr. 1 Sorrel Mare	45.00
" Daniel Lundy Fr. 1 young Horse	49.
" do 1 Bell	.62½
" John Griffith Hatters Tools	21.00
" do 1 oven & lid & Crocks	1.00
" do 1 plough 200 1 flax wheel 200	4.00
" do Verdegris 4.00 Steelyards 62½	4.62½
" do George Cardwell 1 Grindstone 112½ plough 50	1.62½
" William Barr one plough	150
" do 1 pr Drawing Chains 137½ 1 cow 831¼	9.68 3/4
" Joseph Roberts 1 cutting Knife 4.56¼ bridle bit 12 5/4	[illegible]
" do Jug Spirits [illegible] 56¼ Shaving [illegible] /c 67½	1.[illegible] 3/4

" Joseph Roberts 1 cutting Knife 4.56 bridle bit 18 3/4 4.75
" do Jug Spirits Turpintine 56¼ Shaving box /c 62½ 1.18 3/4
" Barnet Camp 1 axe 1.50
" Michel Cardwell 1 Mattock 1.31¼
" Jonathan Scott 1 Frow .93 3/4
" James C. Mitchell 1 Saddle 0.50 .50
" John R. Allison Scythe & cradle 3.00
"Leonard Mcmurray 1 Kittle 2.00
" Ditto 6 Geese 1.43 3/4
" Joseph S. Allison 1 fat Stand 25 wheel bearer 100 1.25
do Grass Seed .93 3/4
" James Allison 1 Kittle 2.75 1 smoothing iron 56½ 3.31¼
" do 1 Flax broke .56
" George Price 1 Sett of Harrow Teeth 4.50
" Joshua Hickey gate hinges 50 1 bar Share plow 4 4.50
" do 10 head Sheep 806¼ 1 Barrel 62½ 8.68 3/4
" Henry H. Collin 1 yoke oxen 21.06¼ 21.06¼
" Jona Vinson 1 yoke do broke since inventory 12.00
" Abrahan Sailers 1 Steer 6 . Red bull 4. 10.00
" Leonard Sailers 1 Sorrel Mare 35.00
" Ann Griffith 1 heifer 625 1 Kittle 1.56¼ 7.81¼
" do 1 chest 3.00 4 chairs do 1.00 4.00
" Elisha Cammron 2 Rawhides 2.06¼
" Thos C. Martin 1 wheel & Rul 175 candle moles & Jug 68¾ 2.43¾
" do 6 Guns 175 2 do 75. 2 do 56¼ 3.06¼
" Enoch Golden 1 pail & Jug .37½
Martin Campbell Bed-S tead & furniture 10.56¼
" Daniel Martin fo 11.18 3/4
" Joseph England 1 Gun barrel 10$ Lock 156¼ 11.56¼
" William Mills 1 coffee Mill 1.50 1.50
P 209 To Franklin M Connell 1 Gunlet .183/4
" Washington Cardwell 6 Geese 1.37 ½

387.31¼

Total amount John X Griffith
his mark
Patience X Roberts
her mark

Recorded 25th January 1836. J. A. Lane Clerk By N. Oldham Deputy Clerk.

Account of Sales of the property of the Estate of William James deceased returned upon oath by Rachel Jones Admx. at January term 1836. Sold on the 3rd day of November 1835.

To William Irwin Leather 2.31¼
" Richard Judson Leather 6.75
" William Baker Shoethread 25 2 Baskets 25 .50
" William Irwin 1 Saddle 650 2 gate hinges 6.75
" Perttyman Jones 1 pr shoes 1.25
" Ebenezer Jones 1 Bible 3.25
" John R. Ellison 3 books 1.75
" George Kelly shaving box /c & 1 Hymn book 1.12½
" William Baker plough & Gears 2.00
" John Prints 1 Mare 60.00
" William Robinson 1 Bridle .50
" James C. Hayes corn 7.06¼

to William Brown 1 cow & calf 9.12½
" William Frisby 1 sow & two Pigs 2.87½
" John Farlow 3 "lws & pigs 5.56¼
" James Basorth 1 hoe .31¼
" Barnabas Harlow Buttons .37½
" " Gunbloth not sold having been loaned out which
Admx. charges hersel f original cost .12½
" Rachel Jones cupboard furniture 12½ Leather 12½ .25
" do Jones ~~Smoothing iron 62½ Tub 12½~~ pocket book 12½ .37½
1 wheel & cands axe & 2 clovis tray & sifter 1.00

Rachel X Jones Admr.
his mark

Recorded 25 January 1836 J. A. Lane Clk. by N. Oldham D.C.

P 210 Inventory of the property of the Estate Zachariah Jones deceased returned upon oath by Thomas ~~Jones~~ at January Sessions A. D. 1836. Towit: One sorrel Mare & Colt, one sorrel horse four years old, one sorel horse six years old, one gray mare & colt four years old, one sorrel mare & colt four years old, one brown four years old, one bay horse nine years old. One filly two years old One sorrel colt two years old, one sorrel mare 16 years old old fifty five head of pork hogs fifty four head of stock hogs one negro man about 23 years old 1 negro woman & child about 33 years old One negro boy about 10 years old One yellow girl about 6 years old, three Small negro boys 2 yoke of Oxen 41 head of Cattle 1 wagon 1 Still & 11 tubs 1 Crop of Corn 24 head of Sheep about 62 bushels wheat 1 Dutch Fan 4 wagon boxes a quanity of horse shoes 1 set blacksmith tools one large kittle a parcel of plough 2 iron wedges a Quanity of plough gear 1 Log Chain 1 grin stone 2 man's Saddles, 1 Side Saddles 5 axes 1 Spade 2 pot racks 7 Hoes 1 frow 3 mattocks 2 Bells 4 augers 1 Cooper adze 1 foot adze & Compass 1 Drawing knife 1 Chisel 1 pr Steelyards 1 hand saw 1 iron for wagon tongue Shoe tools 2 Sides of leather Saddle Bags 3 scythes & Cradle 3 bee Stands 1 Raw hide 2 Cutting Knives 1 Tar barrel 4 Wheel 2 Coffee mills 4 pots 2 Ovens 3 pr fire Dogs a Lot of Spun cotton and some other small articles 1 shot Gun 1 cross cut saw 3 Tables 1 press 1 cupboard 1 clock 1 Looking glass 3 bed and furniture 2 Chests 1 Trunk 2 Slates 1 Box 1 Candle Stick 2 pens of Oats 1 hat 1 Lot of Plank 1 Lot of Fodder Some Rye One shovel 1 Hackle, Seven Bee gums--2 pr Shears, Some Geese & Ducks 341 lb. Bacon 7 more hogs--1 note on Jaber Anderson 21$ due January 21. 1832. good One note on Clement Jordan of $8 due ninty days after 26th May 1834. bad. One note on L. B Fernell $6.60 due 31 July 1834 bad--. 1 note on James T. Hayes for $61 due 1 day March 1834 Credit of 49$ good. 1 note on Elisha Bryant for $25. due 25 Decr. 1835. Signed over by Elijah Nelson doubtful. 1 order from Wm. H. Sullivan to Henry Lyday prostested 1 Note on William Usery for 30$ due Decr. 1835--assigned by Wm. M. Garrah to Z. Jones good. One note on William Gracy due 1 March 1834. bad 1 Note on Elijah Bryant for $50. in trade due 25 December 1835. doubtful--1 order from Wm. Gracy to Connor & Hubert bad.--1 order from J. H. Crowder to Jesse Lincoln $1.95 Doubtful--1 claim (4.99) Henry Adkinson lf $ 3.50--doubtful there is said to be a claim of William Jones deceased of 24 Barrels of corn Doubtful account against David Dean of Sixteen Dollars good a/c against James Baker $7.33 doubtful claim vs. J. H. Hugh $4.50. doubtful balance Judgement vs Richard pirite stayed by William Russel $ 4.25 Claim vs Prettyman Jones $4.20 good-- Thos. Jones Recorded 25 Jany 1836 Admr.

J. A. Lane Ck. by N. Oldham D.C.

P 211 Account of the Sale of the property of the Estate of Thomas R. Paul deceased as returned upon by Jesse Walling sold the 2nd. day of November 1835, towit:

1 set of candle moles to Thomas Walling .62½
1 Bridle do 1.75
1 Bay Horse do 80.00
1 pr. of cloth do 4.50
1 pr Saddle pockets John Fryer 2.25
1 man's Saddle James Walling 6.00
1 Bed & 2 pillows & boulster James Herd 9.50
1 wagon A. S. Rogers 35.18 3/4
1 Set Harness do 15.00
1 do do 15.31¼
1 Chair Henry Chastine .25
1 Curry Comb to William Fryer 1.93 3/4
1 Halter Chain /o Jesse Dodson 2.25
1 Bell James Walling .37½
1 Box of Articles Jesse Dodson 2.50
1 Shot Gun, pouch & Horn William Kerr 12.50
1 Black Mare Jesse Walling 101.00
1 Sorrel horse Hayes Arnold 60.25
1 Gray horse oscar Denton 27.50
1 Shovel & Tongs Jesse Walling 2.06¼
1 Spider Edward Anderson .75
1 pr of Shoes /c Charles Swift 2.25
1 do James Walling .56¼
1 " Boots Jesse Walling 2.37½
2 Bottles & 1 Box James walling 1.00
1 Clock Andrew Cope 5.06¼
1 Blanket James Roberts 2.31¼
1 Box & ohter Articles Jesse Dodson 1.25
1 Bed Quilt Samuel O. Paul 2.00
1 pr Bridle bits Hiram Walling 1.75
1 watch Simon Doyle 10.31¼
1 Razor Box /o Samuel A. Keithley 1.75
1 Brush & Medicine Oscar Denton .68 3/4
1 Dirk Hayes Arnold .31¼
1 do Smith J. Walling 1.31¼
1 Horse /o Creed A. Tayler 1.18 3/4
1 Bag of Oats /c Creed A. Taylor 1.06¼
1 Book William ooch .50
1 Cap William Fryer 2.12½
1 Wagon Cloth James Walling 2.18 3/4
1 do Jeptha Yarbrough 1.06¼
1 vest & Pantaloons Berry Hamblet ✓ .32½
2 Counterpanes Jas. Herd 6.43 3/4
1 cloth coat Samuel O. Paul 1.75
1 do do 7.50
1 Hat do 2.25
1 cap Daniel Richards .31¼
1 Coat Samuel O. Paul .50
1 coat & 3 vests do .50
P 212 1 vest James Walling 1.50
1 Testament William Kerr .62½

1 bible Smith J. Walling .56 1/4
1 Pistol William Rostle 2.50
1 Ditto Berry Hamblet 4.25
1 pr socks Cahrles Hill .50
1 Vest Isham Rogers 1.00
1 pr pantatoons Samuel O. Paul 2.00
1 do do 1.12 1/2
[illegible] Cloth Jesse Walling 2.06 1/4
[illegible]
1 pr. suspenders Creed A. Taylor .56 1/4
1 Table Cloth Samuel O Paul 1.00
1 Map & Book William Kerr 1.00
Some Baize Smith Walling .31 1/4
1 purse Simeon R. Doyle .12 1/2
2 tooth brushes Daniel Richards .50
1 pr Gloves Samuel C. Paull .50
1 Chest Isham Rogers 2.06 1/4
1 Pocket Book Jesse Walling 62 1/2
1 Hammer omitted to be Sold which admr. charges himself .25
Jesse Walling Admr. $474.37 1/2

Recorded 27th January A. D. 1836 J. A. Lane Clerk by N. Oldham Dc.

P 213 Account of Sales of the property of Jeremiah Denton decd returned upon oath by Oscar Denton Admr. at January term 1836. Sold 13th November 1835.

1 tea pot Candle Stick	Samuel Couch	.50
1 Bason & Plates	Anna Gillings	.37 1/2
1 Tin Trunk	R. B. Moore	.37 1/2
1 Pitcher /c	Samuel Couch	.62 1/2
1 Coffee pot /c	S. B. Scoggin	.52 1/2
1 Set plates	Samuel Couch	.75
1 pewter Dish	do	1.25
1 Set Knives & forks	Joseph Jones Jr.	.75
1 smoothing Irons	Thomas Rogers	81 1/4
1 Lot Books	S. B. Scoggin	.25
1 Bible	William C. Denton	3.00
1 Table	S. B. Scoggin	1.00
1 do	Susannah Rogers	1.87 1/2
1 pr Steelyards	Isaac Denton	.75
1 Trumpet /c	John Smith	.18 3/4
1 Clock	A. J. Sims	.25
1 Table	Berry Hamblet	1.00
2 Crocks /C	L. B. Farris	.62 1/2
1 Jar /c	Madison Moore	.31 1/4
2 do	Joseph Jones Senr.	45 1/2
3 pails	Samuel Couch	.37 1/2
1 Tubb	A. Gettings	.43 3/4
1 Meal Bag	William Shuster	.62 1/2
1 man's Saddle	Wm. Knowles Jr.	2.12 1/2
1 do	Thomas Green	.50
1 do do	Smith Cantrell	4.93 3/4
1 Bridle	L. B. Farris	.87 1/2
1 Sotne Hammer	Thomas Robinson	1.06 1/4
2 Augers & Handsaw	John Cantrell	1.00

1 plane	Smith Walling	.25
1 Coffee Mill	John Jones Jr.	1.00
6 Chairs	James Holland	1.56¼
2 do	A. Gettings	.31
3 dO	Archebald Jutson	.75
2 slays	L. B. Farriss	1.56¼
1 Barrel & Plunder	J. Jones Senr.	.81¼
2 Gimblets /c	Benton Denton	.51¼
1 Jug	E. Denton	.12½
1 Tray & Sifter	A. Gritting	.75
1 Barrel /c	B. Denton	.43 3/4
1 half Bushel A. McGowen		37½
P.214 1 pr. Spurs	John Cantrell	.43 3/4
1 Shovel	J. Humphey	1.00
2 H es	Thomas Green	.31¼
1 Pitch fork & hoe	Oscar Denton	.25
1 Mattock	J. Humphrey	.75
1 Singletree & Clevis	S. B. Scoggin	.43 3/4
1 Doubletree /c	Tho. Green	.37½
1 pr Strichess	E. Rogers	.31¼
1 Scythe	Josh. Mason	2.06¼
1 pr Warping bars	A. Hutson	.25
1 frame & Spools	B. Denton	.43 3/4
1 Prs. Gears	A. McGowen	.75
1 do	S. Cantrell	.37
1 do	do	.68 3/4
1 do	J. McDaniel	.61
1 Grindstone	S. Walling	.37½
1 Bed & furniture	S. Couch	10.25
1 do	James Herd	15.00
1 Oven /c	A. Gettings	1.12½
1 Small pot	do	.31¼
1 Frying pan	G. Gawn 62½	.62½
1 Skillet & lid	S. Beasley	1.06¼
1 pot	do	1.00
1 Large pot	J. Dobkin	2.93 3/4
1 Loom	E. Rogers	4.68 3/4
1 Wheel	John Rigsby	.37½
1 Wheel & Craddles	S. Denton	.50
1 Razor & Strap	Thos. Rogers	68 3/4
1 do	B. Denton	.43 3/4
1 Glass hone /c	do	.18 3/4
1 pr. pot hooks	J. J nes Senr.	.37½
1 Trunk	do	.25
1 Bureau	J. Cantrell	10.25
31/2 Bushels wheat	J. Roberts	3.50
1 Cupboard	S. Cantrell	6.31¼
1 plow	S. B. Scoggin	1.31¼
1 do	Thos. Green	1.00
1 Side Saddle	J. W. Copeland	3.56¼
1 Bowl	J. Knowles	6¼
1 Bell	W. C. Denton	00.53¼
1 yoke Oxen	S. Couch	.33
1 wagon	Thos. Green	17.75

1 Heifer	S. Gawen	5.25
P 215 1 Steer	Lewis Philips	8.00
1 Cow & Calf	J. Dobkin	10.06¼
1 Ditto	A. Gettings	13.00
1 Ditto	J. Derrydield	12.12½
6 sheep	William Beshears	7.06¼
3 hogs 1 choice	S. Couch	19.25
3 do 2nd do	J. Denton	18.68 3/4
2 do 3rd do	A. Dillon	11.56½
2 do 4thdo	Tomington Fifer	10.00
2 Shoats 1 do	James Dillon	4.12½
6 do 2nd do	William Overton	12.56¼
9 do 3rd do	James Dillon	9.56¼
1 Bay horse	do	71.00
1 Sorrel Mare	Gr. Rogers	48.00
1 Black do	do	65.06¼
1 Wheat fan	P. Wright	14.00
1 Pile Rye	William Freeman	3.00
1 pile Oats & fodder	Gr. Rogers	1.12½
1 Pack oats	William Bysharea	5.00
1 Cutting Box	J. Hujphrey	2.183/4
1 Set fire dogs & tongs	R. Mason	1.75
1 pr Saddle Bags	G. Rogers	2.06¼
3 Bee Gums	Sarah Denton	3.25
1 pile Corn	B. Denton	9.00
1 Axe	G. Rogers	.62½
50 Bushels Corn	J. Walling	13.18 3/4
1 pile Corn	Isaac Denton	20. 08
2 Barrels Rotten corn	A. Gettings	.75
2 Troughs	Ox. Denton	.25
1 meat trough	S. Couch	.25
1 Keg	A. Gettings	.12½
200 acres land	Smith Walling	1200.00
601/2 do	Jude B. Moore	200.000
1 Cash Note on Jas. A. Moore doubtful		& 10.00
The amount this Sale is $2006.07½		2006.07

Oscar Denton Ex.

Recorded 27 Jany 1836. J. A. Lane Ck. by N. OldhamD. C.

P 216 Nuncupation Will, James Young Decd.

State of Tennessee }
White County } January 14th A. D. 1836.

Be it remembered that on the Seventh day of January in the year of our Lord eighteen hundred and thirty Six in the County and State aforesaid at the late residence of James Young Merchant of Said County and durin his Sickness, the Said James Young now deceased, being of sound and disposing m mind and memory did make this following written or nuncupatived Will and disire--That William L. Young my brother and equal partner in trade Shall manage and carry on the concern, pursuing the course the two formerly pursued. Six years and at the end of Six years my four younger brothers Robert Stanfreed, Yound, Andrew Logan Yound, Miston Yound and Joseph Harrisson Young to have my Share of the proceeds they rendered Services as required. And I want you and uncle Crowder Cemaning Ruben Crowder to attend to it, and Uncle Crowder to do the writing therein or at and there time, and the undersigned understood the Testator that it was his wish that they should bear witness and see that it was fulfilled and carried into execution hereby attest the Same this day above at which time it was written by the Said Richard Crowder.

Richard Crowder
William L. Young

State of Tennessee }
White County } April Sessions 1836 of the County Court of White County.

This day the death of James Young Merchant late of the town of Sparta was suggested, and at the Same time the within writing was produced, purposing to be the nuncupative will of Said James Young deceased.— Where upon the Same or like manner was proven by the oath of William L. Young and Richard Crowder in whose presence the Statement was made by Said James Young concerning the dispositon of his property as he wished and they particularly called upon and that the Said James Young was at the time of making Said Statement and giving Said directions of Sound and disposing mind and memory. and that the said Instruction and directions concerning the disposal of his affects, was by Said William L. Young and Richard Crowder reduced to writing within three days after the death of Said James of Said instructions and directions as aforesaid in his last P 217 illness and Shortly before his death, which is decreed by the court to be properly and Sufficently proven and ordered to be recorded. Given at office 11th April A. D. 1836. Test Jacob A. Lane Clerk of White County Court

Recorded and examined 23rd April A. D. 1836
Test. Jacob A. Lane Clerk of White County Court.

An amount of the Sales of the property of Robert Goade Decd. returned upon oath by John Franklin Admr. at April Session 1836.

Charles Reeves to Shucks and 3 Barrels of Corn	7.62½
William Overton to 3 Barrels Corn	6.03
John Wilson to 3 Barrels Corn	6.00
Edmond Harper to balance of Corn	12.65
All of which are Submitted this 11th day of April A. D. 1836	32.27½

John Franklin Admr. of Estate of Robert Goade Decd.

Recorded and examined 23rd April A. D. 1836. Test—Jacob A. Lane Clerk White County Court

Assignment of provisions to the widow of Wm. Brown Decd. returned on oath by Anthony Sibrell and Mark Lowery, two of the Commissioners at April Session 1836. of the White County Court.

State of Tennessee }
White County } iss.—

We the undersigned Commissioners having been appointed by the County Court of White County to assign and Set apart one years provisions for the Support and maintainence of the widow and children of William Brown Deceased having met at the Said Widows residence and proceeded to set apart and assign provisions as follows towit: two thousand five hundred weight of

Pork 200 Bushels corn 2 Stacks fodder, ten Bushels wheat, Seventy pounds Sugar forty pounds Coffee 1 Bl. Salt of 6 Bushels fifty pounds picked Cotton, fifty pound Wool, the family to be furnished with a Sufficant Quanility of Shoes all of which is respectfully Submitted. Given under our hands and Seals this rth day Febry. A. D. 1836.

Anthony Dibrell (Seal)
Daniel Clark (Seal)
Recorded and examined 23rd April A. D. 1836Mark Lowrey (Seal)
Test Jacob A. Lane Clerk of White County Court.

P 218 Inventory of the property of William Carroll Decd. returned on oath by May J. Carroll Admx. at April Session A. D. 1836. One note on William Austin made payable to Cuetus McDowell for \$2..2½ due 3rd Apl. 1833. Doubtful. One note on Thomas Gann and Sopha Gwan for three hundred doooars due 1st March 1836. Good One note onThomas Gwan and Sopha Gwan for one hundred and twenty five dollars in Merchantable horses valued at trade rates due s5th December 1835. One note on John Hall for two hundreed doooars. with credit of forty dollarsendorced on Same bearing interest from the date Sworn 2nd June 1832, and due two years thereafter doubtful One note on Menkins Green payable to Wm. Cochrane for one dollar in Cotton due 17th Sept. 1831. bad. One note on Joseph Dalton for five dollars due the 1st day of April 1835. good One note on David Derling payable to Joseph Turney for eleven Barrels of Corn on Same due 10th Novr. 1833 doubtful. One note on F. W. Capps for dollars due 25th December 1830. Bad. One note on Matthew Brady for five dollars due 25th December 1834.Bad One Bell worth 1\$. Omitted to be Sold The Black 2 year old filly and Gray horse. Stated as sold. on the proceeding page, were received in discharge of the note for onehundred and twenty five dollars in Merchantable horses on Thomas and Sopha Givan Due 25th Decr. 1835. May J. Carroll
Recorded and examined 23 April 1836. Test--Jacob A. Lane Clerk
White County Court.

Account of the sales of the estate of Moses Godard deceased returned upon oath by George Sparkman Administrator at April term 1836.

17 head of Hogs sold to Arnold Moss	\$17.00
1 Bay Mare sold to Sampson Godard	25.00
2 old meal Tubbs sold to same	.12½
1 Rifle Gun and untensels sold to Elijah Hill	12.50
1 Cotton Wheel 1 flax wheel & 1 bottle Sold to Same	.62½
1 Candle stick & 1 handwas sold to Elijah Hill	1.18
1 Bell and 1 Bottle Sold to John M. Carter	.87½
1 falling axe sold to William Sparkman	.50
1Mattock sold to Joseph Mitchell	.75
1 Auger Sold to William L. Mitchell	.68½
1 pr farming Gear sold Zachariah Simmons	1.37½
1 Feather Bed bed Stead & Card & furniture sold to same	12.25
1 side Iron & Chest 1 Table 3 head of Sheep sold to Same	6.37½
1 Feather bed and furniture Sold to Tilman Brown	7.62½
P 219 6 pewter plates 1 pewter Dish 5 or 6 Knives and forks Sold to Tho. Roberts	2.00
1 plow Sold to James Moore	1.12½
1 Chin Sold to Pleasant Hogg	.25
1 cow and Calf Sold to William Sparkman Jr.	11.56¼
1 Oven & L d 1 Kittle & Hooks Sold to Jesse Hopkins	7.25
1 Sorrel Colt Sold to James Hollingsworth	25.00

One note on Jesse Hopkins due the 10th day of March 1836 11.00
All of which is submitted this 11 day of April 1836.

George Sparkman Admr.
of the Est. Moses Godard Decd.

Recorded and examined 5 May 1836 N. Oldham Clerk White County Court.

Account of the Sales of the property of the Estate of William Carrol decd. returned M. J. Carrol admx. at April Sessions A. D. 1836.

1 Bed & furniture & Bedstead Sold to Mary Jane Carrol	2.00
Big wheel small table & Chest & toilet glass do	3.25
Churn, Water pail, Tin bucket, Small pot. oven & Lid skillet	1.00
Smoothing iron pot rack and fire Dogs do	.50
2 Jugs 1 Jar 1 axe 1 Walnut table 1 Side Saddle do	3.00
1 Hand Saw Sold to Joshua Hickey	1.12½
1 Man's Saddle to Thomas Dewise	16.37½
1 Fancy Clock to Mary Jane Carrol	10.50
1 yearling to Lewis Turner	2.62½
1 cow to Asa Certain	10.62½
1 Dark Chestnut Stallin to Joshua Hickey	115.00
1 Brown do to same	185.00
1 Black 2 years old Filly Mary Jane Carrol	13.50
1 Gray Horse Nelson Hewett	72.25
1 Carry all Wagon to Mary Jane Carrol	107.
Total	243.75

Mary Jane Carrol Admx.

Recorded and examined the 5 May 1836 N. Oldham Clerk
White County Court.

Report of John Walker Guardian to heirs of Kendal Savage dec. made upon oath at April term 1836. Towit:
No attention since last report John Walker Guard.
Recd. 5 May 1836 N. Oldham Clerk White County Court.

P 220 Account of the Sales of the property of the estate of William Brown deceased returned James Thomas & Jno. Brown Admr. at April term 1836 Towit: 1 Bed & furniture 500 1 do do 500 to Catharine Brown 10.00

1 Bed & funiture $5.00 ' Chairs $1.00 3 Tables $1.00 do	7.00
1 Loom $1.00 Kitchen funiture & Shovel $1.00 Table funiture $2.00	4.00
1 Side Saddle $5.00 1 pr Saddle bags 2.00 2 Wheel & Real 50 do	7.50
1 Scythe & Cradle 1.00 1 Frow 25 1 Coffee mill 50 do	1.75
Smoothing Iron, Cotton Cards, Sheep Shears, & Snuffers 50/	.50
1 Sifter 25 1 Iron pot rack 50 1 Axe 25 Large kittle1.00	2.00
1 Hammer & Princes 25 2 old axes & 1 Gimlet 25 do	.50
2 plows & Gears 1 Bull tongue 2 hoes 2 [illegible] Singletrees do	1.00
60 head of Stock Hogs 9 Sheep 1 Heifer do	35.00
1 Heifer 3.00 9 geese 1.00 1 Jug 2 crocks 1 pitchter 1 Jar .50	4.50
and at the Same time negro Bony was hired to Catharine Brown until the first of January next 1837 for	40.00
	113.75

1 Negro boy Bony One not4 executed by Drury Smith to Samuel Fitzpatrick for $58.00 in Current Bank Notes exd. 1st. Decr. 1819 and due 1 January 1820. Dispuate------ One due Bill executed by George W. Campbell 22nd June 1833 for $3.00 Doubtful James Thomas
Jno. Brown
Admrs. of Wm. Brown ded.

Recorded and examined the 5th day of May A. D. 1836.
Test N. Oldham Clerk of White County Court.

Report of Settlement made by pmissioners with John Franklin Admr. of Robert Goard ded. returned at ay term A. D. 1836.

Towit find Admr. Chargeable for property sold at First Sale	32.27½	
find Admr. Chargeable for property Sold at Second Sale	78.85	
Debit	111.12½	
Credit admr. by order of Court for the following sums		
To wit for Receipt Marked A.	7.50	
" " " B.	31.93 3/4	
" " " C.	6.56¼	
" " " D.	5.00	
" " " E.	.40	
" " " F.	5.00	71.40
Allance made by Court for Services	15.00	
	$39.72½	

Leaving balance in the Admr. Hands of $39.72½ whi h is by law bound to account for****
Montgomery C. Dibrell
David Snodgrass Coms.

Recorded 5 May 1836 N. Oldham Clerk.

Report of Settlement made by Commissioners with Daniel Walling & Isaac Taylor Executor of the estate of William Fisher ded. May term 1836.

The Executors stand chargewith the following sums towit:

No. 1 Amount of Sales returned to White County Court		569.20¼
No. 2 Amt. notes returned do		376.43
		945.66¼
Credits		
By Wilson Upchurch receipt No. 1	60.00	
By Nancy Fisher do No 2	60.00	
By Samuel A. Moore do No. 3	60.00	
By Jacob A Lane do No 4	3.28	
By do do No 5	1.75	
By Jno. Fisher recpt to Dannil Walling (legal Heir)	69.77	
By David L. Mitchell recept for tax No. 7	.45	
By David Young do - No. 8	2.62½	

Daniel Walling produced the notes as charged in the account against himself and Isaac Taylor Executors as aforesaid as charge in Item No. 2 and heretofore returned by executors as ensolvent and desperate with the exception of one note on James Jaxton for Ten ollars which said Walling says he has given out for collection and money not made on it to his knowledge.

Amt.	376.46	
By Cullen E. Jacob receipt No. 9	6.00	
By Isaa c Taylor receipt which we think reasonable	15.00	
By Danuel Wallings account for his attention to Said estate which we thinkreasonable	27.00	682.30½

Leaving in the hands of Executors this Sums 263.35 3/4
If the Court should allow the account of the said Walling there will still remain in the hands of Said Executor the Sum of two hundred Sixty three dollars fifty five & 3/4 cents that is Availble and due Said estate. We well here, by the request of Isaac TAylor one of the Executors, suggest that he holds the receipt of his Co--executor D niel Walling, in full of the money or effects of Said estate that had went int. the hands of Said estate that had went int. the hands of Said Taylor as executors and thereby releases S id TAylor for any liability of Said estate as regards his the said a Isaac Tylor liability to the heirs of Said Said estate, the notes as Numbered in the Second item marked No. 2 charging the executor is also in the hands of Said Executor Daniel Walling to make collections if it can be done of which is respectfully submitted to the worshipful court now in Session May the 2nd 1836. By the Commissioners John Jett
Samuel A. Moore
Lewis Pittet

Recorded 5 may 1836 N. Oldham Ck.

P 222 Report of Settlement made by Commissioners with Thomas Hill Senr. Guardian to the Heirs of ames Hill deceased at May 1836.

Guardian to the said Heirs Dr. Agreeable to his return made at January term 1822 being paper No. 1 the Sum of 254.26 3/4
Cr.
By a receipt from Claiborn Hill one of the Heirs of Said James Hill Deceased 63.50
By a receipt from Thomas J. Hill another of the Heirs of Jas. Hill deceased 63.50
By a receipt from James M. Hill another of the heirs of as Hill deceased 63.50 190.50
$63.76 3/4

Leaving a balance due to the Heirs of Sixty three dollars Seventy Six and three fourth Cents All of which is Submitted. iven under our hands and Seal this 9th day of March 1836. Joseph Cummings Jr. (Seal)
Lewis Pettit (Seals)
Recorded 5th day of May A. D. 1836. Test N. Oldham Clerk
of White County Court.

Report of John Mason Guardian to James Howard a minor heir of James Howard deceased returned upon oath at oaty at June term 1836, Towit: That since the last return made by him as Guardian His in the year 1836 he paid Richard Nelson Esq. for Robert Howard deceased in favor of said James and others Compluinants the sum of 10.00
Paid Ann Howard toward her Dower in the lands of Said Robert Howard deceased so for as James is interested 13.25
23.25

Said Guardian has received since last return money belonging to Said James his ward of the money allowed same James & Jesse Bullock by the Commissioners who divided the Land 9.32½
He also has received from Ignatious Howard ADmr. of Said Robert Howard ded. part of the share of S id Infant in Said estate 5.30
$12.62½

Said Guardian has not made any interest on Said Sum of $12.62½ cents but he paid it out in part satisfaction of the said sum of $23.25 paid out by Said Guardian as above John Mason
Recorded 10th June 1836 N. Oldham Clerk.

The above is a just and true account of the property of the deceased So far as has come to my hands. June the 6th 1836. John R. Gann Admr.
Recorded 10th June 1836 N. Oldham Clk.

Report of Commissioners assigning one years provisions to the widow of ~~Zacharia Jones deceased at June term 1836~~ 1836.
~~Towit: One hundred and fifty Bushels of Corn Ten Choice Hogs~~ Twenty five Bushels of Wheat Seventy five pounds of Bacon four hundred pound of Beef two Barrels Salt one with the head out the other three hundred and fifty eight pounds and thirty dollars worth of Sugar & Coffee and what chickens is belonging to the Said Estate also Cabages potatoes. Given under our hands and Seals this 31st day of October 1835. Isaac Tayler (Seal)
Recorded 11th June A. D. 1836 William Fisk Senr. (Seal)
N. Oldham Eli Sims (Seals) Clerk

Report of Commissioners assigning one years provisions to the widow of Jaber Anderson deceased at June term 1836.
Towit: Four pork Hogs one barrel Salt all the corn raised on the plantation supposed not to be more that fifty Bushels and all the oats and potatoes raised on the farm chickens & Geese and five dollars worth of Coffee & Sugar. Given under our hands and Seals this 31st October 1835.

Recorded 10th June A. D. 1836	Isaac Taylor (Seal)
N. Oldham Clerk.	William Fisk (Seal)
	Eli Sims (Seal)

Report of commissioners assigning one years provisions to widow of William Jones decd. at June term 1836. Towit: 100 Bushels corn 8 shoats ½ barrel Salt what chickens and Gese belongs to the farm also five dollars worth sugar & coffee. Given under our hands and Seals 31st Oct. 1835.

Recorded 11 June 1836	Isaac Taylor (Seal)
N. Oldham	William Fisk (Seal)
Clerk	Eli Sims (Seal)

P 225 Report of the Settlement made by commissioners with Robert L. Mitchell and William H. Baker Executors of the estate of Edward Holmes deceased at June term A. D. 1836.

Executors are charged with the following notes & acts DR.

To 1 Note on Mediens A. Long 27 Nov. 1832 due 6 Mos after date 1830 18.00
" 1 Due bill on Julies Sanders March 8th 1830 not good 3.00
" 1 Note on Medicus A. Long due July 9th 1832
With credit indorsed on the same for $11.50 having balance due on said Note 6.50

To 4 notes of hand executor by R. T. Baker each note for $25. one due on 1833 one in 1834 one in 1835 one in 1836 100.00
1 Note on R. T. Baker executed 6 January 1832 due 1st Nov 1832 with a Credit on Said note of $30 having balance of 20. 00

Amount of Sale of property as returned to Court by R. L. Mtvhell on of the Executors 321.59
property Sold and not returned in the above named sale and not returned to Court 51.50

The hire of negro boy John to William Baker for the year 1834	34.00
The hire of negro Girl Caroline to J. Jenkins for the year 1834	36.00
The hire of negro Girl Eliz a & Jefferson to R. L. Mitchell for year 1835	51.00
The hire of negro Boy Jefferson to R. L. Mitchell for the year 1835	22.00
To the hire of Caroline to Daniel Calrk for year 1835	50.00
To the hire of John to William Baker for year 1835	36.00
The negro wommmnEliza was hired to Nancy HOlmes for 1335 which the executors said the negro woman was sick and rendered no service therefore no charge is made for said hire negro woman for said year .	
To the hire of negro Girl Caroline for 1836 due 25th Decr. 1836.	48.50
To the hire of negro Boy John for 1836 due 25 December 1836	50.00
To thg hire of negro Boy Jefferson for 8836 due 25th Dec.	30.00
Mrs. ancy Holmes the widow retained the following negroĕs belonging to said estate towit: Caroline John Jefferson from the 14th of Fevruary 1833. to the 9th day of November 1833. being eight months and twenty five days and the executors admit that the hire of said of negroes was worth this sum which they charge themselves with	56.62½
The Executors represent and shew to the Commissioners that after they had taken and returned and Inventory of the property belonging to the estate and they had advertised the said property for sale that Nancy Holmes the widow dippose of the following articles of property included in articles of property encluded in the Inventory at the private Sale and madd use of the proceeds thereof towit: two coverlids worth $12.00 That she also Killed and made use of one Steer belonging to the estate Worth $8.00 which sums the executors has charged themselves. with	20.00
P 226 To the rant or use of plantation for 1833 to Nancy Holmes wich the executors has also charged themselves with	20.00
To the Hire of negro Girl Eliza 26 days to Robert L. Mitchell in the year 1835	2.60
	977.21 3/4

Cr. By the following Receipts & vouchers towit:

No. 1	By	Jesse Lincoln account $10.25	$10.25
No. 2	"	Carrick & Leftwich Respt.	$12.75
No 3	"	ancy Holmes "	168.18 3/4
No 4	"	Anthony ibrell's clerk"	5.75
" 5	"	Nancy Holmes "	5.00
" 6	"	William Fisks "	2.62½
" 7	"	George W. Easthams Account	4.00
" 8	"	William Fisks receipts	.62½
" 9	"	N te lifted by R. L. Mitchell from Carrek & Leftwich	10.37½
" 10		J. A. Lanes recpt	7.50
" 11		JJames Hayes account for coffin	4.50
" 12		Eli Sims Receipt	3.00
" 13		Cash paid Robert Gamble on note	79.97½

No 14 By R. A. Mitchell Exr. paid Lane Lane & Anderson 11.58 3/4
" 15 " D. L. Mitchell Receipt for Tax 3.09 1/4
" 16 " Edward Holmes note & Eli Sims to
Levi Oliver paid R. L. Mitchell 5.62½
" 17 " By J. A. Lane receipt 3.30½
" 18 " William G. Sims receipt for tax .35
" 19 " David P. Flower account 11.00
" 20 " 2 Receipts from William G. Sims 2.02 3/4
" 21 " Levi Oliver Receipt .87½
" 22 " Thomas Williams account for Schooling 2.50
" 23 Cash paid Carrick & Leftwich on note 1.18 3/4
" 24 " Nancy Holmes receipt 20.00
" 25 " Rovert S. Mitchell account 2.50 378.64
The executors agree that they ought to be charged 598.57
with receipt of Nancy Holmes No. 24 20.00
618.57

State of Tennessee }
White County } Pursuant to an order of the worshipful County Court at May Sessions 1836 appointed the undersigned Commissioners to Settle with Robert S. Mitchell and William Baker executors of the estate of Edward Holmes deceased do certify that we met in Sparta on the 30th May 1836 in the court house when the above named executors presented us debts P 227 and Vouchers as in this account and the papers as filed & mentioned, the court will proceed that the execurors has prodéced their accounts which is not credited in the account we find in the hands of the executors the sum of six hundred and eighteen Dollars fifty Seven cients of Available funds due said estate. Given under our hands this 30th day May 1836.
Recorded 11 June 1836 John Jett
N. Oldham Clerk. David Snodgrass
William Bruster

Inventory & Sales of the property of the estate of George Allen decd. and returned upon oath by Joseph Herd Admr. at July Temr A. D. 1836. Inventory one Negro an named Anthony a slave
Inventory one negro Man Named Dick a slave
" one negro woman named Esther a slave
" one negro woman named Suck a slave
" one negro child named Charolteet a slave
" one negro child named Sally a slave
Sold property as follows on 5th May 1836 Vis:

1 case of Bottles sold to Samul L. Tury	2.25
1 Lot of Tools sold Isaac Adcock	3.50
1 Lot of Augers sold to Levi Bosorth	.50
1 Anville & file sold to James McGuire	2.06½
1 pr Steelyards sold to Saml. S. Allen	.87½
1 Frow sold to William Beasley	.37½
2 Thmahawks sold Samul H. Allen	.75
1 Mattock sold Levi Bosorth	.75
3 Hoes to Phebe Allen	.75
1 Broad Axe sold I. W. Allen	.75
2 Falling Axes and Tomahawks to Samuel Allen	1.00
1 Lot Chains to Samuel Allen	1.06¼
1 Stone Hammer & wedge to Saml. Strong	1.50
2 plowes to James McGuire	.50

1 Hackle to Phebe Allen	1.25
1 pr Sheep Shares and candle moulds to L. Bosorth	.50
1 plow to Zach. Lefever	1.12½
1 Lot of Irons sold to same	2.25
1 Scythe and cradle sold to Phebe Allen	2.00
1 do do Isaac Adcock	1.62½
1 Mans Saddle to Levi Bosorth	9.37½
1 Sheep Skin sold to Emery Bennett	1.06¼
1 Lot of Wool sold to Phebe Allen	1.00
1 side sole leather & deer Skin to S. H. Allen	2.75
1 Side do to John S. Allen	2.12½
P 228 Amt Brought over	
1 side sole leather sold to Jno. W. Allen	2.18 3/4
1 side do James McGuire	2.06¼
1 Lot of Leather sold to Jesse Allen	.50
1 Raw hide to John M. Whitley	2.06¼
1 Lot Deer Skins to same	1.56¼
1 Gun Barrel to William Allen	8.00
1 Book to Allen Dunn	1.00
1 Shot Gun sold to George H. Allen	1.00
1 Scrap Book sold to John G. Allen	1.87½
1 Lot Books sold to Phebe Allen	.50
1 Candle stand & Sticks sold to W. H. Allen	2.50
1 Large Jug to Jno M. Whitley	.50
1 large Pitcher to Jno. W. Allen	.50
1 Lot of Tin sold to Phebe Allen	.12½
1 check rul sold to James Perkins	1.37½
1 Flax wheel to Nathan Bosorth	2.37½
1 Wheat Fan to Same	16.50
1 Ciders Barrels to Saml. S. Allen	.75
1 cotton wheel to Nathaniel Steele	.37½
1 do to Phebe Allen	.50
1 Gigg sild to Allen Dunn	.62½
6 Bee Gums to Phebe Allen	6.00
1 cupboard and furniture to same	10.00
1 patent clock to same	5.00
1 Bureau to same	5.00
1 Bedstead & furniture to same	10.00
1 " " do	10.00
1 " " do	5.00
1 Trunk to do	.50
1 do 50¢ 7 chairs 50 to do	1.00
1 Horse to same	32.00
1 colt Sold to Jesse Allen	56.00
1 Red Cow & Calf sold to Phebe Allen	10.00
1 " do do William Allen	9.00
1 Heifer to Phebe Allen	6.00
1 White cow & calf sold to Same	8.00
1 Heifer Sold to Hannah Allen	8.25
1 Red Heifer to Jesse Allen	5.37½
1 white do to John G. Allen	3.75
1 Red Bull to James Easthern	9.25
1 small Bull to James T. Hayes	4.12½
8 head of Sheep to Saml. Allen	8.87½

P 229 Amount Brought up

1 yoke of Oxen Sold to John M. Whitley	36.00
10 first choice Hogs to Phebe Allen	9.00
10 second choice do to Emory Bennett	10.00
9 third do do to same	5.25
1 ox cart to James Davis	7.68 3/4
1 Large Kittle Sold to Saml. Allen	3.81½
1 do do Jame F. Hayes	3.50
1 Log Chain do Isaac Adcock	3.75
1 Lot of Kitchen Funriture to Phebe Allen	2.00
1 Large Pot to James T. hayes	2.00
1 Pan sold N. G. State	.62½
1 Grindstone to J. W. Allen	1.50
1 Loom to John M. Whitley	2.62½
1 Table to Phebe Allen	2.00
1 do " "	[illegible].06¼
1 Rat trap " Orven Davis	.25
1 negro boy Anthony hired to Tho. Leak for 3 months	32.00
2 Negroes Dick & Esther hired to P. Allen for 3 months	17.00
3 negroes Viz: Suck and 2 children hired to Same 3 mos.	10.00
Sold at private sale 2 hogs heads of Tobacco to Johnson & Rayburn after deducting for less /c amounting in all this sum	106.87½
Total amount	$556.37½

Recoded 7 July 1836 Joseph Herd Admr.

Report of Commissioners assigning one years provisions to widow & family of Joseph Parker deceased made at July Sessions A. D. 1836. Towit: 75 lb of Bacon--3 hogs (choice) 30 Bushels of Corn, Ten Bushels of wheat ten pounds of wool fifteen pounds of Cotton 5lb Flax, 10 lb Coffee & 16 lb. sugar. Given under our hands & Seals this 4 July 1836.

David Snodgrass
Recorded 7th July 1836 M. C. Dibrell
Samuel Brown

Report of commissioners assigning one years provisions to Widow & family of George Allen dcd. made at July Term 1836. Towit: we set apart Bacon supposed to be 300lb. 50 lb. Brown Sugar 25lb. coffee 3 Bushels Wheat what soap and lard there is on hand what corn there is one hand supposed to 100 Bushels and six first choice hogs an account of these not being a P 230 sufficuncy of Bacon for the support of Said family we set apart the six hogs mentioned above all of which is respectdully submitted. Given under our hands and seals this 5th day of May 1836.

William Glenn)
Richard Crowder) Coms.
David Snodgrass)

Report of commissioners, assigning provisions for one years to the widow and family of William Dubcab deceased made at June term A. D. 1836. Towit:

We assign and set apart the corn on hand and all the samll grain growing One cow Beast for Beef and the use of three cows and calves for milk, and as much of the Hogs as will do her and family till killing time and then one thousand pounds of pork

This 4th day of June 1836 William Hitchcock (Seal)
Recorded 2 Sept. 1836

N. Oldham Ck. Ebner Jones (Seal)
William Kerr (Seal)

In the name of God Amen! I Thomas Curtis do make and publish this my last will and testament being in Sound mind and memory. I give my body to the grave and my Soul to God who gave it--Item first--I give and bequeath to my beloved wife Mary Curtis my land and plantation whereon I now live, all my cows and Stock of every discription also all house hold and Kitchen furniture my tools of all kind I also give her my books also my ready money in hand or due from any source, and desire her as above to have full possession of the above articles above mentioned in peace from my death during her natural life to dispose of as she pleases before or at her death. Assigned and delivered in the presence of Barnett Kemp and Mary Kemp this 3rd day of November 1833.

B. Kemp) Thomas Curtis (Seal)
Mary X Kemp) I appoint and request John Alerson Jr. to act as
her mark ( ) Executor to this my last will & testament.

State of Tennessee)
White County) July Term A. D. 1836

This day was proclaimed in open Court a writing purposting to be P 231 the last will and testament of Thomas Curtis deceased late of the County of White and the due execution and Publication thereof as the last will and testament of the said Thomas Curtis deceased was proven in open court by the oath of Barnett Kemp one of the subscribing witness thereto for the purposes and things therein mentioned and that the said Thomas Curtis was at the date of the execution and publication thereof of sound and disposing mind and memory. Given at office the 4th July 1836.

Test. N. Oldham Clerk of White County Court

State of Tennessee)
White County) September Term A. D. 1836

This day was produced in open court a writing purposing to be the last will and testament of Thomas Curtis deceased late of the County of White and the due execution and publication thereof as the last will and testament of the last will and testament of the said Thomas Curtis deceased was proven in open court by the oath of Mary Kemp the other subscribing witness thereto for the same purpose--and that the said Thomas Curtis was at the date of the execution and publication thereof of sound and disposing mind and memory whereupon it is ordered to be recorded. Given at office the 5th day of September 1836. Test N. Oldham Clerk of White County Court.

Recorded 30th Sept. 1836.
N. Oldham Clerk

Report of Joseph Herd Guardian to Susannah Bryan Infant child of John Bryan Jr. deceased made upon oath at Sept. term A. D. 1836.

Reports that his ward has entermarried James Mason since which time Viz: July 20th 1836 he has had a final Settlement with said Mason and has produced his and Susannah Mason receipt in fuol of that date which receipt is here filed as part of this report marked exhibit A. September 5 1836

Joseph Herd, Guardian

Exhibit A.

Received of Joseph Herd Administrator of John Bryan deceased and Guardian to Susannah Bryan heir at Law of said Bryan decd. the full amount of all the estate of all the estate of Said deceased due from said Administrator and Guardian Received by us this 20th day of July 1836.

James Mason

Attest William Rainey   Susannah Mason
Recorded 6 Oct. 1836   W. Oldham Clerk.

P 232 Report of John H. Anderson, Guardian for Mattheas Anderson, Mary Anderson and Reuben Anderson infant children of William Anderson deceased returned of oath at September term A. D. 1836. as follows towit:

To rent of Brick house in Sparta for the year ending 20 Decr. 1831	$50.00
To hire of Negro boy Sam for year ending 4th Nov. 1832	49.00
To hire of boy Amos ending same time	56.00
To hire of negro woman Lydia ending same time	40.00
To hire of Negro Girl Riggy for yeqr ending Same time	12.00
To rent of two unemproved lots in Sparta for the year ending Same time	3.00
To this sum received for rent of farm in the Hickory valley for year ending 1st. January 1832	25.00
To rent of farm in the Barrens for the year ending 1 Decr. 11832	48.25
To hire of Negro man Amos for the year ending 4 Nov. 1833	56.00
To hire of negro woman Lydia Same year	30.00
To hire of negro boy Sam same year	50.00
To hire of negro Girl Peggy same year	15.00
To rnet of farm in the Barrens for the year ending 1 Jany 1833	37.52½
To hire of boy Amos for the year ending 4th Nov. 1834	56.00
To hire of boy Sam for Same year	50.00
To hire of Girl Lydia same year	35.00
To hire of Girl Peggy for same year	20.00
To rent of farm in the barrens for the year ending 1 Jany 1834	67.62½
To rent received for brick house in Sparta from 7 Febry 1833 to 1 Jany 1834	25.00
To rent received for part of Brick house in Sparta for 28 days commencing 2nd Augt. 1834	1.00
To rent of one Room in brick house in Sparta from 8 Nov. 1834 to 18 July 1835	7.00
To rent of one room in Brick house in Sparta from 29 July 1834 to 29 Nov 1835	26.66
To hire of Negro boy Sam for same year	50.00
To hire of negro Girl Peggy for year ending 4th Nov. 1835.	25.00
To hire of Sam up to 1st January 1835	6.25
To hire of Lydia & boy Amos from 4 Nov 1834 to 1 Jany1836	107.62½
To hire of Girl Peggy from 4th Nov. 1835 to 1 Jany 1836	4.00
August 20. 1835 To rent of room in the brick house 2 weeks	1.00
To rent of farm in Hickory valley for the years 1833, 1834 & 1835 exclusive of repairs this sum	4.27
To rent of farm in the barrens for the year ending 1 Jany 1836	67.50

To interest on the forgoing Items, up to the 5 Sept. 1836	137.52½
To rent of the farm in the barrens for the year ending 1 Jany 1836 part of the farm only being Cultivated	21.62½
To Interest on the same upto 5 Sept 1836	.85
up	$1185.71 2/3

P 233 Amt brought up	1185.71 2/3
To rent of Brick house in Sparta for the year ending 20 Decr. 1232	50.00
To interest thereon from 20 Decr. 1832 to 5 Sept. 1836	&11.10
Debit against Guardian	1246.81 2/3

Credits

1831 May 7. By reapirs done on Kitchen in Barrens	3.00
1832 Jany. 1 By repairs on farm H ckory Valley	20.00
1831 Oct. 29 By amt. paid for taxes of estate 1830	23.50
183. Oct 25 By cash for putting 39 panes glass in Brick house	1.25
1834 paid Jacob A. Lane Clerks fees for appontment of Guardian	1.75
1833 By repairs on the Barrens farm	22.02½
1834 By repairs done on same farm	16.00
" July Lock bought and to brick house town	2.00
1835 Sept. 8 By Lock bought for same house	1.12½
1836 Aug 18. By Taxes paid for estate of Wards for 1831, 2, 3, 4, & 1835	39.33 1/3
1836 Sept. 5 By interest CAlculated on the foregoing Credits to this date——	20.29¼
In favor of Guardian	
	150.27½
Leaves a bal of	1096.54¼

against said Guardian for Rents & hire of negroes. Said Guardian begs leave further to report that commissioners have settled settled with him and John W. Roberts administrators of William Anderson deceased and Reports a balance remaining in the hands of Said administrators after paying all debts including interest up to the date of Said report. the sum of $1298.16 3/4. The Court at the same time allowed said admr. for their Services $50.00

John H. Anderson paid fee to Clerk for appointment as Admr. of Eliza Anderson deceased one of the distrubuters of Wm. Anderson deceased one of the distrubuters of Wm. Anderson deceased per receipt marked A. 1.00

The administrators paid the Clerk fee recording said report & Settlement. .50

The Court allowed Commissioners for making Said Settlement 4.50 56.00

over $1242.16 3/4

P 234 The Guardian John H. Anderson who is also administrator of Eliza Anderson deceased one of the Children and Distrebuters of William Anderson deceased here retains as such admr. the sum $327.88½ the amount of his account of his account here filed Marked B. as part of this report which being deducted from the sum of $1242.16 3/4 leaves in

the hands of the Guardian of the said Sum reported by the commissioners aforesaid the sum of 914.28¼
To which add the sum with which he is chargable for rents and hire of negroes /c 1096.54¼
Total Amt. 2010.82½

Said Guardian John H. Anderson further reports to the Court that he has Charged his Wards as follows towit.
He is entitled to, for boarding & washing furnished and done for Matthas Anderson & for money expended for Clothing tuition /c as per account here filed Marked C. and made part of this Report this Sum 189.50
He is entitled for boarding & washing furnished and done for Mary Anderson and for money expended Clothing tuition /c as per account here filed Marked D. and made part of this report this sum 535.85

He is entitled for boarding & washing furnished and done for Reuben Anderson and for money expended for clothing tuition /c as per account here filed Marked E. and mad e part of this report . The sum 401.68¼
These sums charged against Matthias Anderson Mary Anderson and Reuben in accounts Marked C. D. E. an to be taken out of and deducted from their Estate as before Shown to be in the hands of said Guardian in proportion to the Amount of each of their accounts.
These was a Contract between Said Guardian and James Bray in relation to the occupation of the Hickory Valley farm which contract was not complied with by Bray--he has not yet made reparation but promises to settle and pay what ever is right. If he shall do this then Said Guardian will bring whatever he may receive from that Some into his account as such Guardian. Should there be any items omitted with which Said Guardian is properly Chargeable he will on dixcovering the error or omission correct the Same. All which is most respectfully submitted
John H. Anderson
Recorded 6 Oct. 1836 Test N. Oldham Clerk

P 235 Report of a Settlement made by Commissioners with John H. Anderson and John W. Roberts Administrators of the estate of William Anderson deceased returned upon oath at September Term A. D. 1836.

DR.

1830 Sept. 11 To amount of Sales pr. Account returned To October term 1830 White County Court 938.49 3/4
Nov. 4 To amount of Second Sales of Said Estate of this date returned at April term 1831 269.74½
Nov. 4 to amt for which the negroes belonging to Said estate were hired from this date for one year returned Apl. 1831 138.25
The following Amounts have been received on note and accounts Contained in the Inventory returned at October term 1830 . 1834 July 22nd Received from Hannah Anderson on his note 20.00
Received of John & Charles Bencents on their note as follows 1831 Apl. 8th $8.50, 1832 March 19 21.12½

Received of William Usery on his note to William Anderson for Cash Viz. 2 Oct. 1834. $5.00 Decr. 15 th $5000 1831 Febry 8th $10. 20.00

Received of Josiah Cole 2nd Decr. 1831 on his note for corn due 1st Nov. 1830 this Sum in part 13.12½

Received on Jacob A. Lanes note 29th July 1836 in full 7.10

Received of William Usery on his note to William & Matthais Anderson 1831 Apl. 30 $5.00 1834 $6.50 3/4 March 24 $6.85¼ 18.45

Received of Mernican Wade on his account in full his account Inventoried and other items Fe. 2 Decr. 1831 36.65½

Received of Joseph Alevatus by way of his proven account of 29th June 1830 4.75

The following sums of money have been redeived on the accounts returned in the Inventory as created pending a partinship between Wm. Anderson ded. and Morgan Dewese all of which belonged exdlusively to the estate of Said Anderson Viz:

Received of Charles Dibrell Senr. in January 1834 1.50

Received of Emory Bennett 29th March 1831 .50

Recd. of Richard Judson 5 February 1831 .62½

Received of Wm. Anderson M. C. 14 June 1832 4.20

Received of Asa Certain 25 Sept 1830 .31

Recd. of R. M. Ewin 2 Oct. 1830 2.50

Recd. of Joseph W. Glenn 26 June 1831 .50

Received of George Hutson same .35

The Balance of the parternship Accounts as above are not Collected. Some of the Debters saying they have paid to Deweese Some being bad, and no means in the power of Admrs. to enforce payment Dewise having left the Country. Received of Anthony Dibrell 5 January 1835 Amount Act. 38.38½

Received the amount of a Jery Claim 29 October 1831 1.50

P 236 Amount over

Received of John Newman on his Account in part of A. Gamble 12.12½

To Amount of Property sold pr list of Sales returned to October Term A. D. 1831 63.59

1614.26½

VOUCHERS to CREDIT of Administrators CR.

1831 Feby 28 By amt paid Joseph Kerr his a/c No 1 4.90 3/4

" Apl. 18 " amt paid John Vencont do No. 2 4.25

" Jany 5. " " " Nathl. Bramblett do No. 3 10.00

"1830 Sept. 15 " " " Doct. Madison Fisk do No .4 12.00

" Apl. 13 By amt paid Joseph Kerr in full No. 5 12.00

1831 May 14 " " " John Jett Shff. for taxes 1827 and 1828 of Said Anderson recpt No. 6 29.46 3/4

1831 Sept. 24. " " " James Cooper No. 7 1.25

1831 Decr. 2 " " James Young in full No. 8 6.56¼

Meucan Wade in full No. 9 46.50

1832 Jany 14 " " " Wm. Anderson (M. C. in full No. 10 5.50

1831 Aug. 22 By amount retained by John W. Roberts

for balance due him for Services in carrying on the Salt in all for William Anderson deceased after deducting $72.79 2/3 which he as a partime was owing said Wm. Anderson estate in the Saltwell concern this Sum 52.20 1/3

John W. Roberts has another claim against the estate of Said Wm. Anderson D d. but his papers being in the State of Mississippi or lost he cannot how bring it in. 1832 Jany 14. By Amt. returned by John H. Anderson one of the Administrators for money owing by said Deceased to ane & Anderson proprutors of a News paper pup /c in Sparta 5.45½

March 1 By Amt paid William J. Bennett No. 11 14.00

[illegible] do No 12 2.40

1831 Decr. 1 By Cash paid by John H. Anderson Admr. of Wm. Anderson ded. to the Admr. of Mathais Anderson Decd 23.00

1832 March 4 By Cash paid as above 22.07 3/4

" all of which will appear in No 13 45..07 3/4

July 14 By Amount paid A. Tibrell Bank agen for White County receipt No. 14 2.33 ½

Oct. 10 By amount paid to John Givson for crying at sales See receipt No. 15 6.00

1834 May 15 By fees paid acob A. Lane Clerk No. 16 2.50

1833 Decr. 2. By Cash paid by way of interest on note in Bank 1.54

P 237 1834 June 3 By Cull & interest on Note I. B. McCormich in Bank 2.43 3/4

Decr. 3 By Same Same 1.93½

These last three Items are paid as the part of Wm. Anderson ded. 1835 Jany 18 By Cash paid William usrey on a Decreed of the Chancery Court Receipt No. 17 43.31¼

28 By cash paid as last above do No. 18 40.

Feby 17 By Cash paid as above do " 19 16.68 3/4

June 3 By Cash paid M. C. ibrell Clerk of School Commissioners the balance of William Anderson part of note in Bank Receipt No. 20 14.00

Sept 5 By Cash paid Jesse Lincoln a/c in full No. 21 11.62

1830 June 29 By Cash paid Joseph Alevatus do No. 22 4.75

1835 Aug 12 By " paid Costs to Clerk of Chancery Court on Suit of Usery receipts No. 23 23.18

1836 Aug 19 " Ca sh paid N. Oldham Clerk fees No 24 1.80

1832 Decr. 29 By Amt Doct. Fisks act. for attendan ce on negro Mioles per acct. receipt No. 25 9.00

1831 Feby 20 By Amt Joseph Kerr Accy do No. 26 6.70

1830 By Cash paid William Bruster for articles furnished the family of W. Anderson Ded. 1.09

Sept 14 & 15 By Amount bought by Eliz a Anderson a Distrubutee at the sale of porsonal property of the Deceased 141.68½

Nov. 4 By amount boyght by Eliza Anderson a Distributee as above 2.25

By ount bought by John Gipson and kept by Eliza Anderson .60

Amount of Credits 576.02½

To amount of Interest calculated on the monies in the hands of the administrators (Anderson & Roberts) from the end of two years from their appointment up to 5 Sept. 1836. 259.91

Whole amount of Debets	$1874.18 3/4
From which sum deduct the amount of Credits above	576.02½
Leaves a balance in the hands of the Admr. of Principal and interest up to 5 Sept. 1836	1298.16 3/4

The administrators hold a note on William Simpson for One hundred dollars with interest for five years which note will be due the 4th day of June A. D. 1841. This note was not returned in any Inventory and is payable to John H. Anderson Guardian for the heirs of William Anderson dcd. but it was given for personal property of Said William Anderson dcd. at the Saltwell in which said Silliam Anderson decd. seized and the hire of the Slaves belonging to his estate (except for one) are not included neither does the Said John H. Anderson who is also Guardian for Matthias Anderson, Mary Anderson and Reuben Anderson infant children of Said William Anderson deceased bring into this Settlement and account the charges which he has as such Guardianfor the board Clothing tuition/c of his wards but he reserves all these matters to be brought into his account against his said Wards on a Settlement. Hence it may be that the above sum of one thousand two hundred and ninety eight dollars 16 3/4 cents may be matually diminished on such settlement being made. There is also allowance for services of the administrators herein contained. The amount of such allowance being left to the discrition of the Court. The following notes and accounts are returned in Inventories but are not yet collected, they being bad Viz:

One note on Walker Bennett due 19 Nov. 1829	2.00
One note on Morgan Dawise to Isaac Taylor for	3.61½
One note on James R. Robinson to W. & M. Anderson due in Jan. 1832	6.00
One note on David Davis to Same 22 Jan. 1832	
All the note of Isaac Cole not accounted for in the foregoing statement.	
P 238 One note on Isaac Cole payable in Corn /c due 1 Nov. 1830	32.50
One note on James Furginson for	1.00
~~Part of account on Joseph~~ Alevateus Viz:	1.85
~~An account on John Supplanter~~.	1.91
James W. Glenn account not collected	1.56
An account on John Cruise (bad) for	5.31
Amounting to	$

Those accounts if collected in future will created and additional charged against the administrators.

Alexander B. Lane certifies that he made the calculation of the Interest in the foregoing account, and he deams it accurately calculated but it was not counted with precission as to the time in some instances throwing off odd days and in others including a few days but to take it as a whole if mistakes in calculation have intervened the error if any he thinks is against the administrators.

Alex. B. Lane.

We the undersigned Commissioners appointed by White County Court to Settle with John H. Anderson and John W. Roberts administrators of the estate of the estate of William Anderson decd. do hereby certify that we have examined the foregoing Settlement and Acco nt with the Documents and Vouchers therein refined to and we believe the same to be Correct and beg leave to report accordingly-- We would recommend $50.00 as a reasonable sum to be allowed the administrators for their Services in Settleing said estate Given under our hands and Seals this 5 th September 1836.

William Bruster (Seal)
John Jett (Seal)
Joseph Herd (Seal)

Recorded 6th October A. D. 1836 Test N. Oldham Clerk of White County Court

P 239 Report of A Settlement made by commissioners with John Walker Guardian to the heirs of Kindal lavage decd. returned upon oath at October Sessions A. D. 1836. There came to the hands of Said Guardian has paid out the following sums of money and performed the Services as set out below on behalf of Said estate for each of which Items he produced proper Vouchers towit:

		Cr.
1	paid for coffin for Farmelia Savage	2.50
2 "	fees and charges to Jacob A. Lane	8.25
3 "	Nathan Haggard for Services in Law	47.50
4 "	A. Dillion for papers in overton	1.62½
5 "	Funeral Clothes for Parmelis	2.50
6 "	John Jett	52.99
7 "	Taxes in Overton County	1.56¼
8 "	Land tax	174
9 "	Same	.74
10 "	Same	.71½
11 "	Same	.92½
12 "	Same	.73
13 "	Same	.76
14 "	Paid Henry H. Atkinson	3.97
15 "	Paid costs of Sent Vs. Oliver	61.62½
16 "	paid William Goose Clerk	.25
17 "	Clerk of Overton	1.75
18 "	A. ibrell for Drawing money	2.37½
19 "	I. B. McCormick	10.00
20 "	Joseph Hunter	9.00
21 "	A. B. Lane	5.00
22 "	Taxes	.70 3/4
23 "	Same	.69 3/4
24 "	N. Oldham	.25
25 "	N. Oldham	.75
26 "	William Butler D. Sheriff	1.50
P 240 27	John Walker account for services 69 days @ $1.50 $103.50	129.23
27	Paid William R. Savage Legatee 16.50	16.50
" "	John G. Savage do	20.00
" "	William R Savgge do	1.75
" "	I. G. Savage do	2.50
" "	Lucy Savage Schooling	1.00
" "	Turner Lane commissioner	1.00
	Total Payments	$365.66¼ 365.66¼
	Due John Walker Guardian	$236.43 ¼

We further say that the sum of $129. 23 in the hands of the Guardian ha s been subject to interest from the day of its payment--We also See tha t the Guardian has paid out large sums of money to a much greater amount than what he received and that it would be just to allow him interest on his payments from their Several dates and because we think that the interest would at least equal that of the sum in his hands, we have set the one against the other and leave the Subject of interest untouched. Given under our hands and Seals the 1 day of Oct. 1836

Recorded 7th Oct. A. D. 1836	Anthony Dibrell (Seal)
Test . Oldham Clerk of	Turner Love (Seal)
White County Court	William Bruster (Seal)

I list of Sales and Inventory of the personal property of Joseph Parker deceased returned upon oath by John Parker Admr. at October term 1836. Viz:

Sold to	John Parker one bed & furniture	18.00
"	Thompson Johnson 1 Stone Jug	.12½
"	Lewis Hooten 1 Grindstone	.06¼
"	Ca lin Brown 1 Lot wool 32½ lb	5.92
"	Polly Parker 1 Loom & equipage	5.68 3/4
"	do 1 Lot wool 32 lb @ 25 3/4 ¢	8.24
"	do 1 Bed & furniture	16.00
"	John Parker 1 countepane 1.00 Hackle 25	1.25
"	Polly Parker 5 Chairs	.75
"	John Parker 1 Bottle	.12
"	John Massey 1 Basket & wool	.62½
"	Polly Parker 1 Bedstead & cord	.50
"	Tho Nicholas 1 Lot Geese	6.00
P 241	Polly Parker 1 Tub & Churn	.50
"	do 1 Lot ware 1.00 1 Lot Hogs 15 Choice $31.	32.00
"	Thomas Bohannon one Lot 15 hogs	18.25
"	John Parker 1 Barrel	.81¼
"	Polly Parker 1 Barrel 1.40 1 Trough Soap 50	.90
"	do 1 B arrel & Salt 225 2 Jars of fat 2.12½	4.37½
"	John Massey 35 Bacon 42 do 8¢	6.51
"	do 40 lb do	3.20
"	Josiah Turner 50 lb Bacon @ 10¢	5.00
"	John Massey 59 lb do @ 10¢	5.90
"	Ditto 1 Box Irons	3.12½
"	Robert Denny 1 Lot of Tools	1.31¼
"	William Hudgins 1 hand Saw	1.50
"	Mason Watts 1 Foot adze	.43 3/4
"	Jesse Elliott 1 Cutting Knife	1.56¼
"	William Hill 1 Large Auger 50 1 Frow 31¼	.81¼
"	Henry Eller 2 Reap hooks	.25
"	William Hill 1 Bradd Axe	2.62½
"	Polly Parker 1 Patton	2.25
"	E. B. Rose 1 meat axe	.25
"	William Mash 1 Brin scythe	.25
"	Thomas Nicholas 1 pr Steelyards & jointer	.37½
"	Jesse Elliot 1 mowing Scythe	1.87½
"	George Howard 1 Little Wheel & Reel	1.00
"	Robert Denny 1 Stone Jug	.12½
"	Solomon Whilite 1 Set pewter plates	3.12½
"	Stephen Watson 1 pewter Dish 75 1 pewter basin81¼	1.56¼
"	Joseph Grimes 1 pewter Basin	.86½

Sold	Henry Eller 1 Large Dish	1.00
"	Manuel McKinney 1 Jack Screw	1.00
"	Coleman Brown 4 Barrels	.25
"	John Parker 4 do 37½ 1 do 6¼	.43 3/4
"	Pååley Parker 1 Stock & plow	.81¼
"	John Massey 1 Mattock	1.00
"	Polly Parker 1 Weeding hoe	.87½
"	Madison Johnson 1 do	.12½
"	William Nash 1 do	.62½
"	John Parker 1 plow & Stock	.50
"	Polly Parker 1 do do	1.00
"	Reuben Whilhite 1 Barshare plough	4.12½
"	Madison Johnson 1 pitchfork	06¼
"	Thomas Bohannon 1 pr Gears	2.00
"	Polly Parker 1 pr do 2.06¼ 1 frying pan 56¼	2.62½
"	John Parker 1 Tea Kittle	1.50
P 242	Lewis Hooten 1 Large pot	1.06¼
"	Elijah Hooten 1 Oven & Lid	1.68¾
"	Joseph Hooten 1 Kettle	1.00
"	John Wilhite 1 do	1.25
"	Polly Parker 1 Lot Castings	.50
"	John Parker 1 Lot Castings	.50
"	Polly Parker 1 Small do & Lid	1.81¼
"	George Howard 1 Large Kittle	4.12½
"	Polly Parker 1 Little Wheel	2.18 3/4
"	Thos. Bohannon 1 Large Wheel	1.12½
"	Polly Parker 1 do	1.12½
"	Aaron England 1 Blind Bridle	1.31 3/4
"	George Howard 1 pr arting [illegible]	1.43 3/4
"	William C. Johnson 1 Bridle	2.56¼
"	Polly Parker 1 Smoothing iron	.56¼
"	James Bryant 1 do	.50
"	Polly Parker 2 pr cotton Cards	.50
"	Henry Eller 1 pot rack	1.56¼
"	Joseph Hooten 1 pr pot hooks	.6¼
"	Polly Parker 1 Coffee mill 50 1 Lot Lumber 75	1.25
"	Jesse Elliott 1 Table	1.43 3/4
"	Thomas Bohannon 1 Chest	1.00
"	Polly Parker 1 Box	.06¼
"	John Parker 1 Trunk 50 1 Tim Box 50	1.00
"	James Bryant 1 Candle stick	.07¼
"	Polly Parker 1 Set cup & Saucers	.25
"	William Goodwin 1 Table	.37½
"	Polly Parker 8 plates	.50
"	Thomas Nicholes 2 pitchers & 3 glasses	1.00
"	Wm. K. Bradford 2 bottles	.12
"	Resiah James 1 Large Pottles	.50
"	Polly Parker 1 Set Knives & forks	1.00
"	do do 1 Lot glass ware	.62½
"	John Park 1 Lot Books	.75
"	polly Parker 1 Small Pitcher 183/4 1 cupboard 10.00	10.18 3/4
"	do 1 Bed & furniture	20.00
"	Willis 34 Bacon 10¢	3.40
"	Thompson Johnson 47 lb do 11¢	5.17

Sold to Barton Roberts 61 do 12½ 7.62½
" Isaac H ward 1 cow & calf 14.62½
" Polly Parker 1 Do 11.62½
" Clarks Peter 1 Basin .18 3/4
" Polly Parker 1 cow & calf 16.25
" John Parker 1 wagon yoke & chain 61.50
P 243 John Parker 1 gray Mare & colt 82.25
" Polly Parker 1 mare & colt 142.50
" Bartlett BElcher 1 Steed horse 201.50
" Lewis Turner 1 lot of wheat 3.12½
" John C. Owen 1 wheat Stack 6.00
" Thoma s Littel 1 Stack Rye 2.00
" John Farley 2 Steers 17.00
" Mason Watts 1 work Steer 18.00
" Richard Pool 1 cow & yearling 12.50
" William Nash 1 Heifer 4.00
" Resiah Jarvis 1 cow 12.00
" Hiram Harvey 1 do 11.75
" Resiah Jarvis 1 Brown Steer 5.81¼
" William Hudgins 1 Bull 3.00
" " do 1 Heifer 3.56¼
" John M. Key 1 Curry comb .31¼
" Elisha Camrow 1 harrow 4.00
" Peter Goolsby remainder of corn at 56¼¢ p Bu. 13.00
" Thompson Johnson 1 Bag .50
" Polly Parker 1 do .25
" William Hudgins 1 Sack .12½
" Aaron England 1 Saddle 2.37½
" Polly Parker 1 Do 10.00
" William Nash .50
" Polly Parker 1 coverlid .50

Total amount 930.63
Credit by mistake charging Tho. Bohannon 1 large wheel 1.12¼
929.50¼

A list of notes and accounts belonging to the estate aforesaid Towit: One note on John Anderson for $92.50 due 22 January 1837 Good One note on Manuel Robertson and Samuel Dyer for $50. due 25 Decr. 1836 Good One note on Jeremiah, Daniel & Reuben Walhite and James Snodgrass for $100 due 1 September 1836 good. One on L. Pharis payable to James Pharis for $12. due 17 August 1832 Bad an account on Nelly Parker for $10. Good One do on Ramsom Gear for $10.80 good John Parker
Administrator

P 264 Account of the Sales of the property of Wiliam Duncan deceased returned upon oath by Susanah Duncan admx. at Oct. 1836.
Sold to the widow the following property towit:
1 Sorrel Mare and young colt $61. 1 Sorrel Mare 2 years old $50
111.00
6 head of Sheep 7.25 1 Loom 2.00 1 big wheel reel
& cards 1.00 10.25
1 cutting Knife & box 1.30 2 Bee hives 2.10 3.40
½ dozen Chairs 1.00 2 beds bedsteads & furniture 4.00 5.00
1 Trunel bestead bed & funiture 50 1 Looking glass .75
2 piggins 1 pail churn corn & meal tubb 1.00

4 pots, 2 ovens & Lids one Skillet & Lid wpr pot hooks 1 fire shovel & smoothing iron 5.00
2 Axes 2 plows 2 pr Chains 2 weeding hoes one Sprouting hoe
1 pr Hames 2 clevis 1 Swingletree 1 wedge 2 false coutters 3.00
1 Bridle & Saddle 50 1 Bridle 25 2 Jugs & t crocks 50 1.25
3 Geese 75 1 cow & calf 7.60 1 cow & calf 9.50 1 Heifer 9.50 27.35
2 Jars 10¢ 1 Trunk 50 1 chest 25 2 plows & stocks 93¼ 1.78 3/4
1 Table 1 coffee pot 5 plates 1 Dish 1 Set knives & forks 5 Spoons 2 pitchers 1.00
Amount of widows purchase $170.28 3/4

Sold to John E. Bussell Mattock	1.50
" John Massa 1 cow & calf	15.37½
" William Kerr 2 steers	19.18 3/4
" Daniel Martin 1 cow & calf	10.18 3/4
" Elijah Elmore 1 heifer	3.25
" Abraham Saylors 1 Bay horse	85.50
" Daniel Martin 1 corn note on Riley Jones for 24 Barrells [illegible]	27.00
" John Bussel 1 Spotted Sow	4.00
	166.00

All sold on 17th day of September 1836. on a Credit of 12 months. The Beels mentioned in the Inventory were on the Stocks & Sold with them-- One glass bottle mentioned also was broken before the Sale.

Susanaah Duncan Admx.

Recorded 19th Oct. 1836 N. Oldham Clerk.

Account of the Sales of the property of Joseph Henry deceased returned upon oath by George Bohannon Admx. with the will annexed at October term 1836. towit:

Sold to G. Bohannon 4 Beds & furniture	$15.00
Cupboard Furniture @ 3.00 Kitchen furniture @ 7.50 1 Chest 4.75	15.25
8 Chairs 187½ 1 pot 50 1 plow and hoe 50 1 Side Saddle 11-50	14.37½
1 Table 50 3 Bee Stands 6.87½ 2 Cows Calves & heifers 29.25	36.62½
19 hogs 40.00 1 mare 32.50 7 head of Sheep 8.18 3/4	80.69 3/4
1 pr. Gears 2.00 1 Still and Tubbs $61.62½	63.62½
P 245 1 Tract of Land Sold under the Will	500.37¼
12 head of Geese 3.00 1 pr Saddle Bags 2.50	5.50
1 Coffee Mill and Shaving Glass	.50
Cash on Hand	61.00
	792.56¼

1 Cotton Wheel Sold to S. Madewill	.50
1 Flax Wheel To J. Jackson	1.50
1 Pot and hooks to R. Whitaker	1.00
1 mattock & Sang hoe	1.43 3/4
1 axe 1 Shovel plow 1 Bull tongue	4.00
1 pr. Stretchers T Robinson	1.00
1 handsaw 2 augers & 1 Chisel to D. Bartlett	2.25
1 pr Steelyards to S. Madwell	2.00
1 Hammer penchers &c do	.62½
1 Saddle William Martin & 1 Set Shoe tools 75	5.25
1 Log Chain to Leweis Philips	4.00
2 Bee Stands to W. Bartlett	2.50
1 do J. C. Huddleston	.75

4	Bee Stands G. W. Henry	4.25
3	do M. Mllian	6.06¼
1	do Nathan Bartlett	2.00
1 Bull	S. Madewill	9.00
13 head of Hogs	M. Welch	80.00
1 Little Horse		18.50
1 pr Gears	J. Hyder	1.25
1 Cutting Knife & Box	J. Jackson	2.81¼
1 Scythe & Craddle		2.25
1 negro woman (Lauris)		60.50
1 Saddle (J)	S. Madewell	4.50
		@010.50¼

his
George X Bohannon
mark Admr. with the will annexed

Recorded 19 Oct. 1836. N. Oldham Clerk

P 246 Inventory of the estate of William Glenn deceased made upon oath by Wm. Glenn admr. at November TErm A. D. 1836 Towit: Five Beds bedsteads and furniture, two Clocks, two pots 3 ovens 2 Skillets, 1 Kittle, 1 pot rack, 1 Smoothing iron, 1 Set of fire Dogs, 1 fire shovel, 1 Loom, 4 slays 2 Cupboards, 1 Looking Glass, 1 Coffee Mill five Cests 1 Disk, 6 Chairs two Tables 2 Cotton Wheels, Wheels 1 Flax wheel, 2 pr Cards, three water pails, 1 washing Tub, 2 Bibles, 1 Justice Manuel 8 other Books 4 Dishes Ten plates 9 Cups and saucers 3 Glass Tumblers two bottles 1 Set cup Plates 1 pitcher 1 pepper box 1 Set Knives, & forks 1 Set Spoons, 1 Slate 4 Saddle 2 men & 2 womens 2 Saddles Blanket 1 pr Saddle B gs, 1 pr Steelyards, 1 Set Black Smith tools 3 Horses, 2 mules 13 head of Cattle, 61 head of Hogs, 1 yoke of Oxens, 1 cast two new waggon wheels and the tires, 1 waggon Bed, frame 1 Scythe & Craddle 3 Sycles 2 Set of Double Trees, 1 Log chain 4 pr hames, 3 pair chains 7 plows 3 Cutting knives 1 feed trough 1 flax hackle 6 Barrels 3 calves 2 Grindstones 9 Bee stands 4 Chopping Axes 1 broad axe 2 handsaws 1 Iron Square 10 Augers 7 Chisels 2 Drawing 3 plains 2 Raw hides 4 Weeding hoes 2 grubbing hoes 7 Sheep 2 Sidesole Leather 3 Samall pieces of upper leather 1 Reel A C op of Corn fodder & roughness Rye and Oats the quanity not now known but will be before given in when ascertained, a number of Goats the number not yet known but will in like manner be Stated in due time 1 Sugar trunk 2 Unbrellas Some Waggon timber 29 Geese 1 pr Sheep Shears 1 pr cloth Shears 12 Warping Spool 2 pr pot hooks Seven negro Slaves Towit: Peter a man grown Dinah a woman, Violet a woman, Jerry a boy, Malinda a Girl Caroline a Girl and Malinda a Girl Caroline a Girl and Malinda a Girl

Cash on hnad	$74.25
1 note on William Singleton due 1st March 1836 purposed good	10.00
1 do on Hale Doubtfull	15.50
1 on William Roberts doubtful probably in Solvent	10.12½

1 on Richard Crowder due 1 May 1837 good $125. One on Adam Clouse & others due 1st Oct. 1836 good $80. one on David L. Mitchell due 1st March 1837 good $65. One on William G. Sims due 26 Sept. 1836 good $70. One on William Earles due 2 Sept 1836 $1.50 One on Moses Cantrell due 15 Oct. 1836. presumed good $35.

One on Emory Bennett due 1st March 1837. Presumed good $12 One on William Cantrell & others due 1st June 1837. good $40. One on James Towsend ded. due 12 Jany 1835 doubtful $3.00 One on David Jackson

due 21 Febr. 1831 doubtful $1.50 One on Thos. L. Williamson & others due 25 Decr. 1836 good $10. O e on Henry C nnon due 1 March 1837 good $35. P 247 One on John H. King due 22nd May 1836 Doubtful $1.80 O e on David H. Mitchell infavor of Henry Neel due 15 Oct. 1832 good $61.37½ Besides the foregoing their are accounts due to Said Glenn by book account which the administrator and administratrix have not as yet had time apportunty to examined but which shall hereafter be carefully examined and faithfully and correctly Sated in another Inventory which shall be furnished as soon as practicable William Glenn Jr. Admr.
Recorded 16th Nov. 1836 Test. N. Oldham Clerk of White County Court

Additional account of the Sales of the estate of George Allen deceased returned upon oath by Joseph Herd admr. at November Term A. D. 1836 Towit:

Esther being aged Sold to John Allen for	150.00
Charlotte negro Girl do Daniel Clark	145.00
Dick negro man do Phebe Allen for	256.00
Anthony negro man do George W. Allen for	700.00
Susan negro woman Ditto Phebe Allen for	507.00
Sally negro Girl do Phebe Allen for	331.00
	2387.00

Making for the six negroes the aggregate sum two thousand three hundred and eighty Seven dollars Sold on a credit of Twelve months from the 10th day of August 1836. Given under my hand this 7th day of November 1837.
Joseph Herd Admr.
Recorded 16th Nov. 1836 Test. N. Oldham Clerk of White County Court.

Report of Commissioners assigning one years provisions to the widow and fammly of William Glenn deceased made at Decr. term 1836. Towit: All the corn now on hand except Sixteen Barrels, twelve of the choice Bacon H gs, one Beef S eer and what potatoes is on hand what cotton and Flax is on hand one side of Sole Leather 1 side upper Leather 100 lb. sugar 50 lbs coffee 7 Bushels and 200 lb. flour the sugar coffee & Salt to be provided on as good terms as possible out of part of the monies now on hand all of which after being duly sworn. We have Sit our hands this 24th Nov. 1836
Recorded 5th Jany. 1837

Eli Sims }
Richard CRowder } Coms.
William Bruster }

P 248 Report of Settlement made by commissioners with Daniel Williams Executor of William isher Deceased returned upon oath at December Term A. D. 1836. To amount of available funds in the hands of the Executor as charged said Executor in a former Settlement made by commissioners by an order of court at May term 1836 265.35 3/4

To amount paid by James & Alexander Dillion		1.00
To Cahh paid	Alexander Moore	.06¼
" "	Thomas Roberts	1.00
" "	Robert Mason	6.50
2 "	John Cunningham	1.37½
" "	Archebald Jutson	1.00
" "	Hiram Lewis	1.00
" "	Phinias B. Wright	6.00
" "	John Fisher Senr.-	25.00
" "	Stephen A. Charles	4.87½
" "	Wamon Leftwich (Jury) claim	1.50

To Cash from Thomas Mayberry 19.77
" " Anthony Dibrell 11.00
$343.44

Credits
By cash paid Christopher Wright pr receipt No. 1 11.00
" Lewis Pettels Receipt No. 2 3.00
" Samuel A. Moore No 3 3.00
" John Jett 4 3.00
" David L. Mitchell for Receipt 5 .50
" do do do 6 .16 3/4
" Clerks do 7 1.00
" " " .25
" Daniel Wallings account for Services rendered as
Executor Since 1 ast Settlement 3.00
" Commissioners .50 34.41 3/
309.02¼

We the undersigned commissioners find in the hand of the executor Daniel Walling after allowing them three Dolars for his Services as executors and three dollars to each commissioners for two days Services each and fifty cents to the clerk for recording this report the sum of three hundred and nine dollars two and a half cents of the available funds of Said estate, said Executor crying he has not been able to collect any of the Insolvent Debts as has been reported in a former Settlement witness our hand & Seal this 12 Nov. 1836. John Jett (Seal)
Recorded 5 Jany 1837. Mathias Jutson (Seal)
Joseph Herd (Seal)

P 249 Report of Settlement and appointment of the effects of the estate of George W. Hankins deceased made with John R. Glenn administrator of Said Estate upon oath at December term 1836.

To amount of Sales of the property of Said Estate 51.81¼
By Amount of funerel expences pr receipt 8.12½
" amt. allowed admr. by the court 6.00
" " paid John W. Ford per voucher 1.50
" " " Nicholas Oldham Clerk do 2.25
" " Commissioners for services in Settling 3.00 22.37½
29.43 3/4

Apportionment
To Lewis Evans Debt $17.12½ less on his debt 5.34 bal 11.78½
" John R. Glenn Debt 3.12½ do .97 3/4 2.14 3/4
" Colbert Arnold do 2.31¼ do .72¼ 1.59
" Harmon Little do 8.50 do 265 do 5.85
" William Bruster do 2.56¼ do .79 3/4 do 1.76½
" Greenville Templeton 9.13 do 2.84½ do 6.28½
Amt. Debts $42.75 amount loss 13.33½ 29.42¼
.01½
29.43 3/4

Given under our hands t is 26 Nov. 1836 Richard Crowder
Recorded 5 January 1837 Joshua Mason coms.
Eli Sims

Report of John Pennington and Sarah Dyer Guardian to the four youngest children of John Dyer deceased made upon oath at January Sessions

A. D. 1837.

To amt notes /c on hand 1 January 1836	879.31
To Amt received since then	63.70
	943.01

Credit

By this amount paid lerk for recordaing report	.50
Bal	942.51

This 2nd Jany 1837. John Pennington
Recorded 5 any 1837 Sarah Dyer Guardian

P 250 Report of J hn Gillentine guardianto Willima F. Carter made upon oath at January Sessions A. D. 1837.

In hand on note on obert Anderson due for	$42.37½
Interest on the S me	1.89
One note on Warren & Debrell due	35.00
One note on Freich Woxley & William Fryer due wqs paid	15.00
I terest on the same	.07½
One note on Andrew Bryan due 3rd February next	7.50
And Cash on hand	31.42½
	133.26

He has also received form the former Guardian the following negroes, Susannah, Sally and Thomas Although they are sometime knowh by other names yet he has given their names by which they are commonly known -- he has also received the Land belonging to said ward and rented the same to Isaac Denton for the term of three years for the Third of the necessary repairs. He has also paid the Taxes on the Land & negroes 2.12½

He has also paid for Guardian Bond	.50
One day attendance renting out land	1.00
	3.62½

Recorded 5 January 1837 John Gillentine Guardian

Report of Asa Certain Guardian to AlphonzaManisa Holmes Minors heirs of Edward Holmes ded. made upon oath at January Sessions A. D.1837. Nothing Came to his hands except the Land of Said wards shich he has as yet failed to rent out Asa Certain Guardian
Recorded 5 January 1837.

Report of Thomas Hill Guardian to the heirs of James Hill Guardian to the heirs of James Hill decpased made upon oath at anuary term 1837 No Alteration Since last report. Thoams Hill Guardian
Recorded 5 anuary 1837 N. Oldham Ck.

P 251 Report of Thomas Stepe Guardian to Glassberry Stepe made upon oath at anuary Sessions A. D. 1837.
This land which descended to his ward in White County is now under his control, but is Connected with other Land and of difficult to rent out until a division takes place unless all be rneted together which he will endeavor to do. He has received for rent of the year 1836. & preceeding yx year 7.64
Thos. Stepe Guardian
Recorded 5 anuary 1837

Report of Samuel Brown Guardian to Robertson Dryer, Claborn Dyer John C. Dyer and Louisa Dyer infant Children of John Dyer deceased made upon oath at January Sessions A. D. 1837 Amount on hand 1 day anuary

1837 $1142. 61½ 1142.61½
Deduct for Services of Lane & Anderson paid 10.00
1132.61½

Recorded 5 January 1837 Samuel Brown Guardian

Report of Wamon Leftwich Guardian to Malinda Rowland made upon oath at January Sessions A. D. 1837 No. change since last report except h the following
Paid to Carrick & Leftwich for wearing apparel Since 13 January 1836 to present date 63.63½
he has also within that period paid for necessaries 4.25
67.88¾

On the 18 day of May 1836 he received of her funds 144.66
and also on 30 day July 1836 received 20.00
164.66

Recorded 5 January 1837 Wamon Lefterwich Guardian

P 252 Account of the Sales of the property of William Glenn deceased returned by William Glenn Jr. Admr. at January Sessions A. D. 1837.
1 Bed and furniture 15$ 1 Bed and furniture $15 1 Bed & furniture $10 40.00
1 Bed & furniture $12 1 Bed & furniture (small) $4 1 Cupboard 9$ 25.00
cupboard furniture & table $2 1 small table 50¢
1 chest 50¢ 1 chest 25¢ 3.75
1 Chest 50¢ 1 Dish 25¢ 1 chest 25¢ 1 chest 12½ 1.25
1 clock $10 1 Clock an old endeffrent one 50¢
1 side Saddle $10 20.50
1 man's Saddle $15 1 sidle Sadle $5 1 man's saddle $15 35.00
1 pr Saddle Bags 1.75 1 Umbrella and old one 25 1 Umbrella 50¢ 2.50
1 Slay 50¢ 2 Slays 50¢ 1 Kid Skin 50¢ 1 do 56¼ 1 do 100¢ 3.06¼
1 Kip skin 4.75 1 Side upper Leather 3.12½ 1 side do 3.18 3/4 1 Bible 2.00 13.04
1 old Bible 50¢ 1 Justices Manuel 1.50 1 Gum Dovinted med 1.25 3.25
1 Book .50 1 do 43 3/4 1 do 25. 1do 31¼/ 1 do 25¢ 1 do 50¢ 2.75
1 Book 25¢ 1 Lot old books 1.37½ 1 Slate 25¢ 1 pr. Steelyard 2.80½
1 side sole Leather 2.00 8 Barrels corn $12. 8 do 13$
1 Grindstone 50¢ 27.50
1 Grindstone 1.50 1 Bee Stand $1.00 1 do 50 1 do 2.0 0
1 Do 1.25 6.25
1 Bee Stand 50¢ 1 do 25 1 do 12½ 1 do 75 1 Rawhide 2.00 3.62½
13 Shoats 14.00 7 Hogs 24.62½ 1 Mule 50$ 1 HOrse $78.25 231.87½
1 Colt 19.93 3/4 1 Cow 6 1 cow 10.06¼ 1 cow 10.25
1 yearling & bell 3.25 59.50
1 Bull 6.12½ 1 cow lw. 1 Steer 8.87 2 Steer 8.87
2 Steers 14.12½ 1 cow 18. 1 cow 10.50 62.26½
3 sheep 3.25 300 bundles oats 4.00 300 do 3.00 12 goats 10.00 1 Sow 50¢ 20.75
1 Sow and pigs 1.00 1 Lot Hogs 31.06¼ mare 25.00 1yoke oxen 20. 1 Cart 21$ 98.06¼
1 Log Chain 2.00 1 Set Black Smith Tools 35.00
2 Wagon Wheels & tire 19.00 56.00
1 Loom 2.00 1 cupboard 2.00 1 Flax hackle1.00
1 [illegible]
1 [illegible]

1 Reel 5.01 cotton Wheel 25 10.57½
1 Goat Skin 25 1 pot and old oven 75 1 Lot old casting
2.00 1 Kittle 3.00 6.00
1 Frow 75 2 plows 1.18 3/4 1 do 2.00 1 do .75 1 do 3.75
1 old do 12½ 8.86¼
Chairs plates & other Artifles 2.00 1 Sickle 37½
1 do 43 3/4 1 do 37½ 3.18 3/4
old Barrels can's & jugs 1.00 1 plow 112½
1 hand saw 50. 1 Boot tools 2.00 4.62½
1 Currying knife 18 3/4 1 Axe 37½ 2 pr Gearing 2.00
2 pr back bands 1.50 4.06¼
Double Trees 1.31¼ Cutting box & knife 2.06 ¼
Scythe & cradle 1.56¼ 4.93 3/4
1 cutting Knife 18 3/4 old axes 50 1 Hoe .25
1 do .25 1 do .25 1 do .18 3/4 1.62½
1 Axe 25 1 Grubbing hoe 56¼ 1 wagon tongue hound and
axletree 2.56¼ 3.37½
Wagon bed from 1.00 axletree 25 Brin hood .25 Rings and
Steeple 62½ 2.12½
1 plow 75 1 Jug. 25 1 Singletree 25 a lot of old
spools hoe gridiron /c .50 1.75
1 looking glass 25 1 Barrel .50 1 do .25 Tanning leather
6¼ Cotton Card 12½ 1.18 3/4
11 Geese 1.00 18 Geese 2.00 wagon Tumbler 2.00 Stake fodder
1.06¼ 6.06¼
1 Stack fodder 1.00 1 do 1.wt 1 do .75 1do 2.00
1 do 1.75 Lot fodder 1.00 6.75
Two trough 81¼ 3 sheep 2.00 1 plow 5.60 2 pocket books 43¼ 8.85
1 pocket book .25 1 pot rack 2.51½ Bushel 31¼ 2650
bundles 1 hoe 25 1.06½
300 Bundles fodder 1.87½ 2650 bundles of oats 26.50 3 bushels Rye
1.12½ 29.50
1 Hog 3.00 1 pr Sheep Shears and 1 p cotton do 62½ 3.82½
Total 824.80

P 253 There was also found in Cost of which the administrator had no knowledge at the time of returning his first Inventory this sum $11.65 making in all of cash on hand $86.90 1 County Claim not mentioned at first for the sa e reason $5.00 William Glenn Admr.
Recorded 6 January 1837.

In the name of God, Amen! This the 14th day of September 1836 I James Robinson of the County of White and State of Tennessee calling to mind the mortality of my body and that it is once appointed for man to die, do make and publish this my last will and Testament in Manner and form following towit: princopally and first of all I recommend my precious and immortal Soul unto the hands of Almighty God. that gave it me and my body to be buried in a decent and Christian burial and as to such worldly estate where with it hath pleased God to bless me with in this world After my just Debts and expences are paid And first of all the use of the land and negroes to be for the use of my beloved wife Leah Robinson except Burton, and thisnegro above named I do will and bequeath unto my son Priston, Robinson extra of an equal share of the estate and my wife

Leah is to have the use of the Negroes and Land during her widowhood, and as the children comes of age, she is to give everyone two hundred Dollars worth of property equal to that Polly Pryor got. And my beloved wife is to have the use of the Distillery and all the Stock as she has to pay the children twohundred dollars in property as they come of age-- And there is one thousand Dollars in Cash in hand that she is to keep at interest and the Interest is to be for the schooling of the Children and the Capital to br continued and at her death or Marriage to be equally divided amongst the heirs and at the time that Preston comes of age the above Thousand Dollars to be equal divided amongst the heirs. And if said Preston should die or become of no account said Preston Robinson to have Five Hundred dollars extra of the rest of the heirs in his room and Stead and if Said Preston Robinson should die, his part to be equ ally divided amongst the heirs--and I further give her the rest of the house hold furniture as I did the rest day and date first above as witness my hand and James T. Robinson (Seal)

Test Samuel Johnson
Edmond Stamps

State of Tennessee
White County January Term A. D. 1837
Be it remember that this day was exhibited in open Court a writingpurporting
P 254 to be the last will and testament of of James T. Robinson late of county of White deceased whereupon also appeared in open Court Samuel Johnson and Edmond Stamps subscribing witness to said writing and proved on oath the due execution and publication of Said writing to be the last will and testament of the Said James T. Robinson for the purposes and things therein mentioned and that at the date of the Execution and Publication thereof the said James T. Robinson was of Sound disposing mind and memory which with the autherilication thereof is ordered to be recorded Given at office the 2nd day of January A. D. 1837
Recorded 6 January 1837 Test N. Oldham Ck.

Report of Assignment of Provisions by Commisssioners to the widow and children of John M. Rottan deceased made upon oath at July term A. D. 1837.
Towit: 7 midlings of Bacon weighting in all about 130 lbs there being no corn on hand we allow her a Claim on the proceeds of the sale of said estate sufficient to pay for forty Bushels of corn and fifty pounds of Flour and twenty pounds of Ginned cotton, two shoats and two hogs to weigh 150 lb each when fatted also two Beehives and the honey therein. Given under our hands and Seals the 20th day of May 1837.

Thomas Wilson (Seal)
Edmond Cunningham(Seal)
Thomas Frasure (Seal)

Recorded 22nd September 1837 Test N. Oldham Clerk

Report of John Mason Guardian to James Howard made upon oath at September Term A. D. 1837 That there is no alteration therin since his report at June term A. D. 1836 -- 4 Sept 1837 John Mason Guardian
Recorded 21st September 1837 Test N. Oldham Clk.

P 255 Report of assignment of provisions by commissioners to the widow and children of David L. Mitchell deceased made upon oath at June Term A. D. 1837. Towit:

All the corn and Bacon now on hand, and all the Sugar and coffee on hand all the Flax and wool on hand and Money sufficent to purchase 50 lb Cotton, Forty dollars in Cash to purchase pork and money to purchase Six Bushels Salt and fifteen Dollars to purchase Shoes for use /o the present crop which she is cultivating all of whixh is respedtfully submitted 5 June 1837.

Recorded 21 st Sept 1837 A. Dibrell Test. N. Oldham Clk. Thomas Robertson Danl. Clark

Inventory of the Estate of John M. Rotan deceased returned upon oath by Dan Griffith admr. at May term 1837.
Towit: Five head of horses, nine head of cattle, two Rifle Guns, two feather beds furniture, and about fifty head of hogs one clock, one cupboard, one table, one set of plates, one set 6f Knives and fords, one dutch oven, one Skillet two weeding hoes three plows, one poll axe Six Bee hives about 100 lb. Bacon Given under my hand this 5 day of May 1837

Dan G$_r$iffith Admr.

N. B. Years privisions taken out of the above for widow and orphans

Dan G$_r$iffith Admr.

Recorded 21 Sept 1837 Test N. Oldham Clk.

I^{N}ventory of the Balance of the effects of the estate of James T. Robertson deceased returned upon oath by Leah Robertson admx. at Ap ril term A. D. 1837.

Cash on hand	1300.00
Cahh notes on different persons Amt. to	181.89
	1481.89

Leah Robertson Admx.

R corded 2 Sept. 1837. Test N. Oldham Clk.
P^e 256

Inventory of part of the property of the estate of Berry Hamblet returned upon oath by Elizabeth Hamblet Executrix at July term A. D. 1837 Towit: Two horses, two large oxen, two plows, and two pair of G ar two Log Chains, one ox yoke 3 serigs and three steeps one clock, one looking Glass, two Axes one foot adze 3 Augers, one hand saw 40 Stock hogs three cows two calves 4 beds and bed steads and furniture, three Bee Stands two negro men Jack & Jeff, one cupboard, one Burau, one table, one candle Stand, one Sett knives and forks, one coffee pot one washing kittle, three ovens, one skillet, one pr of pot hokks, one man's saddle, two Decanters tw two pitchers 30 Sheep 36 Ducks 6 Tin cups 1 Razor and Strap 1 Grindstone one coffee mill 6 Glass tumblers one Shelf 1 pr Dog Irons, one Shovel 1 pepper Bag one mug two big wheels one little wheel, four peacocks, one water pail 10 chairs 4 weeding hoes two Scythe and cradles one loom two setts of Tea cups and Saucers The foregoing Inventory is not full as it has been impossible for the administratrix to ascertain fully the amount of Debts other due to or from the Estate but she promises by next court to furnish a full settlement and one that willain all respects will comply with the law as nae as possible or as fully as may be in her power

Elizabeth X Hamblet Exr.
her mark

Recorded 21 st September 1837 Test. N. Oldham Clerk,

Report of William Glenn Guardian to Patsey & John W. Glenn infant heirs of William Glenn deceased returned his report upon oath at February term 1837 towit: two negro Girls Viloet $700. belonging to his ward Patsey Malinda $500. belonging to his ward John W. Glenn--He further states that he has hired Violet to Srah Glenn for 40$ the present No Sicurity taken as She said Sarah Glenn is entirely Solvent and the said Guardian has enough of her property in his hands to make the deal entirely Secure all of which is respectfully submitted 6th February 1837
William Glenn
Recorded 21st September 1837 Test N. Oldham Clerk

Account of the Sales of the property of the estate of Berry Hamblet deceased returned by Executrix upon oath at Augst. 1837.
Sale on the 20 July 1837.
Pleasant Taylor bought one Cupboard $10.00 John L. Price 1 young Gray horse 76.00 Addison Dillon 1 Gray horse 88.00 James Randalls 1 Log Chain 4.00 Addison Dillon 1 Log chain 4.06¼ Jesse Dodson 3 Rings 1.00 Spencer Holder 1 Tract of Land 624.00 Jeremiah Webb 1 Frow .50 Ozae Denton 2 Augers .75Jeremiah Webb 1 do .37¢ Spencer Holder 1 foot Adze.62½ Edward Anderson 1 Scythe blade & Rings 2.31¼ Morgan W. Bryan $2.62½ Lisles Earles 1 Bee Stand 2.45 Jeremiah Webb 1 pr Saddle Baggs $4.00 Pleasant Taylor 1 Clock 10 Pleasant Taylor 1 Waggon 80.00 Larkin Yates 1 y9ke of Steers 25.00
Total $935.50 Elizabeth X Hamblett Exex.
her mark
Recorded 21st September 1837. Test N. Oldham Clerk.

Report of Joseph Herd Guardian to the heirs of Benjamin Bowman Dcd. made upon oath at Sept. Term 1837. 20th Nov. 1836.

To William Bowman	126.43
" Jackson Bowman	126.42
" Jeremiah Bowman	126.42
" Nancy Bowman	126.42
Narcissa Bowman	126.42
Making in all the sum of	632.10

All of which is loaned out at 6 pr Cent interest Dr. for Rent from 1st Jany 1834 to 1 Jany 1837. $46.00 making for each Ward the sum of $9.20. Cr By cash paid Lawyer Lane $5. Cash paid Recd. Petit for Repairs on farm $18.70 Ca sh pr Appt. as Guardian 50¢ Paid Taxes 1834 &1835 & 6--$3.28 3/4 Cash paid Nancy Bowman for Schooling boarding & Clothing said Wards form 1 Jany 1832 to the present date $188.33½
Cr. by cash paid Clerk for this return .50¢ in all $310.32
This 4 September 1837. Joseph Herd Guardian.
Recorded 21 September 1837. Test N. Oldham Clerk.

Account of the Sales of the property of the estate of David L. Mitchell deceased returned upon oath by David Snodgrass Admr. at June term A. D. 1837 In Part
Sold to Ann Mitchell the following property towit:
One press and furniture One Bureau and falling leaf table two beds and Bed steads and furniture, One other bureau one Clock One looking glass, One Cribb One tea board, one trunk one tin Box, One Candle stick, Sixteenchairs

One Umbrella one Parasol, one history of the Christian Church one Geography one Bible all for $70.00. Also two Beds and furniture and Bedsteads, one Saddle martingale, Bridle and Blanket one flax wheel and Reel two smoothing Irons 1 pr Steelyards four pr Cotton Cards, one set warping spools one Sa sage stuffer and two slays 1 Disk one Barrel one set of Aud Irons one Loom 6 crooks four Dutch ovens one pot rack, one brass Kittle, one spice Morter, & Pistle two Cotton Wheels One Churn, One Tubbfor four pails, three pots one tin Bucket Aug in all to $25. Also Six head of Sheep $7.50 2 cows and one Heifer 31$ $38.50 " 10 head of hogs $15. 1 Mare &colt $106. 1 mare $20. $141.00. Also 3 Bee hives 5.56½ 1 large Kittle & 1 Saw for $6.00 $11.62½ old to Elixha Cannon 1 shovel plow 1.62½
Sold to Charles Meeks 1 pair fire Irons.50
Iron tools 2.00 sold to Matthias Nichols

Dutch Oven & Ball $1.00	Jaber G. Mitchell
2 Iron Wedges $1.00	James Williams
1 potrack 1.25	Jaber G. Mitchell
1 mattock $1.00 5 hoes 2.25	
1 plow .75 $4.00	Same
2 other plows $4.12	Barrett Lee 1 Scythe
& cradle 1.50	Jaber G. Mitchell
1 Grass blade 1.00	James Williams
1 Scythe $3. 1 Spade & Da	
Drawing Knife $1.50 2 pr	
Steelyards $3.00	David Snodgrass
1 handsaw 1.00	Charles Smith Jr.
2 shuttles and temples.18¾	Barnett Lee 2 plains 1.00

P 259	Sold to Jaber G. Mitchell 2 pr Gears	3.50
"	James Godwin 1 Lot of Bridles	.62½
"	James Cook 2 Grubbing irons & rope	.50
"	Allen L. Mitchell ½ price of Cross cut saw	2.00
"	Barnett Lee 2pr hames	.50
"	Jacob Anderson 1 Patent Plough	7.50
"	William L. Mitchell 1 Axe	.25
"	Jaber G. Mitchell 1 Axe	.75
"	James Hayes 1 Whiskey Barrel	.50
"	Lucy Claybrooks 1 Log Chan	5.00
"	Elisha Cannon 1 ox wagon $80. 1 yoke Steers	115.50
"	William Bruster 3 Dry hides	6.56¼
"	Robert Love 1 Carry all Wagon	20.50
"	Allen S. Mitchell 1 Cow and Calf	15.06¼
"	James Snodgrass 1 Cow	8.75
"	Anderson S. Rogers 9 head of young Cattle	36.62½
"	Thomas Little 22 head of hogs	19.37½
"	Alfred Hamblin 22 head of hogs	17.50
"	James Cook 15. head of Pigs	3.75
"	James Walker 1 Gray Mare & Colt	75.00
"	Daniel Clark 1 Sorrel Mare and Colt	53.50
"	James Snodgrass 1 Sorrel Filly	58.00
"	David Snodgrass 1 Mans Saddle	6.25
"	Jaber G. Mitchell 1 Mans Saddle	20.00

" Woodson P. White 1 Cutting Box 4.62½
" Danl. Clark 1 of Doct Guns Books 1.31¼
" Danl. Clark 1 Justice's Manuel 2.00
" Daniel Clark 2 Vols. Laws of Tenn 8.00
" James Cook 2 Arithmetic for .25
" Anthony Dibrell one poplar table 2.00
" David Snodgrass 1 Lot Razors /c 1.50
" John Overeby part of Barrel Tar 2.00
" Sundry person Belts 14 pr all for 1.75
" Jaber G. Mitchell 10 head of hogs 7.00
" Jaber G. Mitchell 1 Large Kittle 4.00
" 1 pr Saddle bags 1.00
" Samuel Turney 10 window and
door frames 10.00
" Samuel Turney 1 Set house Logs 30.00
5000 shingles $15.00 3000 Rails $30. 130 feet
Sheeting plank $1.00 85 feet Scanting $1.00 77.00
Cash on hand $144.00 Red from A. Keethley $30.25 from A. Bryan 15$ from
M. Nichols $2. form Bartlett $1.20 193.28 3/4
$1095.03 3/4

D. Snodgrass Admr.
Recorded 21 Sept 1837 Test. N. Oldham Clerk.

P 260 Report of settlement by commissioners with Wmmm Leftwich admr. of James N. Rowland deceased made upon oath at June term A. D. 1837. we find the administrator charggenbel with the following amount of the effects that came to his hand belonging to said estate this sum 1606.62½
to Interest collected belonging to said estate 15.03
$1621.65½

Credits for Money disbursed towit:

No. 1 Dalton Guardian receipt to children of M. Dalton 164.66⅓
" 2 Paid Jesse N. Shaw a Legatee 164.66⅓
" 3 " Robert Rowland do 164.66⅓
" 4 John Warren do 164.66 ⅓ 164.66⅓
" 5 Margarett Rowland do 164.66⅓
" 6 John W. Ford do 164.66⅓
This sum due Malinda Rowland which the Admr. has charged
as Guardian to Said Malinda Rowland 164.66⅓
" 7 Paid Robert Mills as pr. Bill 5.00
" 8 George C. Flowers 30.08
" 9 William Biggs 3.75
" 10 William Bilamson 5.25½
" 11 Sampson Inight 1.25
" 12 William T. Brittain 4.50
" 13 Receipt returned on Saml. P. Howard 40.00
" 14 C. Guin as per Receipts 17.25
" 15 I. B. McCormick 5.00
" 16 Allowance to Administrator 84.71
" 17 paid to Clerk 1.05
" 18 R. Nelson 5.00
Leftwichs distrebu ioned share 164.66⅓
paid to John Rowland 14.50
Paid Bruster for enclosing ansere in Equity 1.00 1535.93
There is yet in admr. hands 85.72

There is yet due to the heirs of John Rowland deceased who was one of the Legatees this sum $143.05½. Said administrator has paid to each Legatee $7.16 over their respective Shares(with the exception of John Rowland heirs to whom none has been paid except $14. which was paid to Said Rowland or with which he was charged in his life time.) Which overplus of Said sum of $7.16 each Leagtee is bound to refund to the said admx. with the exception of the heirs of said John Rowland.

Richard Nelson
Anthony Dibrell

Recorded 21 September 1837. Test. N. Oldham Ck.

P 261 Report of Settlement made by Commissioners with the administrator of the estate of Thomas williams Deceased made upon oath at May term A. D. 1837. to wit:

Administrators Stand charged according to the Clerks certificate with $3057.46 3/4

Credit with the following receipts exhibited to wit:		
Joseph England Receipt for	283.18 3/4	
Thomas Williams	283.18 3/4	
Samuel H. Williams	283.18 3/4	
Edmond Stamps	283.18 3/4	
Altasard Williams	283.18 3/4	
Jesse Elliott	283.18 3/4	
John Jett receipts for taking Dispositions	5.00	
William McKinnys receipt for Servide as Coms.	3.00	
J. A. Lane receipt for Registing Deed	1.00	
Burrill expences	7.68 3/4	
Lincoln & Carrick receipt	.60	
James Hutson probate proving away from estate	44.50	
William Kinnard Probate Same	14.12½	
Lewis Bohannon Receipt for	3.08	
Alexander B. Lanes Acct. attending to law Suit	10.00	
Edward Wims one of the heirs received	283.18 3/4	
Robert Officer one of the heirs received	283.18 3/4	
Paid for Whiskey for Sale	7.00	
Paid for Sundries for Widow laid off by coms.	13.00	
do for 400 lb. Pork	12.00	
James T. Holmes acct for the estate	25.00	
Cash paid for a Beef for Widow	8.00	
Cash paid Crier of the Sale	4.00	
J. A. Lane Receipt	2.12½	
Same do	1.62½	
William CRants do	1.50	
Edmond Stamps pro ate proving from estate Millers note amounting to	3.50	
Cost on Said Suit	.50	
Probate of Robert Officer for paying J. A. Lane	1.00	
Widow notes by order of Court	426.31¼	
Administrators Servicew by order of Court	100.00	
Beddels Recpt for a note of J. W. Jones	4287½	3032.57
Bal due estate from Admr.		24.88 3/4

Robert Officer Charges for $16. not allowed.
We the undersigned Commissioners do hereby certify that as far as we have examined the papers, we believe the above to be correct Given under our hands and Seals this first day of May 1837. William Little, David Snodgrass, Elisha Cannon, Coms.

Recorded 21 Sept. 1837 Test. N. Oldham Clerk.

P 262 Report of a Settlement made by Commissioners with the administrators of the estate of John Dale deceased upon oath returned at September term A. D. 1837.

	Dr.		
No1 Sales of Property returned at Jany 1834		337.04¼	
No 2 Same	same	710.90	
Money received for Ferriage		6.47	
" collected from John L. Price		5.00	
" collected forn Trent C. Conner & others a ppears from the papers		599.37½	
	Debit	$1658.78 3/4	

Credit

By money expended in attending to the admr. and time amounting to which was Consented to by the parties being present	257.70¼	
By monies paid out by Daniel Dale Admr. as appears from Exhibits from No. 1 to 17 inclusive herewith filed amting to	179.01	
By money nd time expended by Pleasant White one of the admr. attending to said business	56.37½	493.09¼
Leaving a balance of		1163.69½

Yet in the hands of the administrators. All of which is humbley submitted 5th July 1837. Joseph Cummings Jr., John Gillentine Coms.

Recorded 21st September A. D. 1837. Test N. Oldham Clk.

P 263 Report of a Settlement made by Commissioners with John Witt Administrator of the estate of Dempsey Fenner decd. made at April term A. D. 1837. Towit:

	Dr.	
To amt. of Sales of the Property pr Certificate of clerk	255.72	
To Cash on hands	788.70	
To Debits collected	12.31½	
Debit	1056.73½	
1 Receipt from W. G. Thockmorton	$35.00	
2 Receipt from George D. Howard	249.56 2/3	
3 Receipt from R. B. Fenner	249.56 2/3	
4 do do	85.00	
5 Receipt from George D. Howard	85.00	
Burriel expences	6.00	
Attending to the business of Said estate including all fees (as Adm r.)	35.00	745.131/3
Leaves a bal of		311.60

Yet in the hands of Administrators. Wm. B. Cummings, William Anderson Coms.
6 March 1837
Recorded 21st Sept. 1837 Test N. Oldham Clk.

Report of Edward B. Pollard Guardian to James and Rachel Glenn infant heirs of William Glenn deceased made upon oath at February term

A. D. 1837. Towit:
For his ward James Glenn he has received one negro man named Peter estimated at 600.00
Said negro has been hired out for the present year to David Fisher of Cannon County and taken bond with Isaac Adcock Security for the same 84.00

For his ward Rachel Glenn he has received one negro Girl estimated at $300. Said negro girl is small and could not be hired out to advantage. She therefore remains with the owner the present year—All of which is respectfully submitted
Recorded 21st September 1837. Edward B. Pollard
Test N. Oldham Clerk

P 264 Report of a Settlement made by Commissioners with Jesse Walling Administrator of Thomas R. Paul deceased made upon oath at August term A. D. 1837. Towit: Dre
The Admr is Chargeable with the amount of sales returned at the January term 1836. this sum 474.37½

Credit

By one note given as a fee to Lane & Anderson advin in Said estate	10.00
By note executed by Thos. R. Paul to Sarah Paul	26.53
By n. Oldhams Receipt No. 1	1.15
" do 2	2.00
By Joseph Herds Receipts do	2.00
" Joseph W. Roberts do feeding 4 horses 48 days	1.00
@ 1/6 per day each	48.00
" Administrators account for his trouble and expence to the affairs of Said estate which we think reasonable and ought to be allowed by the court	25.00
By this Sum paid commissioners for compensation for one day Service makint this Settlement	3.00
	355.69½

After Deducting the amount of vouchers and all expences claims by said administrator in the settlemeny of Said estate we the undersigned commissioners find a balance of money in his hands amounting to the sum of Three hundred and fifty five Dollars and Sixty nine & ½ cents We also See a receipt of Samuel O. Paul one of the heirs of Said estate in the hands of said administrator for the full amount of his part of said estate but no amount Specified which we think the admr. is entitled to ~~a credit for which is not here deducted out of the above~~ amount. Witness our hands this 7th July 1837 John Jett
Recorded 21 September 1837 Thomas Green
Test N. Oldham Clerk of White County Court

P 264 Report of a Settlement made by commissioners with the Administrators of the estate of James Isham deceased made upon oath at September term A. D. 1837 Towit:

Russel Gist one of the Admr. at a former Settlement Dr.	34.25
Nancy Isham on former Settlement (admr.) Dr.	50.21½
To amount of Rents and Land warrant Sold in the hand of Administrator	84.88
Debit	169.34 3/4

By receipt to A. B. Lane by Nancy Isham No. 1	4.01	
" " Jesse Lincoln do No 2	50.00	
" Tax receipts to D. L. Mitchell No. 3&4	1.00	
" Receipt to J. A. Lane by do N. 7	63.50	118.59
Bal due David L. Mitchell at former Settlment	37.02½	
By receipt of Henry Isham by D. L. Mitchell No 5	5.25	
" " Samuel Turney recpt No. 6	10.00	
" Taxes 1827, 28 part 1830,31&32, 33, 34	4.56½	
" Receipt to J. A. Lane No.8	8.26½	55.10½
	173.69½	
Nancy Ishams account vs Estate	$118.59	
~~To this sum paid her by Thomas Meeks~~	30.00	
" " do John Meek	4.88 3/4	
" her note returned to her	50.21 3/4	
Due N. Isham	33.48½	
David L. Mitchell acct vs Estate $55.10½	55.10½	
By corn received of Rent	13.91½	
" land warrent sold	4.82	
" note on Kirk & Taylor	11.75	
" " on J. Randals & I. G. Mitchell	10.37½	30.37½
Due Dl L. Mitchell	24.75	
Russell Gist Dr. to the Estate this amount on formey settlement not accounts for	34.25	
to corn from sale of corn	10.00	
Due estate the sum of	$44.25	

but says he has paid thirty Dollars and will furnish receipt or not or affidavit so that after which if done will leaving him owing fourteen Dollars twenty five cents. we find the estate owing Nancy Isham thirty three dollars forty eight and one half cents Also we find P 236 said estate owing the estate of David L. Mitchell twenty four dollars Seventy three cents ($24.73) we find form a statement of Joseph Gooch and papers in his possession, that the plantation whereon James Isham levid at his death was sold by verture of an execution and bought by Jesse Lincoln who agreed that the administrator might swap places with him and he gave five hundred and fifty dollars to boot which he paid over to A. B. Lane and Jesse Lincoln for Debts they held against the estate of James Isham Which was all for the benefit of the heirs all of which we report Given from our hand and seal August 14th 1837.

Recorded 21st Sept 1837. Thomas Green

Test N. Oldham Ck. Jesse Walling

Account of Settlement made by Commissioners with Oscar Denton Executor of the estate of Jeremiah Denton Deceased returned upon oath at August term A. D. 1837.

To amount Sales returned at January term 1836.	$1996.07 ½	
To one note on James Moore Doubtful	10.00	2006.07
	Credited with	
By one note given to Lane as a fee	5.00	
By one receipt of Thifer	1.00	
By one " J. A. Lane No 1	2.50	

By one receipt of J. A. Lane No 2	.50	
" payment of Dibrell	14.75	
" one receipt of James Walling	8.00	
" " " " Jesse Lincoln	.87½	
" " " " William Knowles	1.37½	
" " " " S. Baxton	1.00	
" " " " for tax of 1835	1.02½	
" James Simpson	.75½	
" " " " Lewis Evans	.59½	
" " " " Lewis Phillips	.25	
" " " " William Hickman	1.08	
" " " " William Glenn	4.33½	
" " " " Joseph Herd	4.00	
This amount to Executor for his trouble in settling the affairs of Said estate which we think reasonable and ought to be allowed by the Court	74.87	
By Compinsation to Coms. in Settling 1 day each	3.00	
" Receipt from N. Oldham	1.15	
" Note on James Moore sholly insolven	10.00	
Debit up		2006.07
P 267 By receipt from W. C. Denton one of the Legatees	230.00	
" John D. Denton do	230.00	
" order from Jeremiah Gettings	24.00	
" Receipt " Daniel McDanial	120.00	
" " " Samuel Couch	119.62½	
" " " George Rogers	119.62½	
" Daniel Dewise	15.00	
" Sarah Denton	230.00	
" Adam Mean	15.00	
" Anna (Thomas) Gettings	1.00	
" Amt of one bay horse released by court	71.00	1312.07½
" Balance	693.99½	

After deducting the amount of Boucers and all expenses as Claimed by said Executor in the Settlement of Said estate we the undersigned Commissioners find a balance of money in his hands to the sum of Six hundred and ninety three Dollars and ninety & ½ cents. Witness our hands and Seals this 29th day of July 1837. Jesse Walling
Recorded 23d September A. D. 1837 Thomas Green
Test N. Oldham Clk.

In the name of God, Amen: I Berry Hamblet of the State of Tennessee and of the County of White. being sick but of sound mind and memory do hereby make this my last will and Testament First, I commend my body to the dust, to be burried in a decent Christian like manner, and my Soul to God Who gave it. And touching my Worldy Estate wherewith it hath pleased God wherewithit hath pleased God to bless me; I bequeath in the following manner Towit:
For the love and affection I have for my beloved wife Elizabeth Hamblet it is my will that my wife Shall have and enjoy all my estate both personal n and real estate during her natural life or widowhood, after paying all my just Debts It is my will and desire that my wife Elizabeth Hamblett shall have

the power and privilage to sell and dispose of any part of my estate, either real or personal should it be necessary for the payment of my debts, or the support and maintainance of my Children. It is my will and desire that if it should become necessary for any part of my estate to be sold by my wife for that purpose. I wish my two negro Boys ack and eff to be kept by my beloved wife Elizabeth to work for her support and the support and (support) miantainance of my children. I will and bequeath to my
P 268 wife Elizabeth a childs part out of my estate after all my deb s are paid should my wife Elizabeth marry again before my children all become of age it is my will and desire in the event of my wifes marrying, that at the tim she marries she shall then draw from my estate the part I have allowed to her , t at is an equal part with each child out of my Estate. If my wife h should marry I wish then my two negro boys hired out and the hire of the same to be equally divided between all of my children. If my wife should remain in widowhood during her life. I wish her to keep both my negro boys hired out and the hire of the same to be equally divided between all of my children If my Wife should remain in widowhood during her life. I wish her to keep both my negro boys to work for her support and maintainance of my children. It is my will and desire that if it should become necessary for any part of my estate to be sold by my wife for that purpose. I wish my two negro boys Jack and Jeff to be kept by my beloved wife Elizabeth to work for her support and the support and (Support) maintainance of my children. I will and bequeath to my wife Elizabeth a childs part out of my estate after all my debts are paid, should my wife Elizabeth Marry again before my children all become of age, it is my will and desire in the event of my wifes marrying, that at the time she marries she shall then draw from my estate the part I have allowed to her, that is an equal part with each child out of my estate. If my wife should marry I wish then my two negro boys hired out an the hire of the sae to be equally divided between all of my children. If my wife should remain in widowhood during her life I wish her to keep both my negro boys to work for her support and maintainance. It is my will and desire at my wifes Death that all of my Estate shall be equally divided between all of my children. I hereby constitute and appoint my beloved wife Elizabeth Hamblett Executrix to this my last will and testament, and I hereby disannull disolve and revoke all former wills or executors by me made. In Witness whereof I have hereunto set my hand and Seal this 5th day of July 1836. All enterlematior mad e before this will was signed. Signed Sealed and acknowledged in presence of us.

Berry X Hamblett (Seal)
his mark

Test. Trent C. Couver
John Wallis

State of Tennessee }
White County } May Term A. D. 1837.

This day was produced in open court a writing purposing to be the last will and testament of Berry Hamblett deceased was this day proven in open Court by the oath of Trent C. Couver subxcribing witness thereto for the puppose therein mentioned and that at the date of the execution and publication thereof the said Berry Hamblett was of sound and disposing mind and memory. Whereupon also appeared in open court Elisabeth Hamblet, who appointed executrix in said last will and testament of her deceased husband Berry Hamblet and undertakes

Burthew and execution of Said will and testament and thereupon took the oath required by law and together with James Rndals Senr. and Joseph Herd entered into and acknowledged bond in the sum of Three Thousand Dollars conditioned as the law requires Given at office the 1st day of may 1837 Test. N. Oldham lerk of White County Court Recorded 23rd Sept 1837. Test N. Oldham Clk.

P 269 State of Tennessee }
White County }

I Sampson Goddard being of Sound and perfect mind and memory do make and publish this my last will and testament in manner and form following towit: first I give and bequeath unto my beloved wife Catharine Goddard all my personal property or effects consisting of what it may after my just debts being paid out of Said personal property. I also give and bequeath unto to my daughter Eliza Jane and My beloved wife Catharine Goddard all my real estate so long as my wife remains a widow, and when her widowhood ceases, then the real estate to belong entirely to my beloved daughter Eliza Jane Goddard the real estate consisting of one piece of Land Whereon I now live to hold to her the said Eliza Jane her heirs and assign forever-- Lastly I hereby appoint my Said beloved wife sole executrix of this my last will and testament, hereby revoking all former wills by my made. In witness whereof I have hereunto set my hand and affixed my seal this day of arch A. D. 1837. Signed Sealed published and delivered by the above named Sampson oddard to be his last will and testament in the presence of us we have hereunto subscribed our names as witnesses in the presence of the Testator Witness Sampson X Goddard (Seal)
Joseph Cummings Jr. his mark
James Goddard

State of Tennessee }
White County } May term A. D. 1837.

This day was produced in open Court a writing purposing to be the last will and testament of Sampson Goddard late of the County of White deceased and the due execution and publication thereof as the last will and testameh of Sampson Godard deceased was proven in open Court by the oath of Joseph Cummings Jr. and James Godard Subxcribing Witnesses thereto for the purposes and things therein contained, and that at the date of the execution and publication thereof the said Sampson Goddard was of sound and disposing mind and memory. whereupon apeared in open Court Catharing Goddard who is appointed sole executrix in Said Will and testament of her deceased husband Sampson Goddard, and undertakes the burthen and execution thereof and thereupon to the oath required by law and together with James Goddard Joseph Cummings Jr. and Elijah Hill entered into and acknowledged bond in the sum of Three hundred Dollars conditioned as the law requires . Giva at office 1st day of May 1837. Test N. Oldham Clk. of White County Court. Recorded 23 Sept. 1837. Test N. Oldham Clk.

P 270 Inventory and Sales of the estate of nathan Bartlett Deceased returned upon oath by William Bartlett Administrator at September term A. D. 1837.

Nathan Bartlett Senr. to 1 Kittle		3.00
" "	1 Pott	1.50
Same	1 oven & two lids	.50

Lewis Huddleston 1 Scythe blade	1.37½
William Whitaker 1 pr hooks	.06¼
Nathan Bartlett Senr. 1 Skillet	.25
Same 1 oven & hooks	1.12½
William Bartlett 5 plates & Dish	2.13 3/4
Campbell Bohanon 1 dish & candle moulds	.81¼
Joseph Bartlett 1 Bason	.68 3/4
Nathan Bartlett 1 churn	1.12½
Nathan Bartlett Jr. 1 cow & calf	14.12½
David Wiser Jr. 1 cow & calf	12.62½
Robert Officer 5 Steers	51.00
Daniel Bartlett 2 Steers	12.51½
William Whitaker Senr. 1 Heifer	8.00
William C. Johnson 1 Red cow	12.00
William Bartlett 1 Hackel	2.87½
Joseph Bartlett 1 Looking glass	.37½
Henry Johnson 1 Coffee Mill	.25
Nathan Bartlett Senr. 1 pr Steelyards	1.75
James Roberts 1 Horse	85.00
Joseph Pryor 1 Filly	87.75
John Johnson 1 mare & colt	140.00
Joseph Graham 10 chocie Sheep	17.00
Mathew England 1 yoke of Steers	.50
Nathan Bartlett 1 coffee pot	.18 3/4
Daniel Bartlett 1 Reap hook	.50
Nathan Bartlett 1 pr waffle Irons	1.93 3/4
Same 1 axe	2.62½
Samuel Ayers 1 axe	2.50
Jesse Y. Kirkindale 10 lb wool	3.70
Nathan Bartlett 10 lb wool	3.80
Joseph Bartlett 10 lb wool	3.75
Nathan Bartlett 10 lb wool	3.80
Nathan B. Marchbanks 1 Bee Gum	2.56¼
Campbell Bohanon 1 Bee Stand	1.81¼
James Bartlett 1 Grindstone	.31¼
Moses Robertson 1 Reel	1.06¼
James Bartlett 1 cupboard	17.00
Nathan Bartlett bowles cups & saucers	.56½
P 271 James Bartlett Spoons plates	1.00
William Bohanon 2 Glass Tumblers	.25
Hudson 1 pitcher	.25
Nelson Oxendine 1 Table	3.06¼
Craven Maddux 1 Saddle	12.00
Lewis Bohannon 1 Bridle	.50
Mathias Welsh 1 Log chain	3.12½
James Jackson 1 pr. Gears	2.12½
James Bohanon 1 pr Gears	1.00
John Henry 1 Basket	.18 3/4
Lewis Bohanon 1 Spade	1.18 3/4
Nathan Bartlett 1 Big wheel	1.00
George Thomas 1 Staple & ring	1.00
Matthias Welch 1 pitcher	.18 3/4
Robert Officer 1 crock	.25
Solomon Madewell 1 Jar	.25
Daniel Bartlett 17 lb cotton	1.70

James Jackson 1 Bridle	.25
Samuel Johnson 2 crocks 50 1 pitcher 50	1.00
William Bohanon 3 crocks	.50
Bounds Terry 1 meal Bag	.50
William Bartlett 1 meal Bag	.75
James Bartlett 1 Table	.25
Nathan Bartlett 1 Pale	.12½
Joseph Bartlett 1 wagon	39.00
Joseph Bartlett 2 Salt Barrels	.12½
Joseph Bartlett 1 Stretcher .62¼ 9 sheep 10$	10.62½
Thomas Boahanon 1 Pale	.19
Samuel Madewell 1 set warping Spools	.68 3/4
Dudley Hudgins 1 axe	.50
Solomon Madewell 2 sets weaving gears & slay	.50
George Thomas 49 lb Bacon	4.90
Samuel Aynes 49 3/4 lb do	4.96
Goodman Madewill 67 lb. do	6.70
William Bohannon 1 pr fire Dog	.41
Campbell Bohanon 1 Water pto	.37½
Joseph Prior 1 chest	5.12½
William Whitaker 1 Scythe	.25
Daniel Bartlett 1 Brier Scythe	1.81 ¼
Simon Shanks 1 mare	30.25
Joseph Pryer 1 cutting Box	3.00
Same 1 Flax Wheel	3.00
George Thomas 1 auger	.68 3/4
P 272 Jacob Hyder Jr. 1 auger	.13 3/4
William Whitaker 1 pr. Sheep Shears	.62½
Moses Grant 1 Plow	1.00
Dudley Hudgins 1 plow and screw	.56¼
William Hudgens 1 plow	.86¼
Daniel Bartlett 1 plow & screw	.50
Moses Robertson 1 Grubbing hoe	.50
James Bohanon 2 clevis	.37½
Thomas Boahnon 1 Piggin	.12½
Nathan Bartlett 1 hoe 58 1 Drawing Knife 1.00	1.50
Campbell Bohannon 1 sedge	.56¼
Thomas Welch 1 do	137½
George Thomas 1 Tomahawk	112½
Daniel Bartlett 1 box Iron	.25
Nathan Bartlett 1 Ring & hoe	.62½
Jacob Hyder 1 Bell	.37
Nathan Bartlett 1 handsaw	1.62½
Nathaniel R. Marchbanks 2 Chisels	.18 3/4
Joseph Bartlett 1 quart measure	.50
Henry Bohanon 1 Loom	8.56¼
Jacob Hyder 1 plow & Singletree	1.81¼
Daniel Bartlett 2 singletrees	.68 3/4
Robert Officer 1 Sifter	18 3/4
James Jackson 2 hoes	.75
William Bohanon 1 coffee pot	.20
Nathan Bartlott 1 Bar 2 horse plow	4.00
Joseph Pryor 1 hide 1.18 3/4 1 do 5.00	6.18 3/4

William Hunter 1 Riddle	.62½
Helson Oxendine 1 Churn and Cover	.18 3/4
Joseph Bartlett 1 Wheat fan	13.25
William Daniel 5 Busheäs Wheat	5.00
Robert Officer 5 do	4.37½
Nathan Bartlett 5 do	5.00
C. Maddux 5 do	5.00
Henry Sevimuly? 5 do	5.00
J seph Graham 5 do	4.75
Robert Officer 5 do 4.50 or 4.95	9.45
James Bartlett 500 Bundles oats	5.00
Same 500 Bundles	5.00
Nathan Bartlett 500 do	5.00
James Bartlett 1 pen Straw	1.00
Wm. Bartlett 1 do	.50
M ses Grant 1 Lot Flax	1.25
James Bartlett 7 Barrels & Guns	2.00
P 273 William Bohanon 1 peice of Leather	2.00
Henry Bohanon 27 Bacon	2.88
J seph Bartlett 56½ lb do	5.65
Benjamin Dickenson 27½ do	2.52
Helson Oxendine 32½	3.25
Joseph Twior 3 Flat canns	.25
William Barttett 1 Barriel of Soap	4.00
James Bohanon 1 Barrel	.31¼
Samuel Madewell 1 Jug	.18 3/4
Nathan Bartlett 1 do	.18 3/4
Goodman Madewell 1 Barrel	.06¼
Nathan Bartlett 1 Goard	.12½
Goodman Madewell 1 Lot of Lard	1.12½
Joseph Barttlett 1 Soap trough	.06¼
Samuel Johnson 3 chairs	.56½
M ses Grant 3 chairs	1.00
Benjamin Dickerson 3 chairs	.93 3/4
Black Jacob Barrel & rosin	.50
Henry Bohanon Spooling frames and temples	.25
Willima Bohanon 1 Barrel & mill	.41¼
William Bartlett 1 Bushel corn	.65
David Whitaker 3 Barrels	.18 3/4
Solomon Madewell 2 do	.50
Thomas Bohanon 2 Hogs	12.81¼
Daniel Bartlett Stock of Hogs	101.50
William Hudgins 1 Bread tray	.12½
Nathan Bartlett 1 saddle Blanket	1.56¼
Nathan Bartlett 1 Gallon bottle	.62½
J seph Bartlett 1 pr. saddle bags	3.62½
John Madewell 5 Bushels corn	3.00
William Daniel 5 bushl. do 3.00 5 do 3.18 3/4	6.18 3/4
Robert Whitaker 5 do	3.25
John Huddleston 10 do	6.50
Robert Whitaker 5 do	3.25
Nathan Bartlett 5 do	3.25
James Bartlett 5 do	3.25
John C. Huddleston 5 do	3.25

James Bohannon 5 do 3.25
James Robertson 5 do 3.25
Andrew Jacdson 5do 3.25
Goodman Madewell 5 do 3.25
Soloman Madewell 5 do 3.25
Henry Sininuly (?) 5 do 3.24½
P 274 Amt brought over James Robertson 5 Bushels corn 3.23½
Andrew Jackson 5 do 3.23½
James Bartlett 8 do 5.20
Joseph Pryor bought this sum to be due 10 Augt. 1837 23.12½
Nathan Bought 22.56¼
Inventory William Bartlett Dr. to Est. 150.00
James Bartlett Dr. to affidavt made by Nathan Bartlett deceased 60.00
Claim on James Bohanon 5.00
Money on hand 30.00
William Bartlett Admr. Recorded 1 Nov. 1837 Test. N. Oldham Clk.

In the mane of God Amen I James Madewell of Whote County and the State of Tennessee, being Sick and weak but are of perfect mind and memory thanks be given unto God Calling unto mind the Mortality of my body and Knowing that it appointed for all men once to die, do make and ordain this to be my last will and testament. that is to say, principably and first of all I give and ~~recommend my Soul into the hand~~ of an Almighty God, that give it and my body I recommend to the earth to be buried in dessent Christian burial at the description of my Executors nothing doubting but at the General resurrection I shall receive the same again by the power of Almighty God and as touching such worldly estate wherewith it hath pleased God to bless me with in this life, I give devise, and dispose of the same in the following manner and form that is to say princible and first of all I give and bequeath unto Polly Madewell my dearly beloved wife all my land and other propertys her freely to be possessed and enjoyed and raise all he children upon during her widowhood but if she shall marry to any other nam it shall be longer hers, but shall belong to my three boys James Madewell Junr. Pleasant Madewell Juison Madewell but all the rest of the property to be equally divided among the rest of my children and her I do hereby revoke and disannuel all other Wills any way before mentioned, ratifying this to by my last Will and testament dated this tenth day of P 275 January in the years of our Lord One tho sand eight hundred and thirty seven.

James X. Madewell (Seal)
his mark

Signed Sealed and delivered in the presence of David Robertson
Amis X Madewell
His mark

State of Tennessee }
White County } November Term A. D. 1837

This was produced in open Court a Writing perposting to be the last will and testament of James Madewell late of the County of White deceased, and the due execution and publication thereof as such was proven in open Court by the oath of Aunis Madewell one of the subscribing Witness thereto for the purposes & things therein mentioned. And that the said James Madewell was at the date of the execution and publication thereof of Sound and

disposing mind and memory. And at the same time made oath that David Tobertson whose name is subscribed to said last will and testament as the other witness, did sign his name hereto as witness at the request and in the presence of the testator at the date of the execution and publication thereof and that the said David Robertson is now deceased--which the court deem sufficient and order the same to be recorded. Given at office the 6th November. Test N. Oldham Clerk of White County Court.
Recorded 11 Nov. 1837. Test N. Oldham Clk.

In the name of God Amn. This 30th January 1837. I David Robertson of White County and State of Tennessee being Sick and weak, but of perfect mind and menory thanks be give unto God, Calling unto nind the mortality of my body and knowing that it is appointed for all men once to die, do make and ordain this to be my last will and Testament ~~that is to say principbly~~ ~~[illegible]~~ and recommend my Soul unto the hand of an Almighty God that give it, And my body I recommend to Earth to be buried in dessent Christian burial at the description of my Executors nothing doubting but at the General Resurection I shall receive the same again, by themighty power of God and as touching such worldly estate, wherewith it has pleased God to bess me with in this life, I give, desire and dispose of the same in the following manner and form. That is to say give and bequeath how to my dearly beloved wife Nancy Robertson all the land and other propertys, endorsing her life time or widowhood but if she should marrd, then no more to be herne Exdeceal, then to belong to James Robertson and William Robertson and Thomas Robertson Elizabeth Robertson Ten Dollars, Isaac Robertson one Dollar, William Patton One Dollar, David Robertson One Dollar, Thomas Cox, Signed Sealed and delivered in Presence of us. David Robertson (Seal)
John X. Madewell
her mark
Aunis X Madewell
his mark

State of Tennessee }
White County } October term A. D. 1837

This day was exhibited in open Court a Writing purposting to be the last Will and Testament of David Robertson lot of the County of White Deceased and the due execution and publication thereof was proven in open Court by the oath of John Madewell and that at the date of the execution and Publication thereof as such, the Said David Robertson was of Sound and disposing mind and memory which is ordered to be recorded. Given at office 2nd. October A. D. 1837. Test N. Oldham Clk. of White County

State of Tennessee }
White County } November term A. D. 1837.

This day was produced in open Court a Writing purposting to be the last Will and Testament of David Robertson late of the County of White deceased and the due execution and publication thereof was proven in open Court by the oath of Aunis Madewell the other subxcribing witness thereof for the purposes and things therein mentioned. And that at the date of execution and publication thereof the said David Robertson was of sound and disposing mind and memory. And the same having been at the October term of this Court 1837. In like manner proven by the oath of John Madewell for the same purpose All of which is ordered to be recorded.

Given at office 6th. November A. D. 1837. Test N. Oldham Clk. of White County Court
Recorded 11 Nov. 1837. Test N. Oldham Clk.

P 277 Inventory of the Estate of John Massa Senr. Deceased returned upon oath by John BAssa Jr. Admr. thereof at November 1837.
Towit: Six head of cattle 9 head of Hogs one mare saddle and Blanket and Bridle--two Beds and furniture--One Chest 3 Bedsteads One large Kittle 2 potts 2 ovens & lids 2 plows One Axe one Coffee pot One hlaf dox Pewter Plates One Coffee Mill One Basmn 2 Dishes 3 Geese Some peices Chains and Clevises

John X Massa Jr.
his mark

Recorded 11th November 1837 Test. N. Oldham Clk.

Inventory of a part of the Estate of Mecajah Taylor deceased returned upon oath by Creed A. Taylor Administrator Thereof at November term A. D. 1837 Towit: One dark bay or Chestnut Sorrel horse supposed to be worth $75. One Man's Saddle supposed to be worth $20. One bridle worth about 75¢ One Rifle Gun worth about $10. One Pistol worth about $5.00 One receipt on arris & Barrel of GAllatin Mississippi for the Collection of two Notes one on G orge W. Price, due the 1st January 1837 for one hundred and twenty five Dollars, the other on Drury W. Tucker and Isaa c Fife for One hundred thirty five Dollars due 1st Decr. 1836. Said receipt is dated April 5th 1837. And whether said Notes are good or not, the administrator does not know, owing to the remote distance at which the makers live from White County Tennessee the amount besides interest is $150. (ought to be $250000) Also one other receipt on Fulton and Shackleford for collection of two N tes one on O. W. Saxton and M ses Goff for $140. dated 5 Nov. 1835 and due on the 25 day of December 1835--One note on D. W. Dillahey J el Hudgins and John S. Bottles whether they are solvent or the administrator does not know for the reason above assigned said last mentioned receipt is dated at Canton Mississippi March 31st 1837--And amounts in all to $340. be besides lawful interest--Also one receipt on David Dean and William Moore for the Collection of the following notes towit: One on William Millsap due Oct. 1 st. 1837. $65. O e on Benjamin Davis due 1st Octo. 1837. $27.50 One on Robert G. Anderson due 25 Decr 1836 $20. with a credit of $16.25 cents which credit is dated 23 Sept. 1836 And another credit on the same of $8.37½ cents dated May 3rd. 1837. two other note on Seith Cosby due April the 4th 1837 for the sum of $70. each One other note of Thomas Richards due Decr. 1st 1837 for the sum or $200. The whole of said receipt besides lawful interest amounts to the sum of $57.87½ as the Debts specifidd in said receipt does not know as to their Solvency for the reason before given. Also one note on Bryan & Moore due 4th Sept. 1837. for the sum of $129.56¼ said last mentioned note is entitled to some credit s the amount is not Known to the administrator, but they shall be given as soon as they can be ascertained--Also one note on John Jett due yth June 1837. for the sum of $25. Both the last mentioned Notes are considered good and the Makers Solvent, one note on James Bray (solvent) due May 1st 1837 for the sum of 1.75. Also one note on Memordudum on W. L. Young and Brothers, which they alleged they have paid, how the fact is affeant (?) does not know, for $50. He has a number of other notes which are beleived to be on mean who are intensely insolvent; which however shall all be set out in an amended inventory which he will exhigit ot the next

court. together with every fact required by law to be stated and which would now be set out, if time would permit. Creed A. Taylor
Recorded 13th day Nov. 1837 Test N. Oldham Clk.

Inventory of the Estate of Azariah Long deceased returned upon oath by George Clive Admr. at December term 1837 Towit: 1 Barshare plow 1 Coutler, 4 hoes 1 Iron wedge 1 reap hook 1 cutting knife 1 lot old iron 2 small Kegs 2 small Tubbs 1 old Chain 1 pr Saddle Bags 1 pot & hooks 1 pr Steelyards 1 Bale box, 12 old cider Barrels 1 black Horse 1 saddle 1 Bridle 1 froock coat 1 over Coat 1 pr pantaloons 1 sheet 2 vests 1 pr socks 2 Hats 1 pr legings 1 Brier Scythe 1 pr Boots 1 sifter 2 baskets 2 bales shoe thread 2 small books 1 pamphlet 1 cot bed stead 2 common bedstead 1 shaving Glass 2 Razors and case 2 chair frames 2 Barrels apple Brandy 1 pr spectacles 1 Morocco pocket book, cash found on hand $24.55 1 note on Thomas Grissum for $20. due 1 June 1835 1 note of $2.25 on Terna Tenleton due 18th Nov. 1835 1 account on Jas. H. Jenkins for $59.90 due August 1836. 1 acct on Jas. Godwin for $14. due June 1836. 1 acct. on Hunter & Harlow for $3.50
1 act on W. M. Young for $8.75 this sum due by George Clive payable 1 March 1837. $42.1 note on S. Bramblet $10.75 July 6th 1836.
P 279 Recorded 19th Decr. 1837 George Clive Admx. of A. Long Decd. Test N. Oldham Clerk. of White County Court.

Account of the Sales of the property of Azariah Long Decd. returned upon oath by Geo Clive admr. at December term 1837.

Rhodwn Doyle 1 Barshare plow 4/6	.75
Henderson McFarland 1 pr saddle bags	1.31¼
George Clive 2 Tubbs	.50
Rhodum Doyle Lot old Iron and 2 Kegs	.94 3/4
John Wallis 1 pot & Hooks	2.18 3/4
George Clive 2 Hoes c 3/2 Ditto 1/6	.75
John Gracy 1 pr Steelyard	.81¼
Harman Mayburn 1 Bale box and 1 Barrel	.62½
John Wallis 1 Black horse & Bridle	5.50
Ditto 1 Coat	.50
H. McFarland 1 Blanket Coat	.50
John Wallis 1 pr Pantaloons	.25
Ditto 1 shirt and vest	.25
H. McFarland 1 Vest and pr Socks	.25
Hayes Arnold 1 Hat 181¼ 1 Ditto 2.06¼	3.87 2/4
Rhodum Doyle 1 Saddle	4.50
H. McFarland 1 pr. Leggings	.06¼
John Wallis 1 Brier Scythe 50 1 pr Boots 75	1.25
Rhodum Doyle 1 Coutlef	.25
William Waller 1 Sifter	.31¼
George Clive 2 Baskets and 2 cow Bulls	.12½
George Clive 3 Books .25 1 Cott Bedstead .50	.75
Rhodum Doyle 1 Bedstead	.50
George Clive 1 Bedstead 50 1 old chain 9d	.62½
Ditto 2 Chair frames 12½ 1 Bl Brandy 11.52	11.64½
John Gracy 1 Glass	.87½
William P Jones 2 Razors & case	.37½
John Gracy 11 cider Barrels	2.75
William Waller 1 Barrel Brandy	11.02
John Bryan 1 pr Spectales	.12½

Rhodum Doyle 1 Iron wedge .53
Recorded 19 December 1837 $55.32
Test N. Oldham Clk. George Clive Admr.

P 280 Report of Settlement by Commissioners with George Clive Admr. of the Estate of Azariah Long deceased returned upon oath at the December Term A. D. 1837. Towit: we find the administrator Chargabde as follows to amt account of Sales $55.32 To this amount as appears from another Documents produced 200.70
We find him entitled to the following credits as appears Satisfactory vouchers here produced 138.18½
We find yet in his hands the sum of 117.33½
to be distrrated according to law all of which is Respectfully submitted this the 4 th day of December 1837. John Wallis }
Madison Fiske } Commissioners

He further charges said estate for his services in administrating said estate the sum of $20. which we think reasonable and respectfully recommend its allowance by the court. John Wallis }
Recorded 19th December 1837 Madison Fisk } Coms.
Test N. Oldham Ck.

Inventory of the Estate of Mary Wallis Deceased December County Court 1837. John Wallis Administrator in omplain with the law in relation to Inventories submits the following statement towit: that the interlate has no property or effects of any description except on Claim to the following described property which is envolved in Law as the records of the Circuit and Chancery Court will show in the suits now pending between John & Pleasant Wallis and this affeant who is the legal representative of the said Mary Wallis--How said suits may terminate is of course uncertain One negro man Named Morris, wishes to be distinctly understood that the claim to said property is disputed as set forth. John Wallis
Recorded 19th Decr. 1837 Test. N. Oldham Clk. of White County Court

P 281 Report of Settlement by Commissioners with John W. Simpson Guardian to the minor heirs of Abraham Conner Decd. returned upon oath at December term A. D. 1837. Towit: To Cahs in the hands of Guardian up to this date towit 1st. Decr. 1837 $63.71 3/4
Notes in the hands of Guardian not collected and due the Estate by the heirs of Jugh Connor, William Connor Elizabeth Connor, Nancy Garner 59.52½
All of which is submitted John Jett, Thomas Green
Recorded 19th December 1837. Test N. Oldham Clerk of White County Court.

Additional Inventory of the Estate of Misajah Taylor deceased returned upon oath by Creed A. Taylor Admr. at the December term A. D. 1837. Towit: One note on Hiram Peterson executed the 8th day of Febry 1833 made payable three months after date (Insolvent) for 80.00
One note on Thomas J. Crumpton executed 6 April 1833 (presumed to be ensolvent.) 10.00
One note on George W. Price executed 29 March 1833 (out of the Government & cannot be collected 12.00
One note on James A. McFarson executed 5 March 1833 (ensolvent for balance) 4.00

One note on William Kirvan dated 18th October 1833 (Involvent) for 2.50
One note on James Anderson dated 5th October 1834 (removed) balance due .50
One note George W. Price executed 29th March 1833 removed from the Government from 6.00
The above notes are not deemed collectable, but if they ever should be collected, they willbe accounted for to those intersted Creed A. Taylor
Recorded 19th December A. D. 1837. Test N. Oldham Clk. of White County Court.

P 282 Account of the slaes of the property of the Estate of Micajah Taylor Deceased returned upon oath by Creed A. Taylor Admr. at the December term A. D. 1837.

1 curry comb sold to Creed A. Taylor for	.12½
1 Bridle & Martingales Sold to Hiram Taylor	.75
1 Man's Saddle & Blanket sold to Hiram W. Taylor	18.00
1 pr. Saddle Bags to William Taylor	2.00
1 Rifle Gun sold to Joseph Mitchell for	15.12½
1 Pistole to Furg Walam Jr. for	.25
1 Pistol to Joseph W. Roberts	7.00
1 sorrel horse to William B. Taylor for	100.00
1 Razor and Strap to William Taylor	1.00
1 Trunk to William Taylor	3.00
	147.25

All of which property was sold for the above Sum on a 12 months credit and the payment second by note and personal security.
Creed A. TAylor
Recorded 19th December A. D. 1837. Test N. Oldham Clk. of White County Court.

Account of the slaes of the property of the Estate of John Massa Senr. Admr. at the December term A. D. 1837
Corneleus Hickey 1 cow $8.25 George Price 1 pr Strechers .62½ Corneleus Hickey 1 Mattock .75 William Baker 1 muley Heifer 5.75 William G. Martin 1 Heifer 6.06¼ William Baker 1 Bull Calf 1.81¼ Corneleus Hickey 1 plow .31¼ William Baker 1 Bull Calf 1.25 George Price 1 Basket & tools 1.00 Presley Bussell 1 Swingletree & Clevis .62½ $26.43 3/4
John X Massa Admr.
his mark
Recorded 19th 1837 Test N. Oldham Dlk of White County Court.

Account of the Sales of the property of the Estate of Webster Hutchins Decd. returned upon oath by Benja Hutchins one of the Admr. at the December term 1837. Towit:
Mary Hutchins the widow 1 Bed & furniture $9. Anna Hutchins 1 Bed & furniture 10.00 Anna Hutchins 1 fallin leaf table 9.00 Mary Hutchins 1 side Saddle 19.00 Mary Hutchins 1 Cupboard & Shelfware 10.00 Anna Hutchins 1 Chest $1 Mary Hutchins 1 Looking Glass .50 William Frisby 1 Cloc 11.25 Mary Hutchins 1 pot & Castings 4. Mary Hutchins 1 Loom & thread 2. Anna Hutchins 2 Wheel & Reel 1.00 William Montgomery 1 Man's Saddle $8. Mary Hutchins 1 Axe 1. 1 Bag Wool .50 $1.50 Thomas Jones Jr. 1 Lock Chian 2.75 John D. Clouse 1 hand Saw .87½ 1 hoe .50 $1.37½

Mary Hutchins 1 Lot tools 1.00 John D. Clouse Plow /c 1.50 Bird Bozorth to Sundries 1.68 3/4 Aaron Hutchins 1 mattock 1.37½ 1 plow .75 1.62½ Joshua Adcock 1 plow 1.00 William J. Russell 1 Reep hook .50 Levi Bozorth 1 Auger .50, John J nes 1 plow William J. Russell 1 Bee Gum 1.00 2.50 Isaac Adcodk 2 Bee Gums 4.50 1 do 1.75 5.75 George W. Pirtle 1 Bee Gum 2. John J nes Senr 1 do .75 John J nes Jr. 1 do 1.43 3/4 ary Hutchins 9 head of Hogs 10.00 Isaac Adcock 1 Lot choice hogs 11. 3d Lot 7.00 $18.00 James Redman second Lot hogs 8. John Jones Jr. rth Lot hogs 5.12½ 5th Lot 6.25 $11.37½ Aaron Young Rifle un 21. Aaron Hutchins 1 scythe & cradle 2.37½ james Cogar 1 Cart 18.87½ Isaac Adcook 1 Bull Yearling 4. Wm. R. Tucker 1 Steer 7.75 1 heifer 9.50 $17.25 james Redman 1 Bull 5.37½ James Cogar 1 cow & calf 15. Isaac Adcook 1 yoke of Oxen 37.00 Anna Hutchins 5 head of Sheep 1. Wm. R. Tucker 1st Choice 5 sheep 7.50
P 284 John Witmoth 5 Sheep wnd Choice 6.00 James Young 3 do 3d do 3. John Redman 1 Still & Tubbs 31.25 ary Hutchins 30 Geese 5.37½ Judemon B. M ore 1 Filly 68.12½ Mary Hutchins 1 colt 45.00 1 Mare 25. 16 Bl. Corn $72. Benjamin Hutchins 1 pr Drawing Chians & hames 2.00 James T. Hays & Jno. Cantrell 1 Iron Wedge Couther /c 2.00 Mary Hutchins 1 note on Tho. Mayes $30. avid Morrow an account Doubtful 4.50 Samuel H. Allen 1 note doubtful 50 William McGarrah one account .50 $514.12½

Benja X Hutchins Admr.
his mark

Recorded 19th December A. D. 1837 Test N. Oldham Clk. of White County Court

Report of assignment of privisions by commissioners for one year to the widow and family of John Massa Senr. decd made at January term A. D. 1838 towit: One cow, five hogs, all the corn and fodder & shucks and oats one bushel of Salt, Ten pounds of Coffee, twelve pounds of sugar, and all the small grain that is growing on the plantation by her having it taken care of wherefore we do subscribed our names this 15 Decr. 1837.

Recorded 5th January A. D. 1838. Test N. Oldham Clk. of White County Court.

J. Allison
John Taylor
James M. Nelson

Report of Samuel Brown Guardian to Robertson Dyer, Claiborn Dyer, John C. Dyer, Alfred Dyer & Louisa Dyer heirs at Law and Minor Children of John Dyer Decd. made their report upon at January term A. D. 1838. that on the first day of January 1838. has in his hands which he is accountable for as Guardian as aforesaid $1293.54.

Recorded 5th January A. D. 1838 Saml. Brown
Test. N. Oldham Clk.

P 285 Report of assignment of one years provisions by commisioners to the widow and family of Webster Hutchins decd. returned at January term A. D. 1838. Towit:

Ten head of Choice hogs belonging to the estate two Cows and Calf one small heifer for Beef, one Barrel of Salt 25# coffee 50# Sugar two Bee Gums, what little Wheat there is on the farm about one Bushel and all the corn that is on the field lying west of the orchard all of which we have this day laid off and set apart for the purpose above mentioned. Given under our hands and Seals this 18th day of September 1837. Eli Sims
Recorded 5th January A. D. 1838 William Irwin Coms.
Test N. Oldham Clerk of White Court.

Report of John Gellintine Guardian to William F. Carter made upon oath at January term A. D. 1838 towit:
O e note on William Wallis for hire of boy Thomas $26.75 One note on John Kirdlan due this day for hire of Girl Sall. $12. one note on Andrew Bryan for the hire of Girl Susan $11. one note on Issac Denton for rent due 1 Sept. next said Denton had the use of one half the farm to build a cross fence and repair the buildings, the house got burnt afteward and I was compelled to have a house built shich reduced the rents it being built for and in consideration of part of the rent $13.87½. Interest on $129.63½ the amount of Cash in my at last settlement $7.77½ $71.40
Disbursements:
Paid William B. Cummings for Schooling $2.60 Paid Carrick for Necessary merchandise $7.56¼ Paid W. & J. Kirklan do $11.37½ Paid J. T. Bradley Shff for tax of 1837 $1.79¼ $23.33 Due ward $48.07 Add cash on hand at last settlement 129.63½. Making in all $177.70½ in Cash on hand and notes besides property reported at my lastreport. All of which is respectfully submitted 1 Jany 1838. John Gillentine Guardian
Recorded 5 January A. D. 1838 Test. N. Oldham Clk.

P 286 Report of Settlement made by commissioners with Thomas Hill Guardian to the heirs of James Hill deceased made upon oath at January term A. D. 1838 towit: Thos. Hill Drs. to the heirs of James Hill deceased agreeable to his last return as it appears by the Certificate of Clerk in the sum of $63.76 3/4.
Credits
By a receipt of Claiborn Hill one of the heirs of Seaborn Hill who was an heir of the estate of James Hill deceased No-- $21.18 3/4 By a receipt of James M. Hill one of the heirs of Seaborn Hill who was an heir of the estate of James Hill deceased $21.18 3/4. By receipt of Thomas J. Hill by his attorney Joseph Duncan who being one of the heirs of Seaborn Hill he being an heir of the estate of James Hill deceased 21.18 3/4 $63.56¼ Leaving a balance in the hands of the Guardian of (.20½) Twenty and one half cents all of which is respectfully Submitted this 30th Decr. 1837.

Joseph Cummings }
Lewis Pettet } Coms.

Recorded 5th January A. D. 1838 Test N. Oldham Clk of White County Court

Report of John Pennington and Sarah Dyer Guardian to part of minor heirs of John Dyer deced. made upon oath at January term A. D. 1838 Towit: That they have in their hands notes to amt. of $1030. 36 3/4 And out of the funds of their wards they have paid for the following purpose the following sums towit: Paid for recording report last January 50 paid for Schooling Wards, & ½ taxes $13. Paid Sarah Dyer her part of his rent /o $10.50 By one half the loss of the hire of Ann to Carrick for the year 1838. having been hired at $40. $5. $29.00 In hand of the Guardians $103136 All of shich is respectfully submitted 1 January 1838.
Recorded 5th January A. D. 1838 John Pennington Guard.
Test N. Oldham Ck.

P 287 Report of William Hill Guardian to his own Children made upon oath at January term A. D. 1838 towit: He states that on the 29th day of November 1836 he received for Said minors the following sum which was due them from the estate of James Chisum and James S. Chisum decd. towit--$929.72½. And that on the 9th day of December 1837. he received their part in full of of the proceeds of the sale of James Chisum land this being all of their part of Said Sales that have as yet come to his hands $1180.40. And on the said 18 day of Decr. 1837 he received for them from Robert H. Vernon Admr. of James S. Chisum $180.00 Received also interst on the 400$ part of the items first above mentioned being 6 pr Cent per Annum this sum $24. Total $2649.12½

Credit

Allance to Guardian by County Court for monies actually expended See order Court 1 Jnay 1838s And also his account annexed to this report $55. All of which is respectfully submitted 1 January 1838.

William Hill Guard

Recorded 5 January A. D. 1838 Test. N. Oldham Clk.

Report of Asa Certain Guardian to moniga & Alphonsa Holmes heirs of Edward Holmes decd, made upon oath at January A. D. 1838 towit: He states that he has been wholly unable to rent out the land and get anything for it after making use of every execution in his power. And now in order to get the fencing rebuilt and repaired he has leased it for three years from today (Jany. 1, 1838) to Nicholas Bennett who is to make a good fence all round it and make a Cross fence, all of whichhe is to do for the use of the princes, this being the best he could do for the heirs the negroes towit: Caroline (with a young child) and Jefferson he has hired them out for the year 1838. Caroline is hired to Nancy Holmes with good Security for $52.00 Jefferson to Emory Bennett with good security for $61.50.

Asa Certain

Recorded 5th January A. D. 1838 Test N. Oldham Clk. of White County Court

P 288 Account of the Sales of the property of the estate of John Hailey Decd. made upon oath by William Hailey Admr. At January term A. D. 1838. Towit: One sorrel Mare sold to Jeremiah Witt for $50.00 One feather bed & Stead Samuel Moore Jr. $7.18 3/4 One Man's Saddle sold to Jeremiah Witt $4.25. One pr Saddle Bags to Saml Moore 1.01 One Skillet sold to Alexander Harris .37½ Six head of Sheep sold to Daniel Hollinsworth 8.25. One pr Sheep Shears to Same .62½ One pr hames & Clevis to Same $1.81¼ making in all the sum of $74.26. sold on a twelve months credit. The above is a true return by me this 1 day of January A. D. 1838. William Hailey Admr. or Estate of John Hailey decd.

Recorded 5th January A. D. 1838 Test N. Oldham Clk.

Report of William Templeton Guardian to John Davis a Minor heir of William Davis Deceased upon oath at Febry TErm 1838. To amount of cash received $77.00. To Interest thereon for 8 years at 6 pr Cent $36.96 on hand 1 January 1838. $1113.96

William Templeton

Recorded 8th Febry 1838 N. Oldham Clk.

Account of the Sales of the property of the Estate of Richard G. Jay decd. returned upon oath by James A. Jay admr. at February term 1838. One stud Horse sold to James A. Jay $140. James A. Jay one man's saddle $10.50 Bartlett Belcher one saddle & Blanket $10. William Jay one cross cut saw $3.62½ . George W. Henry one pr Chains $1.50 William jay one axe $1.75 James A. Jay one Dreging knife $1.37½ Thomas Elms one Book & map $1.56¼ John Johnson one pr Martingales $1. $176.31¼

James A. Jay Admr.

Recorded 8 February 1838 Test N. Oldham Ck.

P 289 Report of William Glenn Guardian to Martha and John W. Glenn minor heirs of William Glenn decd. upon oath at February term 1838 that up to this date there has come to his hands as Guardian deducting expences of which he has an account of the Estate of Martha Glenn the sum of $24.77½ and likewise as to John W. Glenns Estate in like manner deducting expences of which he has the account there has come to his hands $38.93 3/4 All of which has been loaned our according to law upon interest to John Cantrell with Adam Clouse for Security that is the amount received for John W. Glenn The amount belonging to Martha Glenn still remains with Said Guardian. The negro Girl belonging to Martha Glenn, the said Guardian has hired to himself the present year for the sum of $45. and is also to pay her taxes. The negro Girl belonging to John W. Glenn is about eleven years of age, and he has left her with the mother of said John W. Glenn as a compensation to her for the supporting the said John W. Glenn the present year. The land belonging to said Wards has been sold for the benefit of Said Wards by order of the Judge as will appear form the record of the Circuit Court all of which is respectfully submitted. William Glenn Guardian
Recorded 8th February 1838 Test N. Oldham Clk W. C. C.

Report of Edward B. Pollard Guardian to James L. Glenn and Rachel Glenn minor heirs of Wm .Glenn decd made upon oath at February term A. D. 1838 that he has not rece ved the hire of Peter, that belongs to J. L. Glenn but that it is in good hands, tha amount after deducting expenses of which he has account is $80.72½. That of the Estate of Rachel Glenn he has received $10. which has been expensed for Merchandise. The negroes are not hiere out for the present year but he inteds to hire them as soon as circumstances will admit in all respects to do his duty. The land has been sold by an order of the Circuit Court all of which is respectfully submitted E. B. Pollard Guardian
Recorded 8th Febry 1838. Test N. Oldham Clk of White County Court.

P 290 Report of Elsa England Guardian to James England Aaron G. England, Amyr England, Wisley England, Rebecca & Jane England minor heirs of Elijah England decd m de upon oath at February term A. D. 1838. That nothing as yet has come to her hands that can be said to belong to the said Wards for this reason. They the wards aforesaid never have applied to have the Lands divided which descended to them as the heirs at Law of Elijah England deceased nor has said Estate as yet been divided into distrubutive Shares so far as regares the personal property. She promises the Court that so soon as a dividson Shall take palce she will properly and faithfully report the condition of the Estate of her said Wards. She further states that in Character as Adm nistrator she has fairhfully watched over Said Estate and preserved it and kept it together for the interest of Said Wards and will use equal diligined as guardian is preserving and reporting according to law whatever may come to her hands in Character of Guardian

Elsa X England
her mark

Recorded 8th February A. D. 1838
Test. N. Oldham Clk.

Report of Settlement made by commissioners with the admr. & admix of Zachariah Jones deceased made upon oath at Febry term A. D. 1838. The amount of Sales and due the Estate was $5473. 28½ cents now collected. And the vouchers presented to us by the admx. & admr. is $473. money paid out by them. We also allow the admr. & admx $100. for Services rendered by them

and we as commissioners charge one dollars each the debts due to the estate and uncollected are as follows. One note on Clemet Jorden for Eight Dollars due the 28 May 1834. One note on L. H. Pernell Six dollars & Sixty Cents due the 31 July 1834. One note on Elijah Bryant for twenty five Dollars due 25 Decr. 1835. One note on William Gracy due 1 March 1834 which is seven Dollars eighty Seven and a half cents. One note on Elijah Bryant for Sixty Dollars due 25 December 1835. One order from James H Crowder to Jesse Lincoln for one dollar & 95 cents. One claim on I. H. Hough for four hundred and fifty Dollars which debts are doubtful. Given under our hand and Seals this 3rd day of February 1838. James T. Hayes
(Seal) John Taylor
(Seal) W. R. Tucker

Recorded 6th February 1838. Test N. Oldham. Clk.

P 291 Report of the Sales of the property of the Estate of Andrew Hampton deceased made upon oath by James Snodgrass administrator at the Fermuary Term A. D. 1838. Sold to the widow Hampton 2 Beds and furniture $2.00 1 Table and Dresser $1.00 Oven and one pot $1. 1 Jug and 1 jar$0.50 $4.50. 1 Lot of old irons to James Walker .25 To Wm McKinney 1 Blind Bridle .75¢ 1 Blind bridle .50¢ 1 Halter chain .50 $1.75.
To John Flatt 1 Halter chain .62½
" Jonathan Hampton 1 shot Gun 3.12½ 1 pr Gears 1.75 1 pr strechers 2.25 1 Blind brown horse $0110 1 Stak fodder 1.87½ $19. Anderson Abshire 1 Halter Chain .75¢ 1 pr Gears 1.62½ $2.37½ John P Bradley 1 waggon and heird Gear 68. 50 Meekin Taylor 1 Mare $.52 1 Stakfodder 1.72½ $53.72½ Bartlett Belcher 1 Stack fodder 4.59½ Thomas Little 1 Stack oats ¢ .83½ per hundred Ditto 1 Stack do c 87½ do $4.40
James Snodgrass 1 Lot corn 50 Bushels c .43 3/4 $2188½ do 1 Lot do 24½ do c .30 $7.35 $ 29.22½ $188. 94½
James Snodgrass Admr.

Recorded 9th February 1838 Test N. Oldham Clk.

Account of the Sales of the property of the estate of John M. Rottan decd. made upon oath by Dan Griffith Administrator at March term A. D. 1838. sold to Cynthia Rottan household and kitchen & furniture $20. 2 head of Hogs $5 2 Sows and 8 pigs c 500 $10. 1 cow & calf $10. One Cow & calf $8. 1 Mare $10. $28. $58.00 William Rottan 1 coffee mill. 31¼ S. Evans 1 Mattock. 87½ Bryan Jones 1 axe .37½ Wm. Rotan 1 plow & 2 hoes .75 W. Rottan 1 plow 1.00 do .31¼ do 2 augers .68 3/4 do 1 Drawing Knife .50 do Grindstone 1.50 George Tucker 1 Bee Gum 2.50 Wm. Rottan L Bee Gum 1.31¼ Bryan Jones 1 do 1.00 David Dempsy 1 Bee Gum 1. do 1 do .31¼ Keaton Tucker 1 Bee Gum 1.25 Riley Jones 1 Rifle Gum $13. Rottans Harry 1 Rifle 12.25 Wm Rottan 1 Clock 7.25 George Tucker 1 heifer $7.50 Dan Griffith 1 heifer $4. do 1 colt $17. Joseph Fifer ~~1 mare 25.75 $121.18 3/4 $163. 43 3/4~~
P 292 Amount over $163.43 3/4
John Frasure 1 Colt $50.25 Laban Foster 1 mare 49.50 Jesse Dodson 1 cow & Calf 9.62 ½ Josiah Frasor 1 Cow 15.48¼ do 1 Cow 10.62½ Dan Griffith 14 hogs 49.14 Bryan Jones 1 Sow & 6 Shoats 4.93 3/4 $144. 45½ $332.95¼
Dan Griffith Admr.

Recorded 17 March 1839 N. Oldham Clk.

In the name of God Amen. I John Farley of the County of White and State of Tennessee being very sick and weak in body but of perfect mind and memory thanks be given unto God, calling unto mind the mortality of my

Body and knowing that it is appointed for all men once to die do make and ordain this my last will and testament, that is to say principally and first of all. I give and recommend my soul into the hands of Almighty God that gaveit and my body I recommend to the Earth to be vuried in a decent Christian burial at the descretion of my Executors, nothing doubting but at the general resurrection I shall receive the same again, by the mighty power and as touching such worldly estate wherewith it hath pleased god to bless me with in this life. I give, demise, and dispose of the same in the following manner and form. First I give and bequeath to Malinda my dearly beloveed wife my whole estate that consists of perishable property, household and kitchen furniture farming tools and tools of every description to have and to enjoy for her own proper use and use of my heirs by her during the time of her remaining my widow I also request and desire that she may have the sole use and benefit of all the lands and tenents that I am seized or in any way possessed of or may in anywise or manner accue to me or my bodily heirs from whatever source during her widowhood above named and further I desire that she may have the ~~use labor hire or the benefits in anyway arising from my~~ negro boy Given for the term of her natural life or widowhood for her use and benefit of my Children that the young may be raised and all educated which I give in Charge to my executors But if my beloved Malinde in her presence should think fit to change her situation by matrimony I do desire that my executors shall allot to her a reasonable portion of my Lands and tenements property and profits for her comforts and use and the balance keepand use by my executors for the use of my Children should my beloved wife or my Executors as the Case may be discover as my
P 293 children grow up that there is any thing to Spare over and above what will raise the rest let it be alloted to them as so much of their propotional part and when they shall all come of age I desire that each of them shall inherit equally and alike of my effects. Also I constitute ~~ma~~ make and ordain Simson Cash Senr. m y sole Executor of this my last will and testament all and Sangular to be managed. And I do hereby utterly disallow revoke and disannul all and every other former testaments, will, Legadis, bequests and executors by me in any wise named, willed and bequests and executors by me in any wise named, willed and bequeathed, ratifying and confining this and no other to be my last will and testament. In witness whereof I have hereunto set my hand and Seal this the tenth day of January in the year of our Lord One Thousand eight hundred and thirty
P 293 eight.

his
John X Farley (Seal)
mark

Signed Sealed, published, pronounced and declared by the Said John Farley as his last will and testament in the presence of us who in his presence and in the presence of each other have hereunto subscribed our names.

James H. Pass
William Farley
Simson Cash.

State of Tennessee }
White County } March term A.D. 1838.

This day was produced in open Court a writing perposting to be the last will and testament of John Farley late of the County of White deceased and the due execution and publication thereof as such was proven by the oaths of James H. Pass and Simson Cash two of the suxcribing witnesses thereto for the purposes and things therein contained and that the said John Farley at the day of the date of the last will and testament aforesaid and the publication thereof was of sound and disposing mind and memory all of which is ordered to be recorded. Given at office the 5th March A.D. 1838. Test N. Oldham Clk of White County Court Recorded the 17 March 1838 Recorded the 17 March 1838 Test N. Oldham Clk.

P 293 I John Crook, being of sound andperfect memory do make and publish this my last will and testament in manner and form following: Item first, I do give and bequeath unto my beloved wife Rebecca Crook Onethird part of all my cleared land situated lying and being in the County of White and State of Tennessee together with a sufficient number of acres of Timbered land as near adjacent thereto as the same can be laid off to answer the purpose of all necessary repairs for fuel &C for and during her during her natural life, said third part of my cleared land to be so laid off as to include my mansion and other out houses where I now reside and also the Spring now used by me, and it is my Will and desire and I hereby direct that my executors herein after named lay off bey Metis and bounds to my said Wife Rebecca the land and premises devised as aforesaid. Item second--I do give and bequeath unto my son John Crook and my daughter Elizabeth Young all the rest and residue of my lands, temements and heredelament situate lying and being in the County of White and State of Tennessee except the part bequeathed as above to my wife Rebecca to them the said John Crook and Elizabetn Yount (?) and to their heirs forever. And at the death of my wife Rebecca I do further give and bequeath to my Said Children John Crook and Elizabeth Young and to their heirs forever all that part of my land bequeathed above to my wife Rebecca to be equally divided between them at the death of My Said Wife Rebecca and none of the lands hereby divided to said Children John Crook and Elizabeth Yount are to be divided until the happening of Said event towit: the death of my Said wife Rebecca--Item third** I give and bequeath unto my wife Rebecca Crook and her heirs forever my negro Girl slave called Edy and her increase, also my negro boy named Simon, also my negro girl slave commonly called Little Edy and her increase, Also two beds and furniture, two Cows and Calves, Six head of other Young Cattle out of my Stock, also on ten Gallon Kittle One pot also one Horse tobe selected by her out of my stock horses also the Crockery and Delfware which she may claim also six head of Sheep to be selected out of my stock of Sheep also two Sows and pigs, also four Killing hogs also two wheels, one Reel, also what pewter she chooses to take, two chests and one clock. I also devise and bequeath to my beloved wife Rebecca Crook in addition to the foregoing property one years provision for herse & family which I direct my executors to lay off and Set apart her and in the event there should not be a sufficiency of provisions on hand at my death for that purpose my executors are directed to supply the deficancy with any funds belonging to my estate which they may have in their hands. Item fourth: It is my Will and desire that all the rest residue and remainder of my personal propeety of shat kind and nature so ever not already particulary devised (my negroes excepted) be sold by P294 my executors at public auction to the highest bidder on a credit of twelve months-- And the money arising from said sale together with what may be collected by them of the Debts due me and directed to be applied in the first place to the extinguishment of all my just Debts, should a surplus remain after paying all my just Debts, I then and in the event give and bequeath to my Daughter Jane Goolsby Twenty Dollars, should a surplus still remain after paying my just Debts and after paying my Daughter

Jane Goolsby twenty Dollars above devised to her. then and and in that event I give and bequeath to my Grandchildren towit the children of my Son John Crook and the children of my Daughter Elizabeth Yount and to the heirs of my said Grand Children forever said remaining Surpluss to be equally divided between my said grand Children to be paid to them respectively by my executors as they Severally arrive at the age of Twenty one years-- tem-- It is my Will and desire that my negro slaves Teythena, Vice, Phillis, Chanty, Little Vice, (being two of the same name) Anthony and a negro child called Mary Jame, and the increase of said negro slaves be sold after my death either privately or publicly by my executors as they may ceem best on a credit of Twelve months, and it is my desire that m y executors in making sale of Said negroes, select for them, masters who will treat them with Humanity. The money arising from the sale of my Said negroes, I give and bequeath to my said grand children towit: The children of my Said Son John Crook and the children of my Said Daughter Elizabeth Yount to them my Said Grand Children and their heirs forever to be equally divided between them, to be paid to them by my Executor as they respectivel ly arrive at the age of twenty one years. Item 2-- I give and bequeath to my Grand Son John Crook Child of my Son John Crook my negro boy named William to him and his heirs forever and lastly --I hereby nominate and appoint my friends William Hill and Samuel Brown, Executors of this my last will and testament hereby revoking all former Wills by me made. In witness whereof I have hereunto set my hand affixed my Seal this 29th day of December in the year of our Lord one thousand eight hundred & thirty four.

his
John X Crook Senr. (Seal)
mark.

Wigned Sealed published and declared by this above named John Crook Senr. tobe his last will and testament in the presence of us who have hereunto subscriber our names as witnesses in the presence of the testator. The word "my" in the second line from the bottom on the first page, the word "my" in the seventh line from the bottom of the second page inserted and the word "to" in the bottom line of the same page erased before.

Signed
William Mills
John W. Mills

P 295 State of Tennessee | April term A.D. 1838.
White County |

This day Samuel Brown one of the Executors of John Crook Senr. deceased produced in open court a writing purposing to be the last will and Testament of John Crook Senr late of the County of White and the due execution and publication thereof was proven in open Court by the oath of William Mills and John W. Mills subscribing witnesses thereto for the purposes and things therein mentioned and that the said John Crook Senr. was at the date of the execution and publication thereof of sound and disposing mind and memory which is deemed by the court sufficiently proven and ordered to be recorded. and it is ordered that Samuel Brown and William Hill the executors named in Said Last will and tesatamentwho take upon themselves the burden of the execution thereof have leave until the next term of this court to qualify, give Bond and Security /C Given at office the 2nd day of April A.D. 1838. Test. N. Oldham Clk. of White County Court. Recorded the 4th day of April 1838. Test. N. Oldham Clk.

Letters Testamontary on John Farleys estate

State of Tennessee ‖
White County ‖ At a County ourt for the county aforesaid on the first Monday March in the year of our Lord 1838. Whereas the last will and testament of John Farley late of the County of White deceased hath been exhibited to the said Court and proven in due form as required by law whereunto in the same manner, have been qualified as Executors Simpson Cash. These are thererore to empower the said executors to enter into and upon all and singular, the goods and Chattels right and credits of the said deceased and then into his possession take wheresoever the same may be found in this state and are Inventory to return into this court within the time limited by law and all the Just debts of the Said deceased to pay so far as the said Estate will extend or amount to witness Nichols, Oldham Clk of White County Court. Recorded 6th April 1838.

N. Oldham Ck.

P 296 State of Tennessee ‖
White County ‖

I James Goddard being of Sound and perfect mind and memory do hereby make and publish this my last will and testament in Manner and form following: first I give and bequeath unto Moses Mayes the son of Silby Mayes which child is about fourteen months old all the right tittle and claim that I have unto two certain tracts of Land lying in White County and on the waters of the caney fork and on the South side of the same, both of Said tracts is adjoining one is called the Dry hollow place containing thirty acres, the other is one hundred acres tract of school Land that I bouyht from George Sparkman and if the above named Moses Mayes should die, then and in that case the above named Land to be sold and equal divide to be made of the money to my brothers and sisters, I hereby appoint Daniel Hollingsworth my executor of this my last will and testament hereby revoking all other wills by me made. In witness whereof I have hereunto set my hand and Seal this 12th day of February 1838.

James Goddard (Seal)

Witness Joseph Cummings Jr. Moses Hollingsworth.

State of Tennessee ‖ April term A.D. 1838
White County ‖

This day Joseph Cumm ngs Jr. produced in open Court a writing purposing to be the last will and testament of of John Goddard late of the County of White deceased and the due execution and publication thereof was proved in open Court by the oath of J seph Cummings Jr. and Moses Hollinsworth subscribing witnesses thereto for the purposes therein contained and that the said James Godard was at the date of the execution and publication thereof of sound and desposing mind and memory all of which is ordered to be recorded. Given at office the 2nd day of April A.D. 1838. Test. N. Oldham clerk of White County ourt. Recorded 6th April 1838 N. OLdham clk.

Letters of Testamentoary on James Goddards Estate.

State of Tennessee ‖
White County ‖

At a county Court for the County aforesaid on the first Monday in April in the year of our Lord 1838 whereas the last will and testament of James Goddard late of said county deceased hath been exhibited to the said court and proved in due form as required by Law wherinto in the same manner have been qualified as executor Daniel Hollinsworth

P 297 These are therefore to empower the said executor to enter into, and upon all and Singular the goods and Chattles rights, and credits of the said deceased, and thereinto his possession take wheresoever the same may be found in this state, and are Inventory to return into this court within the time limited by Law and all the Just debts of the said deceased, to pay so far as the said estate will extend or amount.
Witness Nicholas Oldham clerk of our said Court at office the first Monday in April A. D. 1838. And in the 62nd year of American Independence
Test. N. Oldham Clerk of White County Court.
Recorded 6 April 1838.
N. Oldham Clk.

Letters of Administration on Wm. McConnel Estate
State of Tennessee }
White County } } March term A.D. 1838.
Where as on this the 5th day of March A. D. 1838. was suggested in open Court the death of William McConnel late of the County of White deceased and that he departed this life intersta e whereupon James McConnel was appointed administrator. These are therefore to empower the said daministrator to enter into and upon all singular the goods and cattels rights and Credits of the said Deceased and therein into his possession take wheresoever the same may be found in this state and are. Inventory to return into this court within the time limited by law and extend or amount to. Witness Nicholas Oldham Clerk of White County Court at office the first Monday of March A.D. 1838. Test N. Oldham Clerk of Said Court.
Recorded Apl 1838 N. Oldham Clk.

Letters of Administration on John Crook Senr. Est.
State of Tennessee
Where as the last will and testament of John Crook Senr. late of the County of White deceased hath been exhibited to the County Court of said County and proven in due form as required by law, and Samuel Brown and William Hill the executors named in said Will having appeared in open Court and relinquished and renounced there right to act as executors whereupon Anthony Dibrell was duly qualified according to law administrator with the last Will and testament annexed of the said John Crook Senr. deceased. These are therefore to empower the said administrator to enter into and upon and singular the goods and Chattel rights and Credits of the said deceased and then into his possession take wheresoever the same may be found in the state and an Inventory toreturn into this Court within the time limited by law and all the just debts to pay so far as the said estate will extend or amount to—. Witness Nicholas Oldham Clerk of White County Court at office the first Monday in May A. D. 1838. And of American Independence the 62nd year. Test. N. Oldham Clerk of Said Court. Recorded 9 May 1838. N. Oldham Clk of White County Court.

Inventory of the property of the Estate James Godard deceased returned upon oath by H. Hollinsworth Admr. at the May term A. D. 1838. Towit: Cash of hand in Bank notes $13. One bed and furniture and a Bedstead, one pair farming Gear and plow Two hundred and Sisty Binds of Fodder, one Stack of Oats, One chair, one bridle-- his
Recorded 28th May 1838 Daniel X Hollinsworth Admr.
Test. N. Oldham Clk. mark

Inventory of the property of the estate of William McConnel deceased returned upon oath by ames A. McConnel Admr. at the May term A.D. 1838. Towit: Two Judgements against Thomas Clark of Jackson County both amoujting to the sum of $90.00. Out of which I have received the sum of $50.00. Yet due $10/00. Also One Bureau, One Watch. James McConnel Admr. Recorded 28th May 1838. Test N. Oldham Clk.

Account of the Sales property of John Massa Senr. deceased returned upon oath by John Massa Admr. at April term A.D. 1838 towitt:
P 299 He States that two sales took place one on the 22nd day November 1837. And one on the 30th day of March 1838. Sales on 22nd Nov. 1837 were as follows Cornelius Hickey 1 Cow 8.25 George Price 1 pr. Stetchers .621 /2 do 1 mattock .75 Wm. Baker 1 Jursy Heifer 5.75 W.G. Martin 1 Heifer 6.06 ¼ do 1 Bull Calf .81¼ Conelues Hickey 1 plow .37½ do 1 do 1.25 George Price 1 Basket & tools & plow 1.00 Washington Irwin 1 Oven & Lid .18 Hannah Massa 1 pot .31¼ P. Bussel Swingletree & Clevis .621/2 do 1 Oven & Lid .811/4 H. Massa 1 Smoothing iron .31 ¼ do 1 pot .25 do 2 Beds 5.81¼ do 1 Seive .43 3/4 do 1 cupboard and some litlle furniture 1. $18.25 $16.17 $34.42½ amount of first Sales.

Sales 30th 1838.
Corneleus Hickey 1 bed 1.12 ½ Jesse Williams 1 Axe 1.43 3/4 do 1 Churn .21 do 1 Sadle 4.75 Hannah Massa 3 Chairs 1.00 Adam Massa 1 Bridle .62 Sally Roberts 1 Kittle .62½ Jesse Williams 1 Blanker .65 do Hoe .61/4 H. Massa 2 Geese .75 Jesse Price 1 Bedstead .63 Adam Massa 1 Bedstead .94 Adam Massa 1 sickle .61/4 John Massa 1 Beadstead 1.01 John Stwart 1 plow stock 3. $2.75 $10.18 Amt Sale $13.04 Amt. Sales $47.46½.

The said Administrator states that by reference to his Inventory of the perishable property of said Estate it will be some of what said Estate consisted. And he states that the following articles of said estate were taken from him by Executors to satisfy debts that were in Judgement previous to the death of his enterstate-- Said Inventory was returned as early as the November term of Said Court 1837 and is upon record. He will also state that one of the six head of Cattle mentioned in said Inventory was laid off and assigned the widow as part of her years provision one of the (?) mentioned in said Inventory died before the Sale. The balance of said Cattle were taken to satisfy the execution that will be named below Robert L. Mitchell against John Massa and Washington Irwin against Said Massa Judgement by Emery Bennet Widow as a part of her years provisions. One of them was lost without any fault of the Administrator--The Mare mentioned in Said Inventory was taken by executors to satisfy a Judgement of Lewis Euans against Said John Massa deceased. Therefore it was out of the power of said Administrator to sell the said property at the administrators Sale it having been taken his said Inventory of the property at November term 1837 he has found a note on John Simmons for two Dollars and twenty five cents-- whether said note is good or whether said Simmons is solvent or not he does not know but will Collect and account for said note if it can be collected.
Recorded 28th May 1838. John Massa Administrator.
Test N. Oldham Clk. of White County Court.

– Letters of Administration on the Estate of C. Mason decd.
State of Tennessee

Whereas on the 4th day of June term of White County Court 1838. was suggested in open Court the death of Caleb Mason by appointed by said Court Administrator and aministratrix. These are therefore to empower the said Admx.
P 300 and Admr. to enter into and upon all and Singular the goods and Chattle rights and Credits of thedeceased and then into their possession take wheresoever the same may be found in this state, and Inventory to return into this court within the time limited by Law. And all the just debts of the said deceased to pay so far as said estate will extend or amount to. Witness N. Oldham Clerk, of White County Court at office the first Monday of June A. D. 1838. And of the Independence of the United States the 62nd . Test N. Oldham Clerk of Same Court. Recorded 6th June A. D. 1838. Test. N. Oldham Clk of White County Court.

P 301 Letters of administration on Coleman Brown's Estate.
State of Tennessee.

Whereas on the 4th day of June 1838 being thr June term A. D. 1838 of White County Court the death of Coleman Brown late of the County of White was suggested and that he departed this life enterstate. Whereupon James Brown was qualified as Administrator. These are therefore to Empower the said James Brown Administrator to enter into and upon all and Singular the goods and Chattle rights and Credits of the deceased and them into his possession take wheresoever the same may be found in this state, and an Inventory to return into this Court within the time limited by law and all the just debts of the deceased to pay so far as the Said Estate will extend or amount to--. Witness Nicholas Oldham Clerk of White County Court at office the first Monday of June A.D. 1838. And of the Independence of the United States the Sixty Second year. Test. N. Oldham of White County Court. Recorded the 7th June 1838 Test. N. Oldham Clk.

Inventory and Sales of the Slaves of the Esta e of Isaac Clark deceased returned upon oath by Jessd A. Bounds Admr. Debonisnon (?) with Will annexed at the June term A.D. 1838. Towit:

Sold one Negro Benjamin		$735.00
" " " Peter		880.00
" " " Girl Chaney		674.00
" " " " Susan		400.00
" " " Dick		776.
" 2 " Phill		501.
" " " Harry		592.
To hire of negroes 1 month	6	22.
		$4560.

Negroes Barbara & Anderson & Rebecca retained by the widow Nance Clark, Sold on the 15th May 1838 - Jesse A. Bounds Admr.
Debonisnon
Recorded 5th July 1838. Test N. Oldham Clk of White County Court.

P 302 Inventory and account of Sales of the property of the Estateof John Crook Senr. deceased returned upon oath by Anthony Dibrell ADmr. with the will annexed at the June term A.D. 1838 Sold 29th May 1828.

1 Gray Mare	$30.50	1 waggon	23.00
1 " do	58.00	3 hides	6.06¼

1 Bay colt	27.50	50 # Bacon	7.00
1 yoke Steers yoke		286 # do	34.87½
& Bell	47.75	10 Bushels Rye	5.00
1 do	37.00	1 Scythe and cradle	2.50
1 Bull	4.87½	1 Man's Saddle	19.25
2 Muley cow beasts	9.25	1 woman's do	26.00
1 stray Steer posted		1 old Man Saddle	2.00
time not out	5.00	1 ~~large~~ Kittle	5.00
1 cow & Calf	13.25	pot	3.25
1 do do	11.00	2 ovens	.62½
1 cow & 2 Calves	16.50	1 Steer Kittle	.75
1 cow Calf & Bell	9.25	1 oven & lid	1.43 3/4
1 do	11.50	1 pot	2.00
27 head hogs	82.50	1 axe	1.00
2 pet Lambs	1.18 3/4	12 Beestands	25.12
15 head Sheep	20.00	1 Schthe & Cradle	2.00
15 do do	17.00	1 axe	2.12½
32 do do	32.00	1 wedge	.31
1 Stack fodder		1 Log Chain	1.75
& 1 piece	7.18 3/4	chairs	3.00
1 do do	4.50	1 Jack Screw	2.93 3/4
2 Mattocks	1.81¼	1 Tar Buckett	.06¼
2 ploughs	2.00	2 Bells	1.00
3 Bull tonges	3.50	1 pr. Steel	.43 3/4
1 Grind Stone	.62½	old hoes axes /C	1.00
1 Tar Barrel	.12½	3 shovel ploughs	1.81¼
1 Loom & Gearing	4.56¼	pewter Bason /C	2.50
Harness	.97½	1 pr. Steelyards	1.75
1 Little Wheel	1.18 3/4	Books	.30
1 do do	2.75	4 Reap hooks	.25
1 Big Wheel	.50	1 half Bushel	.37½
Riddle /C	1.00	2 meal Bags	.81¼
1 Hackle	2.06¼	2 do do	.93 3/4
Basketts & Sundial	.31¼	½ Bushel dried apples	.25
~~1 Barrel~~ & Apples	.75	4 Crocks	.24
Auger drawing knife /C	1.63	1 axe	.51½
P303 Foot adze and Law	1.06¼	1 Lot crooking ware	1.06¼
1 Bugle	.18 3/4	3 Chairs	.68 3/4
1 Bed & furniture	10.00	1 watch	5.25
1 cutting Box	2.12½	1 Barrel	.37½
1 pr Saddle Bags	1.31¼	1 Jug	.25
1 Bed & furniture	13.06¼	Dog iron pot rack /C	3.50
1 do do	12.12½	pot racks /C	2.18 3/4
1 do do	14.56¼	1 pr Gears	2.25
1 Lot of bed coathes	4.25	1 pr do	1.00
1 Box	.12½	Bridle Bitts /C	2.06¼
1 Horn Glass	.50	Bason Tub /C	.25
Leather	12.18	Looking Glass	.68 3/4
1 coffee Mill	.50	1 Table	.50
candle Sticks	.25	Mattock & Hoe	1.00
Delph Ware	5.00	1 Skillet	.37½
1 Razor and Strap	1.00	1 do	.62½
pewter ware	4.12½	1 smoothing iron	.37½
373/4 lb Wool	13.59 3/4	1 do do	.65

1 negro woman & child835.00   2 Bells   1.25
1 " " Vice 600.00   Short corn /C   7.40
2 " " Charity & Philis
1600.00
1 " boy Anthony 700.00
1 " Mary Jane 435.00
5241.40   Amount of Sales.

List of Notes towit:

One note on E. Wooten due 2 Nov. 1837 for	$10.00
One on John T. Graham due 10 Jany 1837	50.00
" " Samuel Brown due 14th Febry 1837	100.00
" " Hiran Bowman due 19th Octr. 1837	3.60
" " Thomas Scarlett due 11 Octr. 1837	6.34
" Receipt on Const William K. Bradford for note on S. Price due 27 March 1987	20.00
One note on J. A. Carrick S. Brown & W. Hill due 1 Jany 1839	100.00
Cash in ilber	16.45
Do in Bank N tes	16.00
1 Accopr on David Manslyl (bad) for	2.16

Anthony Dibrell Admr with the Will annexed
Recorded 5 July 1838. Test N. Oldham Clk of White County Court.

P 304   Inventory and account of the Sales of the property of the Estate of Caleb Mason deceased returned upon oath by Joshua Mason one of the Administrators at the July term A.D. 1838.

Margarett Mason to	1 Lot Cupboard and furniture	$1.50
" "	1 Table .25 1 wheel & Cards .50	.75
do	3 Chairs .50 1 Side Saddle & Bridle	2.50
do	1 Bed and furniture 2. 1 Bible .50	2.50
do	1 Hymn Book .12½	.25
do	1 Razor and Strap .25 1 handsaw 06¼	.31¼
do	2 Augers .06¼ 1 Drawing & Chisel.06¼	.12½
do	1 Slate.06¼ 1 Weeding hoe .12½	.18 3/4
do	1 Sprouting hoe .12½ 1 Weeding hoe.06¼	.18 3/4
do	1 Sproutting hoe .06½ 1 pr Gears 1.50	1.56¼
do	1 plow .43 3/4 4 Pails 5 Crocks 1 Churn 1.00	1.43 3/4
do	1 Tub 12½ 1 Barrel and Yoke .37½	.50
do	½ ushel measure .06¼ 1 Clock 8.00	8.06¼
do	1 Cutting Knife & Box .37½ 1 plow and Gears 4.00	4.37½
do	1 Cutler & Band .62½ 1 Swingletree/¼	.87½
Sally Dasner	1 Bedstead .12½ 1 Weeding hoe .06¼	.18 3/4
Joshua Mason	1 Round Shave 1 pr Pinchers	.25
Robert Mason	1 Pr Saddle Bags	2.50
Avery Norris	1 Axe	.25
Levi Jarvis	2 Barrels .37½ 3 Cherry plank 06¼	.43 3/4
Joseph Glenn	1 Doubletree	.25
Joshua Mason	1 Saddle & Blanket	5.00
Edward Gleeson	1 Scythe & Cradle	1.75

John M. Little 1 wagon 50.00
Edward Anderson 1 yoke Oxen 31.50
T. A. Badger 1 Horse 87.00
Robert Mason 1 Lot Boards .18 3/4
Nancy Glenn 1 Bay Mare 100.00
$304.43 3/4

One note on Levi Jarvis payable in a horse or horses due 1 October 1839 for $100. believed to be good. One on Robert Glenn due 25 Decr. 1838 assigned by L. Jarvis to Caleb ason for $50. good. One on Samuel Jones due 25 Decr. 1838 for $ 5.00 Doubtful One Judgement on Greenville Templeton rendered 17 March 1838 by Richard Crowder Esqr. for $95.83¼ Good. One acct on Jesse Lincoln for $18.40 Doubtful--One a/c on Robert Glenn Jr. for $26.50 doubtful--One a.c on Elizabeth Wilson for $1.00 doubtful. O e do on John arlow for $0.75 Cash on hand $7.50 JoshuaM ason Admr. Recorded 6th July 1838 Test. N. Oldham Clk.

P 305 Account of the Sales of the property of James Godard deceased' returned upon oath by Daniel Hollinsworth Admr. at the June term A.D. 1838. of White County Court.

Edmond Goddard 1 plow .43 3/4
J. Hollinsworty 1 pr Gears 1.37½
John Stipe 1 Bridle .81¼
William Sparkman 1 Chair .37½
Edmond Godard 260 Fodder 2.43 3/4
Grief Smallman 1 Stack Oats 2.50
William Hailey 1 Bed & furniture 20.12½
Sold 19 May 1838 $27.94¼

Daniel Hollinsworth Admr.
Recorded 6th July 1838 Test. N. Oldham Clk.

Report of a Settlement made with George Bohanon Administrator with the will annexed of Joseph Henry deceased before the Clerk of White County Court in vocation towit:

Dr. to amount of account of Sales returned at Oct. term 1836 $1010.50¼

Cr. By this amt. paid the Clerk of White County Court pr receipt 3.75
By amt. paid clerk for fee of Settlement and recording the same 2.50 6.25
Bal remaining in hands of admr. of $1004.25½

The Administrator claims a credit for fifteen dollars for his Services as administrator which I think reasonable and submit it to the Court for this confirmation all of which id respectfully submitted August 1, 1838. N. Oldham Clerk of White County Court.
Recorded 24 August 1836 N. Oldham Clk.

Account of Sales of the property of William McConnell deceased returned upon oath by James A. McConnell Admr. at August term 1838. Towit: Sold on 21st. July 1838
One Watch $10. One Bureau $7.37½ $ 17.37½
Recorded 24th Augn 1838. J. A. McConnell Admr.
Test N. Oldham Clk.

P 306 Report of Commissioners on assignment of one years provisions to the widow and family of Caleb Mason deceased made at August term A.D. 1838 Towit: All the bacon on hand two hogs and to have out of the proceeds of the same money enough to buy one hundred pounds pork, ... the corn that is on hand, and money enough out of the proceeds of the sale to purchase twenty five Bushels more, and twenty pounds Coffee to be purchased out of the proceeds of the sale and also twenty five pounds of sugar and also One and a half bushels Salt to be purchased with the money arising from the sale of other property. All of which is most respectfully submitted August the 6th 1838.

John Humphreys
James Rendals
Levi Jarvis Commissioners

Recorded 24 August A. D. 1838 Test N. Oldham Clerk.

Letters of Administration with Will aneexed of Wm. Lewis Decd.
State of Tennessee)
White County) Whereas on the 3 day of September A.D. 1838 the death of William Lewis late of the County of White was suggested and the due Execution of his last will and testament was duly proved and no provision being made for an Executor whereupon Benjamin Lewis was appointed by the Court Administrator with the last will and testament of the deceased annexed. There are therefore to empower you the said Admr. to enter into & upon all and Singular the goods and Chattle rights and Credits of the deceased and then into his possession take wheresoever the same may be found in this state. And an inbentory to return within the time limitted by law and all the just debts of the deceased to pay so far as said Estate will exrend or amount to. Witness N. Oldham Clerk of White County Court at office the 1st Monday in September A. D. 1838. And of the Independence of the United States the 63 year.
Test N. Oldham Clerk of White County Court.
Recorded 6 Sept. 1838 Test N. Oldham Clerk.

P 307 Letters of Administration Pendentatited on John Crook Dcd. Estate.
State of Tennessee) October Term A.D. 1838
White County)
Whereas at former term of this Court the death of John Crook Senr. late of the County of White was suggested in due form and now for reasons appointing to the satisfaction of the Court, it is ordered by the court that Anthony Dibrell Esquire be appointed Aministrator Pendentalita of the said John Crook Senr. deceased. These are therefore to authorise you the administrator oaforesaid to enter into and upon all and singular the goods and Chattle rights and Credits of the said deceased and there into his possession take whereever the same may be found in this state. And shall will and truly administer the said Estate according to law during the pendencey of a certain suit in White Circuit Court where in Jacob Yount and wife are plaintiffs in contesting the validety of the last will and testament of the said John Crook Senr. Deceased and the said Aministrator aforesaid at office the 2nd day of October A. D. 1838. Test N. Oldham Clerk of White County Court. Recorded 3 Oct. 1838.

Letters of Administration on Samuel Jackson Dcd. Estate.
State of Tennessee. Whereas on the first day of October A.D. 1838 being the October term 1838 of White County Court the death of Samuel

Jackson late of the County of White deceased was suggested in open Court and that he depacted this life intestate whereupon Zachariah Anderson has been appointed and quadified as administrator. These are therefore to authorise and empower the said admr. Zacharaiah Anderson to enter into and upon all and singular the Goods and Chattle rights and Credits of the said deceased and them into his possession take whereever the same may be found in this state. And an Inventory to return into this court within the time limitted by law. And all the just debts of the deceased to pay so far as the said estate will extend or amount to. Witness Nicholas Oldham Clerk of Said Court at office the 1st day of October A.D. 1838 Test N. Oldhan Clk of White County Court.
Recorded 3rd Oct. 1838 N. Oldham Clk.

P 308 I stephen Farley of the County of White and State of Tennessee planter do make and publish, this my last will and testament hereby revoking and making void all former wills by me at anytime heretofore made and first I direct that my body be decently intered in a manner suitable to my condition in life. And as to such worldly estate as it hath pleased God to intrust me with. I dispose of the same as follows, first, I direct that all my just debts and funeral expenses be pai as soon after my decease as possible out of any monies that I may die possessed of, or may first come into the hands of my executors from any portion of my estate real or personal Secondly I give and bequeath unto my dear wife Mary Farley all of my goods and chattles lands and tenements during her life time-- Third I give and bequeath unto my Semen children Obedience, Williams, Thomas, John, Jeremiah, Nancy & Stephen and at the death of my dearly beloved wife Mary Farley the whole of my property both real and personal beit of what Kind, nature or quality Sowen to be equally divided between these my above named children. I do hereby make ordain and appoint my dearly beloved Son-in-law Thomas Fallent & Jeremiah Farley my dear Son executors of this my last will and testament. In Witness whereof I Stephen Farley the said testator have to this my Will Written on one Sheet of paper set my hand and Seal this the eight of October in the year of our Lord One Thousand eight hundred and thirty Seven. Stephen Farley (Seal)
Signed Sealed and published in the presence of us who have subscribed in presence of the Testator and of each other Moses Lynnville
William Goodwin
Pleasant Lernville.

State of Tennessee }
White County } September term A. D. 1838.

This day was produced in open court a Writing purposting to be the last will and testament of Stephen Farley late of the County of White deceased, and the due execution and publication thereof as the last will and testament of the said Stephen Farley deceased was proven in open Court by the oaths of William Goodwin and Pleasant Lynville subscribing witnesses thereto for the purposes and things therein contained. And that the said Stephen Farley at the date of the execution and publication thereof was of Sound and disposing maind and memory. All of which is ordered to be recorded. Given at office the 3rd September 1838. Test N. Oldham Clerk of White County Court. Recorded 8th October 1838. Test N. Oldham Clk.

P 309 In the name of God, Amen: I William Lewis of the county of White and State of Tennessee being sick and weakley in body but of sound

mind and disposing memory, do make and ordain this my last will and testament in Manner and form as follows, first, and in the first place, I give my oul to Almighty God who first gave it me and my body to the dust whence it came to be buried in decent Christian burial at the descrition of my executors hereafter named--and as touching my worldly estate which it hath pleased God to belss me with, I dispose of in the following manner. First, I give to my Daughter Polly Rigsby one Dollar. I give to my Son Benjamin Lewis all my right, title claim and interest to the land where now lives. I give to my Son Hiram Lewis all my right title claim and interest to the land he now lives on. I give to my Son Russel One dollar. I give my Duaghter Betsy Hutchings one dollar. I give to my daughter Kesiah Rigsby one dollar. I also leave to my beloved wife Sarah Lewis my plantation together with the whole of my household and Kitchen furniture, also my part of the present crop. I wish it to be understood that myself and my Grandson James W. Julian have got an Article respect fully the present crop and I want it fulfilled on my part, my wife to enjoy Said property during her natural life, and all my suprlus property to be sold and my Executor to take care of the money arising therefrom and the interest of said money to be applied to the support of my wife and should it not be sufficent for her support so much of the principal as may comfortably maintain her must be made use of be it understood that the money arising from the sales of the property and all the balance of my Cash Notes when collected are included in this Case. Further I will that as quick as convenience will admit after the death of my wife that the property which lend her that may be left be sold and the money arising therefrom together with anyother money which may be left if any be equally divided among my Children and Grand Children above mentioned each Grand Child to be equally divided among my Children and Grand Children above mentioned each Grand Child to be equall with a child in confirmation whereof I I Constitute and __________ and my sole executor to this my last will and testament, revoking and disallowing any other Will or Wills heretofor made by me. In Witness whereof I have hereunto set my hand and Seal this 1st day of August 1838. Wm. W. Lewis (Seal)
Edward Pollard, John R. Glenn.

State of Tennessee }
White County } September term A. D. 1838.
This day was exhibited in open Court a writing purposting to be the last Will and testament of William Lewis late of the County of White deceased and the due execution and publication thereof as the last Will and testament of the Said William Lewis deceased was proved in open Court by the oath of Edward B. Pollard and John B. Glenn Subscribing witnesses thereto for the pupposes and things therein mentioned and that the said William Lewis was at the date of the execution and publication thereof of Sound and disposing mind and memory. All of shich is ordered to be recorded. Given at office the 3 September 1838. Test N. Oldham Clerk of White County Court. Recorded 8 Sept. 1838. Test N. Oldham. Clk.

Additional Account of the sales of the property of the estate of Jacob Robinson dcd. returned upon the oath by A. Dibrell one of the Exr. of the Said Estate made at September term A. D. 1838. towit:

To 1	Negro Girl sold to Robert Hewlet	$300.
1	" boy " " Nathan Bartlett	350.
	Sold pork this amount	315.
	Sold Beef " do	40.

One account on John Dyer 21.02½
Hire of negroes 477.
Cash received of Rosewell Pool in 1836 200.
$1603.02½

Recorded 8th October 1838 Anthony Dibrell Exr.
Test N. Oldham Clk.

P 311 Report of a Settlement made with Susannah Duncah Administrator of William Duncan deceased made before the Clerk of White County Court on the 22 day of August 1838. And confirmed by White County Court at Sept Term 1838. To amount of acct. Sales returned Oct. 1836 $336.28 3/4
To a mount collected on Claim returned in Inventory
Towit Note on Alevatirs &Burnatt for 4.00
" Acct on J. Alevatus 3.35
" note on Riley Jones 5.00
This amt received of two claims vs. Hanks 12. 37½
To amt account vs. A. Dibrell for plank /c 23.37½ 48.00
384.28 3/4

Credits
By amount of William Bruster act. 2.00
" " S. K. Robinson " 2.00
" " Lane & Anderson note 5.00
" " H. W. Richardson act 30.00
" " W. L. Young & Brother act 7.18 3/4
" " Henry Waddle act 2.20
" " Shf receipt for Taxes 1835 1 .58½
" " do 1836&1837 .63½
" " W. Bowman asse Note 20.00
" " George Elmore affedt 2.25
" " Sharp R. Whitty recpt. 4.00
" " N. Oldham 2 receipts 2.75
" " Notes to A. Dibrell 50.00
" " Clerk for making settlement $2.00
and recording same .50 2.50 $131.71
This sum of 252.57 3/4
Remaining in the hands of the Administratrix besides some Claims uncollected The admx. charges for 1 pr. Drawing claims as unproperly sold $1.25 and also the sum of Twenty Dollars for her services in Settling the estate of the deceased which I think reasonable and beg leave further to report that Some of the vouchers presented by the administratrix are riot in regular form but I have examined her upon oath touching such vouchers--all of which is respectfully Submitted this 3 day of September 1838.
Test N. Oldham Clerk.

P 312 Inventory in part of the property of William Lewis deceased returned upon oath by Benjamin Lewis Exr. of said Estate at the September term A. D. 1838. Towit yoke of oxen 25$ 1 cow and calf 10$ 1 do $12 1 heifer $8. 1 heifer$5.60 1 do $4 23 head of Stock hogs $23 1 Sorrel Mare $40 1 sorrel colt 57.50 1 pr Saddle Bags $2.50 1 Mans Saddle $4.00 1 cross cut saw $11.00 3 plows hoes $1.00 4 hoes 2.50 1 Bar Share plow $1.50 1 singletree .62½ 1 ox yoke .75 3 Augers $1.00 1 Foot Adze & Handwas $1.00 2 drawing knives 2 chisels 1.25 1 Hgwel & 2 round Shaves and cows $1.00 3 axes 1 Iron wedge 5.00 1 Sett of Gear 1 pr drawing Chains 1.62½ 1 Log chain $4.00 1 Frow .50 1 Jack plain & fire plain and Jointer Bitts

$1.00 shoe tools and 4 pigings 1.50 1 Brier Scythe .50 3 Bitts 2.00 200 bind Flax 4.00 1 Still and Tubs 15$ 1 pr Steelyards $1.00 1 large pot 1.50 1 Large Kittle 2.50 1 pot, oven & Lid 1.37½ 1 Frying pan. 37½ 1 do .75 2 small pots & Skillet & 2 pr pot hooks 1.75 1 key hole Saw 2 files .50 2 Smoothing Irons .87½ 1 clock $10. 1 Dining Table $7.00 1 chest $3. 1 cupboard & furniture $7.50 3 Beds and furniture $300 9 sitting Chairs 2.25 1 Loom $4. 1 Lot of plank & Scantling $12. 1 pr fire dogs--1 pot rack $1.00 1 Seive .75 1 Large Wheel and two small ditto $3.00 1 Iron Wedge .50 1 cutting Knife and Box 2.00$ $359.37½. The foregoing return of an Inventory is incomplete as it lacks a return of the debts due to and from the estate but this shall be given at the next term the same is correct as far as it goes 2nd September 1838. Benjamin Lewis Exr. of William Lewis Decd.

Additional Inventory of the Est. of William Lewis is deceased made at the Octoberterm A. D. 1838.

One Note on David & James Coga for		103.00
" " " Emory Bernett	"	50.00
" " " E.J. Pollard	"	21.00
" " " William Rigsby	"	4.00
" " " David Fisher	"	100.00
" " " Wm. Blackburn	"	3.00
" " " David McIntosh	"	10.00
" " " Wm. Rigsby for 30 Bushels Corn		271.

his
Benjamin X Lewis Exr.
mark.

Recorded 10 Oct 1838 N. Oldham Clerk.

P 313 Account of the Sales of the property of William Lewis deceased returned upon oath by Benjamin Lewis Exr at the October term A. D. 1838 Towit:

One note on Dennis Julin for	$15.71
" " " James W. Julin	19.12
" " " John Rigsby	50.25
" " " Hiram Lewis	115.61
" " " Canady Rigsby	18.00
" " " Russel Lewis	42.50
" " " John Hutchins	10.12½
" " " William Rigsby	2.00
" " " Edward B. Pollard	3.31¼
" " " George W. Julin	12.18 3/4
" " " Sarah Lewis	24.75
" " " W. Sorrels	.50
	$314.06¼

Recorded 10 October 1838
Test N. Oldham Clerk. of White County Court.

his
Benjamin X Lewis
mark
Exr. of W. Lewis dcd.

Report of a Settlement made with Anthony Dibrell one of the Executors of Jacob Robinson Deceased made before the Clerk of White County Court and Confirmed by Said Court at its September term A. D. 1838. Towit:

Dr. To amt. account of Sales returned at Jany 1829	494.06¼
" Sale of Negro boy Abram to J. Hunter	400.00
" " " girl to R. Hewelt	300.00
" " " boy to N. Baftlett	350.00
To amt Sales to be retd. at September term 1838 besides sale of negroes	953.02½
	2497.08 3/4

Credits

No 1	By receipt of Tho. Simpson	505.	
2	" " " A. B. Lane agent	84.27½	
3	" " " Reuben Robinson	68.00	
4	" " " George W. Gibbs	50.00	
5	" " " Jacob A. Lane	27.00	
6	" " " Robert Cox	101.25	
7	" " " David Ames & Lane	27.00	
8	" " " J. J. Hayes	76.22	
9	" " " J & D. Snodgrass	11.04	
10	" " " Joseph Hunter	63.68	
F 314	To amt Debit brought up		2497.083/4
11	" " " Saml Brown Ad of Lyor	143.00	
12	" " " J. Dalton	20.00	
13	" " " Kyle & orr balance	57.37	
14	" " " Thomas Sto e bal Judgt	35.16	
15	" " " A. Burk and others	235.51	
16	" " " John Warren	10.00	
17	" " " Paid Nelson & Anderson atc.	15.00	
18	" " " Joseph Hunter	87.00	
19	" " " Hannah Anderson	20.00	
20	" " Mary McGhee	5.00	
21	" " William Daniel	1.37½	
22	" James Fedk	15.60	
23	" " George Long	15.00	
24	" " John Robinson	3.37½	
25	" William Pryor	4.97½	
26	" John C. Farley	61.18 3/4	
27	" Charles McGuire	2.00	
28	" Henry McKinney	3.00	
29	" George Long	15.00	
30	" John England Const	52.36½	
31	" Noah Phillips	5.43½	
32	" George Long	7.00	
33	" Defoa & Avery	269.91	
34	" William Rutledge	8.00	
35	" Madison Fiske	25.00	
36	" do do	85.00	
37	" Ignateus Howard	4.50	
38	" John W. Roberts	17.34½	
39	" Samuel Brown	20.81½	
40	" Balor Hardin	6.00	
41	" Jonathan Scott	32.91	
42	" William Glenn	26.74	
43	" do do	5.12½	
44	" Thomas J. Pistol	4.80	
45	" John W. Roberts	34.32	
46	" A. Dibrell Bank agent	53.	
47	" A. Dibrell	32.	
48	" Jesse Lincoln	71.46½	
49	" do do	100.00	
50	" Anderson Estate	102.14	
51	" Waman Leftwith cert Suit	34.60	
52	" Cost in case of Nespect	8.13	

53	"	Clerk A. Dibrell for cost & Hinges	65.90	
P 318	To amount over			$2497.09½
No 54	"	receipt Lane & Anderson	15.00	
55	"	Ellis & Plulan Atto.	5.00	
56	"	A. Dibrell Expenses in Tuscaloosa attending to case Robinson against pool 8 days @ 2$ per day	16.00	
57	By this amt cost in the case of Walter vs Dibrell & Ames Exrs. exhlusive of the cost of the Supreme Court which stands atainst the executors this sum		67.41	
58	By receipt of J. A. Lane		4.00	
59	" "	N. Oldham clerk	3.25	
	A. Dibrell one of the Executors charges for his Services which is submitted to the Court		100.	$3098.76½
		Balanced due Executor		601.67½

over and above the means which has come into his possession. The Executor Anthony Dibrell shows that there is yet a Claim of about $2.00 due the estate which he thinks will be available by the 1st October next--All of which is respectfully submitted for the confirmation of the Court this 14 August 1838. N. Oldham Clerk of White County Court. Recorded 10 Oct. 1838. Test. N. Oldham Clk.

Account of the Sales of the property of William Lewis deceased returned upon by Benjamin Lewis the Admr. at November term A. D. 1838.

James W. Julin and John D. Clouse note for	$16.75
John Hutchins & William H. Baker note	3.06½
Hiram Lewis & John D. Clouse note	1.75
George W. Julin & Hiram Lewis Note	.75
Sally Lewis and John Hutchins note	.56½
	22.87½

Recorded 7 Nov. 1838   Benjamin his X mark Lewis Admr.
Test N. Oldham Clerk.

P 316 Report of Settlement made with Joseph Herd administrator and Phebe Allen administratrix of George Allen deceased made before the Clerk of White County Court in vacation returned and confirmed by court at Nov. term 1838. To amount account sales returned at July term 1836. $558.37½
To do do returned at Nove. term 1836-1837 Debits $2945.37½

Credits

By Lanes receipt No. 1	1.50
" Tho. Leaks do do 2	5.00
" James Easthan do 3	1.00
" John Young do 4	2.00
" R. Martin do 5	43.78
" James Coger do 6	4.50
" James Davis note 7	7.42
" Benjamin Hutchins receipt 8	1.50
" Dennis Neal do 9	3.75
" Jesse Allen Senr. Note 10	16.91
" Jesse Nestels do 12	7.07
" M. Fish do 13	12.50
" Samuel Allen do 14	90.45
" Samuel A. Allen do 15	21.34½

www.ingramcontent.com/pod-product-compliance
Lightning Source LLC
Chambersburg PA
CBHW080234270326
41926CB00020B/4229
9780788477751